AUGUST BOURNONVILLE
The Complete Ballet Libretti

Abdallah.

Ballet i 3 Acter

af

August Bournonville.

Musiken componeret af **Paulli**.

Decorationerne af Dhrr. **Christensen** og **Lund**. Costumet tegnet af Hr. **Edw. Lehmann**. Maskineriet anordnet af Hr. **Weddén**.

Opført første Gang i Marts 1855.

Kjøbenhavn.
Forlagt af J. H. Schubothes Boghandel.
Bianco Lunos Bogtrykkeri.
1855.

August Bournonville's libretto for *Abdallah*

AUGUST BOURNONVILLE
The Complete Ballet Libretti

Translated from the Danish by Patricia N. McAndrew

DANCE BOOKS

These translations were first published in issues of the journal *Dance Chronicle* (editors Jack Anderson and George Dorris) between 1979 and 1983.

The present revised edition was published in 2024 by:

Dance Books Southwold House Isington Road Binsted Hampshire GU34 4PH

© 2024 Patricia N. McAndrew

ISBN: 978-185273-188-5

CONTENTS

A Chronology of Bournonville's Stage Works Ballets and Divertissements, Individual Dances, and Stagings of Operas and Plays	1
Scenarios and Cast Lists	12
Acclaim to the Graces	12
Soldier and Peasant	12
Victor's Wedding, or the Ancestral Home	15
Faust	19
The Veteran, or the Hospitable House	27
The Tyroleans	33
Valdemar	37
Don Quixote at Camacho's Wedding	48
Hertha's Offering	57
The Isle of Fantasy, or from China's Coast	58
The Festival in Albano	64
The Fatherland's Muses	69
The Toreador	74
Napoli, or the Fisherman and his Bride	81
The Childhood of Erik Menved	88
Bellman, or the Polska at Gronalund	98
The Oresteia	100
Kirsten Piil, or Two Midsummer Festivals	109
Raphael	115
The New Penelope, or the Spring Festival in Athens	122
The White Rose, or Summer in Brittany	124
Old Memories, or a Magic Lantern	126
Conservatoriet, or a Proposal of Marriage through the Newspaper	131
The Irresistibles	137
Psyche	139

The Kermesse in Bruges, or the Three Gifts	144
Zulma, or the Crystal Palace	149
The Wedding Festival in Hardanger	155
A Folk Tale	162
Abdallah	169
In the Carpathians	177
The Flower Festival in Genzano	184
The Mountain Hut, or Twenty Years	189
Far from Denmark, or a Costume Ball on Board	201
The Valkyrie	208
Pontemolle	221
The Lay of Thrym	227
The Norns	229
Blissful Spirits	237
Cort Adeler in Venice	247
The King's Volunteers on Amager	259
In Memory of Weyse	265
The Mandarin's Daughters	269
A Fairy Tale in Pictures	271
Arcona	278
From the Last Century	289
From Siberia to Moscow	293
Appendix	301
The Sleepwalker	302
The Pages of the Duke de Vendome	312
Paul and Virginia	318
Nina, or the Girl Driven Mad by Love	326
La Sylphide	332
Index	339

INTRODUCTION

In the first volume of his memoirs (1848), Bournonville bemoaned the ephemerality of the choreographic art: "Of a ballet, which has addressed both the gay and the earnest, the young and the old, and brought a kind of excitement into our everyday lives, nothing remains save a libretto! Were it only so much as a sketch, an outline, a venerable ruin, or a skeleton which could give some idea of the true dimensions [of the work]. But– a *libretto*! Hardly more than the scaffolding left over from exploded fireworks!"

When he wrote those words, Bournonville was on the verge of retiring as a dancer, and his future in the theatre was uncertain. He felt that the choreographic works on which he had lavished so much time and care for 18 years would gradually fade from the repertoire of the Royal Danish Ballet and his name would be all but forgotten. Today, a century after his death, Bournonville's name is more widely known than it was during his lifetime: eight ballets and a number of assorted dances still grace the stage of Copenhagen's Royal Theatre, and those "skeletal" libretti – what Bournonville called his "ballet poems"– still exist to impress upon us what a treasure we possess in the Bournonville ballets, to remind us of what has been lost over the years, and – perhaps most important of all – to reveal to us the workings of an ingenious, practical choreographer's mind.

Bournonville's inspiration came from many things and many places: countries he saw, people he met, a stroll in the woods, a novel read, a poem heard, a song remembered. When the jumble of images had sorted itself out in his head and the confusion had cleared, the Danish ballet master would sit down at his desk and write until he had finished his libretto. After completing this first step, he set the story aside for a while. Then he read through it again, and if it still retained his interest, he considered it ripe for composition. After being polished, the synopsis was sent on to the theatre administration for its approval. Once this had been obtained, Bournonville's work with the composer began. While the score was being written, the choreographer worked on the mime scenes and some of the dances. In an essay in *Theatre Research Studies*, the Danish critic and dance historian Allan Fridericia has superbly described the next phase in Bournonville's creative process, emphasizing the importance of the libretto – the written ballet poem – to the finished ballet:

> What we know today as the libretto did not appear until the musical score was completed, the ballet was composed and the rehearsals were finished. Then Bournonville wrote a completely new little book which was published and which could be purchased by the theatre audience .... The procedure indicates

that such vital changes may have taken place during the process that the original libretto could not be used. Therefore Bournonville's small print with descriptions of the action is of great interest. In their carefully considered choice of words they show many details. One might be tempted to write something off as a "florid" sentence, but further study will reveal a lost, but logical feature. Everything indicates something concretely worked out on stage.*

Used in conjunction with correspondence, production records, and rehearsal scores, the libretti also help us to piece together a more comprehensive picture of the Danish ballet master as an artist of national and international caliber. The availability of these primary printed source materials should enable us to assess more fully his place in the world of nineteenth-century European ballet. As his characters and ideas unfold before us, we can begin to compare them with those of other choreographers of his day and finally discover, in part, something sorely missed by many critics today: the setting in which August Bournonville's choreographic "gems" were once displayed.

This book contains the complete extant scenarios for Bournonville's ballets. For a few of his works, primarily divertissements, no printed libretto has survived. For these shadowy works some basic information is given, while the scenarios for the five early ballets based on French originals – *from La Somnambule* to *La Sylphide* – are included in an appendix.

---

*   Allan Fridericia, "Bournonville's Ballet Napoli: In the Light of Archive Materials and Theatrical Practice," *Theatre Research Studies*, Copenhagen, 1972, p. 53.

A CHRONOLOGY[†] OF BOURNONVILLE'S STAGE WORKS:

BALLETS AND DIVERTISSEMENTS, INDIVIDUAL DANCES, AND STAGINGS OF OPERAS AND PLAYS

The following chronology has been prepared from four sources: Dan Fog's indispensable *The Royal Danish Ballet, 1790-1958, and August Bournonville: a Chronological Catalogue of the Ballets and Ballet-Divertissements Performed at the Royal Theatres of Copenhagen and a Catalogue of August Bournonville's Works, With a Musical Bibliography* (Copenhagen, 1961); August Bournonville, *Mit Theatreliv* (My Theatre Life), 3 vols. (Copenhagen, 1848–78); Thomas Overskou, *Den danske Skueplads i dens Historie (The History of the Danish Stage)*, 7 vols. (Copenhagen, 1854–76); and Bournonville's handwritten list of ballets and individual pas and stage arrangements done by him. This list can be found among Bournonville's papers in the Royal Library in Copenhagen and seems to have been drawn up by the choreographer during the early 1850s.

In the chronology presented here, titles of works staged by August Bournonville are given together with the date of first performance or the date on which the Bournonville production of the work had its premiere. Ballets and ballet divertissements are listed by title alone, while operas and plays are indicated as such. The listings for the most part follow those given by Fog in his catalogue. Titles of compositions preceded by an asterisk, however, are not listed by Fog and are entered solely on the basis of their inclusion in Bournonville's handwritten list. Unless otherwise indicated, all of these productions were premiered in Copenhagen.

Acclaim to the Graces (*Gratiernes Hylding*). 1 September 1829
Divertissement.

Fidelio. Opera by Beethoven.   17 September 1829

La Somnambule (*Søvngaengersken*).
Bournonville, after Aumer. Ballet in three acts.

* Pas de Deux Oriental (*partly after another choreographer*). Newspapers from the time record that Bournonville and Andrea Kraetzmer appeared in a pas de deux in "a divertissement in the oriental style" composed by Funck during the previous season.   ? late September 1829

[†]A more detailed, annotated chronology may be found in Knud Arne Jürgensen's *The Bournonville Tradition*, Dance Books, London, 1997.

Soldier and Peasant (*Soldat og Bonde*). Divertissement.	13 October 1829
Princess Isabella (*Prindsesse Isabella*). Play by J. L. Heiberg.	29 October 1829
*Pas de deux from *La Muette de Portici* (*partly after another choreographer*).	22 May 1830
Les Pages du Duc de Vendôme (Hertugen af Vendômes Pager). Bournonville, after Aumer.	3 September 1830
Paul et Virginie (*Paul og Virginia*), Bournonville, after Gardel. Ballet in three acts.	10 October 1830
La Fiancée. Opera by Auber.	22 April 1831
Victor's Wedding (*Victors Bryllup*). Ballet in one act.	23 April 1831
*Pas de cinq from *The Youth of Henry V* (*Henrik den Femtes Ungdom*). Singspiel with music by Paccini and others.	28 October 1831
*Pas de deux from *Zampa*. Opera by Hérold.	30 January 1832
Faust. Ballet in three acts.	25 April 1832
*Pas de cinq from *The Raven* (*Ravnen*). Opera by J. P. E. Hartmann.	29 October 1832
The Veteran (*Veteranen*). Ballet in one act.	29 January 1833
Romeo and Giulietta (*Romeo og Giulietta*). Bournonville, after Galeotti. Ballet in five acts.	27 April 1833
*Pas de deux in *The Carnival* (*Milon's Carnaval de Venise, with some choreography by P. Larcher*).	ballet premiered in Copenhagen in 1823; revived during the 1832–33 season
The Guerrilla Band (*Guerillabanden*). Opera by J. Bredal.	29 January 1834

Der Templer und die Jüdin. Opera by Marschner.	21 April 1834
Nina. Bournonville, after Milon. Ballet in two acts.	30 September 1834
**Pas de deux* for Grahn's debut.	?
Le Pre-aux-Clercs. Opera by Hérold.	28 October 1834
The Tyroleans (Tyrolerne). Ballet in one act. According to Fog, on and after 8 February 1844 this ballet included a "Hamburg-Scottish" and a Galop by Lumbye; in his handwritten list of individual pas, Bournonville records a "Hamborger Skotsk and Finale to *The Tyroleans*."	6 March 1835
Yelva. Play by Castelli and Overskou, after Scribe and others.	9 June 1835
**In Memory of Schall (Schalls Minde)*.	3 September 1835
**Pas de deux in *Herman von Unna*.	? 1835
Valdemar. Ballet in four acts.	28 October 1835
Hans Heiling. Opera by Marschner.	13 May 1836
La Sylphide (Sylphiden). Bournonville, after Taglioni. Ballet in two acts.	28 November 1836
**Pas de trois*, Johansson.	?
Don Quixote at Camacho's Wedding (Don Quixote ved Camachos Bryllup). Ballet in three acts.	24 February 1837
**Pas de trois from *Le Postillon de Lonjumeau*. Opera by Adam.	28 October 1837
Hertha's Offering (Herthas Offer). Divertissement.	29 January 1838
Fiorella. Opera by Auber.	13 February 1838
St. Olaf (Olaf den Hellige). Play be A. Oehlenschläger.	13 March 1838

The Isle of Fantasy (*Phantasiens Øe*). Ballet in two acts and a final tableaux.	28 October 1838
Le Domino Noir. Opera by Auber.	29 January 1839
Aladdin. Play by A. Oehlenschläger	17 April 1839
The Festival in Albano (*Festen i Albano*). Ballet in one act.	28 October 1839
The Fatherland's Muses (*Faedrelandets Muser*). Pantomimic prologue.	20 March 1840
The Toreador (*Toreadoren*). Ballet in two acts.	27 November 1840
Le Dieu et la Bayadère (*Brama og Bayadèren*). Opera by Auber.	7 February 1841
*Pas de Deux a la Taglioni.	? 1841
*Pas de Deux de Retour (Bournonville made his first appearance on the stage after his return from exile in Italy in a pas de deux on 14 October 1841.)	? 14 October 1841
*The Soprano (Sangerinden). Dramatic situation by H. C. Andersen.	? 1841
*Pas de deux from *Robert le Diable* (Robert af Normandiet). Opera by Meyerbeer.	opera premiered in Copenhagen in 1833 with choreography by P. Funck; revived 5 December 1841 with choreography by P. Larcher
*Cracovienne (partly after another choreographer).	?
Napoli. Ballet in three acts.	29 March 1842

William Tell (*Wilhelm Tell*). Opera by Rossini. (*William Tell* does not appear in Bournonville's handwritten list of works for which he did dances or stage arrangements; he does mention Tell in the list in Mit Theatreliv, which was probably compiled in the 1870s. Lefebvre did the choreography for the 1842 production, but Bournonville probably choreographed the revival in the 1860s.) 4 September 1842

Undine. A fairy play after de la Motte Fouqué. 18 September 1842

Polka Militaire. Divertissement. 1 November 1842

The Childhood of Erik Menved (*Erik Menveds Barndom*). Ballet in four acts. 12 January 1843

Les Diamants de la Couronne (*Kronjuvelerne*). Opera by Auber. 17 February 1843

Moise (*Moses*). Opera by Rossini. 20 September 1843

*Pas de Deux, retour de Fjeldsted. ? 1843

Le Nozze di Figaro (*Figaros Bryllup*). Opera by Mozart. 7 January 1844

Les Huguenots (*Hugenotterne*). Opera by Meyerbeer. 28 February 1844

Bellman. Ballet in one act. 3 June 1844

The Oresteia (*Orestias*). Unperformed. ? 1844

Gioacchino. Play be H. P. Holst. 12 October 1844

A Children's Party (*En Børnefest*). Divertissement. 23 October 1844

Hamburger Dans. Pas de deux. ? November 1844

*Parisian Polka for Mme Zrza's benefit performance. 8 February 1845

*The Blossom of Happiness (*Lykkens Blomst*). Play by H. C. Andersen. 16 February 1845

Don Giovanni (*Don Juan*). Opera by Mozart.	new production, 23 February 1845
Kirsten Piil. Ballet in three acts.	26 February 1845
Raphael (*Rafael*). Ballet in six tableaux (*three acts*).	30 May 1845
*Orpheus (Act II of Gluck's opera given as a benefit for the composer Wexschall's survivors).	10 February 1846
Uthal. Opera by E. N. Méhul.	7 July 1846
Polacca Guerriera. Pas de deux.	5 September 1846
Czaar und Zimmermann (*Czaren og Tømmermanden*). Opera by A. Lortzing.	18 September 1846
The New Penelope (*Den nye Penelope*). Ballet in two acts. *The New Penelope* and *The White Rose* are apparently the only completed portions of a projected cycle of four ballets to be called *The Four Seasons, or Cupid's Journey* (*De fire Aarstider eller Amors Rejse*).	26 January 1847
Das Diamantkreuz (*Diamantkorset*). Opera by S. Saloman.	20 March 1847
Maritana. Carnival divertissement	15 April 1847
The White Rose (*Den hvide Rose*). Ballet in one act.	20 September 1847
An Echo of Sunday (*Søndags Echo*). Divertissement.	5 March 1848
Federigo. Opera by H. Rung	23 March 1848
The Lucky Wheel (*Lykkens Iljul*). Play by H. P. Holst.	26 March 1848
Les Mousquetaires de la Reine (*Dronningens Livgarde*). Opera by Halévy	7 October 1848
Old Memories (*Gamle Minder*). Ballet in one act.	18 December 1848

The Wedding at Lake Como (*Brylluppet ved Comosøen*). Opera by F. Glaeser.	29 January 1849
**Gustav III* (*Gustav den Tredie*). Play by M. V. Brun.	4 February 1849
The Conservatoire (*Conservatoriet*). Ballet in two acts (title now spelled *Konservatoriet*).	6 May 1849
Pas des Trois Cousines. Divertissement.	15 May 1849
**Holmen's Old Guard* (*Holmens faste Stok*). Divertissement.	? 16 August 1849
Hussar Dance (*Husardans*). Divertissement	16 August 1849
Masquerade (*Maskaraden*). Play by L. Holberg.	12 December 1849
The Irresistibles (*De Uimodstaaelige*). Divertissement	3 February 1850
**Marsk Stig*. Play by C. Hauch.	15 March 1850
Psyche. Ballet in one act.	7 May 1850
**The Castle of Montenero* (*Slottet Montenero*). Singspiel by N. M. Dalayrac.	revived after 19 years on 24 February 1851
The Kermesse in Bruges (*Kermessen i Briugge*). Ballet in three acts.	4 April 1851
Preciosa. Play with music by C. M. von Weber.	premiered in Copenhagen in 1822 with choreography by Antoine Bournonville; revived 11 May 1851 with choreography by August Bournonville
Zulma, or The Crystal Palace (*Zulma eller Chrystalpaladset*). Ballet in three acts.	14 February 1852
The Nix (*Nøkken*). Opera by F. Glaeser.	12 February 1853

The Wedding Festival in Hardanger (*Brudefaerden i Hardanger*). Ballet in two acts.	4 March 1853
A Folk Tale (*Et Folkesagn*). Ballet in three acts.	20 March 1854
Il Matrimonio Segreto (*Det hemmelige Ægteskab*). Opera by Cimarosa.	new production, 30 May 1854
La Ventana. Divertissement.	19 June 1854
Abdallah. Ballet in three acts.	28 March 1855
Final version of *La Ventana* with final seguidilla after Paul Taglioni	6 October 1856
The Earnest Maiden (*Den alvorlige Pige*). Divertissement.	23 November 1856
In the Carpathians (*I Karpatherne*). Ballet in three acts.	4 March 1857
Lucia di Lammermoor (*Lucia af Lammermoor*). Opera by Donizetti.	3 December 1857
Little Kirsten (*Liden Kirsten*). Opera by J. P. E. Hartmann.	28 October 1858
Polketta. Pas de deux.	31 October 1858
The Fisher Girls (*Fiskerpigerne*).	21 November 1858
El Caprichio. Jaleo.	1 December 1858
The Flower Festival at Genzano (*Blomsterfesten i Ganzano*). Ballet in one act.	19 December 1858
Galop militaire. Pas de deux.	21 January 1859
Tarantella Napolitana. Pas de deux.	1 March 1859
La Polonaise. Pas de deux.	29 March 1859
Lucrezia Borgia. Opera by Donizetti.	15 April 1859
The Mountain Hut (*Fjeldstuen*). Ballet in two acts.	13 May 1859

The Healing Spring (Kilderejsen). Play by L. Holberg.	revived 22 May 1959 with an Intermedium composed by Bournonville
Far from Denmark (Fjernt fra Danmark). Ballet in two acts.	20 April 1860
Divertissement in honour of Wilhelm of Hesse's Golden Anniversary.	10 November 1860
Iphigenia in Aulis (Iphigenia i Aulis). Opera by Gluck.	27 April 1861
The Valkyr (Valkyrien). Ballet in four acts.	13 September 1861

From 1 October 1861 until 1864, Bournonville served as intendant for the stage at the Royal Theatre in Stockholm. A list of operas, plays, and ballets staged by him during that period can be found in Bournonville's autobiography, *Mit Theatreliv*, vol. II, pp. 396–402, and in F. A. Dahlgren, *Anteckningar om Stockholms Theatrar* (Stockholm, 1866).

Il Trovatore (Troubadouren). Opera by Verdi.	10 September 1865
Ponte Molle (Pontemolle). Ballet in two tableaux.	11 April 1866
The Merry Wives of Windsor (De lystige Koner i Windsor). Opera by Nicolai.	14 September 1867
The Elf Maiden (Elverpigen). Opera by Emil Hartmann.	5 November 1867
The Lay of Thrym (Thrymskviden). Ballet in four acts.	21 February 1868
Die Zauberflöte (Tryllefløjten). Opera by Mozart.	new production, 27 January 1869
The Pascha's Daughter (Paschaens Datter). Opera by Heise.	30 September 1869
Cort Adeler in Venice (Cort Adeler i Venedig). Ballet in three acts and two final tableaux.	14 January 1870
Bouquet Royal. Divertissement.	27 January 1870

Scandinavian Quadrille (*Skandinavisk Quadrille*). Divertissement.	6 February 1870
Lohengrin. Opera by Wagner.	30 April 1870
Les Dragons de Villars (*Villars Dragoner*). Opera by Maillart.	19 October 1870
Le Cheval de Bronze (*Broncehesten*). Opera by Auber.	new production, 22 January 1871
The King's Volunteers on Amager (*Livjaegernepaa Amager*). Ballet in one act.	19 February 1871
The Sally from Classens Have, 1807 (*Udfaldet i Classens Have, 31 August, 1807*). Tableau arranged after a painting by C. W. Eckersberg.	? June 1871
A Fairy Tale in Pictures (*Et Eventyr i Billeder*). Ballet in three acts.	26 December 1871
Die Meistersinger (*Mestersangerne i Nürnberg*). Opera by Wagner.	23 March 1872
Robert le Diable (*Robert af Normandiet*). Opera by Meyerbeer.	new production by Bournonville, 19 January 1873
The Corsican (*Korsicaneren*). Opera by Emil Hartmann.	7 April 1873
The Mandarin's Daughters (*Mandarinens Døttre*). Divertissement.	23 April 1873
In Memory of Weyse (*Weyses Minde*). Epilogue with tableaux.	5 March 1874
Iphigenia in Tauris (*Ifigenia i Tauris*). Opera by Gluck.	28 April 1874
Farewell to the Old Theatre (*Farvel til det gamle Theatre*). Divertissement.	1 June 1874
Tannhiuser. Opera by Wagner.	17 March 1875
Arcona. Ballet in four acts.	7 May 1875
From the Last Century (*Fra det forrige Aarhundrede*). Divertissement.	31 October 1875
The Bewitched (*Den Bjergtagne*). Opera by I. Hallstrom.	10 May 1876
From Siberia to Moscow (*Fra Siberien til Moskou*). Ballet in two acts.	7 December 1876

A Memorial Wreath to Denmark's Great Poet　　14 November 1879
(*Mindets Krans til Danmarks Store Digter*).
Cycle of four tableaux honouring Adam
Oehlenschläger

In addition to the ballet divertissements listed in this chronology, Bournonville, in a chapter of his memoirs entitled "Divertissements" (*Mit Theatreliv*, vol. 2), mentions several other small, undated choreographic works. These "bagatelles," as he calls them, must have been done prior to 1865, when the second volume of the autobiography was published. They include *Danes in China* (*De Danske i Kina*), *The Sailor's Return* (*Matrosens Hjemkomst*), *Las Hermanas de Sevilla*, *The Prophecy of Love* (*Kjaerligheds Spaadomme*), and *The Flower Maids of Florence* (*De florentinske Blomsterpiger*).

With respect to operas, Fog, on page 22 of his *Catalogue*, states that he was unable to trace dance arrangements done by Bournonville for the following operas contained in the listing of his works in *Mit Theatreliv*, vol. 3, part 1: Auber: *Le Maçon* (*Muurmesteren*); Boïeldieu: *La Dame Blanche* (*Den hvide Dame*), *Le Petit Chaperon Rouge* (*Den lille Rødhaette*), and *Jean de Paris* (*Johan fra Paris*); Méhul: *Joseph et Ses Frères* (*Joseph og hans Brqdre*); and Mozart: *Die Entführung aus dem Serail* (*Bortførelsen fra Serailet*).

SCENARIOS AND CAST LISTS

ACCLAIM TO THE GRACES

Divertissement
by
August Bournonville
Music arranged from works by
Michele Enrico Carafa, Robert von Gallenberg and Fernando Sor

Performed for the first time on September 1, 1829

Characters

APOLLO	Hr. Larcher
ZEPHYR	Hr. A. Bournonville
FLORA	Jfr. Werning
TERPSICHORE	Mme. Kraetzmer
THE GRACES	Mme. Haack
	Mme. Stramboe
	Jfr. S. Møller

The Graces' Retinue
Geniuses of Joy
Flora's Retinue
Muses
Warriors

The Pas de Trois was choreographed by Auguste Vestris.

* * *

SOLDIER AND PEASANT
(Soldat og Bonde)
Pantomimic Idyll

Composed by August Bournonville

Music composed and arranged by Michele Enrico Carafa, Francois-Charlemagne Lefevre, and Felice Romani

Performed for the first time at the Royal Theatre, Copenhagen, on October 13, 1829

Characters

MARTIN	Hr. Fredstrup
MÈRE MARTIN	Mme. Schouw
VICTOR, a voltigeur, their son	Hr. Bournonville
LISE, his fiancée	Mme. Kraetzmer
ANNA, his sister	Jfr. Werning
A YOUNG SHEPHERD	Hr. Larcher
MARTIN'S CHIEF FARM HAND	Hr. Stramboe

The stage represents a rural area. On one side lies a farmhouse; in the background, a hill.

[**Translator's note**: *Soldier and Peasant* was Bournonville's second original work after his return to Copenhagen in 1829, coming shortly after the divertissement *Acclaim to the Graces* (September 1) and his version of Aumer's *The Sleepwalker* (September 21). In *My Theatre Life* he says of *Soldier and Peasant*

> I had become better acquainted with the public's taste and the Theatre's talent by the time I produced this bagatelle under the name of "pantomimic idyll." I wished to dance a pas de trois (partially after Albert) as well as a bravura solo that Vestris had taught me, and needing a suitable motif, I chose my own homecoming. "Cordiality" had not yet become synonymous with "sentimentality," the French soldier was not so trite a stage character as he later became, and – curiously enough – at that time France and Napoleon alluded quite nicely to Denmark and our king.

The work was a great success and remained in the repertory for many years. Bournonville's choreographic notes for his final revival of the ballet in 1861 have formed the basis for the recent reconstruction of the pas de trois by Dinna Bjørn and Knud Arne Jürgensen.]

Victor has been gone from his family for several years. The defense of his native land has taken him from its bosom, away from his rustic pursuits, his birthplace, and his sweetheart. Peace has now been concluded, and the loved ones he left behind wait with longing for news of his return. The letter arrives. His father seizes it with delight. He reads it, kisses it, and expresses the liveliest joy, which is shared by those around him. "He is coming today!" they all exclaim; and the father, who, in his delight, has regained his youthful vigor and martial spirit, rushes off to meet his beloved son. Victor's mother, fiancée, sister, and the friends of his youth follow the old man, rejoicing over the happy reunion that is about to take place.

Victor has been travelling the whole night through. He has just reached the top of the hill, whence he beholds his ancestral home once more. His agitation mounts with every step and, beside himself, he dashes towards his parents' abode. But, "There is nobody home. No one comes running to give me a fond greeting. Lord! Could it be? I tremble–" Just then a little lad jumps up onto his shoulder and, drunk with delight, he recognizes his youngest brother, whom he greets with tenderness. Then his happy parents, his fiancée, his relatives and friends enter, rejoicing, and embrace the young warrior, who ecstatically throws himself into his beloved's arms. "Victor! Dear Victor! My Victor!" resounds from every side, with various expressions of love, tenderness, and sympathy.

His father bids him tell what has happened to him during his absence. "Shall I tell you?" asks the young warrior. "Well then! Listen! Do you remember how heavy at heart I was when I left you to set off for camp? Do you remember how reluctantly I journeyed hence? But my courage revived when they gave me a weapon and taught me how to use it. I joined the colours. Drum and bugle called me to fight the enemy. With my knapsack on my back, I marched off with my battalion. We soon espied the enemy. There was a battle; cannon thundered, and we looked death in the face. Round about me lay my valiant comrades. I swiftly returned the enemy's fire; we closed ranks and were attacking with charged weapons when a bullet struck my left arm." General dismay. "Oh, it was nothing! Look, dearest," he continues, turning to his fiancée, "see this kerchief which thou tiedst around my neck when I departed! I was wearing it in the hour of peril; with it I bound up my arm, and my wound I then held twice as dear. The enemy fled; we triumphed. Bugles called us back and the general ordered me to step forward. 'Voltigeur! I am pleased with thee.' 'General!' 'Thou hast earned a badge of honour. There, take mine.' I seized it with enthusiasm and hung it upon my breast. Our native land is now at peace; it needs my arm no more, and so I return to the bosom of my family. Father, there is my medal; preserve it as a sacred momento. There is my discharge, Mother; keep it. And thou, Lise. There is my hand; my heart is already thine."

Victor now gives himself up to his love and to his former estate. He takes part in the country people's pursuits, in their dancing and innocent merriment.

* * *

VICTOR'S WEDDING, OR THE ANCESTRAL HOME

A Ballet in One Act
by
August Bournonville

Music composed by Philip Ludvig Keck
(sequel to *Soldier and Peasant*)

Performed for the first time on April 23, 1831

Characters

MARTIN .... Hr. Fredstrup
MERE MARTIN .... Mad. Schouw
VICTOR, their son .... Hr. Bournonville
LISE, his bride .... Mad. Kraetzmer
ANNA, his sister .... Jfr. Werning
PAUL, his brother .... Hr. Hoppe
MICHEL .... Hr. Stramboe
LOUISE .... Mad. Haack
TWO SOLDIERS .... MM. Stramboe and Hammer
AN ENEMY SOLDIER .... Hr. Füssel

Solo Dances

MM. Larcher and Funck, Mad. Bauer and Jfr. Møller

Coryphées

MM. Friis and Bentzen

Young Peasants of Both Genders

MM. Jacobsen, Füssel, Jr., Holm, Nehm, Lund, Borch, Pio, Füssel, Sr., and Mesdames Bentzen, Larcher, Stramboe, Weiner, Bachmann, Fredstrup, Rasmussen, Schaarup

Older Peasant Folk

MM. Weile, Villeneuve, Lundgreen, and Mesdames Møller, Freymann, Johnson, Wolstrup

Enemy Soldiers

MM. Jacobsen, Holm, Lund, Weile

Children

BOYS: Hoppensach, Bech, Lund, Ring
GIRLS: Rinda, Augusta, Sophie, Fjeldsted, Fredstrup 2, Fredstrup 3, AEggers, Weiner 2

A large barn, festively adorned with flower garlands, fully laid tables, and a rustic orchestra. Through the wide gate can be seen a smiling landscape.

Autumn and winter have gone by since Victor's return. Spring, with the appointed wedding day, is at hand. But the enemy army is approaching the frontier; our troops will soon meet them, and Victor's birthplace may become the scene of battle.

The return of the wedding procession from the church is awaited. Martin's servants have completed all the preparations and spend several moments talking and jesting. Soon noisy music is heard, and the joyous procession comes dancing down the hill. Happy and friendly faces greet the young couple beneath the ancestral roof, and loyal handshakes express the warmest wishes.

Martin clasps his children to his breast. "Victor," says he, "behold thy lovely bride. Give me thy word that thou wilt make her happy. And thou, Lise – be a wife such as mine own good woman! My children! Remember to thank the Lord for everything. May his blessing be upon you."

Michel, announcing that the meal is ready, lifts the company out of this solemn mood. "Long live joy! Help yourselves!" The rustic orchestra strikes up and the merry dances lend a most animated touch to the celebration. Dancing groups encircle bride and bridegroom, everyone is filled with the liveliest joy, and the couple is cheered with brimming glasses.

An inexplicable apprehension suddenly strikes the guests, who were previously so merry. They scan one another's faces; they harken, and distant shots fill all of them with misgivings. Victor pricks up his ears. The shots can be heard more clearly now, and he rapidly surmises that the enemy has attacked. Familiar bugle calls confirm this. He climbs the hill, and from the far-off smoke of burning villages, he recognizes the enemy's method of waging war. Filled with indignation, Victor rushes down amidst his friends: "Foreign assailants tread the soil of our native land! Behold yon death and destruction! Harken to our women's cries of terror!" The menfolk have understood Victor's words. They hasten to take up arms.

The trembling bride implores her beloved to avoid the threatening danger: "But a little while ago thou swore to live for me, yet now thou wouldst desert me, perhaps never to return again." Sobbing, she sinks against Victor's breast, but nought can weaken the feeling of what he owes to his ancestral home. The medal he wears imposes greater obligations on him than on anyone else: "Couldst thou love me were I a coward? Weep not, Lise! Feel my heart: it beats without fear."

The father, who has been listening to Victor with joy, embraces his worthy son. He himself has been a soldier and still feels the strength to fight for king and country. Dismayed, Victor tries to remonstrate with him, but the old man remains adamant: he places all his trust in protecting Providence. The dust is soon brushed off his old musket, and Victor's haversack contains reserves of cartridges for both of their rifles. When the son expresses doubts about his father's fitness for military service, the old man – to his astonishment – shows him that he is no way inferior to the young *voltigeur* [a rifleman in a French infantry brigade]. Another fond farewell to the weeping family, and they set off in the name of God.

The tocsin has called the inhabitants of the neighbourhood to arms. They hasten to the ambush whence they will attack the enemy. A band of well-armed peasants passes Martin's farmstead. It is Victor who shall lead them forward. Honoured by this mission, he encourages them to fight the good fight; he inflames their courage to enthusiasm, and they rush off to battle.

The mother, the bride, Anna, and little Paul remain behind in the closed barn. They abandon themselves to their grief and allow their tears to flow freely. Lise, in particular, is disconsolate. With every minute, her anxiety mounts. Her imagination pictures Victor surrounded by a thousand perils; every shot she hears brings death, and in her mind she can already see the cavalry trampling the body of her beloved. The others momentarily forget their troubles in order to comfort the poor girl, but she stares at them wild-eyed and pushes them away, wishing to go off to battle to die at her bridegroom's side. With sympathetic earnestness, the pious mother points out to her that her lack of faith in Heaven's aid is an offence: "And what about me? Would my loss as a wife and mother not be twice as great as yours? My children! We will not despair. Let us take refuge in the Lord! Our prayers for our loved ones shall go with them and strengthen us."

The din of battle draws nearer and passes close to the barn with the clash of swords and flint-shot. The praying group draws ever more tightly together; terrified, they huddle about Mere Martin and imploringly lift their trembling hands to Heaven. The battle moves off into the distance; danger no longer threatens, and with renewed hope the mother embraces her children.

The plaintive groans of wounded soldiers can be heard outside. Lise, Anna, and Paul hasten to help and soon return supporting two valiant defenders of the mother country, whose wounds prevent them from pursuing the enemy. Their injuries are dressed and bound with the tenderest care, and they express their deepest thanks to the kind people. The soldiers can see that they are anxious to know the outcome of the battle. They allay the women's fears and add that a victorious hero is their leader. Mere Martin brings them wine, and they drink a toast with warlike enthusiasm.

The confusion of battle can still be heard at some distance, and in the midst of it resounds Victor's familiar march. "My bridegroom, my son, my brother is not far off!" cries the family, and even the threatening danger cannot prevent them from venturing outside. The wounded soldiers who have remained behind have been listening, however, and every time they hear the refrain of the march, they clink their glasses to the victor and to peace. The womenfolk and Paul return, frightened. They are pursued by enemy troops who are burning and pillaging as they retreat.

The grateful soldiers forget their wounds, promise to defend their benefactors with all the strength that is in them, and prepare to offer valiant resistance. The enemy soldiers burst in, but at that very moment the bugles proclaim: "Victory is ours!" The enemy flees, the barn door is opened, intermingled peasants and soldiers fill the background. With deep emotion, Martin and Victor embrace their loved ones. No one is missing from the ancestral home; tears of joy speak louder than words, and the victor's joy is sent heavenward.

Victor would end this memorable day with joy and merriment. The celebration begins once more. New guests, old comrades-in-arms, have arrived at his wedding, and the dancing does not stop until Victor, with glass in hand, proposes a toast to the father of the country – the hero of the day and of the age.

* * *

FAUST

An Original Romantic Ballet in Three Acts
by
August Bournonville
Music composed and arranged by Philip Ludvig Keck from works by
Jean-Madeleine Schneitzhoeffer, Oreste Carlini, Fernando Sor,
Gaspare Spontini, Gioacchino Rossini, and Carl Maria von Weber

First performed on April 25, 1832,
at the Royal Theatre, Copenhagen

Characters

FAUST	Hr. Bournonville
JOHANNA, a widow	Mad. Schouw
MARGARETHA } her children	Mad. Kraetzmer
VALENTIN	Hr. Larcher
MARTHA, a young village girl	Jfr. Werning
THE MAGISTRATE	Hr. Fredstrup
MEPHISTOPHELES	Hr. Stramboe
URIEL	Mad. Bauer
HOPE	Jfr. Fredstrup

Dances and Subordinate Parts

Genii

Children: Hoppe, Rinda, Augusta, Sophie, Nanna, Fjeldsted, Weiner

Witches

Mesdames Fredstrup, Johnson, Skaarup, Wolstrup, Møller-Freimann,
Eggers, Agnes, Ruff

Evil Spirits

Messieurs Hammer, Weile, Lund, Pio, Borch

Monkeys

Hoppensach, Lund, Ring, Bech, Ruff

ACT TWO

Villagers

Messieurs Bentzen and Friis; Mesdames Møller and Weiner
Messieurs Holm, Nehm, Füssel, Sr., Jacobsen, Lund

Füssel, Jr.; Mesdames Larcher, Stramboe, Worre, Andersen, Bechmann, Rasmussen, Johnson, Wolstrup, Skaarup, Møller-Freimann

Soldiers	**Older Peasants**
Messieurs Hammer and Borch	Villeneuve and Lundgreen

ACT THREE

A MOUNTEBANK	Hr. Jacobsen
A LAD	Hr. Fredstrup
Three Townspeople	Hr. Villeneuve / Hr. Nehm / Hr. Lundgreen
A CHILD	Augusta
ITS MOTHER	Jfr. Larcher

Wandering Gypsies

Hr. Funck   Jfr. Werning
Messieurs Bentzen, Friis, Hammer, Holm
Mesdames Møller, Weiner, Worre, Rasmussen

FAIRGOERS, COMMONERS, GUARDS, CHERUBS

The action takes place in and outside of a German city in the Middle Ages.

ACT I

Faust's study, with book shelves, globes, and mathematical instruments. A table upon which are to be found a number of books and manuscripts, an hourglass, skull, and other things, stands near the fireplace.

 Faust is seated in an armchair. He is surrounded by a flock of disciples, whose positions bear witness to their rapt attention. He has finished his lecture, but still they listen. He politely bids them farewell and they take leave of him with expressions of deep respect.
 Faust wistfully gazes after them and seems to lament his own lack of the very wisdom they seek to learn from him. Brooding, he paces back and forth, restlessly pages through a thick book, and tries to write down a thought, which his pen refuses to reproduce. He opens a window and gazes in rapture at the void beyond. But the celestial globe that revolves beneath his hand gives knowledge only of visible things, and all of his books contain nought but dark speeches about the higher, invisible, and

eternal sphere. He bemoans his waste of time, tears the newly written page into shreds, and despondently sinks back into his chair.

But not in vain shall he have devoted himself to the art of magic. Spirits must come forth at his command, and the heavenly host itself shall reveal the great secret to him. He solemnly conjures up the good spirits. Kneeling, he begs their assistance, and to the strains of a stream of lovely melodies, Uriel, Hope, and a band of genii hover round him.

The angel raises the imploring Faust and promises him all the knowledge that will make him happy; but when the inquisitive man seeks to know what lies on the other side of the grave and beyond the stars, Uriel compassionately shakes his head, gently reproves him for this presumptuous brooding, and, by means of the childlike gaiety of the genii, the fresh flower garlands, and the delicious strains of the harp, refers him to the delights of innocence, Nature, and Art, which ought to enliven and comfort his soul. Uriel meaningfully points to Hope, who amicably approaches Faust, hands him a ring, and bids him remember her.

The genii, perceiving that Faust has been disappointed in his expectations, lovingly hover round him and imploringly point to the precious ring. They gradually vanish but frequently look back with gentle admonition.

Faust, who has long been frustrated in his designs, starts, as if from a dream. A fierce struggle is taking place within him. He has taken the first step into the spirit world and yet he believes himself to be as far as ever from his goal! He defiantly renounces any alliance with the good spirits and calls upon the infernal regions.

The Evil One is not long in coming. Thunder crashes, lightning and red flames illuminate the sinister chamber, and out of a bookcase jumps Mephistopheles.

In deadly earnest, Mephistopheles seeks to learn Faust's request; but when he perceives the terror he inspires, he changes his tone and assumes the guise of Faust's humble servant. He succeeds in ingratiating himself. Faust shows him his books and instruments; Mephistopheles laughs at him, pushes aside the books, and displays the utmost contempt for all studies. His simple signature on a parchment scroll, which Mephistopheles produces, will, according to *him*, open Faust's eyes to true wisdom. Faust is reluctant to sign, but when Mephistopheles offers to transport him to the very place where the elixir of wisdom is made, he can no longer resist his thirst for knowledge; he chooses to go with him, and on Mephistopheles' outspread cloak they travel quickly and easily.

The room vanishes, and the travellers find themselves deep inside a crevice. Small paths wind up both sides of the abyss, and on the ground a cauldron hangs over a fire. It is night, and windy.

An old witch is dozing by the fire. A guenon [a long-tailed monkey] skims the pot; a number of animals of the same sort jump about the cave; they perceive the newcomers and awaken the witch, who flies into a rage at the sight of these uninvited guests!

She seizes a firebrand and pursues Faust and Mephistopheles with it. The latter, however, wrests the brand from her grasp and illumines his own countenance, which the hag immediately recognizes.

She throws herself at her master's feet.

Mephistopheles bids her summon her sisters and helpers to prepare the potion Faust desires. She obeys and strikes the cauldron with her crutch-handled stick. Echo answers.

Over the mountains and down the pathways to the abyss comes a wild noise, and torchlight soon illumines the dark night. Witches, brutes, and evil spirits flock to the place.

The Witches' Sabbat

The potion is prepared and handed to Faust, who bluffly drains the flaming cup. A clap of thunder.

The background opens; rays of light illumine a lovely landscape.

In the shelter of a rose bush, guarded by small genii, slumbers a young maiden clad in white. The genii plait her a garland of white roses and vanish. She awakens and ponders the dream she has had of winged children and white roses. Her playmates enter; she is about to tell them her dream but stops short at the sight of the garland hanging on the bush. The girls take down the wreath, place it on her head, and tell her to choose a sweetheart. She dances with her friends, gesturing several times toward the spot where Faust is standing.

Enraptured by the sorcery, Faust is about to rush over to the floating apparition but is held back by Mephistopheles. The vision disappears but shall become reality when Faust has signed the important parchment. With burning desire, he seizes the dagger Mephistopheles hands him and carves his name in the parchment, while the cave resounds with wild jubilation.

ACT II

The outskirts of a village. To the left, Johanna's house; to the right, a bower. Some distance away can be seen a baronial castle.

It is morning. Valentin is polishing his weapons outside his mother's house. It is her birthday and the happy neighbours hasten to bring Johanna their heartfelt good wishes. Margaretha skips gaily about among the sympathetic friends, and one can readily perceive that she is the pride and joy of her mother and brother.

The village magistrate has chosen this very day to present Margaretha with the chaplet of white roses, the prize awarded to the loveliest and most virtuous maiden of the year. General rejoicing and jubilation, rustic merriment and festive dancing. Valentin's comrade summons him for watch duty while Mephistopheles presents the magistrate and Johanna with an invitation from his master asking them to come up to the castle. They accept with delight and prepare to set out. Margaretha remains at home.

Mephistopheles, who has done everything in his power to weaken the unfavourable impression his singular appearance has made on the villagers, has gradually become more familiar with them and asks them about their customary pastimes. They ennumerate their innocent games but he laughs them to scorn. He shows the lads cards and dice and teaches them how to use them. The girls come and fetch him for a waltz wherein he himself is the central figure and exercises his charm.

A quarrel among the gamers interrupts the waltz every now and then, and even though Mephistopheles tries to satisfy them by filling their cups, they grow more and more heated. Things have almost reached a bloody pass when Faust steps into their midst.

Through his prestige and mildness, Faust has soon restored order, but while upbraiding Mephistopheles for the unrest he has caused, he perceives Margaretha, who had rushed hither upon hearing the noise and now delightedly surveys the friendly young gentleman. He recognizes her as the maid he beheld in the vision Mephistopheles conjured up. Everything around her seems to vanish. She alone captures his eye, and he hardly dares approach this noble creature.

However, his self-confidence soon returns. He hails Margaretha as the Rose Maiden and Queen of the Festival and encourages his vassals to keep on with their merriment, even condescending to take part in their dancing. Margaretha is his partner and scarcely knows how to respond to all the compliments he addresses to her.

Little by little, the dancing groups disperse, and Margaretha finds herself alone with Faust. She is about to leave, but he begs her to stay a few moments longer. He already knows that she is not indifferent to him and therefore ventures to inject a more tender note into his behaviour. Margaretha reproves him for toying with the affections of a poor village girl. She is frightened by his passionate outburst and is only too well aware that if she returned his love he would deceive and abandon her. Faust swears by all that is holy that his intentions are honest, that his riches, rank, heart, and hand shall belong to her. Margaretha resists no longer and, kneeling, Faust kisses her hand.

Mephistopheles reminds his master that it is time to go and hands him some jewels as a present for Margaretha. Faust asks her to grant him a rendezvous this very evening. She refuses, but when he speaks of a sacred betrothal she is won over and promises to come. Faust takes leave of her, followed by Mephistopheles. Martha, who has been spying on the lovers, ecstatically rushes over to Margaretha, and when the latter amicably gives her her hand, she kisses it with awe. Margaretha is astonished at this strange behaviour, but Martha acclaims her as her mistress. Together with Margaretha, she admires the dazzling jewels, hangs them about her neck, receives a pair of earrings, and expresses the liveliest joy.

Johanna comes between them and lectures her daughter on her wicked vanity. She orders her to give back these costly objects and asks her from whom she has received them. Martha tugs at Margaretha's dress. Margaretha is about to lie, but cannot do it. Weeping, she throws her arms about her mother's neck and confesses everything. Johanna asks Martha to return the necklace, anxiously embraces her child, and prays God to keep her safe from temptation. Darkness falls. Margaretha follows her mother into the house.

Martha calls Margaretha back and reminds her of the rendezvous. Mephistopheles slips between them and seeks to instill in her mind the idea of giving her old mother a sleeping draught. Margaretha recoils in horror, but Mephistopheles explains the whole thing to Martha, who, in turn, points out to Margaretha how harmless these drops are. Mephistopheles joins his affirmations to her persuasions, and poor Margaretha is soon lured into doing it.

Mephistopheles is exultant, and in his wild delight he tries to embrace Martha. But she does not understand such jesting and gives him a good clout. The Evil One's eyes flash. He stamps his feet.

Martha becomes frightened, but he once again assumes his obsequious character and is about to resume the waltz from before, but she roguishly eludes him.

Faust hastens to the rendezvous. Margaretha comes out of the house and timidly approaches. She shows her lover the empty bottle which contained the sleeping draught for her mother. This deed lies heavy on her heart. But Faust seeks to drive every dark thought from Margaretha's mind. The most ardent love fills their spirits with bliss unknown, and as the pledge of their betrothal, Margaretha receives that precious ring. Valentin, who is just returning home, surprises them. He can hardly believe his eyes, reproaches his sister, and threatens her seducer with bloody revenge. Faust, who does not know that Valentin is Margaretha's brother and suspects him of being a rival for her affections, draws his sword at the same time as the latter. Mephistopheles restrains the sister, and after a fierce struggle Valentin sinks to the ground in a pool of blood. Margaretha throws herself on the dying man, and Mephistopheles drags Faust away with him.

Margaretha seeks to bind her brother's wounds, but he pushes her away and asks to see his mother. Margaretha runs to fetch her. People flock to the spot and learn from Margaretha, who rushes out of the house with the empty vial in her hand, that Johanna is asleep, never more to awaken. In desperation, Margaretha seizes her brother's sword and begs him to do justice to a murderess and run her through. But the dying Valentin turns away from her in disgust, and his last sigh is a curse. Margaretha denounces herself to the magistrate, who orders her put in chains. But Faust rushes in like a madman, tears his way through the guards, breaks Margaretha's chains, and begs her to follow him. She does not *want* to escape punishment, and when Faust, aided by Mephistopheles, tries to save her by force, she tears herself loose and swoons in the arms of the girls while, by suddenly disappearing, Faust and Mephistopheles manage to escape from the advancing soldiery. General horror.

Now there is no longer any doubt that Margaretha must surely have made a pact with the Devil. Johanna's body, which is carried out of the house, fills every heart with sorrow for her misfortune and with loathing for this unnatural daughter. Death is too mild a punishment for her, and with solemn dread the magistrate calls down the curse of Heaven upon this wretched creature and upon anyone who gives her a drink of water or a crust of bread. He demands that she give back the garland of white roses, tears it asunder, and treads it under foot. When the lost soul wishes to kiss her mother's cold hand, he pushes her far away, unveils the body, and casts the black crape over Margaretha's head. Everyone flees, leaving her to her fate.

ACT III

A marketplace in the town. To the right, a church; in the middle, a Gothic monument.

A fair, and swarms of people. Faust, whose dress and manners are ever more approaching those of his boon companion, enters, accompanied by the latter. His constantly recurring depression shall once more be dispelled at a wine cellar, and a few glasses of champagne have soon restored his high spirits. Margaretha is forgotten, and a roving gypsy girl soon becomes the object of his burning gaze.

A number of gypsies enter and perform one of their fantastic dances. The half-drunken Faust wishes to dance with the girl, and in the meanwhile Mephistopheles lures her former partner over to the bottle. The merriment becomes general, and in the midst of this giddiness the gypsy has all he can do to find his sweetheart. He tears her away from Faust, who laughingly pursues his new romance.

A low murmur spreads among the fairgoers. The dancing stops, the music is hushed. All look at one another in bewilderment, and upstage they see a pale figure, with head enveloped in black and staff in hand. She is immediately recognized as the witch – the accursed one! And though she imploringly stretches forth her hands, she sees naught but loathing on every face. In an instant the square is deserted and everything around her is still as death.

Margaretha raises her eyes to Heaven and gropes her way to a bench, where she ponders her horrible fate. The memory of Faust, however, is not without sweetness for her, and she still possesses the ring he gave her. She looks at it sadly and seems to call her beloved. He does not come, and she soon sinks into the deepest despair. Her mental torments haunt her, disturb her prayers, and place before her the image of her dead mother and brother. She is overwhelmed with grief.

A lad carrying a basket finds her in this pitiful state and compassionately comes to her aid. She can hardly believe that a sympathetic person still exists. Overjoyed, she wishes to kiss his hands and ventures to reveal her need for food. The boy runs over to his basket to fetch her some bread, but one of his comrades comes, seizes his hand, tells him who *she* is, and leads the boy away.

Abandoned, and more than ever pining for food, Margaretha pounds on the door of a house. It is opened; an old man steps out and solemnly orders her to go away. To be sure, he is moved at her plight, but only enough to hand her a garland of roses for the salvation of her soul. She ventures a new attempt at a neighbour's house, but the latter – a rude, unfeeling person – violently thrusts her away and slams the door.

At this moment, a child comes dancing by, sits down on a bench, and is about to devour a piece of cake from the fair. Margaretha begs for a tiny piece of the child's cake, but the boy becomes afraid of her and will give her nothing. She stares about her, and when she sees that she is alone with the child, she snatches the cake. The little one busts into tears. His mother enters but recognizes the outlaw and, terrified, hurries off with her child.

The vesper bell sounds just as Margaretha is about to put the food to her lips. The harmonies of the organ reach her, uplift her spirit, and melt her heart. A stream of tears wet her cheeks. She feels the full burden of her guilt, longs for death, and puts the cake aside. She stumbles upon the black crape lying at her feet, fancies she is at her mother's grave, and kneels in prayer and profound sorrow. She grows ever more weary yet lighter of heart. Penitently, she enshrouds herself in the murky veil, presses the rose garland to her lips, and swoons as the last strains of the organ sound.

Mephistopheles and Faust come walking across the square,

engrossed in intimate conversation. Faust perceives that a woman is lying there and that she must either be dead or in a faint. Mephistopheles indifferently pulls him away, but what can equal Faust's astonishment when he recognizes Margaretha, his beloved... his victim. Love, remorse, and deep compassion awaken in him. He lifts her in his arms and restores her to consciousness by the tenderest caresses. She opens her eyes, recognizes her lover, forgets all her misery, and sees Heaven in his eyes. But the sight of Mephistopheles brings back her dreadful awareness of what she has done. The pangs of death envelop her. She trembles; her knees buckle. She only has time to display the empty vial of poison and point to Mephistopheles before she falls to the ground, lifeless.

Beside himself with despair, Faust draws his sword and fiercely hurls himself at Mephistopheles. But the Evil One seizes it with both hands, shatters it, and tramples Faust in the dust. He scornfully laughs at the misery he sees around him and puts all the blame on Faust. The latter now does everything in his power to recall Margaretha to life – but in vain. He must once again turn to Mephistopheles. He pleads with him, grovels in the dust at his feet, and promises to go with him immediately if only he will save the guiltless Margaretha. This last condition finally leads Mephistopheles to make up his mind, and he touches Margaretha's hand. She lives again – but not the life of the senses. As though transfigured, she looks down at Faust but no longer recognizes him. When he tries to embrace her, she solemnly pushes him away, lifts her hands to Heaven, and Uriel and Hope take her into their arms.

Margaretha follows the heavenly host, and among the clouds encounters two spirits who *maternally* and *fraternally* bid her welcome. Faust sees that there is forgiveness. He tears himself loose from Mephistopheles and rushes toward the light. But punitive cherubs stand at the parting of the ways. *The ring of Hope and Mercy belongs to Margaretha.* Mephistopheles drags *him* down into the abyss as *she* ascends to the home of the Transfigured.

* * *

THE VETERAN, OR THE HOSPITABLE HOUSE

An Original Pantomimic Ballet in One Act
by
August Bournonville

Music composed by Ludvig Zinck

Performed on the occasion of the august birthday
of His Majesty the King, January 29, 1833

Characters

SAINVILLE, Colonel . . . . Hr. Fredstrup
MATHIEU, Miller and innkeeper,
    formerly a soldier . . . . Hr. Stramboe
CATEAU, his wife . . . . Mad. Schouw
LOUISON, their eldest daughter . . . . Mad. Kraetzmer
FIVE YOUNGER CHILDREN . . . . Rinda
                                         Augusta
                                         Nanna
                                         Sophie
                                         Edvard*
COLIN, a mill hand . . . . Hr. Bournonville
A LIEUTENANT . . . . Hr. Füssel
FANFAN, Regimental drummer . . . . Hr. Hammer
TWO DRUMMER BOYS . . . . Hope
                                         Hoppensach
SOLDIERS AND PEASANTS. MILL HANDS AND GIRLS.

Solo Dances

Messieurs Larcher, Funck, Bentzen
Mesdames Werning, Møller, Weiner

The action takes place in Normandy, near a branch of the River Eure, in the autumn of 1815.

    The upper story of a mill by the water. Toward the back of the stage, the roof, which rests on posts, forms a gallery through which can be seen part of the mill wheel outside, together with the steep bank on the opposite side. A small bridge across the stream leads into the house. To right and left, doors give access to the miller's quarters, while through a trap door in the floor, steps lead down to the mill work. A dovecote, a hen house, an innkeeper's sign, and a number of sacks complete the picture.

    Dawn. The mill hands are fast asleep. All is quiet in Mathieu's house. Colin is the only one awake. He is madly in love and bemoaning the fact that his poverty stands in the way of his affection for Louison, the rich miller's eldest daughter. He soon hears an echo of his own sighs. Glancing up, he sees his beloved, who cautiously extends her hand to him from the small opening above the door. He clasps it with devoted tenderness and is enraptured when she allows him to kiss it. They hear her father coming and part.

    Still wearing his nightcap, Mathieu merrily enters and begins his

---

* These are apparently the names of the children dancing the roles at the premiere, but the cast list does not indicate the exact aportioning of roles. The characters are Jeanette, Fanchon, Pierre, Jacques, and Zozo.

day's work with the tankards. He notices Colin, praises him for his alertness, and wakens the other fellows, who immediately set to work. Some of them are to go to town with Mathieu; Colin will remain at the mill.

Cateau and her eldest daughter busy themselves with household chores. Louison, who thinks that Colin is away, displays a dejection that does not escape her mother's knowing eye. Cateau tries to cheer her by having her tend to the small animals, embraces her warmly, and hastens inside to her other children.

Louison tosses grain to the chickens and is about to go up to the dovecote when she catches sight of Colin. Blushing with surprise, she hurries down from the ladder but hardly dares look at her sweetheart, who has brought her a pair of doves as a present. They are symbols of love and fidelity. He offers them to her, and she accepts the gift. They understand one another perfectly and express their joy in merry dancing.

Mathieu comes in just as Louison has granted Colin the first kiss. Enraged, he flies at the bold mill hand and utters the most violent reproaches against his daughter. Touched by the lovers' plight, Cateau joins them in trying to sway the angry father. But it is his firm opinion that, as a poor lad, Colin is not a suitable match for Louison, and, in spite of all their pleas and protests, he pays Colin the wages he owes him and turns him out of his house.

Mathieu indignantly sits down at the table. The trembling Louison does not dare go near him, but Cateau knows how to get him into a good humor: she summons the little ones. Pierre, Jacques, Zozo, Jeanette, and Fanchon gather round their father's chair, hug him, and by teasing and caresses soon restore his good spirits. He embraces Cateau, gives Louison his hand to kiss, and does a round dance with the children, while their mother lays the table. The maids and mill hands gather for lunch. Little Zozo says grace. Workers who are passing by are offered refreshment, and gaiety prevails at the rustic meal.

A boy enters and whispers something in Mathieu's ear. He becomes serious and asks those who are present to leave him alone. They go. An elderly man of noble bearing, enveloped in a cloak and wearing his hat pulled down over his eyes, is approaching the mill. He appears to be a fugitive and asks Mathieu to give him refuge. But when he perceives the latter's embarrassment, he tosses his cloak aside, throws back his hat, and Mathieu recognizes his old Colonel!

Hundreds of memories awaken in his breast, and he would throw himself into Sainville's arms were he not restrained by his reverence for the Colonel. Instead, he kisses the hand which so often led him to victory and swears to risk everything in order to defend his valiant commander. From the Colonel's pallor, the miller can see how greatly he is in need of rest and nourishment. He leads him over to the table, places before him some of the humble fare, fills his glass, and seeks to cheer him with happy memories. With a sad expression, Sainville thanks him while Mathieu keeps his eye on the entrance, lest anyone should approach, and bustles around the gray-haired warrior with a childlike delight and solicitude. But someone is coming! Mathieu quickly opens the trap door to the mill work and hides the colonel down there.

Two small drummer boys with their drums on their backs and clay pipes in their mouths enter and ask for – brandy! Mathieu laughs at them, but with soldierly audacity they demand to be served. They pay, toast, and are just about to empty their glasses when Fanfan, the regimental drummer, struts over to them and with a great deal of affectation lectures them on their bad behaviour. He orders them to pick up their drums and then commands them to march, halt, about face, and beat a roll, while, in order to give greater force to his admonitions, he himself empties both glasses of brandy. His real purpose in coming to the inn is to use the drum roll to assemble the inhabitants of the vicinity to hear the reading of Colonel Sainville's death sentence!

The Lieutenant, who produces the sentence and has it nailed on one of the door posts of the house, gives a description of the Colonel and asks everyone to furnish all possible information concerning the outlaw. He leaves. Mathieu and the peasants stand amazed and dejected. One after another, the peasants return to their homes.

The soldiers remain behind and amuse themselves by drinking and playing cards. The drummer boys dance and a fencing master asks one of the soldiers to cross swords with him. They are in full *assault* when they notice Colin, who is standing in his travellling clothes on the other side of the bridge and seems to be bidding an eternal farewell to the mill. It hurts the good soldiers to see him so crestfallen. They invite him to join them, cheer him as best they can, and advise him to seek consolation by choosing the merry life of a soldier. Fanfan exhausts his eloquence in order to depict the glory and rewards of being a soldier. He succeeds in arousing Colin's enthusiasm, but Louison, who from her window pleadingly beckons to her sweetheart, brings all his efforts to naught, and the soldiers abandon Colin, convinced that he will never amount to anything.

Louison now rushes into Colin's arms. She takes a cross from around her neck and asks him to keep it as a remembrance of her. He searches through his pockets in order to give her something in return. But alas! His poverty is the whole cause of his misfortune! Louison shows him the doves he gave her. She returns one of them to him and asks him to send it back to her with a letter under its wing. They swear inviolable fidelity, embrace for the last time, and take leave of one another with heartfelt grief.

Sainville, who has heard everything from his hiding place, stops Colin at the door. He comforts and consoles him and removes all obstacles from the path of his union with Louison by giving him a number of bank notes. Colin can hardly believe his eyes! He does not dare to touch such a considerable sum, and only by the Colonel's repeated protests can he be brought to realize that it really belongs to him. His joy and gratitude are indescribable. He throws himself at his benefactor's feet and promises to risk life and limb for him. He wishes to tell Louison and her mother of his good fortune, but Sainville bids him keep silent. Colin now considers how he can assemble all his friends, the notary, the musicians, and also return in triumph. Love, joy, and gratitude fill his breast, and he jubilantly flies off to the village.

Sainville looks after the happy Colin with sadness. Everyone will be merry and fortunate beneath this roof; the outlaw's gloom must not spoil their joy. His mind is made up. On a piece of paper, he writes his farewell to Mathieu, places it in the keyhole, sorrowfully looks about, and hastens away. But on the way he meets his host, who is dismayed at seeing him out in the open, and forcibly leads him back to the mill. Sainville tells him of the risk he is running by sheltering him. He reminds him of his wife and children and begs him to leave him to his fate. But in vain! To be sure, Mathieu is shaken at the thought of his family's danger, but nothing can make him forget the sacred obligation of hospitality. He implores the Colonel with a warmth and passion that finally move him. He promises to stay, and Mathieu embraces him with tears of joy. But there is no time to lose. Sainville must once again descend into the mill work.

Deeply moved, and exhausted by his violent exertion, the miller bends his knee and offers a silent prayer to God. Mathieu is strangely uneasy but still feels that "a good deed always has its reward," and he has a premonition of this.

Cateau enters with the children and is surprised to see her husband with tears in his eyes. But he laughs it off, gives the children cakes, and lets them climb all over him. However, his deep emotion returns; he embraces his wife and the melancholy Louison.

He wipes away his flowing tears and runs out, half laughing, half crying.

Mother and daughter now sit down to spin while the children dance around and play jokes. The little boys jump up and down with excitement when they see soldiers march by, and the latter toss flowers across the water into the mill where the children are playing, greet them, and march on.

Zozo wants to make a wreath from the pretty flowers, but he does not have enough of them and therefore runs across the bridge and up onto the road where there is a hedge. Here he picks a number of flowers and imitates the soldiers by tossing the blossoms across the water. But all of a sudden he loses his footing and is hurled into the stream! Terrified, the children run to their mother, who, suspecting the dreadful misfortune, immediately tries to reach the mill wheel but sinks to the floor, unconscious. Mathieu and the soldiers, who from a distance have seen the child disappear, rush to help as people gather at the spot. At the same moment, the wheel stops. Everyone is dumbfounded. Perhaps there is still hope! All hearts beat anxiously. Someone brings the father Zozo's little hat: It is all over!

Unnoticed by anyone, Sainville climbs through the trap door, holding the living child in his arms. (Only he could have stopped the wheel and grabbed the boy.) Zozo holds out his arms to his father. They recognize one another, and Mathieu has his son back! All express the liveliest sympathy. But Sainville points to the unconscious mother. He takes the boy, approaches her, and lays Zozo on her breast. Cateau awakens as from a dream, feels and sees her child, anxiously convinces herself that each of his limbs is whole, and with silent exhilaration presses the boy to her heart. Zozo is passed from hand to hand, lip to lip, and his parents' joy is equaled only by their gratitude for the child's salvation.

Sainville has been recognized! The Lieutenant holds his description in his hand, and, although with visible pain, duty obliges him to seize the Colonel as a condemned political criminal.

Only when Mathieu angrily refuses to hand him over does the Lieutenant order his men to use force. The Colonel has seen this moment approach with quiet composure. But now he advances into the midst of his former brothers-in-arms. He bares his breast and orders them to thrust their bayonets – but they recoil with shame, and he looks down on them with great dignity.

In the midst of this commotion, Colin arrives with his merry band of friends, with his best man and the notary, in order to ask Louison's father for her hand. But his joy must give way to grief and amazement when he sees his benefactor surrounded by guards. He rushes into his arms, pulls him away, and encourages his friends to defend the noble man. But Sainville calls for order and promises to go with the guards. He is already on the road when he asks permission to say good-bye to his old friend. He returns to Mathieu and his family. The good family are bathed in tears. They would give anything to save him, but cold duty calls. Sainville bravely goes to his death, and his last farewell is a benediction.

The Lieutenant receives a written order. He immediately opens it and peruses it with visible emotion. Joy is painted on his face. He rushes over to the door post, tears down the death sentence, rips it to shreds, and respectfully salutes the Colonel.

A general amnesty has been declared! All hearts are filled with the wildest delight. People embrace and congratulate one another, and at a time like this, how could Mathieu oppose the union of Colin and Louison? Their betrothal is the occasion of a new celebration. The veteran will remain for good with this family, whose father and benefactor he has become, and love, fidelity, and gratitude will ever dwell in this hospitable house.

* * *

THE TYROLEANS

An Original Idyllic Ballet in One Act
by
August Bournonville

Music composed and arranged by Chorus Master Johannes Frederik Frøhlich from works by Gioacchino Rossini

Performed for the first time on March 6, 1835

Characters

HERMANN, a tenant farmer	....	Hr. Fredstrup
SOPHY } his daughters	....	Mad. Kraetzmer
HANNCHEN		Jfr. Grahn
PETER } their suitors	....	Hr. Larcher
FRITZ		Hr. Bournonville
A MUSICIAN	....	Hr. Stramboe
A LITTLE BOY	....	Edvard Stramboe

The scene is laid in the Tyrol.

Tyrolean Men

Messieurs:
Funch, Hoppe, Bentzen,
Hammer, Friis, Füssel,
Holm, Lund, Nehm, Weile,
Borch, Füssel, Hoppensach,
Ring, Brodersen, Ruff, Lund

Tyrolean Women

Mesdames:
Bauer, Werning, Møller, Schouw,
Larcher, Fredstrup, Stramboe,
Agnes, Wolstrup, Rinda, Augusta,
Sophie, Fjeldsted, Nanna, Eggers,
Johnsen, Schaarup, Møller

In a fertile valley surrounded by the snowcapped Keiser Mountains lies the tenant farmer's cozy dwelling. The upper story forms a gallery, reached by a steep flight of stairs. Opposite the house is a lovely garden surrounded by a picket fence. Barrels, benches, and farm implements stand round about. Everything in the farmyard gives evidence of order and prosperity.

Hermann has two daughters. They, in turn, have two robust and well-to-do suitors. The father has given his consent; but in the youngest daughter Fritz has encountered so much coldness and indifference, and also such a capricious temper, that he is on the verge of despair. This very day Sophy shall accept the proposal of her more fortunate sweetheart, and on this festive occasion Fritz intends to renew his attempts with Hannchen. He is as charming as he can be. By dancing, caresses, and small gifts – even by her father's intercession – he tries to move her; but in vain. She makes light of everything, and when he forces a ring upon her, she ties it around her neck with a ribbon instead of placing it on her finger. She shakes hands with him as a mark of friendship, but gives him to understand that she never will marry, as she is determined to remain at home with her father and sister. She continues to make merry with the other girls.

Crestfallen, Fritz sits down in a corner, but a couple of his comrades – fine hunters – try to cheer him. They hand him a gun, point toward the mountains, and whisper something in his ear. He rises, smothers his sorrow, defies the cold-blooded beauty with a jovial outburst, and goes off to hunt with his boon companions.

The merry lads and lasses continue to dance until a storm forces them to part and seek shelter.

Fritz, driven home from the hunt, has been forced to take refuge beneath an overhanging rock, but the thunderstorm is soon over and he emerges once again. All of a sudden he hears a low whimpering some distance away. He follows the noise and soon returns, carrying in his arms a little boy (who, to judge from a rather heavy knapsack, must belong to a company of marketers).

The boy is perishing with cold and fright and can hardly see the man who has saved him. The kind Fritz does everything possible to revive him, but his home is far away, and here he lacks all means of help... but surely Hannchen would not refuse to care for the poor little fellow! Fresh courage!

He pounds on the door. Hannchen comes out on the gallery, but is about to withdraw when she catches sight of the unbearable Fritz. He urgently begs her to come to the child's relief; she consents, but only on the condition that Fritz immediately depart.

By the united efforts of the family, the little one is cheered and warmed. He is very shy and timid but full of gratitude toward his benefactors. Sophy and the girls make a great fuss over him, but Hannchen claims him for her own, and he also clings to her. The others go about their business, and Hannchen sits down to spin, asking her little ward to sit at her feet.

The little boy is soon bored with sitting still. He begins to play with the wheel, pulls down the flax, and tangles the thread. Hannchen admonishes him to keep still. He finds amusement in admiring and patting her pretty feet. She becomes angry and threatens him, but he instantly creeps up onto the back of her chair, teases her to make her turn her head around, and steals a kiss. Hannchen now becomes terribly indignant. She grabs a switch and tries to beat the little rascal, but he throws himself at her feet and begs her forgiveness. Her anger soon passes. She can hardly keep from laughing and drops the switch. But, as punishment, he must stand by the garden gate.

While Hannchen is gradually becoming aware of her emotions, the boy has found some strawberries, which he picks and threads on a straw. With this little gift he timidly approaches the angry girl. He smirks and kindly asks that she forgive him and accept the strawberries, in which she finds a most delightful *Taste*.

The boy has plucked a beautiful rose. Hannchen wants it, but he will not part with it. He eludes her, and will only hand her the flower from such a distance that he intensifies her desire by delighting her sense of *Smell*.

She vehemently demands that he give her the rose, snatches it from him, pricks herself with its thorns, and throws it away, overwhelmed by a painful *Sensation*.

The boy consoles the weeping girl and tries once more to give her the desired rose, but she apprehensively turns away from him. He wishes to bind her bleeding finger with its leaves, but she rejects his help. Then a French horn sounds in the distance. The woods are filled with its mellow notes. They force their way to Hannchen's heart. The sounds draw nearer. She listens, and all her senses unite in that of *Hearing*.

The power of harmony has given her whole being a touch of lyricism. Her every movement becomes a lilting dance; her attentiveness, picturesque poses; and she is filled with a mixture of sadness and delight. Suddenly, the French horn falls silent. There is a rustling in the bushes. Fritz jumps out, and Hannchen stands astonished at this unexpected *Sight*.

Hesitantly, and with mounting alarm, she listens to Fritz's pleas. But when he approaches her and tries to take her hand, she evades him, reproaches him for his unwelcome attentions, beckons to the boy, and hurries off.

Fritz is clearly aware of the progress he has made in Hannchen's heart. A bit of jealousy will make his triumph complete. Just then he sees Sophy and a flock of dancing girls. He buys from the boy a number of trinkets that are to be found in his knapsack, and amid dancing and affectionate jesting, he presents them to the merry lasses.

From her half-open window, Hannchen has seen how her suitor is overcoming his sorrow. Piqued, she calls to Sophy, who does not hear her and merrily skips off with the other girls.

Fritz blows kisses to them and becomes deeply engrossed in looking at a medallion, which was also found in the knapsack. Hannchen is curious to know whose picture this is and steals up behind him. But Fritz quickly turns around, ironically bows to her, kisses the medallion while yearningly raising his eyes, and starts to leave. Almost involuntarily, she calls him back to ask if this was a picture of a beloved object. He sings the praises of his new beloved, counts himself lucky, and gaily runs off.

Hannchen is already plagued by jealousy, but it is increased by all the tales she must hear from the young girls, each of whom thinks she has an obvious advantage with Fritz, and, as proof thereof, displays the present he has given her. Hannchen is vexed to the point of tears. Sophy and her sweetheart enter, embroiled in a violent quarrel. The cause of this is the new kerchief she is wearing. They choose Hannchen to judge between them, but she merely overwhelms her sister with reproaches. Sophy demands that Fritz clear her. However, the musicians whom Peter has hired arrive. Confused and indignant, the latter will not accept the explanation and is rude to his sweetheart, who gives him a clout. He strikes the musician, who falls on top of his fiddle. The girls scold Fritz; Hannchen and Sophy cry; the boy roars with laughter; and there is general confusion.

Father Hermann steps into their midst and offers himself as mediator. Everybody rushes to him; each one wants to be the first to speak. They drown out and dislodge each other, and the noise continues to mount until Hermann authoritatively calls for silence.

His sharp eye soon discovers the reason for all this hullabaloo. The guilty one must be punished, and the guilty one is – the boy. But when the little rascal suspects something is up, he takes to his heels, jumps over the garden fence, and flees.

Everyone, with the exception of Fritz and Hannchen, pursues him, and, in many circles, they chase him through the woods.

At last he runs into the arms of Fritz, who hides him in an empty barrel. Here he is discovered by his pursuers, who try to drag him out. But they draw back in amazement when the coarse garb of the Alpine lad is transformed into dazzling raiment, and a pair of white wings unfold from his bare shoulders.

Cupid himself is standing in their midst, and, kneeling, all acknowledge his omnipotence. Confusion ceases, and harmony reigns anew. Smiling, the boy looks down on the girl who was once so cold-hearted. The medallion is seen to be a pocket mirror wherein her own face is reflected. The ring flies off the ribbon encircling her throat and down onto her finger, and Cupid himself unites the young couple. The old father is delighted, there is general rejoicing, and the Tyroleans' festivities continue amid merry dancing.

* * *

VALDEMAR

Original Romantic Ballet in Four Acts

by
August Bournonville

Music by Johannes Frederik Fröhlich
Performed for the first time in honour of the august birthday of Her Majesty the Queen, on October 28, 1835

Characters

SVEND ERIKSØN	Hr. Patges
KNUD MAGNUSSØN	Hr. Holst
VALDEMAR KNUDSØN	Hr. Bournonville
AXEL HVIDE	Hr. Füssel
ASTRID, Svend's daughter	Jfr. Grahn
AGNAR, an old man	Hr. Fredstrup
YNGVAR, a blacksmith } his sons	Hr. Stramboe
ERIK, a fisherman	Hr. Larcher
ELLEN, Yngvar's wife	Jfr. Werning
HEDVIG, Erik's betrothed	Jfr. Fjeldsted
DITLEIF, leader of the halberdiers	Hr. Hammer
A MINNESINGER	Hr. Hoppe

KNIGHTS
LADIES
COMMANDERS
PRELATES
HALBERDIERS
ESQUIRES
GUILD BROTHERS
FISHERMEN
PEASANTS
WOMEN

GIRLS
CHILDREN
SOLDIERS
SPIRITS

Scenery

ACT I:	Forest with the town of Roskilde	(Hr. Wallich)
ACT II:	Great Hall	(Hr. T. Lund)
ACT IV:	Valdemar's tent	(Hr. Wallich)
	Denmark's Future, an apotheosis	(Hr. T. Lund)
	Grathe Heath	(Hr. Christensen)

Costumes designed and organized by Dr. Ryge.

The time is 1156–57.

[**Translator's note**: After the death of the strong and popular monarch Erik Ejegod (reigned 1095 – 1103), Denmark was governed by a series of weak rulers and for a generation was involved in bitter civil wars. On the death of King Erik Lam in 1147, Valdemar, grandson of Erik Ejegod and son of Knud Lavard, who had been murdered by political rivals in 1131, came forward as one of three pretenders to the Danish crown. His rivals for the throne were Svend, a son of King Erik II Emune (reigned 1134-1137), and Knud Magnussøn, whose father was one of Lavard's assassins.

According to the terms of the compact of Roskilde (1157), the kingdom of Denmark was divided, with Valdemar receiving North and South Jutland, Svend Skaane, Halland, Blekinge and Bornholm, and Knud the Danish islands. A few days later, Svend decided to achieve by guile what he could not effect by force of arms. At a banquet in Roskilde, to which he had been invited, Knud tried to have his rivals assassinated (in Bournonville's story Svend plays host of Knud and Valdemar), but Valdemar managed to escape, flee to Jutland, and raise an army with which he defeated Svend at Grathe Heath on October 23, 1157. Valdemar's accession marked the start of a period of stability, growth and prosperity known as the Age of the Valdemars.

The Guild of St. Knud mentioned in the scenario was one of the confraternities which sprang up following the canonization of King Knud II (reigned 1080–1086). These associations bore a half worldly, half religious stamp. Placed under the saint's protection, they were organizations that aimed at helping their members in time of need or peril, providing defense in case of enemy attack, and keeping order in a relatively undisciplined age.]

ACT I

A clearing in the woods by Issefjord; in the background, Roskilde; to the left, a statue of St. Knud; to the right, the blacksmith's house. Here and there, fishing nets and farming implements. Noon.

Agnar, who served under Erik Ejegod, is spending his old age with his sons and amuses himself by telling his grandchildren tales of war. He plays the harp while Yngvar forges a helmet and Ellen winds yarn. The boys, armed with homemade wooden swords, listen attentively to the old man's story and repeatedly hush their little sister, who is seated on her grandfather's knee. But she keeps interrupting them; the children quarrel, and their mother must settle the dispute by taking the little girl.

Hedvig comes from the field with milk; Yngvar and Ellen run to meet her, and the children joyfully hop around her. She greets all of them and reverently kisses the graybeard's hand. A lovely crown of flowers is intended for the saint, and while she adorns St. Knud, the children bring Grandfather the first bowl of milk.

Hedvig sights Erik's boat. All jubilantly hasten to the strand. Erik leaps ashore and into his sweetheart's arms. In his boat he brings a troop of young peasants who are returning from war with leaves in their hats. The kings have been reconciled, the white banners of peace wave over Denmark once more, and the liveliest joy animates every heart. Young and old alike come flocking to the spot, embrace the men who have returned, and give thanks for the long-desired peace.

This day shall see the wedding celebration of Erik and Hedvig! Agnar blesses them, and Ellen serves her old mead in honour of the occasion. Dancing heightens the merriment; the children play the game Agnar has taught them about Rolf Krake and his warriors. Rolf opens the assembly of notables and is murdered by Hjartvar and avenged by Viggo.

Valdemar and Axel come passing by. Awe-struck, the peasants are about to stop the celebration. but Valdemar bids them continue. The boys' game reminds him of the days of his bygone childhood, and he warmly presses his foster brother's hand. The girls vie to see who can run the fastest, and the swains shoot their bows. Valdemar, invited to be president of the Guild, makes the best shot and presents his prize to the bridal couple.

Astrid, Svend's lovely daughter, approaches, accompanied by her playmates. They are carrying baskets of flowers for the impending celebration. All surround the king's daughter with expressions of love and admiration, and her whole manner testifies to the fact that she is worthy of this. She perceives Valdemar, salutes him, and asks why so many people have gathered here. He indicates to her that in this place the day is at once the festival of Love and Peace.

Astrid, too, will embellish this festival. She dances with her maidens; they entwine themselves with chains of flowers. She tries to get the peasant girls to take part in the dancing, but they will not do it. When the Princess, caught up in charming hilarity, finally tosses her garland into the midst of the group of spectators, everyone rushes to grab it. Hedvig is the lucky one and dances with Astrid.

A wrestling match in honour of the Princess begins. Every ounce of strength is called into play, but the blacksmith has soon bested everyone, and nobody dares take him on. With a smile, Valdemar looks at Axel, and this hint is enough for his friend. He will face the victor, who at first modestly withdraws from the noble lord but finally ventures to wrestle him. Here, however, Yngvar has met his match; with a single hand, Axel forces him to the ground. Then, through Axel's half-open coat, he catches sight of the brilliant cross which denotes the head of the Guild of St. Knud. He reverently kneels before his opponent, but the latter quickly raises him to his feet, orders him to keep silent, and gives him the fraternal handshake.

Astrid, Valdemar, and Axel exit, taking with them the blessings of the gladsome people.

Distant martial music calls the throng to the shore. A ship comes alongside; it is Knud, who has come to Roskilde at Svend's invitation. Lightly clad and armed, his knights come ashore first.

Intensely moved, Knud stands upon the beloved coast of Sjaelland. Kneeling, he thanks Heaven, which has granted Denmark peace; with the green bough in his hand, he waves to the people, who stretch forth their arms in blessing. Hope and joy radiate everywhere. Svend enters! Knud can hardly conceal his emotion upon seeing his old opponent again, but, overcoming his rancor, he holds out to him the hand of reconciliation. Svend opens his arms to him, and jubilation resounds among the knights and people.

Knud soon notices that Svend's escort is clad in steel and heavily armed. He expresses his astonishment at this and indicates that he and his men bear the dress and symbol of peace. Svend gives him an ambiguous look, turns to his halberdiers, and asks how they feel about the King's enemies. Wild enthusiasm and crushing gestures throughout the entire host betoken revenge and manslaughter. A bitter smile plays about Svend's lips; he approaches Knud with forced friendliness, but the latter thrusts him aside; the joyous hope is extinct, the old rancor flares up anew.

It is Valdemar! The mediator of peace! Hearts once again beat warmly.

The Emperor commanded that the kingdom should be divided and the kings reconciled. Valdemar has the duty of making peace and seeing to the division. The others want him to choose first. He seizes his arms and swears upon the altar of his native land. Knud follows Valdemar's example, but Svend holds back. Furious, he grips the hilt of his sword, and his devoted halberdiers searchingly await a sign from his hand.

But Astrid and her maidens glide among the fierce warriors; swords and battle-axes are entwined with garlands. Svend, who receives the coat of arms from his daughter, is filled with milder feelings. He fervently presses Astrid to his heart, swears to the peace, and shakes hands to seal the fraternal pact, while a thrill of delight surges through the jubilant assembly.

ACT II

The great hall of the royal castle in Roskilde. In the background, trophies from Thostrup and Viborg (Knud's defeats); to the right, a throne; to the left, a chessboard.

Everything is astir as preparations are being made for the feast. Astrid enters with her retinue. She inspects and approves the completed work, but the trophies should not stand there as a painful memory for Knud. She orders them removed. Ditleif is about to object, but Astrid rushes into her father's arms with pleas and caresses. Svend admires his daughter's sagacity and sensibility of feeling, grants her request, and bids her arrange everything else for the feast. She kisses her father's hand and exits.

Sullen and pensive, Ditleif is leaning against the chessboard. Svend sits down and looks fixedly at the chieftain; he then tests the edge of his dagger and hands it to him. Ditleif takes it, in doubt as to the king's actual intention. But when Svend passes his hand over the chessboard, picks up the king, and holds it out to him, he understands everything. He gives a prearranged signal, and the halberdiers enter from different sides, ready to receive their orders. Svend appears satisfied, distributes gifts and gold to his men, receives their oath, and dismisses them.

Astrid, who has inadvertently witnessed these mysterious doings, steps forth, pale and trembling, and stops Svend, who does not suspect that she has seen what transpired. But her alarm, the confusion that drives her now to the chessboard, now to the exits, leaves him in no doubt as to the fact that he has been betrayed. Astrid does not fear his wrath; she implores him for the sake of his honour, of his salvation, to abandon his vengeful purpose. She shows him the peace treaty he has sworn to uphold; but this only increases his indignation. He tears up the document and utters curses against his rivals to the crown. Astrid tries to flee, but Svend, who suspects that she will warn Knud and Valdemar, threateningly holds her back. Overcome with terror, she collapses at the foot of the throne. The knightly procession is heard. Svend grabs his daughter's hand, lifts her up, and orders her to get control of herself and keep silent.

The court gathers. The guard of halberdiers takes its place, and the noble guests draw near in ceremonious procession. Svend goes to meet the kings, greets them with feigned warmth, and takes them to the high-seat from which he gives a signal for the festivities to begin. Dancing. Valdemar dances with Astrid. He is carried away with delight and does not see all the signs with which she seeks to warn him. Svend leads his guests to table. Ditleif announces that a crowd of peasants is asking permission to view the *taffel* and to crown the noble guests with flowers. Svend permits them to enter. Erik and Hedvig are at their head. They merrily dance about and are a source of amusement to the halberdiers. For a moment this ridicule seems to displease them, but Ditleif satisfies them and orders his men to keep quiet.

Astrid, who has noticed Agnar and the children, has the idea that one of his ballads may be able to give the betrayed a hint. She steals away from the table and goes over to the old man, who is prepared to deliver *Rolf's Drapa*. But Svend has been following her with his eyes, stops the ballad, and orders the crowd of people chased out.

The gentle strains of the harp are now replaced by an impetuous shield dance, and the fumes of wine increase the wild enthusiasm. From the table, the knights rush down among the dancers, cups clink, fraternal kisses seal friendship, and heads swim with joyous intoxication.

It is time that the ladies left the feast. Svend sees Astrid and her retinue out. Astrid is about to plead with her father, but his facial expression crushes her. He watches her every move and gives Ditleif yet another secret sign.

Knud and Axel play chess. Valdemar looks at them, and the knights empty even more cups. All of a sudden Knud stops playing; he feels melancholy and uneasy and cannot be cheered by Valdemar, who tries to get the game going again. Knud feels very strange; he takes Valdemar's hand, places it over his heart as if asking forgiveness, sends his tearful gaze heavenward, and sinks to his friend's breast. Valdemar warmly clasps him in his arms and bids him rejoice with all of them. With this, he beckons the gentlemen and leads them up to the table, where the cups shall be filled anew and drunk to Knud's health.

The signal is given! The hour has come! From every side Svend's halberdiers hurl themselves at the defenseless victims. Death and destruction rain down upon them, and many are run through before they can defend themselves. Axel still has his sword; he looks for his beloved Valdemar, who in the midst of the confusion is fighting with arms he has wrested from the assassins. He then lends Knud his weapon so that he can sell his life as dearly as possible and with gigantic strength grabs Ditleif by both wrists. The chieftain is forced to the ground. Axel tears the sword away from him and plants his foot on his chest. He then sees Knud overwhelmed by the traitors and is about to run to his aid; but Knud falls to the ground mortally wounded. Valdemar has seen his last man fall and fights like a tiger against the gathering horde. No one can conquer the formidable warrior. He cuts his way down to Axel through the body of men and is pursued by the whole band of assassins.

Axel has planted his sword as a cross in front of the dying Knud. He points to the sacred symbol on his breast and claims the right to give the king extreme unction. The midnight bell sounds. The murderers involuntarily pause. All lights are extinguished; only the chandelier is still burning and casts a dull light on the pale faces and gleaming weapons. Unable to await the outcome, Svend has rushed back to the great hall. Fallen enemies lie at his feet, but he starts upon seeing his halberdiers gripped by holy terror, just standing there watching the last, the most important victims. He orders them to finish the job. But the pious Axel, undisturbed in devout rapture, has heard Knud's last confession. The dying king rises, fixes Svend with a transfigured look, summons him before the eternal judgment seat, presses the cross to his lips, and sinks into the arms of Death.

Svend is terribly shaken, but his men soon regain their composure. Swords flash anew, and Valdemar prepares for a desperate struggle. But with lightning speed, Axel jumps up and cuts the chain that holds the chandelier. It comes down with a dreadful crash and is shattered and extinguished in the fall. Pitch-darkness and confusion favour the escape of Valdemar and Axel.

ACT III

The area near Yngvar's house. It is night and a storm is brewing.

Distant pastoral tones echo. The guild brothers gather at the blacksmith's house. Erik and Agnar return from Roskilde, where they were so contemptuously treated. The storm breaks. The guild hall is closed, and while the thunder rolls outside, merriment and the clinking of cups can be heard within.

A flash of lightning reveals a fleeing figure. It approaches! It is Valdemar! Wounded and exhausted, he has escaped death; fainting, he leans on his sword and does not know where he is. Horns sound in the distance; his pursuers are close by, but they will not take him alive! He turns his sword on himself. Thunder rolls over his head; then it is as if a sign from Heaven gave a better intention, a milder hope; he lays aside the steel and prays.

Axel is near him; he listens and gropes in the dark. Valdemar jumps up to defend himself against an enemy but recognizes his faithful friend. What a reunion! What joy! At this moment, love is the only emotion that unites king and subject, and Axel and Valdemar feel what one friend means to another.

Axel becomes aware of the king's enfeebled condition and binds up his wounds with his own linen collar and sash. They find a stone on which Valdemar can rest. But they still do not know where they are. Then Agnar's harp sounds and they remember the smithy from the day before. Axel knocks at the door and Yngvar comes out. He is surprised to see Axel Hvide here so late at night but is horrified to hear what has happened; kneeling, he promises to risk life and limb for Valdemar, and at a sign from him, the guild brothers emerge. They surround the king with expressions of tenderness and awe; they shudder when they learn of Svend's atrocity and vow revenge. Yngvar tosses a bundle of weapons into their midst; they hurriedly arm themselves, and when the horns once again herald Svend's henchmen, they crowd about Valdemar and form a wall around him.

Axel will not have them fight against overwhelming odds; Valdemar can be saved by shrewdness and loyalty. He sends the guild brothers off in different directions with urgent messages. Erik hastens to his boat, Yngvar and Agnar take the king into the smithy, and Axel goes along.

Noise draws closer, and Svend's men are soon roaming through the woods in every direction; all their searching has been in vain. Ditleif gives new orders and hastens off to hunt deeper in the woods.

Some halberdiers stay behind; they are sullen, dissatisfied, and half-drunk. Some of them sit down on a stone to count their gold pieces, while others kick in the doors of Yngvar's house, which they intend to search. Yngvar throws them out and threatens them with his hammer, but Ellen calms her husband and satisfies the soldiers, offering them ale and mead. Axel, who in a coarse peasant frock must do the work of a servant boy, is almost recognized by the halberdiers. But Ellen gives him a cuff, tosses the keys to him, and sends him down in the cellar to fetch more ale.

Yngvar is soon on familiar terms with the troublesome knaves, who do justice to the drink and toast Svend's health and Valdemar's downfall; but now he throws caution to the winds, flings the cup away from him, and defiantly pounds the table so that the tankards roll all over. The halberdiers fume with rage, and the situation looks really dangerous, when the king's approach is announced. They hastily stop drinking and quarreling and get into formation.

Svend enters, followed by Astrid, her ladies, and linkboys. He is very pale and excited. He asks about the fugitives, but his anger mounts with each new report, for no trace of them has been found. He looks at

Astrid suspiciously, but she tries to pacify and soften him. He sends his men off to search in every quarter.

Svend and Astrid are alone. She kneels before the image of the saint, which is illuminated by white tapers; Svend stands in the dark shadows with folded arms. He gazes wildly around him; nowhere can he find peace; the eyes of the man he has murdered are resting on him; it is as if his hands were sticky with blood. He tries to run away from himself until he stops at the illuminated image of the saint. St. Knud's upraised hand, the wound in his side, the pale, noble features all call to mind Svend's evil deed. A convulsive shudder passes over him, he clutches at his temples, and the crown falls off his head. With mounting alarm, he gropes for it, and his fury is only increased by Astrid's tenderness and sympathy. At length he finds his crown, hides it in his embrace, threatens his daughter, and, exhausted, falls to the ground.

The harp is heard again. Astrid summons the old man and bids him to allay her father's anguish with his tones. He eventually succeeds. Svend regains consciousness and embraces his child. But the image of the saint terrifies him once more, and when his men return, having failed in their mission, he himself decides to lead them farther afield in order to escape from this place.

Astrid expects Valdemar to die; she shudders at this thought and tells the harper of her worry. At that very moment, Erik's boat draws near. Axel and Yngvar emerge from the house and a number of guild brothers come running. Then the harper casts off his garb, and Valdemar appears in full armor; Yngvar hands him helmet and gauntlets, embraces his wife and children, and jumps into the boat. Valdemar respectfully approaches the astonished Astrid and, kneeling, presses her hand to his lips. Svend's henchmen are near. Astrid implores the king the evade his enemies. He thanks her warmly, climbs into the boat, and puts off from land, tossing his steel gauntlet onto the coast of Sjaelland as a parting gesture.

The halberdiers flock to the spot, discover the steel gauntlet, and deliver it to the king. Ditleif accuses Astrid of having abetted Valdemar's escape. Svend hears this with mounting rage, and when she fearlessly thanks Heaven for the nobleman's deliverance, he draws his sword on his own daughter. His men rush around him; he shatters the blade, but repudiates and curses the unhappy Astrid, who swoons in her women's arms.

ACT IV

Valdemar's tent. A couch-bed shaded by banners and a table upon which are a lamp and Valdemar's weapons.

Valdemar is asleep and dreaming. He sees his father's sepulchral monument; the runic stones vanish, and in his dazzling raiment Knud Lavard, surrounded by transfigured beings, appears to his son. He looks at him with tenderness while angels dance and play with helm, shield, and sword and bless his beloved Valdemar. He promises him victory, touches his eyelids, and reveals to his mind's eye: DENMARK'S FUTURE. Moments from six centuries appear from the haze, and a distant melody, but one that will be sacred to posterity, calls to mind these words:

> In peace my hair hath turned to gray,
> For the work I've done 'tis God's great fee;
> Thralldom's chains I saw cut away,
> And sons I have who art brave and free.
> (Thaarup's *Harvest Festival*)

The tones die away, the vision disappears, and Valdemar awakens. He sits up on the couch-bed and in a sort of stupor peers into the dawn. His dream hovers imperfectly before him and his heart is filled with dark forebodings. But everything soon comes alive outside the tent; movement in the camp increases; trumpets shrill and Valdemar regains his liveliness and strength. He summons his esquires, who come to help him into his armor. It grows lighter. Axel and the chieftains, all clad in steel, enter the king's tent. Valdemar receives them with warmth and dignity; he distributes banners. His standard he entrusts to Axel. They repeat their oath to risk life and limb for Valdemar and follow him to the decisive battle.

Grathe Heath

Svend, in full armor, is standing on a stone, surrounded by his bodyguard and esquires: he is watching the battle, which is raging some distance away. Messengers come and go; wounded are carried off the battlefield. A band of captured peasants is dragged before him. Yngvar and Erik are among them: they defy Svend and are about to feel his wrath when Ditleif rushes in and demands the king's presence. Svend gives his standard to the chieftain, puts heart into his men, assembles all of them, and leads them off to the fight.

Hedvig detains a young esquire in order to entreat him to loose the cords with which the prisoners are bound. All thank their liberator, with the exception of Erik, who notices how affectionately his fiancée treats the young warrior. Tortured by jealousy, he thrusts her aside and wishes to return to the battle; but when he sees the esquire's face, he realizes how wrong he was and, kneeling, asks forgiveness. Erik does not return to the fray, but the esquire follows his lord.

The tumult of battle draws closer and it is Valdemar's men who are advancing. The fugitives become more numerous; finally Ditleif, too, falls with the standard. Then Svend, with his helmet gone and his mail cut to pieces, joins the ranks of the downhearted.

With the courage of desperation, he seizes the standard and musters his phalanx anew. But Valdemar, at the head of a picked troop, falls upon them with crushing force: those who are not felled are swept away as if by a flood. The standard is trampled in the dust, and Svend, mortally wounded, lies among the vanquished.

Defeated, deserted by everyone, he gives himself up to despair. Then he feels his hand touched by another's: the esquire, who was thrust to the earth by the thundering horde, has risen and hastened to the aid of his lord. He is the only one who has remained loyal to Svend. He gives him rest, staunches the blood, and quenches the dying man's thirst. Svend eagerly drinks from the youth's helmet; but when he raises his eyes he sees long curls hanging down over the lad's houlders. He starts back in amazement and recognizes Astrid! He releases her from his curse; she is the angel at the gates of eternity. The father rests upon his daughter's breast, and her tears wet his pale cheeks.

Victory resounds. Svend awakens from his stupor, gropes for the standard, rises with it, and falls.

A band of rejoicing peasants returns from the battle. They see the fallen Svend and want to seize his weapons. But Astrid forbids them to touch her father's body. They do not recognize her and are about to use force against the defiant esquire when Erik, Hedvig, and the nuns enter from one side, Valdemar and his men from the other. The peasants withdraw and Astrid lays the standard at the victor's feet. She asks for a grave for her father.

Deeply moved, Valdemar grants her request, forgets any grudge he may have had against the dead man, and lays the standard he has won at Svend's bier. When he turns back to Astrid, he starts at seeing her dressed in the black garb of the convent. There will her soul repose; there will she pray for her deceased father and bless Valdemar. The warriors lay down their arms and Astrid follows her father's bier.

Axel enters with the victorious host. Joy and jubilation accompany them. Prisoners are thrust at the king's feet; axes, chains, and yokes hover above their heads, and, prostrate, they await their fate. Everyone's eyes are on Valdemar, who is destined to bear the appellation "The Great": "His hand removes the deadly steel, hurls chains into the dust, and breaks the yoke." Amazed, the victors step back while the vanquished embrace his knees. He raises them up; he has turned enemies into friends. All Danes are brothers. Peace and unity shall consolidate the kingdom; love and happiness shall be spread over Denmark's glorious fields and meadows. Valdemar now receives the crown. He is acclaimed, and, hoisted on shields, he enthusiastically surveys his loyal and devoted people.

DON QUIXOTE AT CAMACHO'S WEDDING
(Don Quixote ved Camachos Bryllup)

An Original Pantomimic Ballet in Three Acts
by
August Bournonville

Music arranged by Ludvig Zinck, including music by
Gioacchino Rossini, Etienne-Nicolas Mehul, Gasparo Spontini,
Jean Schneitzhoeffer, and others

Performed for the first time at the Royal Theatre, February 24, 1837

Characters

DON QUIXOTE	Hr. Hammer
SANCHO PANZA, his armor bearer	Hr. Stramboe
CAMACHO, landowner	Hr. Füssel
LORENZO, innkeeper	Hr. Fredstrup
QUITERIA, his daughter	Jfr. Grahn
MARITORNA, her governess	Jfr. Werning
BASILIO, a young peasant	Hr. Bournonville
PEDRILLO, muleteer	Hr. Larcher
ALDONZA, a tavern maid	Jfr. Fjeldsted
THE PRIEST	Hr. Enholm
DIEGO, barber	Hr. Funck
A MULETEER	Hr. Füssel, Jr.

PEASANTS, MULETEERS, COOKS, BUFFOONS, GUARDS AND CHILDREN.

The scene is laid in a Spanish village.

ACT I

The interior of Lorenzo's inn; to the left, the dwelling-house; to the right, the barn. In the background, a low wall and gate beyond which one sees a lovely mountainous landscape. Afternoon.

Quiteria and her duenna are seated at a table, sewing and reading. Aldonza is standing with them, playing on her guitar a refrain of a romance. Hunting horns are heard close at hand. Lorenzo hurries to the door to greet the wealthy Camacho, who is returning from the hunt with his friends. Camacho sends his party on ahead, orders the slain deer carried in to Lorenzo, and goes with him to pay his respects to the pretty Quiteria. He is most gallant and takes no notice of the embarrassment with which Quiteria receives his compliments. Her father and Maritorna exchange meaningful looks, and the old fellow makes it his business to emphasize all his daughter's talents; but what is particularly to be admired is her dancing. Camacho entreats her to give him a little taste of this, and, though somewhat distressed, she dances to the strains of Aldonza's guitar. Camacho is enraptured by her grace and beauty, and toward the end of the dance he is about to get down on his knees and declare his love for her but she runs inside with Aldonza, and her father holds him back. He now explains his intentions to Lorenzo and Maritorna. The father joyfully embraces him. Camacho does not forget to ingratiate himself with the duenna. He receives pledges of assistance and promises to return soon. The day's work is done. Shepherds lead home their flocks, and muleteers hang the jangling harnesses in the barn. Everyone gathers at the inn to pass the lovely evening. Basilio and Pedrillo are leaders of the merry young people; each one is the cleverest among his peers, and both come to Lorenzo's house with the same interest. Pedrillo is passionately fond of Aldonza; nothing stands in the way of their happiness. But the lofty plans Lorenzo has for his daughter are responsible for the fact that he is loath to see the preference Quiteria shows for Basilio. He would like to prevent them from dancing together but the guests insist on their favourite dances: gay seguidillas succeed one another while groups of playing and drinking guests gather round.

A horn sounds. Sancho enters and his droll figure attracts everyone's attention. He goes from girl to girl with a letter and a locket, looking for the Dulcinea he has already been seeking for so long a time. But the girls, only a few of whom can read, laugh at Sancho and crowd around him with expressions of surprise. Old Maritorna wishes to examine the letter and locket, but Sancho looks her over from head to foot and gives her to understand that he seeks the fairest of the fair; therefore the matter cannot possibly concern her. She responds to this naiveté with a good box on the ear. Sancho, who cannot stand to be beaten, flies into a rage and almost forgets the duenna's age and sex; people come between them.

Meanwhile, Pedrillo and Basilio have grasped what is going on, and since they have already heard of the knight-errant, they acquaint Lorenzo and his guests with the facts.

Don Quixote approaches. Everyone respectfully steps aside. He halts at the gate, orders Sancho to sound the horn, and, immediately taking the inn for a knight's castle, he honours Lorenzo as its possessor. The latter presents the knight to his daughter. Moved by Quiteria's beauty, Don Quixote offers her his service against warriors, robbers, and monsters and promises to obey her every command so long as it does not conflict with his duty to Dulcinea. Quiteria, supported by the roguish Aldonza, plays her part quite naturally, and the knight is delighted with his pleasant reception. He summons Sancho, who has already supplied himself with supper and cannot part from the cask and ladle. He tells him of Quiteria's charm and winsome manner. The armor bearer agrees with his master about this and advises him to propose to her. Don Quixote regards him with astonishment, but Sancho, delighted with his happy idea, calls people to gather round and asks them to compare the image in the locket with the far lovelier Quiteria. He goes even further, tearing up the letter and scornfully trampling it underfoot. In an outburst of the most violent indignation, Don Quixote tears the locket from him, draws his sword, and is about to run the impudent fellow through; but the pleas of Lorenzo and, especially, Quiteria gain mercy for him and only when all have sworn that Dulcinea is unquestionably the superior of the two is the knight restored to calm.

Darkness bids the guests depart. Lorenzo shows Sancho his sleeping place in the barn, while inviting Don Quixote to enter his house. Basilio and Pedrillo receive secret promises of a rendezvous outside the jalousies. Don Quixote thanks his hospitable host but requests the favour of spending the night under the open sky since he considers it his duty to safeguard the castle. Soon all is still.

Leaning upon his lance, Don Quixote romantically gives himself up to the queen of his thoughts. He feels that since beholding Quiteria he is more than ever in need of his unwavering courage and unswerving steadfastness. He tenderly regards the locket and is about to kiss it, but considers himself unworthy to do so. Distressed by Dulcinea's cruelty to him, he kneels and begs for an opportunity to win her through a valiant deed.

A drunken muleteer comes staggering through the gate. He has forgotten his harness and is going to fetch it. Here is an adventure which our knight will not allow to escape him. He waits until the supposed robber is leaving, then challenges him and orders him to drop the stolen goods and fight to the death. The muleteer, who is used to acting first and thinking later, becomes brutal and is about to force his way out with his cudgel when Don Quixote, calling upon his lady and the god of love, drops his lance on the muleteer's head with such force that it snaps and his stunned opponent falls to the ground. Sancho is wakened by the commotion, and Lorenzo and his people come running. The knight presents himself as the castle's deliverer and shows them the enemy he has vanquished. All express fright at the muleteer's condition, but Sancho douses him with water; he regains consciousness and is led away, still wondering what has happened.

Lorenzo tries in vain to get the knight to take some rest. This night Don Quixote still intends to rid the countryside of robbers. He gives his armor bearer the spoils of the last fight, presses his host's hand, and goes out the gate while, shaking his head, Lorenzo closes his door and Sancho prepares his bed with the captured saddlery. Basilio and Pedrillo stealthily enter the gate, one slightly behind the other; each has his guitar and with it gives the prearranged signal.

The jalousies open – Quiteria's on the bottom floor, Aldonza's in the uppermost story. But since the lovers are not expecting to meet here, darkness prevents them from recognizing one another and a misunderstanding almost arises. This is soon resolved, however, and each lover goes to his beloved's window where, to the strains of the guitars, they exchange the most tender declarations.

Don Quixote returns from his rounds; he hears the sounds of the guitars and hearkens. The lovers hide, and Quiteria goes up to Aldonza's room, the window of which is open. Urged on by Pedrillo, the girls address their sighs to the knight, who, convinced that Quiteria cherishes an unhappy passion for him, implores her not to tempt his fidelity to the lady who alone rules his heart.

While Basilio and Pedrillo hug themselves over this scene, Maritorna opens the door and, carrying a candle, comes out to see what is causing this commotion. But the young madcaps blow out her light and there is now double the fun. On one side the ladies beg Don Quixote for a simple squeeze of the hand, which he, after some reflection, does not feel he should deny them. He therefore climbs up on the table that stands under the window and gives them his hand; this they entwine with ribbons. On the other side the duenna is teased by the two ardent lovers, who do not give her a moment's peace but bring out her bad temper. Fleeing from them, she falls over the sleeping Sancho. The latter, who thinks that all the Furies are attacking him, grabs Maritorna and a stubborn fight ensues. Someone is coming. Pedrillo and Basilio run away and overturn the table on which the knight is standing. The girls close the window with a bang, Don Quixote is left hanging by one wrist, and Lorenzo comes rushing out, followed by grooms with torches to illuminate the confusion taking place in his courtyard.

ACT II

The inn from the last act. Dawn.

Music is heard in the distance. The knight and his armor bearer awaken at the same time. Both men think they have been dreaming; they tell each other what has happened to them, and Don Quixote discovers therein a curious blend of magic and reality.

The music draws nearer. It is Camacho, who wishes to pay tribute to his fiancée in festive procession. A troop of villagers dressed in their best comes dancing in. They are carrying staves with the monograms of

Camacho and Quiteria and waving banners with streaming banderoles. While servants deck the house with foliage and flowers, the musicians strike up and girls dance to the sound of tambourines and castanets.

Lorenzo emerges *en déshabillé*, apologizes profusely for his informal attire, and embraces his future son-in-law. Camacho displays the marriage contract while Lorenzo, giving orders to cooks and mountebanks, hastens to complete his toilet. Diego arranges his best wig. The dancing continues; wine is poured; Don Quixote congratulates the rich bridegroom, and Sancho makes friends with the cook's boys.

Lorenzo, who has tried in vain to keep his son-in-law from inviting Don Quixote, takes Camacho into the house. The wedding guests part. Sancho goes off with the cooks.

Don Quixote is standing, lost in thought, when the barber Diego happily and gaily emerges from the inn. He has been well paid for his work and will refresh himself before moving on. Aldonza enters and pours him a cup of wine. After some fooling he takes his leave, sets his brass basin on his head, and is about to depart. But his splendid headdress immediately catches Don Quixote's eye. He takes it to be a costly helmet which he thinks he is destined to capture. He stops the barber and solemnly demands that he hand over the heroic ornament which he has no right to wear. Astounded and frightened, Diego prefers to flee and escapes, leaving the disputed basin behind.

Sancho returns and suspiciously eyes the helmet his master orders him to pick up. He thinks it greatly resembles a barber's basin, but since the knight will brook no objection, he helps him to array himself in his splendid prize. Don Quixote is positively delighted and an abundant lunch helps Sancho to forget all reflections on knightly whims.

Basilio comes rushing in, followed by Pedrillo, who seeks to cool the former's outburst of despair. But this very day Quiteria shall belong to another, and death is the only thing left to the unhappy lover. Pedrillo explains the situation to Don Quixote, while Sancho in his way tries to console Basilio. Quiteria comes out of the house in tears. She disconsolately throws herself into Basilio's arms and both bemoan their cruel fate. Aldonza and Pedrillo take counsel as to how to help the poor couple, and Don Quixote promises to intercede with the father on their behalf. Lorenzo and Maritorna enter and become terribly angry upon seeing Basilio with Quiteria, for if Camacho were to learn of this the whole thing might be called off. This fear supersedes every other notion, and without further ado, Basilio is given the gate.

Camacho and his friends enter. They bring costly gifts for Quiteria but are surprised at her lack of enthusiasm for them.

Lorenzo reassures them of his daughter's feelings, gives her a couple of meaningful looks, several times expresses his impatience with the knight's protests, gives the young couple his blessing, and orders Quiteria to go inside to don her bridal array.

The joy of those present is disrupted by the arrival of the barber and the muleteer. They have brought the guard with them to demand the return of the property that had been so violently taken from them. The muleteer, whose head is swathed in bandages, complains of the humiliation and injury inflicted upon him and has already laid hands on Sancho in an attempt to divest him of the saddlery which the armor bearer considers his lawful prize. The barber points to the knight's head, which proudly displays the brandnew barber's basin. But Sancho shows both teeth and clenched fists while Don Quixote proudly counters every accusation, appealing to the authority conferred by open warfare; furthermore, it is not a basin but a precious helmet for which he will risk a bloody fight. Pedrillo and a couple of other merry lads support the knight's claim, while the barber and the muleteer choose Lorenzo as their arbitrator. The latter, who is bored to tears with his troublesome guest and, moreover, has a bone to pick with him after the previous night's adventure, starts to make rather serious charges. Don Quixote is amazed that a knight and the lord of a castle would behave in such a way, but Lorenzo soon sets him straight by presenting him with a bill for room and board. The confusion mounts. Don Quixote refuses to pay the bill, and Sancho will not relinquish the saddlery. The guard steps forward; one squabbles with the other, and Don Quixote, seeing in this confusion a knot which ought to be cut, forces his way out with his sword. They are about to pursue him, but Camacho, who has thoroughly enjoyed this whole dispute, halts the guard and satisfies the plaintiffs by compensating them for their losses.

Meanwhile, Sancho has been seized and the gate shut. The servants expect to have great fun with the armor bearer. The latter tears himself loose and tries to flee, but they throw a big carpet over him, roll him up in it, and, after four lads have each taken a corner of the rug, they toss the unfortunate Sancho into the air to the endless amusement of Camacho and the dancing youths and to the great chagrin of Don Quixote, who can see his armor bearer's somersaults over the wall.

ACT III

A solitary place in the woods.

Don Quixote is seated by a spring, reading a book. His weapons are lying on the ground. From time to time he looks at the locket, kisses the book, and, sighing, sometimes raises his eyes to Heaven. Sancho enters, half-angry, half-crying, and vehemently blames his master and the whole of knight-errantry for all the ills he must suffer: hunger, thirst, drubbings, being tossed in a carpet, and Heaven knows what else! Don Quixote gently seeks to pacify him. "Your misfortunes will soon cease; a better hope shall smile on you and a principality be your reward." But Sancho will not be consoled. He is more furious than ever, curses the day he followed his master, and threatens to desert him forever. With painful earnestness, Don Quixote looks upon him as someone about whom he has been mistaken; he takes his purse, gives it to him as a reward, wishes him Godspeed, and sadly goes back to his place. But Sancho's good humor now returns; he cannot leave his old master. The gold is weighing down his hand and his soul, and with tears of repentence he softly approaches the knight, kneels at his feet, and kisses his hand. At first Don Quixote hardens his heart. But when Sancho fervently presses him, promising to fight for him and risk anything just to stay with him, he can resist no longer. He raises him up and forgives him with all his heart.

Don Quixote accepts an invitation from Comacho to attend the wedding feast, and Sancho, who can already smell the delicious cooking, is himself again. He impatiently hurries his master and goes off with him, jubilantly skipping for joy.

A field surrounded by forest. In the background, Camacho's house; farther off, the village. In the shade of a number of oak trees, tents with refreshments. A fire with spits. Tables with cakes and fruits. Cauldrons over the fire. Swings and a tall pole with a garland on top.

Everything is astir. Children and old folks stoll about; intimate groups camp in the woods. The cooks are officious; there is loud music, people are swinging, and the prize atop the pole has already been won by the boldest climber.

The procession draws near. A numerous crowd in festal dress surrounds the bridal couple. Don Quixote is among them. Sancho, on the other hand, steals away, and, captivated by the delights of the kitchen, completely disappears amid the bounteous fare. Quiteria is greeted with admiration. Never before has she been as lovely as today; the sadness which blanches her cheeks only enhances her beauty. The procession halts, and from decorated chairs beneath a canopy of flowers the young couple view the ceremonies preceding their marriage. First comes a dance by young girls with flower garlands; next the most stalwart youths – armed with florettes which they dexterously employ for attack and defense – perform in two quadrilles. Finally, a little theatre is brought forward; the director hands the bridegroom a scroll. The curtain rises on a miniature production of the following piece:

THE TRIUMPH OF LOVE AND FORTUNE

A young princess is surrounded by her playmates. Her old father describes to her several suitors, but she rejects all of them and retreats into her castle. Her father exits in tears. Then Cupid enters and seeks admittance to the castle, but the princess denies him entry. Indignant, he empties his whole quiver of arrows against the castle; at last, only tears are left and the princess laughs at his impotence. But Fortune comes to his aid; their forces united, they now storm the castle; it crumbles, the princess begs for mercy and is forced to acknowledge the power of Love. Her father now enters with a good-looking young shepherd, a prince in disguise. Cupid and Fortune declare him to be their chosen one. The old father gives his blessing, and amid a dance of joy the curtain falls.

Those assembled are delighted with this spectacle. The director reaps compliments and applause, and the procession once again gets under way. Pale, dressed in black, with all the signs of despair, Basilio meets the band of people, stops the bridal couple, and gives the tottering bride a look of reproach. He seizes Camacho's hand and declares that he loves Quiteria passionately. He would have given his life for her, but a cruel father separated them in order to follow the dictates of his self-interest; despair is now his lot and death his only refuge. General bewilderment and surprise. The father wants to quarrel but is restrained. Basilio demands that all present bear witness to the love he has borne the woman who will now desert him for another. But to live and see Quiteria in Camacho's arms-that he cannot do. He takes a step back, draws his sword, and stabs himself. Everyone expresses horror. People hasten to aid the mortally wounded man, Quiteria throws herself on top of him, people run for help; in their dismay, Camacho and Lorenzo do not know which way to turn. Blood is streaming from Basilio's chest. He grows weaker and weaker, and when the friar arrives, he announces that Basilio has only a few more moments to live. Basilio then asks to take leave of his beloved. Everyone sheds tears at this sorrowful scene. He has one more wish; to die Quiteria's bridegroom... Camacho, Lorenzo and Maritorna oppose this idea with all their might, but the assembled guests beseech Camacho. Don Quixote supports Basilio's plea, and even the friar feels it would be cruel to deny the last request of a dying man. Camacho finally consents. The clergyman performs the marriage, rings are exchanged, the witnesses sign, and the prayers of those present attend this sad ceremony.

The monk departs and profound sadness prevails. But what can equal the general astonishment when, alive and well, Basilio arises, tears the bloody linen from his breast, tosses aside the mourning cloak, and enthusiastically embraces his bride. The red-eyed Quiteria thinks she is dreaming; without hesitation, Pedrillo throws himself into his friend's arms, and the timorous guests believe they are witnessing a miracle.

"Nay," says Basilio, "no miracle – unless it be that love, almighty love – has inspired me to use cunning to overcome power. This sword only pierced my coat. I am not wounded, but more cheerful and more dauntless than ever, and now nothing in the world shall part me from my beloved."

There are divided opinions about Basilio's act. Camacho and his friends denounce him for his treachery. The father considers the marriage invalid, but Basilio's partisans – Don Quixote among them declare that the marriage is legitimate and that Basilio had every right to dupe those who would oppose him. Tempers flare, the dispute becomes hotter, weapons are drawn, and soon the once-peaceful field is turned into a field of battle. Don Quixote fights like a tiger at the head of Basilio's party and soon drives the enemy before him. The fighting moves farther away and the womenfolk surround the swooning Quiteria.

Some young fellows discover Sancho among the saucepans. They pull him out and encourage him to fight. Although he is not particularly in the mood for war, they still tie one pan lid in front of him and another in back, place a meat fork in his hand, and, thus equipped, lead him into the heat of battle.

Don Quixote and Camacho come on engaged in swordplay. The latter can no longer stand up to his opponent. He stumbles and falls, and the knight is preparing to give him the coup de grace when Basilio and Quiteria jump in and, by their pleas, save Camacho's life.

A group of combatants enter from upstage. Sancho is in their midst and on his copper armor receives blows from friends as well as enemies. The confusion is at its height, but Don Quixote now calls for peace and harmony and effects a reconciliation between the contending parties. Camacho, who owes Basilio his life and realizes that a forced marriage cannot bring him happiness, intends to outdo his rival in magnanimity. He therefore not only forgives the lovers and helps them to reconcile the father, but announces that the whole costly feast shall continue in honour of Basilio and Quiteria. General rejoicing over Camacho's noble sacrifice. Don Quixote is gladdened by the couple's happiness and gratitude, while Sancho takes delight in the delicious wine and roguish girls. Lorenzo blesses his children, congratulations flow in from every side, and a gay dance of joy celebrates the most perfect festival of love.

* * *

HERTHA'S OFFERING
(Herthas Offer)

A Flower Piece
by
August Bournonville

Music arranged by Johannes Frederik Frøhlich

First presented at the Royal Theatre in honour of the august birthday of His Majesty the King, January 29, 1838

Characters

HERTHA	Jfr. Grahn
SPRING	Hr. Bournonville
AEGIR	Hr. Fredstrup
AEGIR'S CHILDREN	Hr. Larcher Jfr. Fjeldsted

ELVES, WOOD-MAIDENS, MERMEN AND MERMAIDS.

The scene is a Danish beech grove by the sea.

Winter vanishes; the first songbird is heard. Spring joyfully returns.

Denmark is beginning to burst into leaf; the beech tree displays fresh leaves, and the sacred oak of the grove spreads its mighty crown of foliage.

Spring lifts the white veil enveloping the slumbering Hertha. She awakens, and woodland elves adorn her with flowers.

The lively Spring arouses love in Hertha's breast. Aegir and his children rise from the sea; from the underbrush wood-maidens steal forth. All rejoice at the union of Spring and Hertha.

Dancing by Spring and Hertha, by the sons and daughters of Aegir.

Hertha and her handmaidens carry forward the year's thank offerings. Aegir, his retinue, and small woodland elves join them. They reverently encircle the age-old trunk which has survived so many winters, delighted them for so many springs, given them shelter from the storm and shade in the summer heat, and from whose loving embrace spring forth

DENMARK'S LOVELIEST FLOWERS.

* * *

THE ISLE OF FANTASY, OR FROM CHINA'S COAST
(Phantasiens Øe)

An Original Romantic Ballet in Two Acts and a Final Tableau
by
August Bournonville

Music for Act One: Johann Peter Emilius Hartmann, with a piece by Daniel Francois Auber
Act Two: J.P.E. Hartman, Ivar Frederik Bredal, Ludvig Zinck, Edvard Helsted, Herman Løvenskjold
Final Tableau: Holger Simon Paulli
Scenery by Aron Wallich and Troels Lund

Performed for the first time at the Royal Theatre in honour of the august birthday of Her Majesty the Queen, Sunday, October 28, 1838

Characters

THE QUEEN OF FANTASY	Jfr. Grahn
FAUNUS	Hr. Larcher
SVANE, a carpenter at Holmen	Hr. Fredstrup
SOPHIE, his wife	Mad. Schouw
MARIE ⎫	Jfr. Fjeldsted
LOVISE ⎬ their children	Jfr. Petrine
JOHAN ⎭	Ed. Stramboe
CHRISTIAN HOLM, Second Mate, Marie's fiancée	Hr. Hoppe
SOREN THE TOPMAN, a sailor	Hr. Stramboe
ANE, his wife	Jfr. Fredstrup
BLOCK, Svane's friend	Hr. Nehm
CAPTAIN OF THE CHINAMAN	Hr. Füssel, Sr.
A SKIPPER	Hr. Füssel, Jr.
A CHINESE POLICEMAN	Hr. Hammer

Solo Dances

RUSSIAN DANCE:	Hr. Bournonville and Jfr. Larcher
CHINESE DANCE:	Hr. Hoppensach
ENGLISH SAILOR:	Hr. Bournonville
BACCHANTIC WALTZ:	Jfr. Nielsen

SEAMEN OF SEVERAL NATIONS, CHINAMEN, CHILDREN, FAUNS AND NYMPHS.

In Act I, the action takes place in Copenhagen and Canton, in the month of January; in Act II, on the Isle of Fantasy and in Copenhagen, in October of the same year.

Prefatory Remark

I ask seafarers to forgive the inaccuracy that, as a consequence of the demands of the ballet and my own insufficient knowledge of the locale, is prevalent in my picture of life in Canton. In spite of everything I have heard and read about the *Coast of China,* for me it still remains the *Isle of Fantasy.*

ACT I

A seaman's dwelling. Two windows and a door opening onto the street. To the right, the tiled stove and a door; to the left, the sleeping chamber. A chest of drawers containing porcelain, a striking clock, a picture showing factories in Canton, a small mirror, a table, and chairs make up the humble furniture. A winter morning.

Marie is already up and working by candlelight. She has lit the fire and made coffee. While tidying up, her eye is caught by the picture showing the place where Christian must be now. She is carrying his latest letter with her and reads it with mounting delight. But her little brother, who has stolen up behind her, unnoticed, snatches the letter, eludes Marie, who tries to grab him, and extinguishes the candle. Father and Mother enter, but all is dark, and they cannot understand what is going on until the shutters are opened and the gray light of dawn penetrates the room.

The mother sets the table for coffee. Marie finishes dressing her little sister while the father converses with Johan about the Chinese picture. It becomes full daylight. One hears the guns of Nyholm. It is Denmark's festival: the twenty-eighth of January!

Block comes to announce that Svane must present himself to the Chief without delay. The women are alarmed, but Block asks them to get their man dressed up, since something out of the ordinary is in the offing. Svane is ready in a moment and hurries off with his old comrade.

Sophie rejoices with her children. She is going to offer the neighbour's wife a cup of coffee, and Johan calls up to Ane in the loft. She answers and hurries down. After a great deal of officiousness and many embraces, she comes to the coffee table.

A troop of Nyboder boys comes to fetch Johan for the public feast; but he dares not leave before his father has returned. Meanwhile, they amuse themselves with dancing, in which Marie and her little sister take part.

Ane, who has earnestly been studying the dregs of her coffee, jumps up in despair and announces that her husband has been lost at sea. Marie vainly seeks to learn whence she has received this doleful news. Ane only answers that Christian has gone down with the same ship. Horror and sorrow on the faces of all, just as Svane returns home.

Everything is explained; Ane's superstition is to blame for all this alarm. Svane brings with him newspapers announcing the ship's safe arrival in Canton, and the joy is heightened by the medal which today rewards Svane's faithful service. Family and friends shall rejoice together. The changing of the guard is heard in the distance, the boys are jubilant, and everyone goes out to enjoy the ceremony of the day.

A square in Old Canton. In the background, the river, and on the far side of the water, the European factories in New Canton. A large number of small craft, Chinese as well as European, cover the river.

The Danish captain of a Chinaman, surrounded by his crew and a number of Chinese merchants, is in the process of concluding the final bargain and paying wages. On all sides, groups of sailors and Chinese. The Danish seamen make purchases for wives, sweethearts, and children. Their Captain informs them that they will weigh anchor today, but before their departure they may still enjoy themselves for several hours and celebrate the twenty-eighth of January. Wine is brought and the solemn toast is delivered to the accompaniment of kettle drums and trumpets.

Søren the Topman, with the Chinese police in hot pursuit, breathlessly dashes into the midst of his comrades, who are ready to defend him. The Captain is forced to step in and demand an explanation. From what he can understand of the Chinese complaints, Søren, impelled by curiosity, ventured farther into the city than is permitted, then created several disturbances and failed to show respect for the authorities, who now want him seized and punished. The Captain promises them satisfaction and pacifies them with a small *douceur*. Søren is given a severe reprimand, which he receives with such a funny look on his face that the Captain has to turn away in order to hide his rising laughter.

Søren now tells what he saw in the great, impenetrable city and announces that he has invited a select company of mountebanks, who shall amuse them with their ridiculous gestures. The merriment becomes general, and Christian bids all of them dance.

The rejoicing is interrupted by the wretchedness of misfortune. That is to say, some Negro slaves have escaped from a ship. They have been recaptured and are now brought back in chains to thralldom and mistreatment. The Danish sailors cannot bear this sight. By their pleas, they seek to move the foreign skipper. Søren even becomes a bit rude to him. But all in vain. Then Christian steps into his comrades' midst and shows them how they shall celebrate this day in worthy fashion. He contributes his mite to ransom the slaves; the brave seamen follow his example. But alas! This sum is insufficient. They stand, downhearted because of their poor showing. But the Captain, who, unbeknownst to them, has witnessed their noble deed, quietly approaches, and *his* aid decides the outcome. The skipper is willing to accept ransom; the chains fall; the blacks are free. They first embrace each other, then thank their rescuers. But the Captain makes them understand whom it is they really ought to thank, and a thousand benedictions flow from the Negroes' lips for their far-off benefactor [King Frederik VI of Denmark] to whom, with childlike tenderness, they send their humble ornaments as a token of gratitude.

With this farewell, the Danish travellers to China leave Canton. The sailors joyously head homeward to the Baltic strand.

ACT II

The Isle of Fantasy. Trees and flowers of a supernatural luxuriance. To the right, a spring which, as a fountain, falls into a porphyry basin. To the left, a throne; in the background, the ocean.

Surrounded by her court, the Queen of Fantasy receives the homage of fauns and nymphs and graces their festival with her captivating dancing. A ship comes into view, and the Queen orders that enchanting fireworks be used to lure the seafarers. All vanish.

A small craft approaches the island. Søren and Christian come ashore and express their admiration for this lovely landscape which, however, appears to be uninhabited; for Søren, who calls through his hands, receives no answer save the echo from the woods. However, he has brought along his gun and asks Christian to go bird hunting with him. But the young sailor, who is carrying a strange glockenspiel, would rather stay at this place in order, through its melody, to dream of his beloved and his native land. Søren goes off alone.

The spring catches Christian's eye. Its crystal-clear waters entice him, and he scoops some water in his hands. But no sooner has he drunk of it than the fairy queen and her feminine retinue stand near him. In swaying dance they twirl Christian around, and in the face of the enchanting Queen he forgets homeland, fiancée, and himself. He is intoxicated by sensual melodies, gives away his engagement ring, and adoringly falls at the feet of the Queen. She hands him a bouquet whose fragrance overpowers him. He falls asleep by the throne, and the fairies dance off in triumph.

A shot is fired, and Søren comes running to see what he has hit. He is dismayed to see Christian lying immobile directly in the path of his shot. He is unable to rouse him. Alarmed and heavy of heart, he feels in need of a cool drink, scoops up some water in his hat, and takes in long draughts.

A magical world is revealed to him, and everywhere temptations abound. On one side, fauns bearing ripe, luscious grapes, brimming pitchers, and golden cups; on the other, a troop of flower maidens with youthful exuberance and charming smiles. In a bacchantic waltz, Søren the Topman hovers between the temptations of love and of the vine, and does not know which side to choose. A richly laid table is brought forward and the prettiest maiden shall share its delights with Søren. But when, enraptured, he turns around to embrace the lovely creature, he finds in her stead Ane, his wife! The magical beings vanish and the couple remains alone. Søren and Ane stand looking at each other for some time, he with astonishment, she with indignation. The man finally plucks up his courage and puts on a polite and friendly face in order to approach his infuriated spouse. But now the storm breaks, with tears, reproaches, and harsh treatment, so that poor Søren is forced to succumb. He resorts to cajolery and unpacks a great number of presents for her. He finally succeeds in making her forget her resentment. Her former gaiety returns and peace is made.

Søren points to the slumbering Christian and expresses his concern. But Ane parts a bush and out jumps Marie in airy garb and with an ethereal lilt. Søren wants to approach her, but Ane forbids him to and orders him to stay hidden behind the trees. She gives Marie the glockenspiel and withdraws to the opposite side.

Marie takes her place near her beloved and plays "Open Thy Window, Maiden Fair!" These strains take Christian back to his fondest memories. He opens his eyes and with surprise recognizes his fiancée, who smilingly eludes him, all the while playing the melody, which on his part is expressed by: "Thy lily hand give me, maiden fair!" and finally, "Thy ruby lips give me!" She cannot resist his pleas and, giving him hand and mouth, dances in her sweetheart's arms with innocent delight.

Søren and Ane come closer to congratulate the young couple, but just as Ane is about to join their hands together, Marie notices that Christian is not wearing her ring, and when he cannot answer her eager questions, she can no longer doubt his unfaithfulness. Ane vents her wrath at the faithlessness of men. Marie takes Christian's ring from her finger and throws it at his feet and, weeping, puts her arms around Ane and sinks into the earth with her.

The desperate lover curses his rashness. Søren tries to console him and wishes to get him to leave the island. But their boat is gone and their ship is lying far out at sea. Christian is overcome with grief. He falls to the ground in a swoon, and Søren brings him water from the enchanted spring. But he has scarcely drunk when he sees himself surrounded by the airy host of Fantasy, who, led by their queen, offer him a crown and all the delights of life. Carried away with excitement, he forgets everything for the magic of the moment. But Søren does not allow himself to be deceived by phantoms again; when he sees that protests are no help to Christian, he grabs him by the arms, constrains him, and blindfolds him. In vain the spirits of Fantasy seek to gain victory, for Søren has the glockenspiel and plays the melody:

> From China's coast to the Baltic strand
> The Danish sailor delights to go.

Christian listens and gropes toward the sounds. He follows where Søren leads him. They are standing near the beach, on the edge of a cliff. Søren now removes the blindfold from his friend's eyes, pushes him into the waves, jumps in after him, and together they swim toward the waiting ship.

TRANSFORMATION

Svane's dwelling in Copenhagen.

Marie, who awakens from a deep sleep, starts up in dismay. She is disturbed by an alarming dream. Her mother worriedly asks the reason for her confusion, but she cannot give any explanation. Only when Ane enters does her memory become clearer, and Fantasy's images drift past her.

She pauses and anxiously feels for her ring. It is still there! The whole thing was only a dream! Marie stands lost in thought; her mother and Ane regard her with concern. Then her father quietly comes in the door and indicates that they are not to disturb Marie. He gives a package to his wife and puts his hands over his daughter's eyes in order to surprise her. Meanwhile, a table is brought in, laden with presents from Father, Mother, Ane, and the children; for today is Marie's birthday!

The most heartfelt joy and good wishes from every side. Lovise has assembled her playmates; they bring flowers, form monograms, and dance around Marie to a melody which contains a happy omen. They hear a discharge of guns. A crowd of neighbours fills the street. Block rushes in with a number of good friends and announces that the Chinaman has been sighted! Marie is almost faint with happiness, but Ane hurries them and tells them to hasten to greet the arriving ship. They get dressed in the utmost haste and now go jubilantly off to the Custom House.

FINAL TABLEAU

The Chinaman is heading full sail for Copenhagen, which comes closer and closer; in front of the ship sails a little yawl with a dinghy astern.
The ship slowly glides past the lovely coast, the roadstead, Langelinie, and finally the splendid harbor of the royal residence, where the ships are festively decorated. The sailors stand in the bow of the ship to greet their sorely missed home. A little boat rows out to meet them; in it are Svane, his family, and friends. Christian and Søren cannot resist their yearning. With the Captain's permission, they swing themselves by a cable from the bowsprit down into the rocking dinghy. The boats meet. The faithful arm embraces its dearest treasure, and joy resounds in the sailor's favourite melody:

> Even thou, proud ocean,
> Thou art many a seaman's grave,
> He loves thee.
> But if his native soil he sees,
> Then wide his arms he opens,
> And cries aloud his sweetheart's name –
> In short, is happy.

THE FESTIVAL IN ALBANO
(Festen i Albano)

An Idyllic Ballet in One Act by
August Bournonville

Music by Johannes Frederik Frøhlich.
Scenery by Christian Ferdinand Christensen

Performed for the first time at the Royal Theatre in honour of the august birthday of Her Majesty the Queen, October 28, 1839

Characters

VINCENZA, a rich widow	Mme. Schouw
SILVIA, her daughter	Jfr. Fjeldsted
GAITANO, a winegrower	Hr. Fredstrup
ANTONIO, his son, Silvia's bridegroom	Hr. Hoppe
AMBROSIO, an innkeeper	Hr. Stramboe
PEPPO, his boy	Hr. Hoppensach
ALFRED ⎫	Hr. Larcher
WERNER ⎬ foreign artists	Hr. Füssel
MÜLLER ⎭	Hr. Hammer

TWO GUESTS	⎰ Hr. Bournonville ⎱ Jfr. Nielsen
AN OLD SHEPHERD	Hr. Nehm
THREE YOUNG ARTISTS	⎧ Hr. Bentzen ⎨ Hr. Ferslew ⎩ Hr. Wiehe
SERVING MAIDS	⎧ Jfr. Lund ⎨ Jfr. S. Nielsen ⎩ Jfr. N. Fredstrup

Solo Dances

Pas de deux of Bacchus and Venus: Hr. Bournonville and Jfr. Nielsen; Tarantella: Hr. Hoppe and Jfr. Fjeldsted
Pas de six: Messieurs Gade, Funck, Busch; Mlles. Borup, P. Fredstrup, Funck

The scene is laid in Albano, three miles South of Rome.*

An elevated open square from which, through the town and some pieces of luxuriant vegetation, one looks out over the Campagna to Rome. To the right, Vincenza's house; to the left, the inn, on which can be read: Osteria con Cucina. Between the two houses, a flight of stairs [leads] from the terrace down into the valley. In the right foreground, a picture of the Madonna is fastened to an old evergreen oak.

Solemn tranquility prevails in the lovely landscape; bells sound from the church. A group of children occupies the foreground; some of them fashion bouquets, others are taught by their older sister to tell the beads of a rosary (Kuchler).† At the same time a young girl with a pitcher on her head comes down the steps of the osteria while an old shepherd devoutly pauses before the Madonna's image. The girl goes to the well, the old man asks for a cooling drink, and the youngest of the children is lifted up to kiss the holy picture.

Some young artists, whose appearance indicates that they are Northerners, climb up to the terrace and stand lost in thought at the sight of this picture. In their wanderings through the environs of Rome they never fail to find subjects for piquant sketches. But it is to Albano that they come most often, for here the scenery is rich not only in glorious prospects but in feminine beauties, and of these Silvia in particular captivates the art-loving youths.

---

* Bournonville is speaking of Danish miles; Albano is actually sixteen English miles south of Rome.

† Bournonville refers to Albert Kuchler (1803-86), from whom this scene is taken. A Danish painter known for his Danish and Italian genre pictures, he travelled to Rome in 1830 and remained there until his death, becoming a Franciscan monk in 1851.

Ambrosio, followed by his waiters and cook's boys, is terribly busy. He is responsible for arranging the entire celebration. He sends his people on various errands, gives Peppo the menu, and is zealously occupied with another piece of paper covered with writing. The artists try in vain to speak to him; he tears himself away and hurries off to tend to his business.

The children and the old shepherd tell [them] that today the lovely Silvia shall wed Antonio, a son of Gaitano, the wealthy winegrower. At this very moment the bells are calling the young couple to the altar. Upon hearing this news, the young painters are filled with inexplicable sadness. Silvia, their ideal, shall marry a peasant! She, whose picture they have not dared to trace, will now give hand and heart to another. But one consolation they will have: Werner seizes crayon and parchment and bids his comrades use all their artistry to capture her portrait at the moment when, awaiting her bridegroom, she changes her headdress and is adorned for the ceremony. They seek hiding places on all sides.

Vincenza leads her daughter down to her childhood playground in the shade of the evergreen oak, beneath the gentle gaze of the Madonna. Here she will receive her bridal array – the white veil, the bouquet of orange blossoms – and from here, accompanied by the joyous cries of the young folk and the blessings of the old, she shall go to meet her unknown fate.

The bridegroom and his father approach. A single glance at the young couple is proof enough that the most heartfelt love has sealed their covenant. The parents settle the necessary details of the marriage contract while the young couple regard each other with silent rapture. "It is time to head for the church." Yet another farewell to [the bride's] home, another prayer to the Madonna, alms for the poor, and the happy little band descends into the valley, where the bells are ringing.

The artists emerge from their hiding places, each with a drawing in hand. One has captured the moment when Silvia sat before the mirror, another that in which she knelt before the Madonna, a third the scene when she embraced her mother. Delighted at the thought of possessing a remembrance of Albano's fairest maiden, they all decide to put off their return in order to attend the merry feast. Meanwhile, their long walking tour has given them hearty appetites, and Alfred proposes that they eat luncheon in the open air.

Peppo and the girls wait on them, while Ambrosio himself brings them *fogliette* of the pearly wine. Muller has fetched a cello from the rustic orchestra, and a guitar is procured. Pipes are lighted,

German Ländler resound delightfully in the Italian air, and the most intimate gaiety seasons the humble repast. Peppo and the serving maids must dance to the improvised music. Ambrosio, who also happens to be a poet, tries to recite the speech of welcome with which he intends to greet the bridal couple, but it is impossible for him to be heard above the noise, which is increased by Peppo's quarrel with the painters, who indulge themselves in pulling his leg.

Jesting, drinking, music, and a mad waltz give this scene a bacchanalian touch.

Tambourines resound in the distance; the sound draws closer. It is the wedding party coming up the hill. A troop of jubilant children surrounds the *pifferari* who, marching ahead of the others, play a Roman folk tune on their bagpipes to the accompaniment of drums, triangles, and castanets. Ambrosio offers his congratulations and presents his poem. Joy has transformed the procession into a surging stream of people. Lads and lasses are carried away by the most fantastic forms of dancing; flower-decked staves and garlands mingle with the motley array of costumes from the various Roman suburbs. People wave banners and handkerchiefs from steps and balconies, while the bridal couple is showered with bouquets.

The young girls remind Silvia of a game in which, according to an ancient custom, the bride, encouraged by the guests, is supposed to flee from her groom, using every possible means of tricking and eluding him. This jesting now begins, and Antonio, who thinks he is about to catch her at any moment, is torn away by the crowd which is heartily amused by his indignation. In the midst of the game he comes to a halt behind the chair that Alfred is sitting on and is transported by the sight of his completed drawing. It is a portrait of Silvia! How did this foreigner come to possess it? Did she pose for someone? Is it a keepsake from her? A thousand thoughts run through Antonio's mind; the pangs of jealousy gnaw at him. He grabs Alfred's arm, tears the portrait away from him, and Alfred only adds fuel to the fire by demanding the return of his drawing. The wedding guests are astounded and cannot understand the reason for Antonio's wrath. But when he breaks through the crowd, drags Silvia forth, makes the most vehement accusations against her, and points to the supposed proof of her infidelity, they are filled with grief and indignation. Silvia assures him that she has not the slightest knowledge of this picture and does not know the stranger. Alfred tries to convince Antonio, but in vain; he only makes things worse, and the enraged man, with upraised dagger, hurls himself at him. The artists rush to help their friend and Werner succeeds in disarming Antonio, which fairly well brings him to his senses. The whole matter is soon cleared up, and the painters display the drawings they made while hiding. The picture that caused the dispute shall belong to Antonio, and, offering their congratulations, the handsome Northerners promise to help enhance the festivities.

Antonio, who is bewildered and ashamed at his impetuosity, has a lot to ask forgiveness for. Alfred embraces him, and Silvia has to begin her married life with a reconcilation scene. Joy returns. The bridegroom bids the foreign guests welcome while the bride gathers their bouquets in her apron. Ambrosio gives the signal for the music, and the dancing begins.

After the lively Saltarella, visiting pilgrims are announced. Alfred points out to them the bride and groom. They plant their staves in the ground; here they have found the goal of their wanderings. They swiftly cast off their hats and cloaks, emerging in the new guise of Bacchus and Venus. In a pas de deux containing attitudes from ancient and modern sculpture, they salute the festival's favourites: Bacchus offers his thyrsus to the young winegrower, while Venus presents her golden apple to the lovely bride.

It is now the bridal couple's turn to dance: everyone displays the most lively attentiveness. Some pick up instruments, others climb up on tables and benches to watch their favourites dance the gay, passionate Tarantella. Silvia entices Antonio with her whirling castanets; Antonio flourishes his red neckerchief. They draw near one another, then move away. She tries to evade him, then roguishly hovers round her kneeling lover. Their ardor increases with the rapidity of the movement; they dance in tighter circles, the tambourines accelerate the racing beat, and dancers and spectators alike are caught up in the dizzying whirl.

Evening falls. Small groups form, and the loving couple strolls about hearkening to the strains of the guitar under the plane trees. Here many gladsome guests sit round a laden table; there three girls and two youths at one time swing in the *canafiola* suspended beneath the gate. To the left, bowls are tossed; to the right, the popular finger game of *morra* is played. Glasses are filled and drained, and everywhere Joy reigns supreme.

A new surprise, a new spectacle is presented to the merry company; to wit, in the arcade below Vincenza's windows, the young artists have arranged a distinctively lighted live exhibition of statues after the works of Rome's leading master.* The Italians recognize their favourite works:

THE STANDING AND KNEELING GANYMEDE,
HEBE,
THE SHEPHERD BOY AND MERCURY,
CUPID AND PSYCHE,
and JASON.

---

* A reference to the Danish-born sculptor Bertel Thorvaldsen (1770–1844) and some of his works. Thorvaldsen went to Italy in 1797 and, except for a brief visit to Denmark in 1819, remained there until 1838.

At the last apparition, a melody reminiscent of a beloved home resounds, while Albano's inhabitants enthusiastically acclaim the genius that shines from the north.

Torches are lighted and the bridal couple shall be escorted home. Antonio and Silvia embrace their parents and pass through the ranks of their friends, where here and there a smile or sigh is hidden but where the most heartfelt sympathy and warm good wishes greet them. From the balcony they once again salute the merry throng which dances around the bridal torch.

* * *

THE FATHERLAND'S MUSES
(Faedrelandets Muser)

A Pantomimic Prologue in One Act
by
August Bournonville

Music composed and arranged by Johannes Frederik Frøhlich
and Niels Gade
Scenery by Aron Wallich and Christian Ferdinand Christensen

Performed for the first time at the Royal Theatre on the occasion of the august presence of Their Majesties King Christian VIII and Queen Caroline Amalia, at the Playhouse on March 20, 1840

Characters

DANIA	Mme. Holst
APOLLO	Hr. Bournonville
TERPSICHORE	Jfr. Fjeldsted
AGLAE	Jfr. Nielsen
ZEPHYR	Hr. Hoppe
FLORA	Jfr. Petrine Fredstrup

Solo Dance

Hr. Larcher

SHADES OF HEROES, SAVAGES, ELVES, JAEGERE, MUSES, GRACES, NYMPHS

The scene is laid in Hertha's grove.

Dances

ZEPHYR .... Hr. Hoppe
THE GENIUS OF ART .... Marie Eydrup
(Jfr. Nielsen
THE GRACES .... Jfr. Fabricius
Jfr. N. Fredstrup
FLORA .... Jfr. Petrine Fredstrup
FLORA'S RETINUE
Mme. Hildebrand, Jomfruerne Werning, Eggers, Bruun, Holm, Funck, and Bincke

Tableaux

1.
THOR .... Hr. Stramboe

2.
TYCHO BRAHE .... Hr. Schneider
CHRISTIAN IV .... Hr. Wiehe
BRAHE'S WIFE .... Mme. Kretzmer

3.
AGNETE .... Jfr. Østerberg
THE ELF-KING .... Hr. Borch

4.
THE HARVEST FESTIVAL .... A Troop of Peasants

5.
JEAN DE FRANCE .... Hr. Hoppensach
MAGDELONE .... Jfr. Fredstrup

6.
AXEL .... Hr. Hansen, Jr.
VALBORG .... Jfr. Andersen
WILHELM .... Hr. Ferslew

7.
DAGMAR .... Mme. Hansen

8.
VALDEMAR II .... Hr. Füssel

THE MUSES
CALLIOPE .... Jfr. Andersen
URANIA .... Jfr. Amundin
CLIO .... Jfr. Rasmussen
POLYHYMNIA .... Jfr. Egense

ERATO	Jfr. Borup
EUTERPE	Jfr. S. Nielsen
MELPOMENE	Jfr. Larcher
THALIA	Jfr. Lund

GIANTS

Messieurs Fredstrup, Füssel, Nehm, Borch, Holm, and Weile

JAEGERE

Messieurs Bentzen, Brodersen, Ring, Hoppensach, Ruff, Funck, and Gade

SAVAGES	Hr. Hammer
	Hrr. Füssel, Jr.

Winter landscape. The gray light of dawn.

Dania sits lost in grief, the lions of Denmark resting at her feet. Behind her throne stand the two savages, shielding her from the harshness of Winter with an ermine cloak.

A group of heroes of antiquity has camped at the foot of a barrow. They keep their eyes fixed straight ahead and lower their ancient arms upon the cinerary urn, the sacred treasure of the barrow.

Driven by storm and cold, the elves come flying out of the woods; they grumble and shiver. Dania beckons them to come to her; she opens to them her maternal embrace and grants them shelter, warmth, and love.

The giants surround Dania. They see her tears and share her pain. But Spring draws near. The first song of the lark echoes and recalls the elves to life and gaiety. The happy little men make haste to welcome Zephyr. He salutes them from the barrow. The vale soon grows green; the woods are adorned with fresh leaves, and Flora comes to offer Dania her finest gifts. But Dania does not rejoice as she once did at the coming of Spring, for her sorrow prevents her from bedecking herself with flowers. Zephyr and the elves, Flora and her retinue, dejectedly surround the grieving mother.

The old heroes, memories of the past, once again step forth. They bid Dania cast off her mourning crepe, with which they in turn entwine the urn. They point toward the barrow whence they came and whither they will now return. They console Dania once more and vanish. The elves plant flowers around the barrow and sympathetically gather round Dania, who regards them with quiet sorrow.

Phoebus Apollo hovers over the ancestral graves; the Muses appear around the menhir of the barrow. Apollo descends into his sisters' midst and summons from the temple of Art the Graces, who bring consolation and lofty delights.

Apollo leads the fair goddesses before Dania's throne. In threes they acclaim their chosen ones: Calliope, Urania, Clio; Polyhymnia, Erato, Euterpe; Melpomene, Thalia, and Terpsichore. The sorrow gradually fades from Dania's brow, and now, as the Graces array her in brighter draperies, the smile returns to her lips. Her shield and spear are brought; she arms herself and is once again as she should be. Apollo beckons, and with renewed strength, Dania enters the temple of Art, where festive jubilation resounds to greet her.

A dance by Zephyr, who, as the messenger of Spring, brings the Genius of Art to the Graces. (Idea from Thorvaldsen)

Flora distributes garlands – each one fashioned from a different flower – to the Muses and bids them offer these blossoms in the temple of Art.

Calliope offers a wreath of oak leaves. On the wall of the temple there appears a tableau vivant representing:
1. "Thor and the Valkyrie" (*Gods of the North*, Oehlenschläger)
   Urania offers a garland of lilies:
2. "Tycho Brahe Receives a Chain from Christian IV"
   Polyhymnia offers a garland of myrtle; Euterpe, one of oranges:
3. *Elves' Hill*, Heiberg, Kuhlau
   Erato presents a wreath of cornflowers:
4. *The Harvest Festival*, Thaarup, Schultz
   Thalia presents a garland of red roses:
5. *Jean de France*, Holberg
   Melpomene presents a garland of white roses:
6. *Axel and Valborg*, Oehlenschläger
   Clio offers two wreaths of everlastings:
7. "Queen Dagmar Solacing the Poor"
8. "Valdemar the Victorious building the land with Law"

Lastly, *Terpsichore* offers a garland of forget-me-nots.

The dancing begins anew. Apollo and all the Muses accompany their youngest sister, under whose leadership Joy shall sit enthroned in Hertha's grove.

The temple opens to reveal Dania, who, shaded by the palms of cherubim and the proud Dannebrog, is seen to bless the Muses and Graces who have nestled in the shelter of the Royal Arms of Denmark.

Translator's Note: The tableaux vivants offered by the muses honour Danish artists or allude to Danish history:

MUSE	OF	PERSON HONOURED
(1) Calliope	Eloquence & heroic poetry	Denmark's bard, Adam Oehlenschläger, for his Eddaic cycle *Gods of the North* (*Nordens Guder*)
(2) Urania	Astronomy	The sixteenth-century Danish astronomer known for his correction of astronomical theories
(3) Polyhymnia	Sacred lyric	The Danish poet, lyricist, and critic Johan Ludvig Heiberg, for his national play *Elverhøj* (*Elves' Hill*)
Euterpe	Music	Daniel Friedrich Kuhlau, composer of music for *Elverjøj*, including a song that became one of the Danish national anthems
(4) Erato	Lyric & love poetry	Thomas Thaarup, lyricist for a popular musical play, *The Harvest Festival* (*Høstfesten*), and Johann Abraham Schultz, composer of music for *The Harvest Festival*
(5) Thalia	Pastoral poetry & comedy	Ludvig Holberg, for his play *Jean de France*
(6) Melpomene	Tragedy	Adam Oehlenschläger, for his heroic tragedy *Axel and Valborg*
(7,8) Clio	History	Dagmar, beloved Danish queen; first wife of Valdemar I
		Valdemar the Victorious, who reigned during the medieval Golden Age in Denmark and established law and order

* * *

THE TOREADOR
(Toreadoren)

An Idyllic Ballet in Two Acts
by
August Bournonville

Music composed and arranged by Edvard Helsted
Scenery by Christian Ferdinand Christensen

Performed for the first time at the Royal Theatre, November 27, 1840

Characters

JOSÉ, innkeeper ....Hr. Fredstrup
MARIA, his daughter, engaged to ......Jfr. Fjeldsted
ALONZO, toreador ....Hr. Bournonville
CÉLÈSTE, solo dancer from Paris ......Jfr. Nielsen
MME. FINARD, her mother ....Jfr. Larcher
MR. ARTHUR } English travellers .... Hr. Füssel
MR. WILLIAM } Hr. Stramboe
PEDRO } young villagers .... Hr. Larcher
PAQUITTA } Jfr. P. Fredstrup

Solo Dances

ZAPATEADO: Hr. Larcher and Jfr. P. Fredstrup
JALEO DE XERES: Hr. Bournonville and Jfr. Fjeldsted
POLONAISE: Jfr. Nielsen
BOLERO À QUATRE: Mm. Bournonville, Hoppe;
Mlles. Fjeldsted, Funck

The scene is laid in a Spanish village on the road to Madrid.

ACT I

The courtyard and garden of an inn. In the background, a wall, broken through in several places and almost completely covered with ivy and vines. The road to Madrid runs past the gate, and on the far side of the road way can be seen a magnificent landscape bordered by distant mountains and a brook which flows through the ruins of a Roman aqueduct.

Afternoon. The innkeeper, José, who is very busy, has not allowed Pedro to attend the bullfight which is to be held this day in the nearest town, and little Paquitta has preferred to stay with Maria, whose feelings of anxiety prevent her from enjoying this favourite spectacle of the Spaniards, for her lover, Alonzo, the young toreador, is to risk his life in what is certain to be a perilous fight. Her good wishes and prayers are with him, and during these anxious moments her guitar provides her with consolation.

Marie and Paquitta sit down beneath a shady plane tree while from the balcony of the inn Pedro surveys the road to see whether his friends will soon return. He is terribly annoyed at having had to stay home on such a day. But when he sees Marie so dejected he gives her flowers with which to bid the triumphant Alonzo welcome, and together with Paquitta he dances to distract and cheer Maria.

The merry Zapateado draws José from the kitchen. He rejoices at the gaiety of youth and embraces his daughter. They hear the clamor of the approaching crowd. It is Alonzo and his friends returning from the festival.

The swarming crowd has formed a triumphal procession around the victorious toreador, who is lifted up by the young lads and carried on their shoulders while the dancing groups of spectators jubilantly praise and applaud him.

Arthur and William, two rich gentlemen who have wagered for and against Alonzo, have followed the crowd. And the jolly Mr. William, who has won his melancholy countryman's money, is not the last to express his admiration. Alonzo hastens to the arms of his beloved. All are invited to take refreshment and spend a pleasant evening at José's inn.

Tomorrow a new fate awaits them, for Maria and Alonzo are to become man and wife. Her father leads them about among the guests, who with brimming cups offer their heartiest congratulations. Happy and relieved to see her fiancé return unharmed, Maria now wishes to learn what happened at the bullfight which all the others witnessed. Alonzo is instantly willing to describe it. But his friends must assist him as spectators in the lifelike picture he will paint of the contest in which he won the prize. Tables and benches are placed in a circle to form a broad arena; the gate represents a barrier, and on the balcony of the house Maria is enthroned as queen of the festival.

MIMED MONOLOGUE

Alonzo represents the elegant toreadors marching across the arena, saluting the crowd with their lances, being received with vociferous applause, flinging their red capes about them, and exciting the admiration of the ladies.

The trumpet sounds the signal for the fight. Silence ensues. Everyone is tense with expectation. The bull roars within its enclosure; it is bated with dagger tips. Alonzo shows how the wild beast bursts from its barrier, runs about the arena, wildly thrusts its horns to every side, paws the dirt with its feet, and halts in the middle of the circle, frothing with rage.

The light picadors attack the bull on horseback, wounding it with dangerous thrusts of their lances. A horse is felled; its rider flees in fright. Other swordsmen enter the circle, excite the bull by the sight of their scarlet capes and mortify its side with their spears (decorated with waving ribbons). A picador who has exhausted his supply of weapons and finds himself pursued by the martyred beast vaults over the barrier, where the people's scorn punishes his cowardice and general clumsiness.

Alonzo now appears as himself; the barrier is opened for him, and the confident matador waves his sword as a token of thanks for the glorious reception he has been accorded. Everyone admires his bearing and the calmness with which he enters the ring. The bull immediately hurls himself at the red cape. By a single turn the matador escapes the deadly thrust. Yet another charge! With a smile on his lips the swordsman places his left foot between the horns and is tossed over the back of his raging opponent. In a picturesque pose he awaits the third charge, then thrusts his sword into the bull's chest, seizes it by the horns, forces the bull to the ground, and slays it with his dagger.

The joy that animates the whole assembly is no longer an imitation and a prearranged drama, but reality. Thunderous applause hails the victor. Maria tosses a garland down from the balcony. Alonzo seizes it, lifts it on his lance, and runs about the ring amid general jubilation. He presents to his beloved the golden chain he has won and as he rapturously embraces her he is greeted with heartfelt sympathy from every side.

The sound of wagon wheels and the cracking of a whip is heard… A post chaise is driven into the backyard. José hastens to welcome the travellers, and the guests curiously gather at the gate. It is two ladies: a young and an old one, very tired, very distinguished looking, and rather displeased with the inn and the company to be found there. They are shown every possible attention, and José sees to their lodgings and refreshments. The ladies, who have noticed that people are gathered here for a fête, do not wish their presence to disrupt it and most graciously let it be known that they would like to attend. The young villagers are rather shy, but José orders dancing to begin and guitars, tambourines, and castanets are immediately set in motion.

The young lady, who while sitting with her glass of lemonade has only now and then deigned to peer at the dancers through her lorgnette, becomes ever more attentive to the charming Jaleo performed by Alonzo and Maria with all the enthusiasm of a couple in love. Enraptured with the lovely movements, she laughs, claps her hands, jumps up, and is only restrained from throwing her arms about the dancers' necks by the older woman's sternness. Finally she can no longer refrain from expressing her delight. She embraces and thanks Maria and Alonzo and begs them to teach her this lovely dance. They are all surprised that such a distinguished lady wishes to learn their rustic dance, but she finds it ravishingly beautiful. From now on all her haughty notions disappear. Her thoughts are totally preoccupied with dancing, and in a moment she will reveal herself to them in her true form. She runs into the house and people ask one another who this curious woman can be. Alonzo finds her most amiable and is genuinely delighted to teach her his favourite dance. Maria, however, thinks it most proper for *her* to instruct the lady. Alonzo opposes her; she remains adamant. He teases her, but their little bickering is interrupted by the lady's return.

As airy as a sylphide in a light, short white dress, she glides into the astonished villagers' midst. It is no longer the affected young lady but Mademoiselle Céleste, who is travellling from Paris to Madrid and intends to capture all hearts with her motto: "*Je suis la bayadère!*" The old lady is her mother, who now abandons her stiff etiquette and, surrounded by women and girls, rejoices at her daughter's talent. This transformation has made the most pleasing impression on those present. Céleste learns El Jaleo and, to repay the friendliness of the company, gives proof of her skill in French dancing. All are astonished at her lightness and grace. They applaud with all their might and fill the intervals with dancing to the clacking of castanets. Céleste wraps herself in her shawl, takes leave of the company with amiable gaiety, and skips into the house, followed by applause and admiration.

The two Englishmen, who immediately after the narration of the bullfight had had their luncheon served on the second floor of the inn, glimpsed the dancing from the window just as Céleste had been learning El Jaleo. They were all eyes, and by her captivating art the young *danseuse* has stolen their hearts.

Darkness falls; everyone goes home. Maria has promised Alonzo a little tête-à-tête at her jalousie, and Mr. William is still sitting at his table, lost in thought. Suddenly he jumps up, exclaiming that never in his life has he seen such a charming girl. His heart is on fire! He will go mad if she does not become his, and he has made up his mind to offer her his hand.

Arthur enters, completely crushed by the storm his soul has had to withstand. He has now found fuel for his melancholia and he melts into sighs and lamentations. The two British types now confide their feelings to each other and soon discover that they centre on the same object. Each thinks he has the advantage over his rival. It goes from opposition to mockery, from mockery to anger, and they almost come to blows.

Alonzo arrives for his rendezvous. Tonight is the last time he will stand outside Maria's window as her lover. Tomorrow he will lead her home as his bride! These thoughts occupy him as the Englishmen rush over to him and choose him as their arbitrator. He advises them to propose – the sooner the better, but *one at a time*. There is a new quarrel on this point. The dice will decide who shall go first, and once again it is William who has the highest number. He is indescribably happy. But Alonzo, who is pulling their legs a bit, consoles Arthur by telling him that he will surely beat out his corpulent opponent. But just who is their "chosen one"?

The Englishmen do not know her name, but a melody haunts them. It is the Jaleo de Xeres. She must be the very beauty who danced with Alonzo. "With me?" "Yes, with you." The Spaniard, whose blood begins to boil, informs them that this girl shall never belong to either of them. Furthermore, he will know how to punish anyone who dares cast eyes on her. Arthur and William give him to understand that their wealth can surely outweigh his pretentions. Alonzo threatens them. The Englishmen swear never to renounce the charming Jaleo dancer. The toreador flies into a rage; the rivals defy him, and the irritated lover draws his dagger. Arthur runs for the guard, and William is in deadly peril when the uproar calls the people of the house and their neighbours out into the courtyard.

It is impossible to find an explanation. Mr. William, who is taken for a base seducer, is accused of mistreating the furious Spaniards. The guard arrives with a rather inebriated gendarme at its head. In his zeal for arresting people, the latter blindly seizes several whom he believes to be guilty, and finally comes to William, who gives him very weighty arguments about the fact that Alonzo tried to kill him. The gendarme pockets the evidence, and without further questions lays hands on the toreador, who, despite Maria's pleas and the resistance of his friends, is marched off to prison amid general confusion.

ACT II

Dawn. Mr. Arthur is already up and about and is arranging with his people that at a certain sign from him they will carry out his orders. They hear someone coming and quickly depart.

A group of young girls enters the courtyard, playing music and dancing. They are carrying baskets of flowers and station themselves outside Céleste's window. It is Mr. William who has assembled them to give beauty a morning concert, thereby introducing his proposal in pleasing fashion. Astonished, Mademoiselle Céleste and her mother step onto the balcony. William explains that all this festivity concerns the captivating artiste and begs her to come down and enjoy her triumph. But when she comes out of the house the little girls have vanished, and only William is standing there.

He now timidly draws near and stammers out his declaration of love. Both mother and daughter are extremely surprised, and Céleste begs him to remember that "she is only a bayadère." But it is her very talent and grace that have captivated William. His expressions grow more impassioned. Céleste can hardly restrain her laughter, and her suitor interprets this gaiety as being to his advantage. He steps forth with renewed courage and offers her his hand and his fortune.

Mme Finard exhorts her daughter to consider this honourable offer. William is so bold as to take Céleste's hand, and in his mind he can already see himself bound for England with his spouse. He vaguely remembers melodies from home and involuntarily starts to dance about.

The young girls emerge from their hiding places and empty their store of flowers at Céleste's feet. In dancing groups they surround the infatuated William, who, kneeling, waits for her to say "Yes."

Maria, in despair over Alonzo's imprisonment, rushes over to Céleste to tell her that William is to blame for her bridegroom's misfortune. She showers him with reproaches, and he tries in vain to convince her of his innocence. Céleste sternly orders that the toreador be released from his captivity. Only then will she see if she can give a definite answer. This hope inflames the enamored Englishman. He promises to bring Alonzo back, even if his freedom should cost a thousand pounds. He sends the little girls on ahead, tells Maria to be of good cheer, kisses Céleste's hand, embraces his mother-in-law [to be], and rushes off, borne on the wings of joy and love.

Céleste and her mother reflect on the new circumstances they are about to enter into. Maria's gratitude for the sympathy Céleste has shown for Alonzo is as great as is the dancer's delight at the rank and riches which will now be hers. José congratulates the young lady and hurries off with his daughter to welcome the newly freed Alonzo. Mme Finard arranges flowers in a large basket while her daughter greets Maria and José.

Arthur steps into the foreground and makes his presence known by a deep sigh. Céleste sees him and goes to the opposite side of the stage. Arthur follows her with his lorgnette. She becomes frightened, calls to her mother, and tries to avoid this strange person. But with his lorgnette focused on Céleste, he dogs the ladies' steps and continues to utter louder sighs. At last Céleste can stand it no longer. She turns around and asks him to leave her alone. In a few words, Arthur expresses his passion and declares his intentions. The mother now speaks up and asks the Englishman to relieve them of his unwelcome attentions. Arthur pays absolutely no attention to the old lady, but turns directly to her daughter. Indignant at the fact that he pays her so little heed, Mme Finard hastily empties the large basket and gives it to her daughter, who has tried in vain to get rid of the troublesome fellow. With a deep curtsy, Céleste hands him the basket. The suitor does not immediately grasp the meaning of this unhappy allegory, but soon perceives that it concerns a definite refusal. His despair knows no bounds. He threatens to kill himself if his request is not granted. The ladies turn away from him with contempt. They are about to flee, but he stops them, throws himself at Celeste's feet, pulls out a pistol, and puts it to his temple.

The frightened Céleste swoons. Her mother flings herself on top of her, and – Arthur quite cooly uncocks his pistol, puts it in his pocket, and claps his hands three times.

His carriage is driven forth, and at a signal from their master, the coachman and jockey seize Mme Finard. Arthur gathers the unconscious Céleste in his arms, and despite obstinate resistance on the mother's part, they get her and her daughter into the carriage. Everything is ready for a perfect abduction when William suddenly rushes in, stops the horses, and summons the crowd of people returning with the toreador.

A frightful commotion arises: Mme Finard cries for help; William thrashes the coachman and the jockey, and the innkeeper demands his money. Overcome by his misfortune, Arthur is assailed with threats and curses from every side. The women gather round the unconscious young lady, and the men have all they can do to keep the angry rivals from coming to blows. Maria finally succeeds in bringing Céleste to her senses. The uproar ceases, and it is now the dancer's choice that will solve the problem.

William's joviality and heartiness, his earlier and better-thoughtout proposal, his speed in preventing the abduction, and especially his obtaining Alonzo's release have given him an essential advantage over his rival. Céleste grants him her hand. Her mother gives the union her blessing, and, accepting his fate, Arthur requests the consolation of being allowed to drive them to Madrid since his equipage is already harnessed.

Everything is now all right. No clouds darken Alonzo's wedding day, and the happy guests congratulate both couples. William is in seventh heaven and gives José a substantial present as a dowry for the young bridal pair. Céleste, who will now leave the theatre and, with a sort of sadness, bid farewell to her airy art, wishes to see once more the Spaniards' lovely dancing. At her behest, the lightest couple performs the lively and graceful bolero, and to the strains of a round dance glowing with gaiety and "the fire of youth,"* the travelllers climb into their carriage and leave this place, which will always remind them of the toreador and his bride.

*   *   *

---

*   The music is Johann Strauss Senior's galop "Jugendfeuer," o p. 90.

NAPOLI, OR THE FISHERMAN AND HIS BRIDE
(Napoli eller Fiskeren og hans Brud)

A Romantic Ballet in Three Acts
by
August Bournonville

Music by Holger Simon Paulli, Edvard Helsted, and Niels Gade
Finale by Hans Christian Lumbye

Settings by Christian Ferdinand Christensen

First performed at the Royal Theatre, Copenhagen, March 29, 1842

Characters

GENNARO, a fisherman	Hr. Bournonville
VERONICA, a widow	Mme. Schouw
TERESINA, her daughter	Jfr. Fjeldsted
FRA AMBROSIO, a monk	Hr. Nehm
GIACOMO, a macaroni seller	Hr. Fredstrup
PEPPO, a lemonade seller	Hr. Stramboe
GIOVANINA	Jfr. Lund
PASCARILLO, a street singer	Hr. Hoppensach
CARLINO, a puppet master	Hr. Stramboe, Jr.
GOLFO, a merman	Hr. Füssel, Sr.
CORALLA } naiads	Jfr. Borup
ARGENTINA	Jfr. Holm

Solo Dances

Messieurs Hoppe, Larcher, Brodersen; Mlles. Funck, P. Fredstrup, Borup, and Bruun

The story takes place in the present and is divided into three tableaux:
1. The *Largo di Santa Lucia* in Naples, in the evening and in the morning
2. The *Grotta d'azzurra* on the Isle of Capri
3. Pilgrimage to the *Madonna dell'Arco* outside Naples

Dances in Act I

Ballabile: Hr. Bournonville; Jfr. Fjeldsted
    Messieurs Brodersen, Funck, Gade, Busch, Ring, and Lund; Mlles. Funck, Borup, Fredstrup, H. Werning, and Bruun

Dances in Act II

Naiads: Mlles. Borup and M. Holm
Mme. Møller, Mlles. Werning, S. Nielsen, Egesen, Eggersen, Fabritzius, Amundin, Rostock, L. Holm, M. Holm
Tritons: Messieurs Hammer, Füssel, Jr., Borch, and Ring

Dances in Act III

Pas de cinq: Hr. Hoppe; Mlles. Funck, Fredstrup, Borup, and Bruun
Tarantella   Hr. Brodersen, Jfr. Lund; Hr. Bournonville, Jfr. Fjeldsted
Hr. Larcher, Jfr. Fredstrup; Hr. Hoppe, Jfr. Funck
Bacchanalian Finale: the entire corps de ballet

ACT I

The bell strikes twenty-four [eight o'clock in the evening]. The tattoo sounds from Castel dell'Ovo, and people are summoned to the Ave Maria. The noise of bustling cuts in again, and the square and beach of Santa Lucia are seen in the glow of lamps, torches and kitchen fires. The bay is shrouded in darkness.

TABLEAU

A tent is stretched crosswise above the street so that only the second story of the houses is visible. To the left, a staircase leading up to the abode of Veronica; to the right, a palace with light gleaming through its red curtains. A group of women and children sit in the doorway while a number of ladies and gentlemen are on the balcony taking refreshments. Common people occupy the foreground: a sleeping lazzarone, three men playing *Morra*, boys roasting chestnuts, and a peasant selling oranges. In the distance a tarantella is danced to the jangling of a tambourine. Mothers play with their children while girls spin on distaffs. Business is good at the macaroni stalls, where people enjoy their evening meal standing up, lying on the ground, or sitting at the tables set up on the sidewalk along the quai. Ladies and gentlemen stroll about centre stage, refreshing themselves at the richly decorated lemonade stall. Groups of children play, beg, and fashion coal hods.

Noise and bustle. Teresina enters, accompanied by her mother. It is immediately apparent that Giacomo and Peppo are in love with the young girl, but her gaze is directly solely toward the sea, where her favoured sweetheart is. Gennaro will soon return from his fishing. In the meantime the suitors overwhelm the mother with compliments and take turns asking for her daughter's hand in marriage. Veronica shrugs her shoulders and indicates that Teresina has thoughts for none save the poor fisherman; still, they may speak to her themselves and try their luck. They propose to the girl, but without success. Indignation on the part of the suitors; mild reproaches from Veronica: and roguishness from Teresina.

The barcarolle announces the fishermen's return. By the light of torches they drag their nets ashore. Everyone gathers round to see their fine catch. Gennaro rushes over to his beloved, but her mother prevents him from embracing Teresina. She points to the wealthy suitors who have declared themselves. Gennaro is burning with indignation; the rivals hurry off to their stalls; Teresina tries to calm her friend, and they both earnestly ask the mother for her consent. A quarrel arises among the fishermen; it is settled by Gennaro, who divides the catch, offering the best portion to the Madonna.

Fra Ambrosio passes among the dealers, asking for alms. Some give him something, others evade him. But the fishermen, led by Gennaro, do not forget the cloister. Touched by their piety, the friar promises to offer prayers of intercession on their behalf, and when Teresina gives him a silver heart for his altar, he blesses the young couple and leaves, wishing them good fortune.

The fish sell rapidly, and Gennaro indulges in a bit of galant joking with his young customers, among whom is Giovanina. His rivals speak ill of him to Teresina – who flies into a passion and quarrels with the pert cook – while pointing out to her mother how foolish it would be to give her daughter to such a madman. But the lover goes over to the infuriated girl and, by slipping a little gold ring on her finger, placates her as if by magic. Peppo and Giacomo are now convinced that witchcraft is involved. They join forces in order to harm their successful rival by means of slander; but the mother can no longer resist the young couple's pleas and their friends congratulate them on their betrothal. Veronica allows her children to take part in the dancing, but feeling tired and sleepy, she retires. Dancing and merriment. But the lovers have so much to say to each other that they must get away from the teeming strand, away from the noise, out onto the water, into the lovely night – where there is peace and quiet! Gennaro fetches his oars, Teresina her guitar, and, unnoticed, they row out onto the bay. People soon perceive that they are missing and espy the light gleaming from their boat. Everyone listens, and in the distance can be heard Gennaro's favourite melody:

Te voglio ben' assai
E tu non penzi a me!

Pascarillo, the Neapolitans' favourite buffoon and street singer, enters with his musician. Delighted, everyone gathers round him, and with a brilliant recitative he prefaces the treat he intends to give his numerous audience. But at the same moment, Pulcinello's march is heard. It is Carlino with his puppet theatre, and the inconstant crowd rushes to greet him. Both artists cannot perform at the same time, yet neither of them will yield. They soon come to blows; Pascarillo upsets the marionette theatre; the puppets fall down, and a fight scene ensues between the director and the outraged singer. Giacomo tries to make peace. The theatre is overturned. Laughter and quarreling. The general confusion is interrupted by a storm. Everyone seeks shelter; shops vanish, lanterns go out, and the square is soon deserted.

The thunderstorm continues to rage. Fishermen come to protect their vessels. They remember that the young couple is out at sea, and a flash of lightning reveals Gennaro battling to reach shore. They run to his aid. The storm abates. People gather from all quarters and the swooning Gennaro is carried ashore. He eventually awakens from his stupor, and his first thought is for Teresina! The trembling Veronica asks for news of her daughter. Beside himself, Gennaro dashes toward the beach. The mother demands that her child be returned to her: everything is clear! Gennaro's rashness is responsible for the lovely girl's death! Teresina has become the prey of the sea; she is the victim of witchcraft! Everyone repudiates, curses, and flees Gennaro, who stands alone and abandoned in the solitude of the night.

The deserted fisherman is filled with despair. He bursts into lamentations and begs the sea, the sky, and the grave which has swallowed his bride to give her back to him. He rolls in the dust. People have rejected him! There is no one to hear his cries! No one is touched by his misery. But the seaman's guardian spirit, the compassionate Madonna, *she* will listen to him! He falls to his knees before her image and begs for help in his hour of need. The sky lightens with the approach of dawn. He sees Fra Ambrosio standing near him, leaning on an anchor. He points toward the sea and urges him to seek his bride with confidence in the Holy Mother he has just implored. Filled with renewed hope, Gennaro seizes the anchor, fetches his oars, and is about to go wither the monk pointed. But the pious father gives him a precious amulet: a picture of the Madonna dell'Arco. This shall aid him in the face of all obstacles, dangers, and temptations and defeat any sorcery.

Filled with confidence and gratitude, Gennaro sets off, and the monk's prayers go with him. The morning sun illuminates his way along the lovely coastline, where smoking Vesuvius can be seen in the distance.

ACT II

Grotta d'azzurra (the Blue Grotto) on the isle of Capri.

The sea swells constitute a prelude. One sees the empty grotto. Its dark pillars form the foreground; the water, with its magical play of colour, fills up the interior of the cave, and in the far background, sunlight pours in through the low and narrow entrance to the grotto.

Golfo enters from the dark interior of the cave. He blows his horn. The call is answered, and tritons come to receive his commands. They bring with them precious objects that have been washed ashore by the storm during the night. Golfo surveys them with indifference, for a secret longing is gnawing at him.

Outside the grotto, lovely music sounds; a large shell comes drifting in. Argentina and Coralla are holding the lifeless Teresina in their arms. The other naiads crowd around to see the new arrival. They carry her ashore and prepare a bed of rushes for her. Her clothing is in disarray, her hair is hanging in strands about her shoulders, and she is clutching her guitar.

Golfo is charmed by her beauty. Coralla brings fragrant herbs which gradually restore Teresina to consciousness. She awakens from her long stupor, looks about her, and is terrified by the spirits of the sea that surround her. She wants to flee, but the deep appears to be her only avenue of escape. The naiads and tritons, looking at her with curiosity, try to calm her and draw her attention to their ruler, the mighty Golfo.

Unable to restrain her tears, Teresina beseeches him to send her back to her beloved Naples, to her bridegroom and the joys of youth. But the Lord of the Bay pours over her head some of the blue water of the grotto. Her clothes take on a silvery sheen; she takes on a new nature and is transformed into a naiad! She no longer asks about her home; she has lost all memory of it. The grotto, the water, is her element.

Coralla and Argentina adorn their new mistress with precious jewels. All vie to do her homage, and she triumphantly dances among them. Teresina observes her guitar, but it has lost all meaning for her; she does not know how to play it any more and carelessly tosses it into a corner. The shrill tones of the conch are more to her liking. She takes up a shell and blows it, and the tritons and naiads perform fantastic dances.

Golfo remains alone with Teresina, whose anxiety mounts with his passion. He offers to share his power and riches with her, but she is unable to return his affection. She avoids his burning gaze.

A boat approaches the entrance to the grotto. It is Gennaro in search of his beloved. Golfo orders that he be surrounded by dangers and temptations. Teresina is taken away, and all vanish into the interior of the cave.

Gennaro rows into the grotto. All is empty and silent. He has misgivings about this mysterious place and looks for his fiancée with a beating heart. But here, too, his search is in vain.

Suddenly he notices Teresina's guitar. How great is his surprise, how indescribable his delight; for she must be *here* or somewhere quite near. Subterranean rumbles echo through the cave and flames burst through the fissures of the rock, but Gennaro is undismayed. The scenes of horror vanish; coral trees spring up before his feet, the naiads emerge from their hiding places, offer him treasures, tempting and warning him in turn. But Gennaro asks that Teresina be returned to him and accompanies his pleas with such enchanting tones that the naiads can no longer resist him and go to fetch their mistress.

Teresina enters but gazes at Gennaro in wonder, without recognizing him. His concern arouses her sympathy, but he tries in vain to remind her of their love, their frolics, or the vows they have made to each other; all memory of her previous existence has vanished. He tries to play their favourite song on her guitar, but its sounds are displeasing to her. However, she will dance for him to the sound of the horn. Gennaro's deep pain piques her curiosity. She asks if he is in love with someone else, and her heart is filled with anxiety. Then Gennaro remembers Ambrosio's gift; trembling with hope, he removes it from around his neck and prays for his beloved. She draws near, seeking to learn the meaning of this image. Kneeling, Gennaro calls upon the Most Holy and hangs the amulet about Teresina's neck. As if by some powerful magic, a new change comes over her; she is filled with a holy rapture. Her cheeks become wet with tears, and every memory is vivid to her once more. She beholds and recognizes her bridegroom and flings herself into his arms.

Golfo halts their escape; his wrath is terrible. Neither pleas nor tears can soften him. Teresina is carried off, and he orders the tritons to crush Gennaro beneath the enormous weight of the giant rocks. But Teresina tears herself loose and clings to her bridegroom. Relying upon the Madonna's aid, she raises the amulet aloft and bids the spirits of the sea humble themselves before the Queen of Heaven.

Golfo, who must yield to a higher power, now permits Teresina to leave with Gennaro and, as a reward of faithful love, bestows upon them the treasures with which the naiads have loaded their boat.

Happy and grateful, the lovers climb into the little bark, salute the inhabitants of the grotto, and sail off.

ACT III

Monte Virgine outside Naples. A bridge connects one hill to the other. A niche in the centre pillar of the bridge contains a picture of the Madonna, and beneath the large arch can be seen the bay and the shore near Vesuvius. It is midday.

Pilgrims are crossing the bridge in solemn procession. They are divided into three groups, each with its banner, the corners of which are held by children. Led by their pipers (*zampognari*), they descend to the plain and devoutly kneel before the Madonna while women and girls strew flowers over their heads.

The pilgrims greet and embrace one another, but the conversation soon turns to the fatal accident that has befallen the young fishergirl, cut off in the flower of her youth. Peppo now reminds them of what he has so often said, and Giacomo has a great deal to relate about the influence of evil spirits on a young girl's fate. All are filled with apprehension and disgust.

This sinister atmosphere is soon replaced by one of delighted surprise when Teresina and her mother enter. They jubilantly rush to greet her and she is overwhelmed with questions which she does not have time to answer, for when Gennaro appears, richly dressed, Teresina declares that it was he who rescued her, and the idea that witchcraft is involved becomes even more firmly rooted in the minds of the bewildered crowd. Gennaro encounters only dark and embarrassed looks. Veronica is soon convinced that her daughter's rescue and Gennaro's affluence are a result of occult arts. All point to Gennaro with loathing, and in spite of the lovers' protestations, they are forcibly separated.

Bewildered and disgusted by all these occurrences, the unhappy fisherman flies into a dreadful rage. Panic spreads. Most of the bystanders flee in confusion; others turn to their amulets. The guard is sent for; but instead of apprehending the sorcerer, they drop their muskets and take to their heels in flight. At last a monk is fetched to cast out the evil spirit. The whole crowd gathers behind the monk, who strides forward, unafraid. He stops, looks at Gennaro, and opens his arms to him! The monk is Fra Ambrosio, who explains to everyone that Teresina's miraculous rescue is due solely to the intervention of the Madonna dell'Arco, patron saint of this day and of this place. Before her image, he now blesses and unites the faithful couple.

The pious rapture gives way to the wildest merriment. Joy spreads to all the guests; the rivals resign themselves to the inevitable and mingle their congratulations with those of Teresina's and Gennaro's friends. The liveliest dances succeed one another until the procession once again sets off to return to Naples. Some young fellows have unhitched the horses from a cart and transform it into a triumphal car for our hero and heroine, who, surrounded by the jubilant throng and crowned with flowers, are driven home amid a bacchanalian finale.

*   *   *

THE CHILDHOOD OF ERIK MENVED
(Erik Menveds Barndom)

A Romantic Ballet in Four Acts
by
August Bournonville

Music by Johannes Frederik Frølich and R. N. C. Bochsa
Scenery by Christian Ferdinand Christensen and Troels Lund
Costumes by F. Westphal

Performed for the first time on January 11, 1843

Characters

QUEEN AGNES OF DENMARK (Erik Glipping's consort)	Mme. Nielsen
ERIK	Augusta Bournonville
CHRISTOFFER } her children	Axel Fredstrup
MERETE	Caroline Lumbye
LAVE LITTLE, knight	Hr. Füssel
JOMFRU INGE, his daughter	Jfr. Nielsen
PEDER HESSEL, THE LORD HIGH CONSTABLE, betrothed to Inge	Hr. Bournonville
DAVID TORSTENSSON, knight, his friend	Hr. Larcher
RANE JONSEN, the King's *valet de chambre*	Hr. Lefebvre
CLAUS SKIRMEN, esquire to the Lord High Constable	Hr. Hoppe
HENNER FRISER, an old seaman	Hr. Fredstrup
AASE, his granddaughter	{ Jfr. Fjeldsted / Fjunck }
GOVERNESS TO THE ROYAL CHILDREN	Mme. Schouw
THE CONSPIRATORS	{ Hr. Stramboe / Hr. Peterrsen / Hr. Wiehe / Hr. Fersløv }

COURTIERS. PRELATES. MONKS. ESQUIRES. SOLDIERS. COMMON PEOPLE. CONSPIRATORS. LITTLE BOYS. LINK-BOYS.

Solo Dances

Pas de trois and *Galopade:* Hr. Hoppe; Mlles. Funck and Fredstrup
Peasant Dance: Hr. Hoppensach and Jfr. Lund

Pas de six: Messieurs Brodersen, Funck and Gade; Mlles. Fredstrup,
    Borup and Bruun
Pas de deux: Hr. Bournonville and Jfr. Nielsen

In Acts One and Two the action takes place in and around Skanderborg; in Act Three, at Viborg; and in the fourth Act, at Ribe. The time is 1286-87.

Having lost his father at the age of twelve, Erik Menved finds his life and liberty threatened by conspirators and is protected by the virtues of his mother and by the people's devotion: *these events are taken from History.*

The delineation of the main characters; the tone and colour of the Middle Ages; the court intrigues; the conspirators in Grey Friars' cowls; Aase's sleepwalking; Viborg Cathedral; the conquest of Ribehuus Castle through dancing: *these things are taken from [B. S. I Ingemann's historical novel* Erik Menveds Barndom].

The concentration of the action; the proposal of motives; the tightening of the dramatic knot through the Prince's kidnapping; the exposition of the plot; the dramatic and mimic treatment of the material: *these are of my own invention.*

With the exception of the first four numbers in Act One, the music is completely original and composed by Frølich. The four numbers mentioned above were written by Bochsa at an earlier date.

There are *four* new settings:

1. Woodland near Lake Skanderborg, by C. F. Christensen
2. Viborg Cathedral (the older one), by Troels Lund
3. The Tower Room of Ribehuus Castle, by Troels Lund
4. The yard of Ribehuus Castle; through the castle gate, a prospect of Ribe, by C. F. Christensen

Costumes designed and supervised by F. Westphal.

[**Translator's note:** After almost thirty years of chaotic civil strife, the glorious Age of the Valdemars (1157–1241) had seen the increase in economic prosperity and the growth of royal power and influence in Denmark and abroad. The death of Valdemar II, "The Victorious," in 1241 signaled the collapse of his empire and the renewal of power struggles among his sons and between Church and State.

In 1282, in an attempt to curtail the royal power, a group of nobles forced Valdemar II's grandson, Erik Glipping (or Klipping) to agree to a Danish Magna Carta. After four years, however, the King was murdered by a group of malcontents who, disguised as monks, are said to have stabbed him fifty-six times as he lay sleeping in a barn after spending the day hunting. Erik Glipping's assassination left the kingdom in the hands of his queen, the highly esteemed Agnes of Brandenburg, who served as regent during the minority of her twelve-year-old son Erik. It is the events surrounding the accession of Erik Menved to the throne that Bournonville, like the Romantic novelist B. S. Ingemann before him, sought to dramatize in this ballet.

Both the novelist and the ballet master were wise to select events from their hero's youth, for unfortunately, the remaining thirty-three years of Erik Menved's reign were marked by clashes with the Church, peasant revolts, and a series of costly and exhausting military campaigns waged in an attempt to revive the empire of the Valdemars. In 1319 Erik died, at the age of forty-five, without issue, although he is said to have had fourteen sons – a sad end for a king whose surname, Menved, signified Bird of Ill Omen.]

ACT I

The guards' room of Skanderborg Castle. To the left, the door to the King's apartments; to the right, that leading to those of the Queen. In the open background, a balcony with stairs leading down to the garden, the regular entrance. Standards and weapons adorn the hall. Early morn.

Rane Jonsen finds the watch asleep in front of the King's door. Two cloaked figures bring him a message and threateningly remind him of a pledge he has made. He dismisses them, wakens the guards, and gloats when he sees their alarm.... Someone is coming! It is old Herr Lave Little. Rane pays him a great deal of attention, praises his appearance, flatters his paternal pride, and, since he knows that Lave desires a commander's baton, he congratulates him in advance on obtaining this distinction.

Linkboys announce that the King has awakened. Everyone begins to stir. The watch is relieved; David Torstensson, the leader of the halberdiers, appears; servants and little boys hurry back and forth, and the hall is filled with courtiers awaiting the King's orders.

Rane seals an important document. He answers the questions of the curious with a meaningful shrug: In this letter the greatly esteemed Lord High Constable, Peder Hessel, who is presently with the army, will learn that he has fallen into disfavour. Everyone is occupied with this important piece of news when the Lord Constable himself enters in complete armor. He greets everyone in joyful and chivalrous fashion, hastens over to his beloved's father, asks about Inge, and rejoices in his return. But everywhere he encounters coolness and embarrassment. Rane presents him with the royal message, the contents of which demand an explanation which the Lord High Constable intends to obtain from the King himself. But the fallen favourite's path is blocked; he is surrounded by feigned compassion, and Rane is already savouring his triumph. Peder, however, shows David Torstensson the King's own ring and this token procures him admittance to the monarch.

The Queen's ladies in waiting, Inge among them, come to await their mistress's commands. A few incidents acquaint us with Lave's love for his daughter and with Rane's efforts to please her. Through the esquire, Skirmen, Inge learns of Peder's return. But far from sharing her delight, her father denounces the Lord Constable as his enemy and demands that she return the engagement ring.

Everyone reverently bows when Queen Agnes enters the room. Her response to their homage is mild and friendly, and she congratulates Lave on his son-in-law's return. Pleading indisposition, the knight removes his distressed daughter. Peder emerges from the King's door completely cleared and honoured with a splendid gold chain. His enemies are humbled; the Queen greets him with grace and favour and invites the gentlemen to attend the feast that is to be given at the castle this evening after the hunt.

The royal children enter, Christoffer and Merete holding on to their governess's hand. Agnes tenderly embraces them and fusses with their clothes. The guards salute Erik, who immediately catches sight of his armorer, Lord Constable Peder, bids him welcome, and congratulates him on his gold chain. He respectfully greets his august mother, who mildly reproaches him for his preoccupation. But one glance is enough to tell her that he knows how much she loves him and he flies into her arms. Today is his birthday. He receives a golden cross from his mother, who, moved, presses her children to her breast. At a sign from her, more presents are brought forward. Overjoyed, Erik puts on the helmet, salutes with the sword, and shares with his brother and sister.

The Queen takes Merete by the hand and goes in to her spouse, entrusting the princes to the Lord Constable's care. Erik gazes after his mother for some time; in his eyes, none is so fair as she.

Skirmen announces some village girls, who wish to celebrate Erik's birthday with flowers and dancing. Aase is among them, and, led by the light and lively esquire, they perform merry dances. A new surprise is in store: the little boys of the castle have formed a small army and march into position with drums beating and banners flying. Erik and Christoffer place themselves at their head, have them perform a number of maneuvers, and lead them in to show them to the King.

Peder remains behind in the hall. He feels his beloved is near, plucks a rose from the Queen's flower garden, and tosses it onto the threshold Inge must cross. Hidden behind a pier, he sees her enter, catch sight of the rose, and thoughtfully pick it up. He jumps out and the lovers joyously run to each other, but during this welcoming embrace the rose's thorn pierces Inge's hand.... She alludes to the love that has "gladdened her heart, caused her pain." Peder tries to take her mind off her distress. Driven by longing, he hastened home, for "Heaven granted a fair wind." But the engagement ring is no longer on her finger! With fear and distrust,... their eyes meet and reproachfully seem to say: "Fair words!"*

Knights and halberdiers assemble in solemn procession. Lave, followed by the senior courtiers, emerges from the King's apartments; a diploma and commander's baton are carried by his side. Pale and trembling with suppressed resentment, he calls forth the Lord High Constable, accepts his oath in the King's name, presents him with his new badges of office, and opens his arms to him as a mark of forced congratulations. But prompted by Rane, the furious old knight gives back to Peder the ring with which Inge had been bethrothed. Startled, the Lord Constable drops it, but Skirmen picks it up and takes it to Inge, and when Peder turns his head he sees that his beloved has put the ring back in its usual place.

The hunting horn sounds. Courtiers hasten to accompany the King; little boys carry the King's falcons, his crossbow, and his hunting hat. The Queen, who has bade her consort farewell, comes out on the balcony to have a last good-bye. Across fields and highways the stately hunting party rides, while in the foreground Rane drags the sinister and vindictive Lave off to the forest with him.

ACT II

A piece of woodland by Lake Skanderborg. To the left, the house of Henner Friser. Twilight.

Henner is longing for his granddaughter, who danced for young Erik along with the other girls. A boat steered by Skirmen is bringing all of them home. But since the boat cannot dock on the shore, the girls are carried up onto the beach, and Henner holds his little Aase by the arm while Skirmen makes his marriage proposal and declares his intentions and hopes. Pestered by the lovers, the old man does not really know how to answer them, but young fishermen and peasants interrupt the conversation with the merry "Proposal Dance."

Hunting music is heard. Skirmen, a bit embarrassed by the approach of the Court, tries to get away. But Ridder Torstensson, with his hunters, bumps right into him, pulls his leg a bit, and inquires for the King. He orders the horns to be sounded. The girls dance to the sound of the horns. From some distance off, the call is answered. Rane comes as messenger of the King to Torstensson, who is to hurry to Skanderborg to order the festivities to begin; the King himself will come later. After some small bits [of stage business], the valet de chambre returns to the hunt,

---

* The romance "Herr Peder kasted' Runer over Spange."

and Torstensson sails across the lake, where the hunters' fanfares echo.

The evening bell sounds. Villagers kneel to Our Lady, while Grey Friars cross upstage in pairs. Everyone goes his way, but Skirmen, who has become suspicious of the monks, persuades Henner to follow them. Aase closes her door, undresses, and says her evening prayers. Rane steals through the woods; he sees Aase through the window, but her candle is extinguished.

The monkish figures approach Rane. He promises to give them a certain signal, then hastens away. The conspirators take council for the last time, but Ridder Lave, who is among them, suffers pangs of conscience and refuses to swear. They fly at him in a rage. Aase, holding a lighted taper, emerges from her door. Smiling at some pleasant dream, she sleepwalks right into the midst of the murderers' swords. Rane's horn resounds: it is the promised signal! The dastards hurry off; Aase remains alone with the unconscious Lave.

The Sleepwalker senses everything that is happening some distance away. In her mind's eye she sees the evil men attack; her anxiety and despair mount; she is crushed, turns, extinguishes the taper, and gently falls to the ground in peaceful sleep.

Henner and Skirmen return without having discovered anything. They see Aase and Lave and revive them. Aase awakens, happy and cheerful; but lave comes out of his stupor and cries out in despair.

He speaks of the King, murder, conspirators, and takes Skirmen with him and rushes off to effect a rescue if there is still time.

Another part of the forest. Dark night, illuminated by a distant conflagration.

The murderers have done their dreadful deed. As a token of victory, Rane brings the King's crossbow and hunting hat. They order him to throw them away and flee in fright. Lave and Skirmen come from the burning barn. They intend to pursue the killers, but halt when they see the King's hunting gear laying on the ground. Overcome with grief, they now decide to bring these sorrowful tokens and news of the horrible deed to the royal castle.

The armory at Skanderborg, festively decorated for a ball and illuminated by countless wax tapers. In the centre stands a throne.

Surrounded by her children and brilliant Court, Queen Agnes receives from Ridder Torstensson the message that the festivities are to commence and that the King will not appear until later. Music sounds, and the ball is opened by a Torch Dance in which pairs of ladies and gentlemen tread a slow and modest dance, while the Queen takes her elevated seat. The dances alternate: first there are three couples, then Peder and Inge perform. Little Erik and his sister Merete lead the great Round Dance, in which everyone takes part. A vague uneasiness brings the ball to a standstill, but it soon regains its former liveliness. Shortly afterward, however, it is interrupted by the arrival of Lave and Skirmen. Trembling and deathly pale, they stand before the Queen; horror and confusion follow in their wake... King Erik has been cruelly murdered on the hunt!

ACT III

Viborg Cathedral. In the centre the staircase leading to the quire. On either side of the quire steps, doors leading to the crypt. To the right, Svend Grathe's sepulchral monument. In the foreground, beneath a canopy of crepe, King Erik Glipping's sarcophagus. The church is illuminated.

The funeral is over. The King's sword and standards adorn his coffin, while on the dark background of the altarpiece the word ANATHEMA is written in glowing letters in condemnation of the hidden murderers. The funeral procession moves off, and Lord High Constable Peder remains alone in the foreground. Inge is kneeling at the altar. Her fiancé is about to approach her, but she indicates to him that, in accordance with her father's wishes, she is to become the bride of Heaven. To both of them this calls to mind the old song about Hr. Aage and Jomfru Else, and it fills their hearts with profound sorrow. But new hope smiles beyond the grave, and at the foot of the altar the lovers pledge their eternal fidelity to each other.

Tormented by pangs of conscience, Ridder Lave, crushed by the curse, rushes back to the church. Beseechingly, his children greet him, but find him just as unbending as ever. After a moment's solitude, he discovers a monk to whom he will confess his guilt. But the latter grabs him violently by the arm and throws back his grey hood.... It is Rane Jonsen! He is hatching a ghastly plot. He needs Lave's help, but the latter turns away from him in disgust. Reproaches, wild defiance, and despair pass between them. Someone is coming! Rane pulls the old knight with him behind King Svend's monument.

Queen Agnes, in deep mourning, enters with her children. A large crowd, composed of people of every social estate, surrounds her. Tender sympathy causes them to shed tears over her grief. After lingering at her late husband's coffin, she collects her strength, remembers her maternal duties, and leads her eldest son up the quire steps. From this height she asks protection for herself and for her children and indicates that henceforth Erik shall rightfully wear his father's crown. The whole assemblage is filled with excitement, and they swear allegiance to the young King.

In accordance with the Queen's wishes, everyone departs, leaving the widow and her fatherless children to their silent grief. But the very thought of the dastardly crime arouses the indignation of the usually gentle Agnes. She becomes violently emotional and calls down the wrath of Heaven upon the killers. Her children fearfully huddle round her.

Impressed by the solemnity of the moment, Erik feels that from now on he must be everything to his mother, brother, and sister. He embraces them, dries his mother's tears, promises his deceased father that he will safeguard his loved ones, and calls upon Heaven for strength and assistance. Beside herself, Agnes reminds him of the circumstances of his father's death and stirs up his anger. She takes the sword from the King's coffin, leads the boy up to the altar, and makes him swear by God, by all the saints, and by his father's ashes that he will seek revenge on the killers!

Lave tears himself loose, rushes up into the quire, throws himself at Erik's feet, and asks to die. But a sign from Rane calls the conspirators forth from the crypt. In a flash, they rush up to the altar, wrench the sons from their struggling mother's arms, drag them away together with Lave, and disappear through the underground vault.

Merete throws herself on her swooning mother. The darkness frightens her and she starts to wail. People come running from every direction. Dismayed at seeing their Queen lying lifeless at the foot of the coffin, they fail to notice that the Princes are missing until Agnes, aroused from her stupor, looks about, wild-eyed, and asks where her sons are. They have been kidnapped! Not a trace of them can be found. Horror and confusion prevail. Pain overwhelms the despairing mother, who once again loses consciousness. Henner and Skirmen have found Lave's scarf and bring it to Inge. She immediately recognizes it: her father is with the children! He will guard their lives! She sees a ray of hope and asks Peder's assistance. Everyone clings to the hope that they will be rescued. The Queen, who with renewed attention has once again been revived, hardly dares to accept the hope that Inge and Peder try to instill in her. A fervent prayer has given her strength and, with the very sword upon which Erik recently swore, she will hasten to her sons' aid. Everyone presses round her with sympathy and consolation. They will follow her to the ends of the earth, rescue the boys from the assailants, and give their lives to save them.

ACT IV

The tower room at Ribehuus. High up, on the left, a prison window. To the right, an iron door; against the wall, a couch with cushion and hangings.

The captive Princes sadly stand listening to their persecutors rejoicing in the castle yard. They weep and think of their mother. But Erik tries to cheer his brother and devises little games. However, they soon grow tired of them. In wrestling they happen to fall against a wall, and the blow releases a hidden spring; the panel turns and reveals a secret door leading into Ridder Lave's prison.

The children are terrified, but Lave approaches them in a friendly manner. They threaten him and call him a murderer! Kneeling, he swears that he was not one of their father's killers. On the contrary, he is willing to give his life to save the children of his King. Erik reassures his brother and with childlike trust shakes the old knight's hand. The children grow sleepy; Lave prepares their bed, helps them to undress, and keeps watch over them.

Hinges creak and keys jangle. Lave retreats to his cell. The leaders of the conspiracy, followed by Rane and a couple of warriors, enter the tower room. By the light of a lantern, they behold the sleeping Princes and agree that if the castle should be taken by surprise, a horn will be sounded. Then – Both of them! They depart.

The panel turns again. Paler than before, but bold and determined, Lave runs over to the children's couch, takes one after the other in his arms, and without waking them carries them into his chamber. The door closes.

The castle yard of Ribehuus. On both sides, stairs leading to the towers. In the background a large gate with iron grilles.

Evening light. Wild merriment among the conspirators; drinking, gaming, and brawling. The leader enters; order is restored. The patrol announces that everywhere the Queen's troops have retreated. The leader turns the command over to Rane Jonsen, gives him the signal horn, calls for order and obedience, and leaves the fortress with a band of picked men.

From the town of Ribe comes the sound of festive music. There is dancing and merriment. It is St. John's Eve, and in the hazy distance motley crowds can be seen dancing over Ribe Bridge by torchlight. The festival always used to be celebrated like this in the courtyard. The well-known songs fill the conspirators with wistfulness and longing, and they entreat Rane until he finally allows them to summon the merrymakers up to the castle. They do not delay, but from the walls sound the ballad of Herr Aldebrand and "There's dancing in the courtyard." Their call is answered: the noise draws closer; the portcullis is hoisted up and the dancing throng comes streaming into the courtyard, dressed in the most fantastic disguises and carrying flower staves, torches, and lanterns and playing shrill instruments. They have brought wine with them. Their joy is contagious, and the castle yard is transformed into a brilliant banqueting hall.

In the midst of the whirling throng, Rane has espied a slender female figure wearing Lave's scarf. It is Inge, who makes herself known to him, pleads for her father's release, and promises Rane that her hand shall be the reward for his magnanimity. Overjoyed, Rane and the lovely mask are caught up in the dancing throng, while the intoxicated fellows drink until dawn.

(The sun comes up over Ribe, and from the merlon can be seen Nibsaaen, the bridge, the town, and the glorious cathedral.)

The dancing continues. The red and white draperies of the girls weave a variegated chain about the whole castle. Presently they are fastened onto the lofty Maypole. There they rise in tight clusters like Dannebrogs. Flower staves, shepherd – and Agnus Dei – staves are transformed into swords and lances, and in the twinkling of an eye, masks fall off, and Peder, Skirmen, Torstensen, and Henner, together with a numerous band, fall upon the conspirators and overpower and bind them. But Rane, who has been expecting a surprise attack, takes a troop of archers and ascends to the heights of the castle. The portcullis drops, and from staircases and windows the attackers are threatened with death. Terrified, the women rush together. Peder and his warriors display the defiance of desperation.... Then the Queen's men scale the outer wall, break through the portcullis, and come storming in with Agnes at their head. All resistance is crushed. The victory is decisive. But a horn sounds shrilly through the din of battle. It is Rane, giving the death signal! Everyone stands as if turned to stone. Agnes drops the sword from her hand. Every heart is filled with terror.

Lave emerges from the tower. He delivers the children into their mother's arms, unharmed. Expressions of astonishment and thanksgiving to Divine Providence.

The traitor is put in chains and led away. The repentant Lave owes his pardon to the children's salvation and Erik's intercession. Peder and Inge are united; the people come streaming in to greet the miraculously rescued children and to congratulate their gentle Dowager Queen. Dannebrogs wave from tower and wall. Joy resounds, and round about the captured fortress a dance is done for

"YOUNG KING ERIK"!

*   *   *

BELLMAN, OR THE POLSKA AT GRONALUND
(Bellmane ller Polskdandsenp aa Gronalund)

A Ballet-Vaudeville in One Act
by
August Bournonville

Music partly after *Fredmans Epistlar*, arranged by Holger Simon Paulli

Performed for the first time at the jubilee performance of the ballet Valdemar, June 3, 1844

Characters*

BELLMAN, a poet . . . . .Hr. Bournonville
THE INNKEEPER at Gröna Lund . . . . .Hr. Fredstrup
ULLA VINBLAD, his niece . . . . .Jfr. Lund
MOLBERG, corporal and dancing master . . . .Hr. Füssel, Sr.
MOWITZ, virtuoso . . . . .Hr. Stramboe

Guests: All the soloists and the corps de ballet

ANACREON . . . . .Hr. Bentzen
CUPID . . . . .Jfr. Eliza Garlieb
BACCHUS . . . . .Jfr. Laura
                                                                          Stramboe

GRACES. FAUNS. GENII. NISSES.

The scene is laid in the vicinity of Stockholm, Anno 1781. [The setting is the Djurgarden, a popular pleasure park.]

Outline

SCENE ONE

Cupid and Bacchus, who have lost their way here in the North, seek shelter from wind and weather. The *nisses* console them, forge arrows for Cupid, and refresh Bacchus with punch. They part as intimate friends.

SCENE TWO

Bellman, the enthusiastic bard of joy, nature, and folk life, comes to spend his Sunday at Grona Lund. He asks for wine, improvises on his

---

* **Translator's note**: This tribute to the beloved Swedish poet-song writer Carl Bellman draws on familiar characters and melodies from his collection *Fredman's Epistles*. The title recalls one of the songs in this volume, "The Fray at Grona Lund." The polska is a popular Swedish dance of Polish origin. Bellman was staged to celebrate the fiftieth performance of *Valdemar*.

lute, teases Ulla; and when she gets angry because he has written a ballad about her, he restores her charm and gaiety by giving a representation of the drunken Fredman.

SCENE THREE

Molberg and Mowitz make themselves known by a couple of characteristic little traits. The musicians enter, Father Berg and Bergstrom among them.

SCENE FOUR

The guests foregather. The innkeeper apologizes for his deshabille. His periwig and coat are missing, and he searches for them in vain. Finally, the guests point out to him Herr Fredman, who is wearing both. Bellman reveals his identity. Mowitz effects a reconciliation. This practical joke puts everyone in the mood for merriment. The orchestra strikes up and the dancing begins: minuet and polska.

FINALE

The innkeeper, Mowitz, and Bergström become angry at Bellman, who seens to have been pulling their legs. Quarreling and a brawl.

The backdrop is changed and now depicts a vineyard where the Graces and genii are gathered round Anacreon. Cupid and Bacchus extend their hands over the disputants, and everyone, with the exception of Bellman, stands as if turned to stone.

The Greek poet beckons to the Anacreon of the North. Graces and genii entwine Bellman with garlands and lead him up the hill, where the golden lyre is offered him. But at this very moment the nisses rise from the earth with a flaming bowl in their midst. The group mentioned above comes back to life, and the dancing resumes with even greater frenzy. Bellman tears himself away from the loftier sphere and rushes down into the turbulent throng. At length, Bacchus hands him the nectar of the gods, and the poet follows thither, where immortality beckons.

* * *

THE ORESTEIA*

A Tragic Ballet in Three Acts

Characters

AGAMEMNON, King of Argos and Mycenae, principal leader of the Greeks against Troy
CLYTEMNESTRA, his queen
ORESTES
ELECTRA their children
AEGISTHUS, the King's kinsman, vice-regent of the kingdom
PYLADES, Agamemnon's nephew, Orestes' childhood friend
CASSANDRA, daughter of Priam, brought as a slave from Troy
EURYMEDON, Agamemnon's charioteer
WARRIORS. COMMONERS. COURTIERS. APOLLO. THE EUMENIDES.

The scene is laid in Mycenae and on the shores of the Aegean Sea. The time is 1183 years before the beginning of our Christian era.

PART I: AGAMEMNON

The royal palace in Mycenae is situated on a hill with a prospect of the city and the distant sea. To the left, the staircase leading to the Palace of the Atridae. To the right, a temple dedicated to Apollo. Palms and bay trees shade the space between the palace and the temple, while bushes and hedges are resplendent with the most luxuriant blossoms.

The Greek fleet is sighted in the distance, and great numbers of people gather to greet the returning warriors. Joy is painted on every face, and while most of them flock to the shore, others stay behind to welcome the victorious hosts with triumphal arches and festive games.

Aegisthus arranges everything for the entry of the King. Together with his sister and his friend Pylades, Orestes emerges from the palace.

---

* Translator's note: This is the only scenario for an unperformed ballet that Bournonville included among the Ballet Poems, where it is placed with the works for 1844. In *My Theatre Life* he says that the subject was suggested to him by "some erudite art-lovers, thinking that mime was better able to assume antique forms than any other form of art" and he was also inspired by the recent translation of Aeschylus' trilogy into Danish by Peter Oluf Brøndsted.

But the inadequate technical facilities of the old Royal Theatre and the limitations of his company made the realization of this ambitious scheme impossible. "However," he concludes, "I believe this libretto can find a place among my finest ballet poems, partly to show that I have not left a higher genre untouched, and partly to give some idea of what could be accomplished if one's hands were not tied."

Their joy is expressed in highly different ways, for while Electra piously offers her thanks to the gods, Orestes burns with longing to throw himself into his father's arms. Aegisthus restrains him and tells him that he must not leave the palace but wait here upon its steps to bid the King welcome. Orestes can scarcely curb his impatience and responds to Aegisthus' feigned friendship with acrimony. But Electra and Pylades allay his hotheadedness and manage to pacify him. The royal children join the people in adorning the entry route.

The sound of martial music grows louder; Orestes is summoned to array himself in ceremonial dress; and Aegisthus takes his place at the head of an honour guard that opens the Triumphal Procession.

Old men and women and children occupy the peristyles of the palace and temple. A host of young men and girls rush forward with palms and garlands; they strew flowers in the path of the arrivals and wave colourful draperies in greeting:

I. A band of musicians.
II. Archers.
III. A four-wheeled chariot holding four suits of armor and a maiden dressed as the Goddess of Victory.
IV. Spearmen.
V. A chariot with precious vessels and golden chests borne by richly clad little boys.
VI. Soldiers with silver shields.
VII. A chariot upon which is borne a golden horse in halfnatural size. Four little boys carrying golden household gods walk at its side.
VIII. The King's bodyguard.
IX. Four priests with golden palms.
X. A chariot with a veiled statue of lifelike proportions; four veiled priestesses sit on the corners of the chariot. In their hands they hold censers. The people kneel as they drive by. (These chariots are driven by prisoners of war.)
XI. The leaders of the Greek army.
XII. A four-wheeled triumphal chariot drawn by four white horses, guided in front by Eurymedon. The chariot has three ledges. Upon the first sit two captured Trojan army leaders in chains; upon the second, Cassandra; and on top, leaning upon his ruler's staff, Agamemnon. On either side of the chariot walk four captured leaders bound in chains, while behind the chariot twenty-four large banners, which wave above the victor's head, are borne in a semicircle.

Jubilant excitement among the people; a serious mien and strict discipline in the army. Trumpets sound from the ramparts of the palace, and the halls of the temple give echo. Deeply moved, Agamemnon salutes his home, his people, and the stronghold of his fathers. He turns toward the temple and promises a glorious sacrifice to the saviour Apollo. Banners are waved, arms rattle, and the people give thanks to the mighty gods. Then Clytemnestra comes out onto the steps of the palace with her children at her side. Assisted by Eurymedon, Agamemnon descends from the chariot and throws himself into his wife's arms. Orestes and Electra cling to their father while Aegisthus kneels, and the orderly ranks of the army are broken up by fervent expressions of welcome.

Those who have been gone for so long a time are joyfully seen once more, and in the midst of the many happy souls stands the King, who now embraces as adults the son and daughter he left behind as children. Everyone seems delighted, save for that maiden in dazzling raiment who stands alone, sadly regarding the children who can enjoy parental affection. It is Cassandra, Priam's daughter, carried off as a slave from her conquered and ravaged homeland. Her youth and beauty arouse the sympathy of all; and only when the King, at his son's behest, grants her freedom and takes her into his house, and when Electra shows her a sister's love, does the rejoicing become universal and complete. Flower girls open the festivities with their dancing, Agamemnon and his queen take their seats of honour, and the games begin.

Orestes and Electra win the prize for grace and lightness and the King presents them with laurels, at the same time alluding to the fact that while the other youths have become hardened in war, Orestes has grown soft in peace. Outraged, Orestes returns the garland to his father and demands his arm ring if he should be proven the bravest in the passage of arms. He now gives proof of his strength and agility. Agamemnon proudly hands him the ring he has won, and Orestes leads the most stalwart youths in the warlike Pyrrhica *pyrrhiche*.

Envoys from the King of the Phocaeans (Strophius, father of Pylades and brother-in-law of Agamemnon) come to congratulate Agamemnon. They bring costly gifts and summon their young prince to return to his home. Pylades is delighted to see his old friends. He longs to embrace his parents, but how will he be able to live apart from his foster brother? Agamemnon, who receives the envoys and their costly gifts with gracious favour, orders Orestes to convey the greeting he sends his royal kinsman (a statue of Peace and a golden palm) and thus accompany his friend. Since the envoys cannot pass the night in Mycenae, he gives his son loyal Eurymedon as a guide.

Agamemnon gives the signal and his soldiers re-form their ranks: the King desires Clytemnestra to distribute the rewards intended for the bravest men; jewels, arms of honour, and laurels are bestowed by the Queen's own hand. The army cheers and the elders of the people embrace the honoured men in paternal fashion. But a host of women are slowly approaching. At their side walk children bearing swords entwined with bands of crepe. Where are they who wielded these swords? Where are the husbands and the fathers? Agamemnon's face grows somber and serious; he orders two shields brought forth, upon whose shining surfaces are engraved long rows of names – "They died for the mother country, but won the palms of immortality." The children kiss the beloved names, which shall now adorn the vestibule of the temple. But the young shall not remain fatherless, for Agamemnon lives and will protect them and their mothers.

Trumpets announce the offering which is to express the victors' thanksgiving. The sacred chariot is brought forth, and at a given sign the statue is unveiled: it is the image of Apollo, executed in gold at Agamemnon's command and intended to adorn the temple at Mycenae. The royal family, the army, and the people kneel with religious fervor, as the priestesses emerge from the temple with flaming altars which are placed about the figure of the god. Dancing girls bring forth the offering of fruits of the earth, and everyone joins in this solemn pageant.

Impelled by a prophetic force, Cassandra, who has remained silent and withdrawn throughout the entire ceremony, asks that she be allowed to dance the sacred sacrificial hymn. She becomes more and more animated; her irresistible charm and the Asiatic character of her movements arouse admiration and captivate hearts. Several people join in the dance and she is soon surrounded by an excited throng. But all of a sudden she stops, seized by pythonine rapture. Everyone looks at her with astonishment; her eyes stare wildly, her limbs tremble, and her spirit seems to commune with some distant storm which momentarily darkens the sky. Agamemnon is alarmed about her; but she grips Electra's hand, pulls her close to her father, and looks with horror at the Palace of the Atridae, where she sees murder and destruction. She points to Aegisthus and Clytemnestra, names them as the enemies of the King, and then sinks powerless to the ground before the image of Apollo. General consternation follows.

The air clears. Clytemnestra, who is the first to regain her composure, seeks to calm Agamemnon; he is soon convinced of Aegisthus' devotion. The priestesses denounce Cassandra as an imposter, and the statue of the god is carried to its consecrated dwelling place. By Electra's care, Cassandra is brought to her senses once more. She has no idea what has happened but everywhere encounters faces burning with anger and revenge. In vain she begs Agamemnon's mercy; Electra's own pleas are fruitless, and, cursed by all, she is banished from their midst and driven away as an evil, sinister creature.

But joy must once again prevail. Aegisthus has had a splendid banquet arranged for the returning warriors. With their friends and relatives they foregather in merry groups, and wine flows in abundance. Agamemnon, who is in need of rest, goes into the palace with the Queen and Electra, and the untrammeled merriment of the people quickly transforms the celebration into a boisterous bacchanal. Aegisthus, who in all his unguarded moments has displayed cunning and uneasiness, takes advantage of the wild confusion to send off, unnoticed, several messengers and sets in motion a plot he has been brooding over for a long time. He encourages the guests to drink and he himself empties a cup amid the drunken hilarity. The wild excitement increases, and Bacchus celebrates his triumph by torchlight.

TRANSFORMATION

The interior of a tent which Eurymedon has erected for Orestes and Pylades.

Agamemnon's old charioteer expresses his devotion to his master's son and utters his delight at the latter's erect stature and prowess in physical exercises. He leaves the two friends alone. They remove their cloaks, bid one another good night, and each goes to his couch, when Eurymedon announces a stranger who, closely shrouded, appears before Orestes and asks to speak with him alone. Eurymedon and Pylades express their mistrust, but Orestes reassures them and prays them to comply with his wishes. They leave, and Cassandra reveals herself as the Outcast, who turns to Orestes as her only friend.

There now follows a scene of amazement, sympathy, and growing passion on the part of Orestes, while Cassandra displays confidence and feminine charm. Orestes has loved her from the first moment he beheld her, and her heart returns his sentiments. But she is trembling with fever; she falters, leans upon Orestes, and recoils in horror as she points with a quavering hand toward the backdrop, which dissolves into a dim fog through which Orestes sees Aegisthus, who, urged on by Clytemnestra, murders the sleeping Agamemnon.

The vision disappears. Filled with horror, Orestes throws himself upon his couch, and regarding the whole thing as a delusion, pushes the unhappy Cassandra away and dismisses her from his sight in disgust. Once again she wraps herself in her dark cloak and withdraws just as Pylades enters. Scarcely has Orestes told his friend of Cassandra's irrational behaviour and described to him the horrifying vision than Cassandra, who has been struck by robbers' daggers, breathlessly rushes in. She throws herself at Orestes' feet and implores him to flee the impending danger. Eurymedon, deadly pale, reports an assassins' attack. They hear the din of battle outside. Orestes lifts the wounded girl in his arms. In the utmost haste, Pylades tosses Orestes' cloak about him, places his helmet on his head, seizes the unconscious Cassandra, and shows Orestes the only means of escape. But Orestes will not abandon his beloved in the hour of death, nor betray his friend in the moment of need. A tender quarrel now ensues between the two friends, but the dying Cassandra herself hastens his flight, and the faithful Eurymedon drags him away.

Pylades, who has carried Cassandra to Orestes' couch, is standing guard over her just as Aegisthus' messengers enter the tent. They mistake him for Orestes, overpower him despite his violent opposition, and lead him away laden with chains.

PART II: THE PROPITIATION

One year later.

The prelude expresses a violent storm, which abates as the curtain rises.

A cypress grove by the seashore. A stormy night. The tempest has splintered and destroyed Orestes' ships, and the pounding waves have cast him unconscious upon his native soil.

Eurymedon, who has swum ashore, discovers his young master and tries in vain to bring him back to life. He himself does not yet know where he is. At length, day begins to dawn and he finds himself standing by a grave. It is Agamemnon's! Overwhelmed by pain, Eurymedon leans against the covering stone and loses himself in silent grief.

Electra and her women come to offer sacrifice at the grave.

Eurymedon is aroused by the sound of mournful hymns. He is recognized by the King's daughter, who anxiously asks for her brother. The old man points toward a thicket, and the women hasten thither in order, if possible, to tear Orestes from the jaws of Death! They succeed! He opens his eyes and recognizes his beloved sister. Expressions of mutual tenderness and joy. Electra leads her brother to their father's grave. She does not need to incite him to vengeance, for Orestes has come to call the murderer to account.

But, alas! Clytemnestra too is guilty. And yet she is his mother! "But," asks Electra, "hast thou strength enough to do this deed?"

Orestes first takes part in the sacrifice, mingles wine and honey in the sacred soil, and then, with the strength of a giant, lifts his father's gravestone. He wields the heavy sword as the women bind the sandals to his feet. However, caution and cunning are needed in order to enter the tyrant's well-guarded palace. Orestes shall borrow Eurymedon's robe and manner, and Electra shall spy out the opportune moment. They hasten away.

TRANSFORMATION

A hall in the royal palace. The ocean can be seen through a colonnade.

Clytemnestra enters, lost in thought. Her women place her loom before her, but the work soon falls from her hands as bitter memories assail her.

The hunting horns sound. The Queen rushes to receive Aegisthus, who, joyous and elated, shows her the captured prey. Among other things, he has shot an old eagle and captured its young. But either on purpose or from clumsiness, the slave who is to display the bird allows his prisoner to escape and it flies through the colonnade out into the open. Clytemnestra is shaken by this omen and the furious Aegisthus wishes to punish the slave, but the Queen intercedes for him and the tyrant dismisses him with scorn and contempt. The slave is none other than Pylades, who must now bear the chains of slavery for having saved his friend.

Aegisthus and Clytemnestra remain alone together, but Reproach soon makes a third party. Neither joy nor love has rewarded their crime, and any consolation they seek to bestow on each other only feeds their internal anguish. Electra appears from the background and Aegisthus, who cannot stand her presence, retires.

Electra begs her mother to tear herself loose from this sinister villain. But Clytemnestra is all too blinded by her passion. Her pride is aroused by her daughter's ideas and she angrily threatens to vent her wrath, when Electra announces an old man who brings a message from Orestes. This name robs the Queen of her self-composure. She is uncertain whether or not to receive these tidings. But maternal tenderness finally wins out. She makes a sign and the old man enters – she recognizes Eurymedon! He hands her Orestes' golden arm ring as a sign of his mission. Clytemnestra hardly dares ask, "Then he is dead? Did he curse me with his dying breath?" "Nay, he loved you always!" "By the gods, what have I heard?" The old man is on the verge of being overcome by his emotions. The Queen orders her people to take care of the traveller, takes Electra by the hand, and enters the palace in order to give vent to the feelings of her heart.

A table is laid for the wayfarer, and Pylades brings him a cup of water. One glance and he has recognized his friend – but with caution, lest he give everything away. He now dismisses the other slaves and throws himself into Orestes' arms. His loyal heart beats with exhilaration, but Orestes' joy is embittered by the sight of Pylades in the garb of a slave. "And Cassandra?" "Alas! She is no more." "Woe to her murderers! Down with the tyrant!" Electra rushes in to report the approach of Aegisthus and brings Agamemnon's sword. Orestes lays it on the table as he drinks to the destruction of the murderers. Pylades goes to assemble the people. Electra embraces her brother, trembling with anticipation. "The hour has come – avenge our father!" She goes to Clytemnestra.

Aegisthus, who is carrying Orestes' arm ring, comes to question Eurymedon, who brought the news of his death. He finds the old man dwelling upon the memory of his deceased lord and king and answering every question with another one about Agamemnon, whose greatness he admired, whose dangers he shared, and whose bounty he enjoyed. Aegisthus grows impatient, but when the old man bursts into lamentations about not having been present to defend his protector and finally calls down the wrath of the gods upon the murderers, he summons the slaves and tells them to cast out this bold creature. The slaves try to lay hands on the supposed Eurymedon, but the latter hurls them to the ground, left and right. Raging, Aegisthus himself tries to drag him to the exit, but receives a kick that knocks him to the floor. The disguise falls away, and Orestes stands before him. The villain tries to flee, but the avenger stops him, seizes his father's sword, and forces the murderer to defend himself. This fierce struggle has summoned Clytemnestra, who tears herself away from Electra in order to throw herself between the swordsmen, where she receives the thrust intended for Aegisthus. The latter escapes. Electra throws herself upon her dying mother. Orestes stands with the sword in his hand, as if turned to stone.

Pylades arrives with the jubilant people. Eurymedon, who has slain the tyrant, throws his helmet and cloak at Orestes' feet. Orestes silences the cries of acclamation which are beginning to burst forth and points to Clytemnestra. She opens her eyes, beholds her son, takes his head in her hands, presses his brow to her lips, and dies. The groups of people display horror and pain.

PART III: THE EUMENIDES

Yet another year later.

A sleeping chamber in the royal palace. Orestes is resting on his bed, at the foot of which Electra (who never dares to leave her brother) is slumbering, with her harp in her arms. On the table a lamp is burning. Crown and sword rest upon a cushion near by.

The stillness of the night is broken by a subterranean hissing. A bluish glow illuminates the chamber, and from every side come darting and gliding slender female forms with wild, long hair; they are carrying torches or vipers in their hands, together with cups of bitterness and sprigs of thistle. They approach Orestes' couch and dance about it in whirling circles. He groans in his sleep, jumps up, and rushes about, everywhere pursued by the frightful beings who menace him. They cling to his robes, show him his dying mother, tear from him the sword which he tried to plunge into his own breast, and dance triumphantly around the desperate man, who sinks beneath the weight of his anguish.

Electra wakens and sees her unconscious brother surrounded by the hideous group. She seizes her harp. Its gentle tones lull the ferocious Eumenides to sleep. They descend to their dark home, and delicious melodies call the tortured man back to life. There follow expressions of sisterly tenderness and love.

Pylades enters and learns of Orestes' state of mind. He tries to cheer his brokenhearted friend. He draws aside the large curtain and shows him the people who have gathered in the early light of morn to see their King. Orestes must exercise justice and show strength. Little by little he regains his composure, sets the crown upon his head, and ascends the throne.

The people draw near with acclamation and festive jubilation, but Orestes halts their joyous exclamations. He calls for seriousness and silence. The accused are brought before him. He learns their offences and – unfastens their chains; for he himself was a greater criminal. Pylades calls upon him to perform feats of arms. The stalwart youths only await the signal, and Orestes is about to take his place at their head. But as he draws his sword he remembers that this very steel killed his mother! His despair verges on madness, and all depart in terror.

Then Electra once again steps forth with her harp. She has gathered round her a host of graceful little children, whose innocent joy shall soothe the mind of the distressed king. Their dancing and games cheer him; jesting, and with marks of affection, he passes through their ranks and personally distributes gifts to the little ones. But when their mothers, who stand hidden, come rushing forth to express their thanks, and the children, shouting jubilantly, throw themselves into their embrace, the pangs of conscience return and the Eumenides lay hold of him with greater force than ever.

Pylades, Electra, and Eurymedon bring the veiled priestess of Apollo. She signals, and the sacred tones of the harp exert their anesthetizing effect on the Eumenides. Orestes is carried to a boat which, rowed by Eurymedon, is steered by the priestess toward the sacred mountain. Pylades stays behind with Electra, who goes back to the palace with her women.

The Eumenides reawaken and perceive that their victim is missing. They break into wild dancing and hurl themselves into the waves in order to swim in pursuit of Orestes.

TRANSFORMATION

The summit of the sacred mountain. At the pinnacle stands the tripod of Apollo.

Exhausted in mind and body, Orestes is led up the steep rock by the priestess' hand. His legs will hardly hold him, but one more effort and he can attain compassionate mercy and implore the God of Light. The mountain is still shrouded in the gloom of twilight. In defiance of the prohibition, Orestes has glanced behind him and the Eumenides once again appear before him in the distance. They come closer; Orestes is about to become their prey, but the faithful hand of the priestess saves him, and he clings to the tripod with trembling hands.

The summit of the mountain glows in the rising sun. Apollo is revealed in all his splendor. Warmth, light, and peace return to the soul of the prodigal. The veil of the priestess falls, the sacred draperies vanish, and she stands arrayed in bridal dress – it is Cassandra!

At a command from Apollo, the Eumenides sink down into the abyss, the tripod glides down to earth with the united pair; its flame becomes the lovers' bridal torch and whirls the people's offerings of thanksgiving up toward the clouds to the Lord of Life and of the Day.

Note: When this ballet is performed on stage, one will be able to see in what way I have interpreted the Greek tragedian, whose division of the subject matter I have carefully followed. In [my treatment of] the story, however, I have been completely independent and have taken great pains to avoid any similarity with the great Noverre's mimed adaptation of the same theme. But the altered fates of Cassandra, Pylades, and Eurymedon must not be ascribed to my ignorance or to indifferent treatment. Their characters are historical, but their situations, especially that of Cassandra, need to be modified if they are to fit into the course of the action in a satisfactory manner. This work is intended for talents of the Royal Theatre, provided that it some day obtains the long-awaited expansion in height and breadth.

* * *

KIRSTEN PIIL, OR TWO MIDSUMMER FESTIVALS
(Kirsten Piil eller To Midsommerfester)

A Romantic Ballet in Three Acts
by
August Bournonville

Music by Edvard Helsted

Performed for the first time on February 26, 1845

Characters

JOMFRU KIRSTEN PIIL, heiress to the manor	Jfr. Nielsen
HERR TØNNES, her guardian	Hr. Stramboe
JUNKER HANS, officer of the Sjaelland cavalry	Hr. Brodersen
RASMUS THE TRUMPETER	Hr. Bournonville
MARTHE, a lady's maid	Jfr. Fjeldsted
HENNING, the steward	Jfr. Fredstrup
NORA, his daughter	Jfr. P. Fredstrup
ELSE, the cook	Jfr. Lund
ESBEN, the gardener	Hr. Edv. Stramboe
TWO MILKMAIDS	{ Jfr Werning / Jfr. Bruun }

Solo Dances and Supporting Parts

Mm. Hoppe, Larcher, Lund, Funck, Gade, Füssel, and Hoppensach; Mlles. Funck, C. Nielsen, Borup, A. Holm, Rostock, and Mme. Møller.

LADIES AND GENTLEMEN. CAVALRYMEN AND PEASANT FOLK. ELF-MAIDENS AND DREAM PICTURES.

The scene is laid a mile and a half from Copenhagen. Acts One and Two take place on Midsummer Eve, 1582; Act Three, a year to the day thereafter.

ACT I

The manor of Skovgaard; through the gate a prospect of landscape and lake. To the right, the family residence; to the left, the steward's. Morning.

Henning rings a bell, calling people to work. Rasmus the Trumpeter pays court to the maids of the manor. Reveille sounds, mustering the cavalrymen who are billeted here. Junker Hans brings Herr Tønnes a new requisition, and while he and the steward express their displeasure at the presence of these troublesome guests, Hans gives a slip of paper to Marthe, who promises to see that her young mistress receives it. Despite the guardian's suspicions, the message reaches its destination.

Tønnes announces to the girls that there should be merriment in honour of his matrimonial project. They do indeed make merry – at his expense – and he becomes highly indignant. The gallant trumpeter manages to halt his outburst; but when the entire crowd of work-people comes to ask permission to celebrate Midsummer Eve, they are angrily refused.

Jomfru Kirsten comes out onto the steps of the château, sees their crestfallen faces, and goes down to console the poor people. She does everything in her power to persuade Hr. Tønnes, for her sake, to allow Midsummer dancing to take place at the manor. The peasants jubilantly hasten to prepare for the celebration, while Tønnes and the steward go down into the cellar to fetch potables.

Scene of chaste and chivalrous love between Junker Hans and Jomfru Kirsten. She gives him reason to hope, and he ardently presses her hand to his lips. At this very moment Hr. Tønnes emerges from the cellar; his surprise is as great as his indignation. But he hardly has time to think before the courtyard is filled with the merrymakers, and the May Dance is gaily performed around the decorated pole.

The officers invite the distinguished residents of the manor to a ball that evening. A St. John's Fool amuses the assembly with his funny leaps, and some amuse themselves by playing with his cap and bells. Junker Hans and Jomfru Kirsten are chosen king and queen of the May. They open the grand Round Dance, which continues amid laughter and jesting while a toast is drunk to the health of the distinguished guests.

ACT II

Jomfru Kirsten's chamber. To the right, an exit; to the left, an ottoman and armchair; centre stage, a table with a vase of flowers; and in the background a large mirror with a curtain.

Marthe is busy attending to her mistress's toilette. Rasmus catches her in front of the mirror. She is offended and reproaches him for his rashness. He promises to mend his ways and is about to seal his oath of fidelity with a kiss when Tønnes sullenly enters, plagued by Henning and Esben. He catches sight of Rasmus, who is presenting a bouquet he has brought Jomfru Kirsten on behalf of the Junker, and rudely dismisses him. Marthe offers to take her mistress the bouquet, but Tønnes has become so annoyed at the trumpeter's boldness that upon seeing himself in the mirror he starts in dismay, tips over the table, hurts his leg, and lashes out at the others, who cannot refrain from laughing. He chases them out and, exhausted, flings himself into the armchair.

Marthe feels sorry for the foolish guardian, who is in love with his pretty ward, whom he torments with surliness instead of making himself pleasing and amiable. He is beside himself, wishes to take revenge on his rival, and is almost driven to despair. The lady's maid tries to turn his thoughts to milder things and gives him a little lesson in the art of pleasing a lady. Tønnes shall present the Junker's bouquet, accompanied by a pretty speech, as if it came from him. Jomfru Kirsten enters and appears embarrassed by her guardian's presence but accepts the bouquet with good grace. Overjoyed, Tønnes asks her for the first dance at the ball, gives the roguish Marthe a douceur, and hurries off to dress for the festivities.

Marthe completes her mistress's toilette, and Kirsten Piil dances before the crystalline glass, which gives back a faithful reflection of her charms. Esben brings flowers, which Marthe shall distribute at the ball. The carriage is at the door. Hr. Tønnes enters in full dress, and the maids of the manor come to admire Jomfru Kirsten in her finery. The chatelaine and her party depart, and Henning follows, after having stolen a few mischievous glances at the pretty cook.

TRANSFORMATION

Festively decorated armory.

The officers' ball is brilliant, but the arrival of Kirsten Piil makes the party complete. Dances both merry and solemn are performed.
Marthe, clad as Flora, distributes her gifts; Tønnes is dogged by misfortune. A young page, who also serves as cupbearer, dances with her, and with lightness and grace they compete in a lively *vexeldands* [changing dance].

They sit down at table; but the trumpet sounds and Rasmus brings orders that the soldiers are to march. The celebration is cut short, and all the officers hasten to arm themselves. Standards and military drums are fetched, and cups are filled in order to drink a toast to the glory and success of the departing warriors.

The trumpeter's sweethearts dissolve into tears and weigh him down with keepsakes and provisions.

Happy and officious, Tønnes orders everyone to drink to a successful journey, and the officers, gathered round the table, bid farewell to their friends and relatives. But in one corner of the room, unnoticed by the others, Junker Hans receives the promise of his maiden fair that she will wait for her knight and remain faithful to him.

ACT III

Dense forest. The stag has been felled. Hunting horns call the party together. It is Hr. Tønnes who does the honours; but Jomfru Kirsten is missing: she has gotten lost, they grow anxious, and people set out in all directions to search for her.

TRANSFORMATION

Wooded vale and marsh with alder thicket. Midsummer Eve. Mist rises from the rushes, and hovering groups of elf-maidens with white veils dance to the sound of the hunting horn,which alternates with the tolling of the evening bell at Gentofte Church.

Kirsten Piil enters, lost in thought; only too late does she realize that she has lost her way. Fear of night overwhelms her, and she is prostrate with heat and thirst; then she hears church bells in the distance and kneels down to pray.

The elf-maidens jump out of the brushwood at the foot of the elevation; they push the branches aside, and a silvery spring gushes forth from the hill. Kirsten Piil is terrified, but their friendliness conquers her fear. They offer her a golden horn, and she "draws a drink from the gushing spring." The airy beings dance for her until she feels her eyelids getting heavy. They prepare her a bed of rushes and flowers, enfold her in their veils, and gently rock her to sleep.

SHE DREAMS:

Time, in the guise of an old man, passes the spring, drains the golden horn which the elf-maids hand him, turns his hundred-year hourglass, and vanishes.

A knight and a lady from the age of Christian V [1670-1699] have a rendezvous at the spring. He carves his own initials and those of his beloved in a beech tree. She picks forget-me-nots, which she meaningfully hands him. But Time overtakes them, they sink into the ground, and their monograms are erased from the bark of the tree.

Time drinks once more from the waters of the spring, gazes wistfully about, and exits to the melody: "In a hundred years all things are forgotten." Beperiwigged dancers and peasant folk from 1783 waltz about a barrel organ in measured circles. A bear trainer shows off his clumsy pupil, while paralytics seek a cure from the miraculous effects of the water. Next comes the curious Jew with his lute; his laughable ballads work wonders, the cripples toss away their crutches, and, dancing and waltzing, all praise "St. John's Day as the festival of joy and Midsummer." The music dies away and the earth swallows up both the virtuosi and their instruments.

Time, gray-haired and bent with age, draws near with hammer and chisel to carve his mark in the hard stone. Elf-maidens hand him the golden horn, which he seizes with trembling hand. But scarcely has he drained it than he is transformed into a vigorous youth with flowing locks and dazzling raiment. Young and bold, he brandishes the fresh beech branch, casts the sands of the hourglass to the winds, and glides away.

Up from the depths of the marsh there rises a railroad; the locomotive starts to puff, and the clanking train carries a crowd of passengers from Copenhagen to Dyrehaven. A Chinese pavilion emerges from the thicket, civilized peasants have bottles of champagne opened, and the capital's *élégants* and their ladies visit the spring and perform a whirling polka to the Nr. 3 of joy and speed. The bell sounds, and in the utmost haste the party rushes off to the railway, which carries them to new pleasures. The train whizzes by, and the noise fades away little by little.

The short Midsummer night gives way to dawn. The elfmaidens vanish but leave the golden horn behind near the spring.

Hoofbeats are heard in the distance. Junker Hans, clad in light armor, climbs down into the vale. He is hastening to his beloved's manor house to appear as her chosen suitor, crowned with triumph and glory. He finds the golden horn near the edge of the spring, drinks of the delightful water, and, looking around, discovers Kirsten Piil asleep in the shade of the tree. He pauses, lost in silent rapture, and, to him, everything seems like a dream. The Midsummer sun comes up. Jomfru Kirsten awakens, tender and charming but astonished to see where she is. She recognizes the spring, but everything she has been or dreamt is still confused in her mind. Then she hears familiar tones: far-off military music, the cavalry's march! They are returning! *He* is with them, and she sees him before her eyes. Surprise and heartfelt joy. She thanks God, who has spared him, and ecstatically sinks to his breast. But this bliss is too much for her; she cannot help weeping and is about to faint. Then Junker Hans fills the golden horn with water from the spring and hands it to his "maiden fair" with the same expression with which he took leave of her a year ago. She drinks from the horn, gazing at her knight with deep emotion all the while. A loyal handshake tells him she has remained true to him, and he places the betrothal ring on her finger.

Hr. Tønnes and his party enter and find Kirsten Piil with the Junker. She presents him as her bridegroom; her guardian cannot withhold his consent, and all vie to congratulate the returning warrior and his happy bride.

It is once again the festival of joy and Midsummer, and the peasants come by to celebrate it as they did last year. Rasmus the Trumpeter is also among them. But, alas! The war has not been kind to him: he has left an eye, an arm, and a leg on the field of honour! Only his heart has remained whole. It still burns for the fair sex, but his old luck has deserted him. The girls turn their backs on him! Most of them have found new sweethearts (among them Else the Cook, who has given her hand to the steward and become the stepmother of Nora, who is to marry Esben). Sighing, he asks for a drink from the gushing spring; it is compassionately given him: but with *the first cup* his eye can see; with *the second* his empty sleeve is filled with a powerful arm. The astonishment mounts. But when he drains *the third cup*, and his faithful Marthe (who is in on the secret) enters with the musicians, his wooden leg starts to dance, and the miracle dissolves into uproarious hilarity. Cupid will never forsake the brave soldier. The day and the spring are dedicated to the Genius of Joy, and the charming woodland vale is destined to become a place of pilgrimage in memory of Kirsten Piil.

RAPHAEL

A Romantic Ballet in Six Tableaux
by
August Bournonville

Music by Johannes Frederik Frøhlich

Scenery by Aron Wallich, Troels Lund, and
Christian Ferdinand Christensen

Performed for the first time May 30, 1845

Characters

LEO X	Hr. Füssel
RAFFAELLO SANZIO DA URBINO	Hr. Bournonville
BERNARDO DIVIZIO DA BIBIENA	Hr. Fredstrup
CECILIA, his niece	Jfr. Augusta Bournonville
GIULIO ROMANO } artists	Hr. Lefebvre
MARCANTONIO	Hr. Larcher
FRANCESCO PENNI	Hr. Gade
GIOVANNI DA UDINE	Hr. Funck
TADDEO, a young nobleman	Hr. Brodersen
FRANCESCO, a baker	Hr. Stramboe
PAOLA, his wife, called La Bella Fornarina	Jfr. Nielsen
LAURA, Cecilia's friend	Mme. Møller
CATARINA, Raphael's housekeeper	Mme. Schouw
PASQUALE, a baker's boy	Hr. Edv. Stramboe

PRELATES, NOBLEMEN AND LADIES, CARNIVAL MASKERS, COMMONERS, PAPAL GUARDS, PAGES, AND SERVANTS.

The scene is laid in Rome in the year 1520.

Settings

First Tableau: A *stanza* in the Vatican	by Hr. Wallich
Second Tableau: A baker's shop and a street	by Hr. Wallich
Third Tableau: A villa	by Hr. Christensen
Fourth Tableau: Raphael's home	by Hr. T. Lund
Fifth Tableau: The Corso on Moccoli Night	by Hr. T. Lund
Sixth Tableau: The picture gallery (older)	by Hr. Wallich

FIRST TABLEAU

The Stanza d'Attila in the Vatican. Doors to right and left. In the background, a window. To the right, scaffolding.

Raphael and his pupils are in the process of completing the fresco entitled "Heliodorus." Cardinal Divizio, his niece Cecilia, the violinist Taddeo, a couple of young ladies, and some models are viewing the work, which continues amid the sound of music and dancing.

The central group of the painting is posed for the last time. The portraits are completed and everyone congratulates the great artist. Ecstatic with admiration, Cecilia chooses him as her squire and gives him her colours to wear. Joy prevails and cups are drained. Taddeo alone is despondent, over the homage Cecilia pays Raphael.

Roman noblemen and papal guards announce the approach of the Holy Father. Leo X distributes rewards. Marcantonio and Taddeo receive honourable laurels, but Raphael must show the Pope around the newly completed *stanza*. They go first to "Heliodorus," then to "Attila." Leo admires the painter's genius, but when his "Peter" is unveiled, showing the radiant angel freeing the apostle from prison, he is filled with holy enthusiasm and falls to his knees before it in admiration. Everyone follows his example and art enjoys its finest triumph.

The great patron recognizes his inability to reward Raphael in worthy fashion. He offers him the accolade, but Raphael modestly declines it; then a cardinal's hat, but, directing a glance at Cecilia, the artist confesses that his heart still clings too much to earthly things. Leo finally asks if he will be his son, his friend! Raphael prostrates himself at the Holy Father's feet, but the latter embraces him, kisses his brow, and places a precious ring on his finger.

The Pope leaves, followed by his court. The young noblemen now abandon their stiff bearing and, amid jesting and gaiety, invite Raphael and his pupils to [share] the delights of Carnival. Old Catarina has forced her way through the ranks of the guard to congratulate her master, but he is badly in need of a moment's solitude.

Everyone leaves and Raphael finally gives vent to his emotions. Is it really he who has completed these works that surround him? No, it is a higher power that guided his brush, a sacred fire that inflamed his imagination. Then Cecilia – her playing of the harp, the ribbon she gave him to wear – these things reappear in his memory and fill his soul. New strains of the harp surprise him. It is Cecilia herself, who, together with her uncle, has come to bid him farewell. They invite him to a feast at the cardinal's villa, then leave. The successful Raphael now gives himself up to the most joyous hopes. Giulio Romano comes to share his delight and, arm in arm, they hasten out into the open air.

SECOND TABLEAU

Francesco's bakery shop. To the left, an oven; to the right, a household altar with a picture of the Madonna and a lamp. In the background, a door and windows.

Girls and women buy bread from Francesco, who plays the wit and gallant and rebuffs young whippersnappers. Pasquale has forgotten to take the bread out of the oven in time. It is burned to a crisp, and the boy is just about to feel his master's rightful anger when Raphael's old housekeeper comes between him and the guilty party and calms the baker by talking about his pretty wife. A gentleman passing by has noticed the picture of the Madonna and asks the painter's name. Catarina proudly names her master, and the art-lover offers Francesco a considerable sum for the beautiful picture.

Paola returns from Mass and distributes alms. Her husband introduces her to the stranger and proposes that they sell the painting. She, on the other hand, is most violently against it. All his remonstrances are fruitless, and while Francesco despondently sees the gentleman out, she shows Catarina a secret that the picture contains. The old woman wants to disclose everything to the husband, but Paola's pleading glance restrains her. Shaking her head, Catarina leaves and the painting once again resumes its accustomed place.

There now ensues a domestic scene between the baker and his capricious young wife. When the indignation is at its height, Pasquale announces a troupe of Carnival merrymakers. The maskers come dancing in, hop about on tables and benches, and fill the house with a noise reminiscent of bacchantes.

Doctors and gypsy girls plague Francesco. Harlequins beat their baubles on his back and small devils yell in his ears. Fornarina is assailed with bouquets and sonnets, and the boisterous crowd does not leave the baker's shop until Francesco is completely worn out. Paola pities her poor husband and tries to comfort him. But she reminds him of important business and helps him to dress, and he hurries off. However, he appoints Pasquale to watch over the house in his absence.

Fornarina perceives that Pasquale is just as reluctant to stay at home as she is to have him there and she succeeds in persuading him to join the Carnival maskers who dance through the streets in noisy crowds.

It is at this time of day that Raphael usually goes past. He enters, pauses, and sees Paola in tears. He cannot refrain from going in and asking the reason for her sorrow. It is the memory of a bygone time, her present position, and Raphael's coolness that are torturing her. He consoles her, finds her as beautiful and charming as ever, and promises to be a true friend to her. Her good humor returns. She bids him sit down, wipes his brow, and gives him some wine. But just as he puts the cup to his lips he is struck by the way she is standing: why, it is Hebe! She hands him the wine jug, takes a cup herself, and falls on his breast like Erigone.

The beautiful model animates the painter's memories. He sets the drinking cups on the table, and as he turns around, Venus stands before him. Enraptured, he hastens to her. But just then she is transformed into the Mater Dolorosa and he bows in awe. He now remembers the days when, leaning on his shoulder, she stood by his easel and was the muse who crowned his work. He tries to embrace her, but she enfolds herself in her veil as Chastity. He modestly draws back, but an outstretched foot and an innocently roguish glance remind him of the bathing nymph. He darts forward, but the timid, kneeling Venus keeps him at a distance. Paola is still in love with him. She confesses her sin before the Madonna and begs forgiveness. But she cannot tear herself loose from her passion.

Raphael tells her this love will be the cause of her destruction, that both he and she have obligations... Fornarina regards him with a look of deep offence... but she soon comprehends that another has supplanted her. Her eyes blaze... woe to her rival, for her jealousy knows no bounds! Raphael's friends come to fetch him for the celebration. He leaves the frustrated woman, who flies into a rage at his departure. But Raphael has dropped Cecilia's ribbon on the floor. Paola finds it and surmises everything. The maskers come and invite her to join them. She quickly dresses and, with despair in her heart, she dances off with the noisy crowd in a whirling Saltarello.

THIRD TABLEAU

The Cardinal's villa, with a magnificent garden and a terrace to the left. In the background, the palace. Afternoon.

The cardinal and some older noblemen are gathered on the terrace, watching the frolicking of the young folk. Surrounded by artists, Raphael is received with homage and friendship, especially by Cecilia, who, to Taddeo's annoyance, singles out the great master at every opportunity. The dancing continues until darkness invites the company to go into the palace. Taddeo remains alone. He is going to leave this place, but he wishes to speak with Cecilia once more.

A masked gypsy wants to tell his fortune, but he turns her away. She perceives his sorrow, but promises him victory over his rival and gives him a ribbon as a talisman. Taddeo recognizes it and tries in vain to discover who the beautiful woman can be. The gypsy waves her tambourine and eludes him.

Cecilia, with her faithful friend Laura, enters the garden. Taddeo bids her farewell, for another has surely won her heart and he cannot endure his rival's triumph. Everything is explained: Cecilia admires the celebrated Raphael; she is captivated by his genius, she loves his art and honours his personality. But her heart belongs to Taddeo alone, and since Raphael has so carelessly tossed her favour aside, Taddeo shall wear it now. Enraptured, he throws himself at the feet of his beloved.

Raphael enters upstage with Giulio and witnesses the conclusion of this scene. He stands as if turned to stone upon seeing the lucky Taddeo strolling through the garden with the two young ladies. He does not know if he is awake or dreaming. Giulio tries to see it from the humorous side. But when he notices that by doing this he only increases his friend's pain, he tells him he must overcome his passion so as not to become an object of humiliation and pity.

The Carnival crowd approaches, and the garden resounds with the life and gaiety that buffets arouse. Surrounded by his friends and young noblemen, Raphael empties glass after glass. Disguised as a gypsy, La Fornarina arouses excitement with her dancing and exercises her old mastery over Raphael. On her arm he throws himself into the whirl of the festival, seeking the intoxication of forgetfulness. Fate brings him face to face with Taddeo: he recognizes his favour and tears it from his rival's shoulder. General confusion. The rivals display their indignation, but the cardinal comes between them. Raphael, beside himself, is led away by his friends.

FOURTH TABLEAU

Raphael's home. His studio, or workroom, in the most elegant style. To the right, a cabinet; in the background, an exit door. Dawn.

Catarina sits slumbering. She is awakened by the striking of the bell and runs to the window, apprehensive about her master's fate. She kneels and prays as Raphael enters the room. He is very pale and, shaking with a feverish chill, responds to Catarina's care only with a forced smile. She dejectedly leaves him. But in a kindly manner he calls her back and asks for a glass of water, which he drinks with a trembling hand. He then sits down on the couch, brusquely dismissing the old woman. He has barely had time to reflect on the events of this night and to cast an eye on his "Saint Cecilia" (that picture in which the ideal of form and tone flowed from the deepest wellsprings of his heart) before Catarina announces Taddeo.

Trembling with rage, Taddeo walks over and stands before Raphael. After some inner struggle, the latter rises with calm dignity and bids him be seated. The proud Taddeo bursts into a torrent of reproaches and threats and defiantly demands that Cecilia's favour be returned. Raphael calmly replies that he knows she prefers Taddeo to him. But he did not indifferently toss aside this ribbon, which is a memento of Cecilia. He will keep it as his rightful possession; for Cecilia shall be as eternally dear to him as is her picture in saintly form. Outraged at seeing his beloved portrayed without her knowledge, Taddeo forgets himself to the point that his noble pride makes him wish to humiliate the artist. Raphael bids him desist. Rapiers are drawn and Taddeo is wounded in the arm.

Frightened, Catarina comes rushing in. She is about to scold, but Raphael thinks only of binding up the wound. This kindness moves Taddeo. But once again there is pounding on the door. Raphael commits him to Catarina's care and goes to receive the stranger. It is Cardinal Divizio! Raphael's honourable patron is sorely distressed at what has happened, but wishes to straighten things out; and since he perceives that Raphael is in love with his niece, he gives his consent to their union.

But Raphael stops him. It is Taddeo whom Cecilia loves and she can only be happy with him. The cardinal is astonished, but Raphael calls his unfortunate rival out of the chamber and speaks warmly on his behalf. Moved by such generosity, Divizio feels a growing admiration for his chosen favourite and grants him what he asks. Taddeo and Cecilia shall be wed. They leave, but Taddeo returns to thank his benefactor. The latter embraces him and wishes to return the disputed ribbon. But Taddeo begs him to retain this keepsake and hastens away, blessing Raphael's magnanimity.

Worn out but at peace, the artist now retires. He has worked and played, fought and won. He has nothing left to desire. He is in need of rest. The faithful Cataraina prepares his bed, draws the curtains, and, when she notices that his sleep is feverish, decides to fetch a doctor.

In his dreams, Raphael sees the Madonna and angels beckoning him.

His disciples quietly enter, draw back the curtains from the window, and regard their sleeping master. They do not wish to disturb his rest, but he awakens of his own accord. His face is transfigured; he greets his friends and feels in the mood to work. Giulio Romano, who has felt his pulse, advises him not to exert himself. But Raphael points to the "Saint Cecilia," which needs the final brush strokes. With anxious forebodings, his pupils go to help him. He stands up and pauses to reflect upon his dream. He will paint; it must be done quickly, for it is almost over. He is seized once again with violent trembling. Giulio supports him, and in his feverish fantasy Raphael leads him over to the unfinished work, hands him his brush, and receives the young men's promises that they will obey Giulio as their master.

Raphael now feels new strength and desire and enthusiastically puts the finishing touches on his picture of "Saint Cecilia." She stands there, completed. Her earthly longing is at an end; her gaze is directed heavenward and a choir of angels calls her to the home of the blessed. Raphael steps back for a moment in order to view his work and falls to his knees in prayer and thanksgiving. He is no longer able to rise. Weeping, his friends carry him to the couch. Catarina returns with the doctors, who order bloodletting, and everyone stands around Raphael with mingled feelings of fright and hope, as he smiles at them with benign confidence.

FIFTH TABLEAU

The Via del Corso. Moccoli Night.

It is the last hour of Carnival. Maskers with candles in their hands swarm about everywhere. They try to extinguish each other's lights. Some attack; others defend. Kerchiefs are aflutter. Hats and bouquets fly through the air and firecrackers burst to the jubilant dancing of the crowd.

The stout baker, who is reconciled with his capricious wife, brings her to the final merriment of Carnival. Everywhere homage and compliments greet the beautiful Fornarina. Venus gives her the golden apple; knights and Saracens fight for her colours and a triumphal chariot awaits her. Francesco shares this honour, but not without new adversities.

Taddeo and Cecilia are the objects of admiration and congratulations. They are showered with flowers and Cecilia's light is the last one burning. Finally it, too, is extinguished, and the signal is given that Carnival is at an end. Then the bells sound from a nearby church. They do not ring as if for a celebration. Giulio Romano and Marcantonio announce their master's death, and with sorrow and lamentation the people, with torches in their hands, join the procession, which passes through the same streets where the festive brands of joy had burned only a short while ago.

SIXTH TABLEAU

The picture gallery in Raphael's palace.

On a raised dais stands a gilt sarcophagus at the head of which Raphael's last painting is held by children dressed as angels. Groups of mourners from all classes fill the hall. (Taddeo and Cecilia. Catarina and Paola.)

Leo X enters. Giulio Romano returns the ring he had given Raphael, and the august patron and friend bestows the laurels of immortality upon THE WORLD'S GREATEST ARTIST.

* * *

THE NEW PENELOPE,
OR THE SPRING FESTIVAL IN ATHENS

A Ballet in Two Acts by
August Bournonville

Music by Herman von Løvenskjold

Scenery by Troels Lund and Christian Ferdinand Christensen

Performed for the first time at the Royal Theatre, January 26, 1847

Characters

AMYNTAS, a chieftain	Hr. Bournonville
LEILA, his wife	Jfr. Nielsen
DEMETRI	Hr. Füssel
NICIDAS	Hr. Brodersen
MARCOS	Hr. Stramboe
HERACLES	Hr. Fredstrup
CONSTANTIN	Hr. Larcher
URSULA	Jfr. Larcher
A LITTLE BOY	Jfr. Walbom

GREEKS OF ALL CLASSES.

The action takes place in Athens in modern times.

ACT I

A chamber in Leila's house. To the right, a window and exit. In the background, a portrait of Amyntas.

Anxious and melancholy, Leila is embroidering a sash for her husband. But two years have already gone by since he went to sea. He was attacked by corsairs and most people think he was drowned; Leila alone believes him to be in captivity. If she only knew where, she would gladly give everything to ransom him. As a widow, she is pitied, and distinguished suitors are asking for her hand in marriage: the mighty Demetri and the talented Nicidas vie to please her. But the vehemence with which they both demand that she make a choice causes her to think of using the same ruse as the ancient Penelope to rid herself of her pressing suitors. She promises to decide in favour of one of them as soon as she has completed the sash on which she is working. The rivals conclude a forced peace and depart.

Night falls. Leila goes to sleep and dreams that she sees Amyntas overpowered and put in chains. His ship sinks and a bloodred horizon broods over the restless sea. But the sky soon brightens; Venus comes sailing past with her son. The goddess motions to the grief-stricken woman and bids Cupid bring Leila the cup containing the nectar of consolation.

Leila awakens. She remembers only the terrible part of her dream and frightens old Ursula by her outburst of despair. But the bells announce the loveliest day of spring. Hymns and the booming of cannon greet the dawn of the Resurrection. Hope awakens in everyone. Young maidens enter carrying green boughs in their hands, and Leila excitedly finishes her task. She throws the sash about her shoulders and rushes off to the festival, firmly convinced that today she will see Amyntas once more.

ACT II

A plain near Athens surrounded by several groups of trees. Midstage, the river Ilissos. On the far side of the river, the ruins of the Temple of Jupiter Olympios. Farther off can be seen the triumphal arch of Hadrian, the city of Athens, and the Acropolis.

The Greeks greet one another with joy and congratulations. They tie the bonds of friendship even tighter and forget old animosities on this solemn day, which is the festival of the rebirth of freedom and of nature. But it has not brought back Amyntas! For Leila there is nought but sorrow and a feeling of bitter loss. A little boy approaches her in friendly fashion and bids her drink from a golden cup. She remembers her dream, drinks from the cup, and immediately takes heart.

Demetri and Nicidas, who have noticed the finished sash, now step forth and demand that she make a definite choice. But at this moment there is bustling among the crowd. It is Marcos, who has returned home with his brave palikars, and he brings – Amyntas! Overcome with delight, Leila swoons, but she is soon restored to consciousness by her beloved's caresses. She throws herself into her husband's arms, kisses his hands, which still bear the marks of the barbarians' chains, and, together with the whole assembly, offers her thanks to Heaven for his salvation.

Amyntas tells of his struggles, his sufferings, and his deliverance by Marcos. "Was it with gold that you ransomed Amyntas?" asks Heracles. "No," he answers, "with steel." The little boy hands the cup of consolation to the dejected suitors. Their spirits are restored, the cup is passed around, joy fills all hearts, and Constantin gives the signal for the dances to begin.

> No. 1: INVITATION TO THE DANCE. (Pas de deux: Hoppe and Jfr. Funck)
> No. 2: BELT DANCE. Motif taken from modern Greek folk life.

(Messieurs Funck, Lund, Gade, and E. Stramboe; Mesdemoiselles Fredstrup, Norberg, Rostock, and L. Stramboe)

No. 3: BRIDAL DANCE. Motif taken partly from modern Greek folk ballads, partly from the twenty-third book of *The Odyssey*. (Pas de deux: Hr. Bournonville and Jfr. Nielsen)

No. 4: BOYS' DANCE. After nature.

No. 5: FINALE

    a) *Parthenon Hymn*. Leila, as Pallas Athena, dances surrounded by symbols of peace, joy, and art.

    b) *War Dance*. The Greeks fight and die for their native land.

    c) *Death March*. Pallas shrouds herself in mourning. The women give the martyr's palm to the fallen and the sons inherit their fathers' swords.

    d) *The Awakening of the Greeks*. The tutelar goddess of Athens tears the mourning crepe asunder, adorns her brow with flowers, and raises the banner of freedom. Swords and olive branches are intertwined and jubilant dances celebrate the memory of THE REBIRTH OF GREECE.

* * *

THE WHITE ROSE, OR SUMMER IN BRITTANY

A Ballet in One Act
by
August Bournonville

Music composed and arranged by Holger Simon Paulli

Performed for the first time September 20, 1847

Characters

THE MARQUIS AND HIS WIFE . . . . . . .Hr. Fredstrup and
                                                Jfr. Larcher

MERE BERNARD .Mad. Schouw
LA BRAVOURE, her son, a sergeant
  in the African *chasseurs* . . . . .Hr. Bournonville
ALIX, her daughter . . . . .Jfr. Fjeldsted
ANTOINE, a young farmhand . . . . .Hr. Hoppe
THE VILLAGE MAYOR . . . . .Hr. Stramboe
JEAN, ANDRE, FRANCOIS,

AND PIERRE	Füssel, Edv. Stramboe, Gade and Hoppensach
ROSE	Jfr. Petrine Fredstrup
A LITTLE BOY	Anna Walbom

Solo Dances

PAS DE DEUX: Hr. Hoppe and Jfr. Fjeldsted
PAS DE QUATRE (The Competition of the Rose-Brides): Mlles, Fjeldsted, Nielsen, Fredstrup, and Rostock
FINALE: Messieurs Funck, Brodersen, Lund; Mlles. Stramboe, Borup, Hammer and Egense

The action takes place in the present.

In Brittany, a number of customs from the Middle Ages have been retained, and they not infrequently come into conflict with present-day institutions. On his estate an old marquis has reinstituted the well-known medieval custom of annually giving a prize to the district's most virtuous maiden, who, though young and pretty, has not yet harkened to the voice of love.

The little god Cupid, who in the course of the year has been travelling the world over in all sorts of disguises, comes from the Spring Festival in Greece to the Corn Harvest in Brittany and exerts his magical influence.

In Africa, Bernard La Bravoure has won a Cross of the Legion d'Honneur and sergeant's stripes and now returns to his native soil to embrace his mother and sister and also to have the young recruits draw lots to see who will join the army. As it happens, all of these swains have sweethearts, each of whom is hoping to win "the white rose" and the dowry, with which they may buy their fiancés' freedom from military service. The conscription and the Festival of the Rose-Bride* here collide and, as a result of Cupid's presence, produce various complications. Even the local authorities are unable to resist his power.

The mayor of the village has an eye for the fair Alix and has promised Mere Bernard that he will take her daughter under his protection.

The drawing of lots takes place before the ceremony, but even the most stalwart lads are reluctant to become soldiers. The sorrow over a chosen number is as great as the joy that is felt at the selection of a free lot, and it is Alix's chosen one who has drawn Number 1. La Bravoure seeks to balance the mood and stirs his countrymen with the paean "*Allons, enfants de la patrie!*"

The master and mistress [of the estate] enter just as the excitement

---

* *In French, rosière* – Trans.

is at its peak, but find that this spectacle has little to do with the festive occasion that has brought them hither. However, they are soon mollified by the villagers' expression of sincere devotion.

The ceremony begins and they move on to the selection of the Rose-Bride, which would appear to be somewhat difficult with so many winsome maidens to choose from. The mayor, who is well aware of Alix's virtuosity in dancing, recommends that the rivals perform a changing dance [*Vexeldands*], wherein the victor shall win the prize. They find the idea charming. The competition takes place and Alix wins the rose and the dowry. Now she can not only choose herself a bridegroom but, by her fortune, can remove all obstacles to their joint happiness. The mayor is disappointed in his expectations, for Antoine is the one she prefers. Her brother's consent and her mother's blessing unite the lovers, and the gracious marquis and his wife open the ball with the young couple.

After the marquis and his spouse have left the celebration, the rejoicing becomes more boisterous and the unknown boy enlivens the dancing with his drum. But – the hour for departure is drawing nigh. The conscripts must leave their homes and they part from their loved ones with heavy hearts. They are already on the other side of the stream when they notice that they have forgotten to take *the boy* along. The drum and the dance beckon them anew. They rush back again into the arms of their friends and have one last whirl before setting off.

*   *   *

OLD MEMORIES, OR A MAGIC LANTERN

A Ballet in One act
by
August Bournonville

Music arranged by Edvard Helsted

Performed for the first time on the occasion of the hundredth anniversary of the Danish Royal Theatre, December 18, 1848

In a hundred years all's been forgot,
So the old ballad goes.
The work of Art lies wrapt in dust,
Moldering away with its laurels.
But the *Idea of Beauty* still endures
And Art itself shall never fade
While from Olympus' lofty peak

Sunlight's rays to its altar stray.

Characters

PHILEMON, one hundred years old .... Hr. Axel Fredstrup
PHILEMON THE YOUNGER,
   seventy years old .... Hr. Fredstrup, Sr.
BAUCIS, his wife .... Jfr. Larcher
LUDVIG, a naval officer ⎫   ⎧ Hr. Stramboe
JOHANNES, an army officer ⎬ their sons ⎨ Hr. Füssel, Sr.
HERMANN, an artist ⎭   ⎩ Hr. Brodersen
CAROLINE, married to Ludvig .... Mad. Schouw
ANNA, married to Johannes .... Jfr. J. Fredstrup
VINCENZO ⎫   ⎧ Hr. Hoppe
CLAUDIUS ⎪   ⎪ Hr. Funck
ANTON ⎬ Grandchildren of Philemon ⎨ Hr. Ed. Stramboe
AGLAE ⎪ the Younger   ⎪ Jfr. Fjeldsted
THALIA ⎪   ⎪ Jfr. Nielsen
EUPHROSINE ⎭   ⎩ Jfr. Funck
LARS ⎫   ⎧ Hr. Hoppensach
GRETHE ⎭ Servants   ⎩ Jfr. P. Fredstrup
GREAT-GRANDCHILDREN, YOUNG AND ADOLESCENT.
GUESTS OF ALL AGES.

The scene is laid at a manor house in the year 1848.

[**Translator's note**: An occasional piece, this work was hastily composed as the Ballet's contribution to the celebration of the Danish Royal Theatre's centenary in 1848. A magic lantern presented to the theatre-loving centenarian, Philemon, produces animated representations of characters and scenes from the masterworks of celebrated Danish playwrights and choreographers, as well as living portraits of "luminaries" of the Danish stage.]

SCENE ONE

Philemon's study.

    Great-grandfather is dozing in his armchair. Grethe busily tiptoes about the room. The old man's son and his wife quietly enter. They learn that he is asleep and give the maid some instructions. With a feeling of deep emotion, the elderly couple approach the father's chair and, while the son reverently kneels, the daughter-in-law winds Philemon's clock. He is *one hundred years* old today!

(Melody by Schulz)

The younger Philemon's sons come to congratulate their grandfather. Grethe brings flowers. The bouquets are handed out. Hermann has arranged a little celebration. Everyone takes their places behind the armchair and, at a signal, render the tune that was Philemon's cradle song.

(*"Dance of the Fairies"* from Gluck's *Armide*)

The old man wakens as from a pleasant dream, listens to the music, and looks about him in amazement. He is overwhelmed with bouquets and congratulations, and only now does he remember that today is his birthday. His heart is gladdened by the familiar sounds and every phrase of the melody ushers in a group from the younger generation: stalwart lads, lovely lasses, little boys and girls, and, last of all, on his mother's arm, the youngest member of the family – the apple of his great – grandfather's eye. His arms filled with flowers, the old man stands surrounded by a joyous cluster of people.

(Melody: *Hvor mon man bedre er end blandt sin Slaegt og Venner / Where Is One Better Off Than Among One's Friends and Relations*)

Philemon's delight is indescribable, but it wearies him a bit. The family leads him over to his armchair and, kneeling, receives his blessing.

Letters and newspapers arrive. Philemon lays hold of a playbill.

Its contents sadden him, for he, who was once an avid playgoer, must now relinquish the pleasure that brightened and beautified his younger days. But Hermann invites him to the festival arranged in his honour. Exciting music in the distance summons everyone.

(March from *Herman von Unna*)

His son and daughter-in-law stay behind to help the old man dress. But father and son now quarrel over a coat, which the former does not want to put on, and Philemon becomes so angry that he decides to stay in his room. Baucis soothes him with a caress and the son must apologize and give in to his father's wishes. They are about to leave when the old man suddenly halts, changes his mind, and asks for his coat. He pretends to chastise his seventy-year-old boy, takes his daughter-in-law by the arm, and departs.

SCENE TWO

A large room arranged for a theatrical performance. To the right, a seat on a dais for Philemon.

Friends, neighbours, and artists, together with all the young people, have gathered, and they heed the advice Hermann gives them so that they may receive the old man in worthy fashion. He arrives.

("Welcome March" from Lagertha by Schall)

A festive reception. Rejoicing and emotion. Graceful dancing by the younger Philemon's granddaughters, who entwine their greatgrandfather with garlands and, as if by enchantment, transport him back to the springtime of youth.

("Bridal Dance" from Lagertha)

A flock of children gather round Philemon, and as a birthday present the youngest of them hands him a Magic Lantern in which he will see his fondest memories of the theatre pass before him. New surprises are in store for him. He is conducted to his seat. The lamp is lit, the lights are dimmed, and the curtain rises.

The playhouse can be seen in the distance. The fairy Armida arrives in her dragon-chariot, extends her wand, and transforms it into an enchanted castle. Holberg and Ewald inaugurate it. The curtain falls, the lights come up, and an Arcadian shepherd and shepherdess in the rococo style dance a pas de deux.

Chaconne, 1760. Motif after Noverre.
(Danced by Hr. S. Lund and Jfr. Rostock)

FLEETING PICTURES OF ARTISTS OF THE THEATRE

1. Rose (deb. 1747). A group from *The Fidget* by Holberg.
2. Schwarz (deb. 1773) and Mme. Preisler (deb. 1778). *Emilia Galotti.*
3. Rosing (deb. 1777) and Caroline Walter (deb. 1762). *Balder's Death.*
    (All of the above to music by Hartmann the Elder)

Norwegian Springdans, 1786. Motif after Galeotti.
(Danced by Hr. Edward Stramboe and Jfr. Laura Stramboe)

4. Galeotti (deb. 1775). Group from *Lagertha.* (Music by Schall.)
5. Bournonville the Elder (deb. 1792). *Rolf Bluebeard.* (Music by Schall.)
6. Chr. Knudsen (deb. 1786). Group of Danish sailors. (Music by DuPuy.)

Hornpipe from the entrée *The Fisherman,* 1798.
Motif after Bournonville the Elder.
(Danced by Hr. Hoppe, Mlles. P. Fredstrup and Amalie Price)

7. Lindgreen (deb. 1790). Group from *Jeppe of the Hill.* (Distinctive melody.)
8. Ryge (deb. 1813). Melpomene carves his name upon a menhir,

while a Giant sounds the Gjallar-Horn. (Heroic ballad from *Hakon Jarl*.)

9. Frydendahl (deb. 1786). Thalia hands him her wreath. Comus groans with laughter, and a Genius contemplates Thorvaldsen's "The Graces." (Music: "From East to West am I loudly praised," from *The Sleeping Draught* by Weyse.)

The Present, personified by three gay young Italian couples (Mlles. Fjeldsted, Nielsen, and Funck; Messieurs Funck, Brodersen, and Lund), summon a merry throng to the festival. The Saltarello is danced to the jangling of tambourines, while fresh garlands form a bower of vine-leaves over the dancers. The younger Philemon brings his father a cup. The refreshing juice of the grape shall strengthen the old man and bring pearls of memory to the surface of the beaker. One after the other, Mature Age, Youth, and Childhood pay their homage to the aged guest of honour (while Weyse's melody "An Artist Strolls by the Tiber's Shores" gives expression to the solemn note in the atmosphere). He salutes the assembled guests and drinks to the health and happiness of the coming generation. The background parts to reveal a group dominated by the all – enlivening Phoebus Apollo – the god of light, warmth, and art.

Characters in the Tableaux and Secondary Groups

	ARMIDA	Jfr. Andersen
TAB. 1:	VIELGESCHREY	Hr. Hoppensach
	PERNILLE	Jfr. Werning
	LEANDER	Hr. Nehm, Jr.
	OLDFUX	Hr. Bentzen
TAB. 2:	ODOARDO	Hr. Füssel, Sr.
	EMILIA	Jfr. Egdrup
TAB. 3:	HOTHER	Hr. Gade
	VALKYRIES	Mad. Møller, Mlles. Amundin and Holm
TAB. 4:	REGNAR LODBROG	Hr. Ring
	LAGERTHA	Mad. Møller
	THE CHILDREN	Gjødesen and Madsen
TAB. 5:	ROLF BLUEBEARD	Hr. Füssel, Sr.
	APPARITIONS	Mad. Stramboe, Mlles. Eggers and Egense
TAB. 6:	SAILORS	Messieurs Stramboe, Füssel, Jr., Borch, Brauer, Stendrup
TAB. 7:	JEPPE	Hr. Hoppensach
	DOCTORS	Hr. Nehm, Sr., Hr. Bentzen

TAB. 8: MELPOMENE .... Jfr. Fabricius
        THE GIANT .... Hr. Füssel, Jr.
TAB. 9: THALIA
        COMUS
        GENIUS

ITALIAN PEASANT-FOLK: Messieurs Busch, Ring, Borch,
                        Andersen, Nehm, Jr., Brauer,
                        Stendrup, Carpentier, Miles.
                        Holm, Eggers, Hammer, Egdrup,
                        Egense, Weming, Amundin,
                        Rasmussen.
CHILDREN: Boys: Scharff, Møller, Paetch. Girls: Olsen,
            Walbom, Nielsen, Holm, Juel, Gjødesen, Madsen,
            Smith, and the youngest of Philemon's grand-
            children – little Thorvald Price.
APOLLO .... Hr. Gade

* * *

CONSERVATORIET, OR A PROPOSAL OF MARRIAGE THROUGH THE NEWSPAPER

A Vaudeville-Ballet in Two Acts
by
August Bournonville

Music arranged and composed by Holger Simon Paulli

Performed for the first time at the Royal Theatre,
May 6, 1849

Characters

DUFOUR, *Inspecteur* at the
    Conservatoire .... Hr. Hoppensach
MAMSEL BONJOUR, his housekeeper .... Jfr. J. Fredstrup
ELIZA   ⎫   ⎧ Jfr. J. Price
           ⎬ *danseuses*   ⎨
VICTORINE ⎭   ⎩ Jfr. Funck
ALEXIS, *danseur* and teacher .... Hr. Hoppe
ERNESTE, first-prize winner in the
    violin competition .... Hr. Funck
RAIMBAUD, a fiddler .... Hr. Füssel

JEANNE, his wife, a harpist			Mme. Møller
FANNY, their daughter			Jfr. S. Price
JULES OSCAR	} students	{	Hr. Brodersen Hr. Edv. Stramboe
ADELE FIFINE	} grisettes	{	Jfr. P. Fredstrup Jfr. Stramboe
LAROSE, restaurateur			Hr. Fredstrup

Subordinate Characters

DANCE PUPILS: Mlles. A. Price, Borup, Hammer, and Egense
PEASANTS: Hr. Füssel, Jr., and Mme. Stramboe
STUDENTS: Messieurs Gade, Lund, Andersen, and Nehm
GRISETTES: Mlles. Weming, Holm, Eggersen, and Lumbye
GUESTS OF EVERY CLASS OF SOCIETY, DANCE PUPILS, MUSICIANS, AND WAITERS.

The action takes place in recent times.

ACT I: The Dancing School of the Paris Conservatoire
ACT II: The restaurant of the Pavillon Henri IV at St.-Germain-en-Laye (three miles from Paris)

ACT I

A salle de danse with almost no furniture. Doors to the sides and in the middle.

SCENE ONE

Dufour, in dishabille, enters, deeply engrossed in reading a newspaper. He is pursued by his housekeeper, who showers him with reproaches to which he does not seem to pay any attention. She wants to know why he is taking such a keen interest in this newspaper. She tears it away from him and discovers that he has advertised himself as an anonymous suitor. Dufour, who wishes to give up his bachelor status, flatters himself with the thought that his personal merits will secure him a favourable match. But Mamsel Bonjour, to whom he had made a promise of marriage in earlier days, becomes disconsolate, curses the faithless fellow, and faints in a chair. In the utmost embarrassment, Dufour grabs a watering can in order to revive the swooning damsel. There is a loud knock at the door, Mamsel jumps up, and Raimbaud and his daughter enter.

SCENE TWO

Dufour and his housekeeper receive the strangers with rather rude hastiness. The old fiddler introduces his daughter as a budding dancer and asks that she be accepted into the Dancing School as a pupil. Without waiting for a reply, he takes out his violin, and little Fanny gives proof of her ability there and then. The merciless judges find her dancing wretched, and Dufour refers these poor artists to the *théatre forain*. Raimbaud is furious, but his daughter calms his righteous indignation and, broken-hearted, they both leave the Conservatoire.

SCENE THREE

Alexis, at the head of a group of pupils, comes dancing in and greets the Inspecteur, who, embarrassed at his dishabille, wishes to leave the room. But the children encircle him, tug at his dressing gown, and play countless little tricks on him. Eliza and Victorine pay him so many compliments that, in ecstasy, Dufour offers them bonbons. The children rush forward to plunder the paper cone. Alexis sprinkles Dufour with the watering can while the ladies laugh at him. At last he becomes really angry and hurries off, pursued by laughter and merriment.

SCENE FOUR

The signal is given for the class to begin, and with the utmost seriousness the dancers all commence their exercises, which are led in turn by Alexis and the female soloists.

Pas d'école with variations

Erneste, a young violinist, enters, exulting over his good fortune. He has won first prize in the Conservatoire's competition and is bringing his laurels to Eliza, the sole possessor of his love. The successful artist is congratulated and embraced. Alexis, who is also a prisoner of Cupid, looks imploringly at the roguish Victorine.

They are to try out a dance for the next opera performance.

Accompanied by Erneste on the violin, Alexis, Eliza, and Victorine perform

A brilliant pas de trois.

The class is over. The ladies take a rest. The children leave to get dressed and people inquire as to the news of the day. Erneste tells them of an amusing matrimonial advertisement; but the matter really gains interest with the arrival of Mamsel Bonjour, since she informs them that it is none other than M. Dufour who intends to enter the state of matrimony in this adventurous way. She bursts into tears and displays the antiquated promise of marriage which she always carries with her.

The young people are struck with the idea of playing a trick on the vain Dufour in order to avenge the deceived spinster. They decide to put in an appearance at the site of his rural rendezvous. Erneste looks at his watch. They must catch the next train for St. Germain. This will be glorious fun. They promise Mamsel Bonjour their zealous assistance and hasten to prepare for their imminent pleasure trip.

SCENE FIVE

Dufour enters, trying to finish dressing as quickly as possible.

Without showing bitterness, Mamsel helps him with his toilet, receives his orders, and hands him his hat and umbrella. Dufour would like to explain, but he hears the train's shrill whistle and rushes off so as not to be late. Left alone, Mamsel gives in to her grief. The children, who have learned that there is to be a pleasure trip, beg Mamsel to take them out to the country. She finds this idea appealing and it fits in nicely with her scheme to thwart Dufour's plan. But who shall pay the costs? The pupils are not at a loss. They break open their money box, quickly dress Mamsel, hop about her, mad with delight, and lead her off in triumph.

ACT II

The restaurant of the Pavillon Henri IV on the terrace at St.-Germain On all sides, tables and garden chairs, boskquets and flower beds. In the background is revealed the glorious prospect across the valley of the Seine to Paris.

SCENE ONE

Larose is busy arranging everything for the evening. Waiters run back and forth. A great many customers are expected at the Pavillon.

A merry crowd of students and grisettes returns from strolling and fishing. They give the host their order for a repast and bring him their catch. Several peasants offer the party donkey rides. This proposal is accepted with delight; riding crops are handed out and, pawing and prancing, they perform a contredanse that, in its gaiety, is reminiscent of Chaumiere's balls and Mussard's masquerades.

SCENE TWO

Raimbaud and his wife sadly gaze after the merry band, who rush off to new delights. There is nothing for them to earn here.

The wife strives in vain to alleviate her husband's deep distress. "Here comes our child. What will become of her?" With a tambourine in one hand and a bouquet in the other, Fanny comes skipping toward her parents. She hands her father the fresh bouquet and tries to cheer him by her dancing. But this only increases his dejection. "Surely she can never become an artiste." A man officiously enters the Pavillon, orders some chocolate, and sits down at a table. The family immediately wants to put on a little concert for him; but he covers both ears with his hands and, irritably giving them some alms, begs them to just go away. Raimbaud has recognized [him as] the *Inspecteur* from that morning. He hides his sensitivity and with dignity puts the coin back on the table, hoping that Providence will grant him a less humiliating reward for his art. The family bows and exits.

SCENE THREE

Alone and engrossed in his plans, Dufour senses the significance of the impending moment, which is to bring him a companion on the pathway of life. The waiter announces a veiled lady. There now follows a scene of "advances," sentimentality, and roguishness. Dufour tries in vain to persuade the lady to lift her veil. This results in a graceful allemande, in which everyone, with the exception of Dufour, recognizes the piquant Eliza. She demands proof of his faithfulness before she will make herself known to him. She allows him to kiss her hand, promises to return, and exits.

SCENE FOUR

The captivated Dufour is gazing rapturously after the departing beauty when a thickset chap, half-civilian and half-soldier, claps him on the shoulder and warns him against proposing to this lady; for if he does, he, as her declared lover, will know how to emphasize his claim. Most unpleasantly surprised, Dufour renounces his earlier expectations and the fellow, who suddenly becomes quite jovial, orders schnapps, forces his rival to have one, and bids him farewell with a vigorous handshake.

SCENE FIVE

Indignant and annoyed, Dufour upbraids Larose, who, being privy to this little intrigue, can hardly contain his laughter. A lady dressed somewhat according to English fashion approaches. A little groom follows after her and obeys her orders. She sits down, peers at Dufour through her lorgnette, and asks if it is he who has made the proposal of marriage in the newspaper. He seems to please this lady. She praises his physique and declares that he must dance the Polka superbly. Dufour, who has never in his life danced the Polka, allows himself to be carried away by the damsel's flattery and hops about with her as best he can. Luncheon is served, but when the service is not prompt enough, Dufour goes inside to hurry the host along. Meanwhile, an elegant Hussar has sat down next to the lady, and Dufour is startled to no small degree when, on his return, he finds his seat occupied and the luncheon in full swing. He becomes livid, but the young couple drinks a toast to him, and with an ironic salute, Victorine polkas off with Erneste, who has arranged both their disguises.

SCENE SIX

Dufour is about ready to die of moritification. He sinks into his chair at the table with his face in his hands, totally exhausted. An elderly, rather corpulent lady enters. She is quite warm and flustered after a long promenade, sits down at the table, pulls the cork out of the bottle, and with a "by your leave..." pours herself a glass of wine, nods amiably to Dufour, and drinks. He does not seem at all flattered by this company, but when she begins to count the interest money she has just drawn out of the bank, Dufour's heart warms. He learns that she is a widow and decides to settle his choice on her. He is so fortunate as to please Madame, receives her "Yes," and rushes off to have the marriage contract drawn up.

SCENE SEVEN

Erneste, Eliza, and Victorine surround and congratulate Alexis on his successful disguise, for it was he who played the widow. Now, once again using the dance as his medium of expression, he performs several tremendous jumps and pirouettes, to the great delight of his comrades. But a numerous crowd of guests arrives at the Pavillon and Larose calls Alexis in so that he can get dressed. The three sit down at one of the garden tables.

SCENE EIGHT

Guests flock to the restaurant. One notices a number of foreign families, Parisians, officers, peasants and laundresses from the neighbourhood, and, finally, the merry company from the donkey ride. The waiters are busy; the tables are filled; and refreshments are being enjoyed by everyone.

Raimbaud, together with his wife and daughter, wishes to make music, but it is impossible for them to capture anyone's attention. They are standing, crestfallen, in the midst of this merry throng when Erneste jumps up, goes over to them, asks to borrow the violin, and tackles it with such virtuosity that everyone is astounded. They all leave their tables and flock to where the lovely tones are resounding. The enchantment of the eye soon mingles with the rhythms of the music. Two graceful sylphides glide into the circle. The garden of the Pavillon is transformed into a stage, the tables and chairs into a gallery and a parterre. The trio is greeted with thunderous applause and admiration for art is blended with acknowledgment of nobility of soul. The tambourine is passed around and filled to the brim with coins and bank notes. The poor family is aided and Fanny is adopted by the pretty *danseuses*, who promise to guide her along the pathway of art.

SCENE NINE

Dufour, who has fetched a notary, enters, out of breath and searching high and low for his fiancée. Eliza and Victorine reveal themselves to have been his first two matches and Erneste the unwelcome cavalier. Dufour, who is at first astonished at these transformations, laughs it off, pretends to know everything, and informs them that he is seriously betrothed to a rich lady. But Alexis steps forth, curtsies, returns his ring, and confesses his imposture. Dufour stands as if turned to stone. Merriment and noise is heard. It is the children from the Dancing School, who encircle and bedeck Mamsel Bonjour with garlands. Dufour returns to his senses and introduces Mamsel Bonjour as his bride. This pleasure party and mutual affection have sealed the bonds between Erneste and Eliza, Alexis and Victorine, and the notary now has three marriage contracts to draw up. General satisfaction. Raimbaud has assembled a whole orchestra and joy is expressed in merry dancing.

* * *

THE IRRESISTIBLES

A Divertissement
by
August Bournonville

Music composed by Hans Christian Lumbye

Performed for the first time at the Royal Theatre,
Sunday, February 3, 1850

Characters

THE COMMANDER IN CHIEF
   OF THE SQUADRON . . . . Mad. Kellermann

THE LIEUTENANTS . . . . ⎰ Jfr. Funck
                                        ⎱ Jfr. P. Fredstrup
                                        Jfr. Juliette Price

Buglers

Mlles. Olsen, Walbom, Nielsen

Hussars

Mlles. Stramboe, Rostock, A. Price, S. Price, Lumbye, Garlieb, Holm, Werning, Borup, Eggersen, Hammer

VICTORIA . . . . .Mad. Møller
ROLF KRAKE . . . . .Hr. Gade

ELVES, WORTHIES, GIANTS.

The stage represents a grove, in the centre of which stands a statue of the Goddess of Flowers. The background is a Danish landscape.

A squadron of hussars enters in platoons, executes a number of evolutions, and makes several swift charges, in closed as well as open order.

They rally round their precious standard, look upon it as something sacred, and swear to defend it to the last man. They hang up their weapons and standard near the statue of Flora, enjoy the rest that comes with peace, and amuse themselves by merry dancing. The goddess calls forth a blossom from the bosom of the earth; elves emerge from the woods with garlands, wherewith they entwine the hussars, and Flora is transformed into Victoria, who tosses wreaths to the braves. Once again, they enthusiastically take up their arms and their standard and march past to the tune of "The Brave Soldier."

The background is filled with memories of antiquity: Worthies float on clouds and hail the younger generation, while one espies Rolf Krake marching across the fire with his giants.

Note

This is not the first time that combat has been likened to a dance, and Danish valour has this in common with that of the French: it does not preclude pleasant merriness. In Napoleon's army there were demi-brigades which bore the names *La redoutable, L'invincible, L'indomptable, L'irrésistible*. Therefore, it is not in jest that this divertissement is called *The Irresistibles*. Should it contain a humorous element, this can be justified as *totally Danish*, because it robs the title of any trace of sentimentality or boastfulness.

* * *

PSYCHE

A Ballet in One Act
by
August Bournonville

Music composed and arranged by Edvard Helsted

Scenery by Christian Ferdinand Christensen and Troels Lund

First performed at the Royal Theatre, Copenhagen, May 7, 1850

Characters

CUPID	Jfr. Stramboe
PSYCHE	Jfr. J. Price
MYRIS } her sisters	Jfr. Funck
LEDA }	Jfr. P. Fredstrup
ZEPHYR	Hr. Hoppe
FLORA	Jfr. S. Price
VENUS	Jfr. Lumbye
APOLLO	Hr. Gade
PLUTO	Hr. Fredstrup
PROSERPINA	Mme. Møller
JUPITER	Hr. Füssel, Sr.
NYMPHS OF FLORA'S RETINUE	Jfr. Borup
	Jfr. S. Price
	Jfr. Garlieb
	Jfr. Borup
THE EUMENIDES	Hr. Lund
	Hr. Stramboe
	Hr. Nehm
THE PARCAE	Jfr. Larcher
	Jfr. Amundin
	Jfr. Fredstrup

THE GODS OF OLYMPUS. NYMPHS. ZEPHYRS. CUPIDS.
SPIRITS AND SHADES OF THE UNDERWORLD. DREAM PICTURES.

FOREWORD

Thorvaldsen's masterworks and Paludan-Müller's charming poem have sufficiently acquainted our public with the meaningful legend of Psyche. It would therefore be superfluous to give a historical introduction, much less an interpretation, of the deep allegory one encounters in every feature of this myth, "where the Soul, seeking an invisible Godhead, is snatched from Death by the omnipotence of Love and led to eternal Life." Such an abstract theme would not have been in the least suitable for representation as a ballet had not poetry and the art of sculpture arrayed it in forms of such rapturous beauty that dance could find no worthier standard for its striving in the footsteps of the fine arts. I myself am aware of such an effort, and it has always been my greatest encouragement when people have perceived in my works something more than the bouquet which dazzles the eye with the splendor of its colours; for it is the fragrance of the flower which is its "psyche."

Training and virtuosity have often been the enemies of Beauty, and their influence has been especially destructive to the true and noble meaning of the Dance. Although my better judgment has always been opposed to the excesses produced by a jaded taste, without giving in to them I have all too often been forced to concede them more than I deemed admissible for art.

But *this time* I have torn myself loose from all secondary considerations. Perhaps I have done so at the expense of that effect which is so tempting in the relationship with the audience. For Psyche performs no *pas d'ecole*; she executes neither pirouettes nor tours de force. The performance becomes no dazzling fireworks display but, if possible, a stroll through a museum where lifelike statues, groupings, cameos, and bas-reliefs alternate with one another. May this attempt in a purer artistic direction succeed and be recognized as a confession of faith in the profession to which I have dedicated by activity. May it help to accomplish the honourable task which has been given the Ballet of the Danish Royal Theatre, that is, "of developing a feeling for Beauty."

SCENE ONE

A hall in Cupid's palace. Through the open door a luxuriant a landscape can be seen. Dawn.

Cupid, (who though invisible to his beloved, has hidden her from his mother's wrath), stands by the slumbering Psyche and regards her with tenderness while the following dream pictures drift past her:

Venus ordering a sea-monster to devour Psyche.

Psyche's initiation into Death.

The Zephyrs carrying Psyche away through the air.

Parents and sisters at Psyche's grave.

But day dawns and Cupid must away. He summons Zephyr and Flora and bids them while away the time for Psyche, always hovering about her invisibly. When evening falls, he will return once more.

SCENE TWO

Zephyr and Flora, together with their retinue, are about to carry out Cupid's orders, but Psyche awakens and they vanish. She is still uncertain whether it is dream or reality that surrounds her. She looks about with mounting astonishment and tries in vain to collect her thoughts. She hears delightful melodies; her couch is adorned with blossoms, and the table is filled with refreshments. But the obliging spirits constantly hide themselves from Psyche's gaze and gather wherever she cannot see them. An unseen hand places a garland upon her head. She perceives it only when she catches sight of her reflection in the brimming cup. Her memory returns; she recalls the circumstances which have borne her away from her ancestral home. She is tormented by a yearning for her loved ones. She wishes to write to them, but who will deliver the letter? She feels dreadfully alone and abandoned. Filled with dejection, she bursts into tears.

SCENE THREE

Flora and her handmaidens are unable to resist Psyche's tears. They reveal themselves to her, and her surprise is as great as her delight. Zephyr reproaches them for having disobeyed their master's orders; but Psyche, who notices his wings, asks him to take a message to her sisters. Zephyr tries to demur, but he is assailed with pleas, eventually gives in, and hastens away. Flora and her retinue finish dressing Psyche and adorn her with flowers and precious jewels.

SCENE FOUR

Zephyr brings Myris and Leda. Psyche throws herself into their arms and overwhelms them with caresses, and they all express the liveliest joy at the reunion. The sisters are astounded at all the magnificence that surrounds them: the splendid palace and the festive repast. They ask if Zephyr is Psyche's spouse; but Flora is quick to correct this error. The merry couple adds life to the festivities. Music is heard and dancing expresses the joyous mood.

SCENE FIVE

Darkness falls. Zephyr reminds the sisters that they must depart. Myris and Leda, who are envious of the good fortune which seems to have befallen Psyche, are furious at everything they see, even at the costly presents they themselves have received. They try to awaken doubt and suspicion in their sister's mind and feign sorrow at the cruel fate that destines her to be the prize of a monster. They counsel her to free herself from his power by lulling him to sleep and then killing him. Psyche listens to their plans with horror. But the hour of departure is at hand; they must leave, and Zephyr takes them back to their home.

The handmaidens help Psyche undress and try to banish her grief. Soon the master will be here – they kiss the lovely maiden good-bye and depart.

SCENE SIX

Filled with forebodings, Psyche is sitting, lost in thought, but starts in fright when she feels a kiss on her shoulder. It is he, the invisible creature "more ferocious than a lion, more wily than a snake."* She manifests fearful anxiety, but the tenderness that accompanies his expressions soon erases her dark suspicions and the presence of the deity fills her with unknown exhilaration.

She takes up the lyre in order to delight her lover with its sounds, and, while listening to its lovely melodies, he discovers the anesthetizing poppy that Myris has placed at the head of her bed. It has an instantaneous effect, and he falls into a profound slumber. Psyche remembers her sister's advice. She fetches a lamp and, with upraised dagger, approaches the bed of the sleeping creature. But what can equal her bliss when in this bewinged youth she recognizes Cupid himself! The lamp trembles so violently in her hand that the burning oil falls upon his shoulder and wakens him. Terrified at finding himself discovered and known, he reproaches Psyche for her curiosity, which has forever ruined their peace. Pleading, she throws herself at his feet and with a thousand caresses tries to atone for her guilt; but Cupid, who has seen through her suspicions and caught sight of the dagger that threatens his life, tears himself loose from her. The messenger of Fate separates them, and the grief-stricken deity abandons the disconsolate Psyche.

SCENE SEVEN

Cupid's palace is transformed into a rocky wilderness. Left to her despair, Psyche is about to kill herself when an old woman stops and disarms her. As a mark of sympathy, she shows Psyche a mirror that reflects her features grown old and wrinkled: "Cupid abandons thee because thou has lost thy beauty. If thou wouldst regain it, thou must fetch it back from the Underworld." Shuddering, Psyche refuses to follow the woman's advice; but the latter throws off her garb and stands before the quivering maiden, not as the amourous Venus but as the wrathful goddess. At a sign from Venus, the Eumenides spring forth. They seize Psyche, who in vain cries for mercy, and carry her down to the Underworld.

---

* The utterance of the Oracle.

SCENE EIGHT

Venus is standing in a luxuriant grove, where she receives the acclaim of Flora, Zephyr, and their retinue. Cupid enters. She knows his sorrow and tries to console him by signifying that he is now avenged. But he is terrified, breaks into lamentations and reproaches, shatters his bow, and wishes to call down the wrath of the gods upon his mother... Venus throws herself into her son's arms and promises to do everything in her power to compensate for the loss of his beloved. But it is too late! She belongs to the Kingdom of the Dead!

Accompanied by his nine sisters, Apollo, the God of Poetry, comes to bring consolation to the distressed. He opens his embrace to the unhappy Cupid, who, weeping, falls on his breast. He encourages him, like Orpheus, to fetch his beloved from the Underworld and bestows upon him his lyre, with which he can overcome the horrors of Death. Cupid feels a resurgence of strength. He enthusiastically seizes the divine harp, embraces his benefactor, is reconciled with his mother, and hastens off to save his beloved.

SCENE NINE

The entrance to Tartarus. A vaulted hall made of rock, illuminated by the reflection of the River of Fire. Pluto is seated on his throne, with Proserpina standing at his side. In her hand she holds the urn containing Psyche's earthly beauty. The Parcae bring Psyche before the sovereigns of the Underworld. Pluto asks her what she wants. Pointing to the urn, she tremblingly asks for the restoration of her lost beauty. Cerberus, who rattles his chains, announces that a stranger is approaching. The Shades are terrified, the Furies rage wildly, and Pluto is astonished at the fact that so presumptuous a man dares approach the abode of Death. He takes Psyche away with him, and Proserpina stays behind with a host of spirits who are to defend the entrance.

Cupid advances; the Shades and Eumenides are forced to recoil before the celestial strains of the lyre, and his pleas soften their wrath.

The cold, unbending Proserpina signifies that Psyche now belongs to her; therefore all of Cupid's efforts will be to no avail. But the all-enlivening god does not allow himself to be deterred by her contempt. He seizes her hand, places it on his breast, approaches her with tenderness, and infuses his warmth into her icy heart. Long-effaced memories, slumbering emotions, once again gain mastery over the Queen of the Dead. Tears fill her eyes; she bows before the power of Love, and enfolds Cupid in her embrace. He is victorious! The Furies and Shades, who, overwhelmed, had fallen before the feet of the magnificent being, rise enthusiastically, lift him in triumph, and lead him to the King of the Underworld.

TENTH AND LAST SCENE

Psyche enters with the treasure which shall restore her lost happiness and disarm the goddess's revenge. She longs to try the magic power; she cannot resist her curiosity and opens the urn... but an anesthetizing smoke arises from it; flames whirl about Psyche; the Parcae already drift past, and the ferocious Atropus lifts her shears to sever the thread of life. But Cupid rushes in, stops the Parcae, and takes Psyche in his arms. He implores the gods to place his beloved among the immortals. When he touches her heart with his arrow, she is restored to life. He presses a kiss on her lips, and butterfly wings sprout from her shoulders. Now they belong to each other forever, and radiant Olympus is revealed to them. Reconciled, Venus leads them to the altar and Jupiter summons them to share in the delight of the gods.

* * *

THE KERMESSE* IN BRUGES, OR THE THREE GIFTS
(Kermessen i Brugge)

A Romantic Ballet in Three Acts by
August Bournonville

Music by Holger Simon Paulli

First performed at the Royal Theatre, Copenhagen, April 4, 1851

Characters

MIREWELT, an alchemist	Hr. Füssel, Sr.
ELEONORE, his daughter	Jfr. Juliette Price
SARA, his housekeeper	Jfr. Larcher
TRUTJE, a townswoman	Jrf. J. Fredstrup
MARCHEN, JOHANNA } her daughters	{ Jrf. A. Price, Jfr. Stramboe
ADRIAN, GEERT, CARELIS } brothers, young burghers	{ Hr. Brodersen, Hr. Hoppensach, Hr. Hoppe
VAN DER STEEN, VAN HOËCK } noblemen	{ Hr. Gade, Hr. Nehm, Jr.
FRU VAN EVERDINGEN, a rich widow	Mme. Møller
POTTER, the burgomaster	Hr. Füssel, Jr.

---

* Every town in the Low Countries celebrates the feast day of the patron saint of its principal church with an annual bacchanalian fair, which in Belgium is called *Kermesse*, after the German *Kirmis* or *Kirchmesse*.

CLAËS, the butler	Hr. Stramboe

Solo Dances

Messieurs Funck and Lund; Mlles. P. Fredstrup and Rostock
NOBLEMEN. BURGHERS. COMMONERS. PEASANTS. MONKS. SOLDIERS. OFFICERS OF JUSTICE.

The scene is laid in Bruges, in Flanders, toward the close of the seventeenth century.

ACT I

A marketplace in Bruges, decorated as if for a fair. To the right, Mirewelt's house; to the left, upstage, a tavern.

Popular rejoicing, with processions, drinking bouts, dancing, and merriment. Adrian and Geert bring their sweethearts to the celebration. Mirewelt, with his daughter, is sitting outside his house. Carelis asks Eleonore to dance, and the young people delight everyone with their grace and lightness. Two young cavaliers, Van der Steen and Van Hoëck, have mingled with the groups of people and arouse bitterness among the young chaps by the flattery they address to the young ladies. In particular, they cause disputes between the brothers and their fiancées, Marchen and Johanna. Their mother, Trutje, tries to settle the affair, but the confusion mounts. There is a positive falling out, and Trutje, who becomes angry, leads her daughters away.

Adrian and Geert are about to leave Bruges. Carelis promises to accompany them, but they must first drink to a successful journey. Carelis goes to don his travelling clothes. Meanwhile, darkness has fallen and Van der Steen, together with some bandits, has decided to kidnap the beautiful Eleonore. Mirewelt and his daughter return from the celebration. All of a sudden, he finds himself overpowered and torn from his child. He is thrown to the ground, and Eleonore, half swooning, is already on her way to the nobleman's carriage when Carelis arrives to lend his aid. At the sound of his outcries, his brothers rush out of the tavern, hit the assailants with cudgels, and free the young girl. Mirewelt's old housekeeper rushes out and by her tender ministrations brings him back to consciousness. His first thought is for his daughter, and he forgets his pains at seeing her safe. She presents the young men who have rescued her, and his gratitude knows no bounds.

Mirewelt learns that the brothers are about to sally forth into the wide world, and he wishes to give each of them a gift to take with him. The enamored but rather simple-minded Geert is given *a ring* that will draw all hearts to its owner; the bold Adrian receives a sword that will always bring victory; while the light-hearted Carelis obtains a *viola da gamba* which will impel everyone to dance. They say good-bye, depart, and empty yet another cup with a festive troop that is marching through the city by torchlight.

ACT II

Mirewelt's study. To the left, a large fireplace and the entrance to the other rooms in the house; to the right, an exit. Upstage, a window.

Eleonore wakens by her father's couch. She and old Sara bustle about him. There is a knocking at the door. Marchen and Johanna, who are worried about their lovers, wish to consult the wise man, and Mirewelt reads their horoscopes. They see, in turn, Adrian surrounded by the perils of war, and Geert reveling in a sybaritic existence. The sisters' despair vents itself in tears, and suddenly they hear a melody which makes them dance in spite of themselves.

It is Carelis, who consoles them with the fact that his brothers still love them and will soon return. They go away reassured, and Carelis is left alone with Eleonore.

He opens the conversation by returning to her a bow that she had lost at the festival. His expressions soon become more tender, and she wishes to leave; but he lures her back, dancing to the magical power of the sounds. When she still wishes to flee from him, he lays aside his viol and goes sadly away. But now it is her turn to call him back. The music unites them both, and they confess their love for each other.

Her father surprises the young couple and is about to burst into reproaches. His daughter's pleas soon mollify him and he gives the young man hope. But first he must endure his trial in the world. Carelis rushes off with joyful confidence.

The stage is transformed into a magnificent garden in the old-fashioned style. In the background, the Castle of Everdingen and a terrace looking out over the water.

Geert has been very well received in Fru van Everdingen's house. The rich widow pays him unusual attention, has him splendidly outfitted, and introduces him to her entourage as her prospective husband. Geert is very much at home in these new circumstances; he is the object of the ladies' delight and admiration and is overwhelmed with bouquets and billets-doux.

The arrival of an unknown officer is announced. It is Adrian, who has performed prodigies of valour on the battlefield and is now feted as the hero of the day. Overjoyed, Geert rushes into his brother's arms and is proud to be able to present him to the whole assembly.

They sit down at table. The butler calls Geert over into a corner to inform him that a veiled lady wishes to speak with him. But what can equal

Geert's horror and astonishment when he recognizes his deserted fiancée. Marchen showers him with anger and reproaches. Her mother and Johanna appear and try to effect a reconciliation. They finally succeed. Geert repents his errors, embraces his beloved Marchen, and as proof that he will never again be unfaithful to her, he gives her the magic ring.

The cavaliers, who can no longer tolerate Geert's arrogance, challenge him to a duel and intend to force him into striking; but when they become aware of Marchen they forget their intention and give *her* their undivided attention. Geert begins to suspect that the power of the ring is causing this, takes it from Marchen's finger, and gives it to Johanna, who immediately becomes the object of the gentlemen's admiration. The poor girl, who is frightened by these half-insane declarations, begs her mother to keep the jewel and steals away. But now buxom old Trutje is assailed with handshakes, kisses, and embraces. She defends herself as best she can and finally bursts into laughter at the sight of half a score of passionate lovers at her feet.

Adrian rushes in to give his mother-in-law peace from the intruders. When Trutje recognizes him, she heartily throws her arms about his neck, thereby arousing the jealousy and ire of the cavaliers. They challenge and attack Adrian. But the latter gives them such a piece of his mind with his sword that, wounded and disarmed, they seek salvation in flight.

The mother and the pairs of lovers express their joy at finding each other again. From this moment on, love will be enough for them, and they are unanimous in agreeing to toss all the enchanted objects into the canal.

But the authorities have been informed of the brothers' doings and have sent guards, accompanied by monks, to exorcise and imprison the supposed sorcerers. The burgomaster himself comes to seize them. They try in vain to defend themselves; in vain, mothers and daughters plead for mercy. Adrian and Geert are dragged away, and the burgomaster promises Fru van Everdingen every possible reparation for the scandal inflicted upon her house.

Act III
Mirewelt's study.

The old alchemist is seated at his chemical experiments and is reflecting on the imagined value of gold. Then Eleonore enters with a flower garland in her hands. It is his birthday, and filial innocence has prepared a little feast in his honour. This makes him realize that no wealth can compensate for the joys of fatherhood.

There is violent banging at the door. An Officer of Justice enters and orders a guard to block the exit. Mirewelt reads his accusation; he is accused of sorcery and sees himself headed for certain disaster. Eleonore clings to her father and falls into despair when she learns from Johanna that Adrian and Geert have already been condemned to the stake. Marchen comes in with Carelis, who is assailed from every side with pleas for the salvation of the unfortunate souls. He does not know where to turn – all of a sudden he receives a divine inspiration, enthusiastically kneels to thank the Lord, and promises them all his help. They hasten away.

Transformation to a large open square on the outskirts of the town.

Crowds of people mill back and forth. Drums beat and a grand auto-da-fé of three sorcerers is announced. Joy and business. Platforms are erected for the spectators. The ladies take their seats. People engage in eating and drinking while the executioners set up the stake and boys compete to see who will have the best view of this spectacle.

The condemned are brought forth. Their grieving relatives take leave of them and vainly beg mercy for the unfortunate men. The sentence is read, and the condemned are led to the stake. Carelis is standing dejectedly in the midst of the judges and dignitaries. "Then you will not grant pardon?" "No, no mercy." "None at all?" "Never." "Well, then!" And with this he seizes his viola da gamba and with a couple of rapid strokes [of the bow] transforms the whole atmosphere. Judges, executioners, ladies, gentlemen, old women, soldiers, and children romp about in the wildest dance. Never has any Kermesse seen such a dance. Everyone dances, leaps, and swings, except for the three condemed men, who are hampered by their ropes and chains. The movements grow faster with every measure of the tearing Galop, which finally overwhelms the crowd, who fall to the ground exhausted. Now it is their turn to beg for mercy, and Carelis grants it on the condition that Mirewelt and his brothers be set free and pardoned. All this is granted. Joy and peace return. Eleonore becomes the reward of faithful love, but so that the viola da gamba should not cause all too great a disturbance, it is to be kept at the Town Hall, to be taken out only for each year's Kermesse. Joy and merriment then spread throughout the old Flemish capital.

*　　*　　*

ZULMA, OR THE CRYSTAL PALACE
(Zulma eller Chrystalpaladset)

A Ballet in Three Acts
by
August Bournonville

Music composed and arranged by Holger Simon Paulli

Scenery by Christian Ferdinand Christensen and Troels Lund

Performed for the first time at the Royal Theatre, Copenhagen, February 14, 1852

Characters

SIR EDWARD	British noblemen	Hr. Füssel, Sr.
SIR JAMES		Hr. Brodersen
SIR GEORGE		Hr. Ring
SIR ROBERT		Hr. Nehm, Jr.
MISS HARRIET, Edward's sister		Jfr. Garlieb
SAMI, master of an Indian pagoda		Hr. Gade
ZULMA	bayadères	Jfr. Juliette Price
ADITSCHA		Mme. Kellermann
AKHBAR, a chieftain		Hr. Funck
TOM, a sailor, Edward's batman		Hr. Stramboe
A CHINAMAN		Mr. Hoppensach
AN ALDERMAN		Hr. Füssel, Jr.
A CONSTABLE		Hr. Nehm, Sr.
A FLOWER GIRL		Jfr. Amalie Price

Dances

Bayadères: Kellerman, J. Price, Fredstrup, Rostock, Stramboe, and S. Price
Brahmans: Gade, Anderson, Fredstrup
Chinese Dance: Stramboe, Hoppensach, W. Price
Festive Dance: All the bayadères; Messiers Hoppe, Funck, and Lund
Hornpipe: Hoppe, Fredstrup, Scharff; Miles. Fredstrup, A. Price, Stramboe, and Borup

In Acts I and II the scene is laid in the British East Indies in 1849; the third act is set in London at the Great Exhibition in 1851.

ACT I

The vestibule of an Indian pagoda sacred to Devendi, king of the demigods. A heavy curtain separates the vestibule from the temple itself.

Sami sits surrounded by the handmaidens of the pagoda, the *devedassi*, who are brought up under the supervision of the Brahmans for the worship of the idol. They make costly materials and shawls and are often called upon to enliven celebrations with their music and dancing (wherefore the Portuguese have given them the name of "bailadeiras," or "bayadères").

Mothers bring their children to Sami, bearing gifts so that he will choose them for temple service. The pretty ones he keeps, but hurries the others out the door.

Gongs sound the call to prayer. The vestibule is cleared of people. The Brahmans assemble, and the curtain is drawn aside. Sacred dances are performed before the image of the idol while sacrifices are brought forth and the smell of incense fills the air. Zulma, lightest and youngest of the bayadères, has attracted the special attention of the master of the pagoda and he hands her a brimming cup as a token of Devendi's favour. But, trembling, the young maiden recoils before Sami's burning gaze.

Akhbar, chieftain of a band of Assassins, is announced. The bayadères withdraw, and Sami welcomes his fanatical guests, promises to aid them, and consecrates their weapons. They follow him into the Holy of Holies. Unbeknownst to them, Zulma and Aditscha have overheard the plot they are hatching. Filled with horror, they are about to flee when, at the exit of the temple, they encounter an English sailor. Bowing deeply, he approaches and shows them a letter he is to deliver to the head of the pagoda from his master, who wishes to arrange for music and dancing.* Zulma suspects that Englishmen are the murderers' intended victims, and she is horrified at the thought. The frivolous Aditscha amuses herself with setting the seaman's heart afire, and Tom allows himself to be carried away to the point of dancing with her. Zulma tries in vain to interrupt their fun, but the loud striking of the gong calls the bayadères away. Aditscha gaily bids Tom farewell and rushes off with Zulma.

Filled with curiosity, Tom looks around and is just about to peep under the curtain when a bamboo stick held by an unseen hand thrusts him back. He tries to flee to right and left, but the Brahmans menacingly block his path. They begin to whirl about with their long sticks, which race over Tom's head like a millwheel so that he is forced to throw himself on the ground in order to escape this deadly whirlwind. Sami and the conspirators intervene and angrily regard the presumptuous foreigner. Trembling from head to toe, Tom produces his orders and the atmosphere changes. Sami respectfully defers to the Englishmen's wishes. Their messenger is treated with courtesy and carried home in a palanquin. In disguise, Akhbar and his fellow conspirators – who have now found a favourable opportunity for carrying out their plan – join

---

*   *Melody: "Steady Boys."

the company of bayadères, and with Sami in the lead they set off for the Englishmen's party.

ACT II

A palm grove on the banks of the River Ganges.

A Chinese merchantman is lying at anchor in the river. Some Chinese have encamped on the river bank, where they are cooking and eating their rice. Tom, who is waiting for his master to arrive, enters and makes the acquaintance of the Chinamen, with whom he transacts a little business.

The sound of a bugle announces the Britons' approach.* It is a Scottish melody that awakens echoes in the hills of Hindustan. A light gig glides over the water and a merry hunting party steps ashore with numerous Indian servants. Sir Edward, a wealthy Scottish baronet, is giving a party today for his friends, the Irishman James, the Englishman George, and the Scotsman Robert. Here they will erect a tent and rest and refresh themselves after the hunt, Sir James constitutes the musical and poetic element in the party, and the gentle sounds of his homeland mingle with sadness of longing with the festive joy.†

Tom introduces the Chinamen, and the British gentlemen purchase a number of objects – among other things, a hat and gown for Tom, who in an access of delight dances and hops about with the Chinamen to the great amusement of the company. The gentlemen depart and Tom sees that everything is arranged. The servants busily scamper from the boat to the palm trees. The tent is erected and an elegant table laid.

Aditscha comes into view behind a bush. She motions Tom to send the servants away. He obeys and happily rushes toward her. But she is no no mood for pleasantry, for his life is threatened by an assassination plot, and only a quick escape can save him. Tom loses his composure. Fearing for his life, he forgets everything else but knows not whither he shall flee. At this moment the Chinamen enter. They are getting ready to sail. Aditscha, who notices that Tom is wearing the same costume as theirs, urges him to sail away with them. And, after having come to terms with them, taken leave of Aditscha, and furnished himself with some provisions from the gentlemen's table, he leaves this wretched country as a deserter.

With Zulma at his side, Sami comes to scold Aditscha, who is always straying from the group of bayadères. But nothing comes of it and she repeatedly chaffs Sami by coming between him and his infatuation for Zulma. The Hindu procession draws near. The conspirators are hidden among the dancers and musicians, and, while they arrange a sig-

---

* "Hurrah for Bonnets of Blue."
† "My Heart and Lute."

nal with Sami, Aditscha points out to Zulma the departing merchantman.

The hunting party returns and is greeted by Sami and his fanatic company. Sir Edward notices that Tom is missing and is a bit annoyed by his absence; but they are waited upon all the same. The gentlemen sit down at table and the dancing begins. Zulma captivates everyone with her grace and lightness. They vie to offer her gifts, but Edward, to whom she hands a golden lotus blossom – which is to be a saving talisman – is the only one from whom she will accept a memento. With indescribable emotion, he places a medallion about her neck. Sami receives a purseful of gold for his troupe and retires with expressions of reverence and satisfaction.

Darkness falls. The gentlemen seek rest inside the tent while the servants sleep in the soft grass. Only Edward lies awake, thinking of the lovely Hindu maid who handed him this lotus blossom with such a strange expression. He hears something and thinks it is Tom who is finally returning. He resolves to chastize him severely. But how great is his surprise when, through the darkness, he discerns two female figures, one of whom approaches him while the other appears to be keeping guard. It is Zulma and her friend! With deep emotion, Zulma runs to him, looks anxiously about, and acquaints him with the danger that threatens his life and the lives of his friends! Edward recoils, especially at the thought that Zulma might be involved in this plot. "Was it with such a plan in mind that you captured my heart and handed me this flower?" With a cry of pain and anger, he hurls it at her feet. But she gives it back to him and signifies that it is intended to be a safeguard for his good fortune. She calls upon the god of gods to bear witness to the fact that she has desired naught but his safety. Moved by her fervor, Edward forgets the impending danger. The magical power of love draws him to her, and he presses a kiss upon her brow. Aditscha rushes in to fetch Zulma. Every moment she stays here is a matter of life and death. She leads her away, and Edward promises never to forget his saviour.

Sir Edward awakens his friends and tells them what he has learned. He orders them to be careful. The servants are summoned. Everyone arms himself in silence and awaits the attack. Akhbar and the conspirators crawl forth from their hiding places. At a given signal they rush toward the tent with daggers raised. But some well-aimed shots fell several of them. The armed servants seize those who are fleeing and the Britons congratulate one another on the fact that the danger has been overcome. Dawn is beginning to break. Edward gives the signal for departure. The ship is made ready, and from the banks of the Ganges the bugle, whose familiar melodies remind them of their distant native soil, resounds once more.*

---

*   "O! Steer My Bark to Erin's Isle."

ACT III

A section of Hyde Park in London. In the foreground, groups of trees on the shore of the Serpentine; farther off, the Crystal Palace.

As the curtain rises, "Rule Britannia" can be heard in the distance. Some sailors are sitting in their gondolas, waiting to ferry strollers over to the plain, while on a bench beneath a shade tree we perceive an officer in Highland uniform at the side of a young lady who is reading to him from a book. The martial music is interrupted by a stanza of the English ballad "Home, Sweet Home." But the march is soon heard with renewed vigor, and people of all classes hurry by in order to see the changing of the guard at the corner in front of the park.

Sir Edward, the Scottish officer, rises and takes the book from his sister, Miss Harriet. He thanks her with a woeful sigh. She tenderly asks him to confide in her, and he shows her the lotus blossom which reminds him of the being who was his guardian angel in his hour of peril. His life was saved, but his gaiety lost, and the thought of Zulma fills his heart with burning longing. "But you cannot understand this. You do not know what love is!" Harriet shyly blushes and at the very moment sees Sir James approaching. Edward's friend and travelling companion adores the lovely Harriet and is, in turn, rewarded with her love. They confess to her brother their mutual admiration, hoping to confirm their happiness by his consent. He agrees to their union. Harriet goes off with her brother, and Sir James, who remains behind, gives himself up to the expression of his delight.

A flower girl is offering flowers and cherries for sale. She is the first to give Sir James a bridegroom's bouquet.* A distinguished Chinaman with a long pipe in his mouth is having tea and with great dignity sits down at a little table while his servants hold a sunshade over his head.

Several Hindus enter, bearing coffers containing East Indian wares for the Exhibition. It is Sami who has come to London to represent the artistic industries of his country. He has brought with him two veiled women, one of whom appears to be the object of his special attention. Driven by curiosity, flower girls approach the Hindu women, offer them bouquets, and get to see their faces beneath the veils – it is Zulma and Aditscha!

Sir James is regarding the people from distant Hindustan with great interest, but Sami is horrified when he recognizes one of the Englishmen who escaped his wiles and might now take revenge on him. The Chinaman, too, becomes uneasy at finding himself in the proximity of the two people mentioned above. To her great delight, Zulma has dis-

---
* "Cherry Ripe."

covered that Sir Edward's friend is here in London. She makes herself known to him and asks him about the one she loves. But Sami, who is anxious to get away, interrupts their conversation and leaves without taking any notice of Aditscha.

For some time the spirited bayadère has been keeping her eye on the mandarin, who tries to hide beneath the parasol. She comes up beind him, snatches away the umbrella, and each is amazed to find the other here. "Tom!" "Aditscha!" "My saviour!" "My merry friend!" What joy! But there must be silence and caution as well, for not only the mandarin's dignity, but the deserter's life are at stake.

Three young sailors and their girls come dancing by, led by a fiddler. Tom is tempted by the sight of their hornpipe, and both he and Aditscha join in. But when the sailors actually start to flirt with the bayadère, the Chinaman forgets his role, gets into a quarrel, and boxes with them, to the great delight of the gathering crowd, who enthusiastically applaud his skill in the noble art of self-defense. The police are about to arrest the troublemakers, but Aditscha, who has gotten hold of Sir James, reveals to him Tom's plight and begs him to post bail for the mandarin. Peace is restored. The Chinaman regains his former dignity and, accompanied by his lady, goes off to the Exhibition followed by the curious mob.

TRANSFORMATION

The interior of the Crystal Palace, seen from the Indian and Chinese exhibitions. Toward the background a, dais with an organ-pianoforte. Divans and benches. Tightly-packed crowds of visitors.

Sami leads Zulma to the Indian Division, which is attracting general attention because of the costly shawls and the personality of the exhibitors. Several members of the Jury for Industry are making notes about the most singular objects. Sami is discomforted by Aditscha's absence. Zulma has recognized Sir Edward, who stands as if turned to stone upon seeing her. Miss Harriet is concerned about her brother, who tenderly presses her hand without explaining himself. Zulma follows them with her jealous gaze. "That lady is certainly his sweetheart, maybe even his wife!" Quavering, Sami once again catches sight of an old acquaintance from the Ganges, and this nervous tension is broken only when Aditscha comes dancing in front of her mandarin. Highly indignant, Sami is about to reveal the Chinaman's secret. But since Tom also has knowledge of the Hindu's treachery, they agree to keep silent, and with suppressed anger each goes his way and is soon engulfed by a numerous crowd.

Sir Edward has returned. He stands so that, unseen by the crowd, he can be observed by Zulma, who asks him to take back his medallion, since she will leave this place and soon die of grief. But Harriet enters on her lover's arm. Edward joins their hands in his and introduces the young couple to his friends. Zulma hardly dares believe her own eyes. Edward asks his sister to play his favourite piece on the organ-pianoforte. The others join in his request, and she consents. A tightly packed crowd of listeners surrounds the dais.

The foreground is completely given over to Edward and Zulma. Aditscha keeps a modest distance [from them]. Harriet plays "Memories from the Ganges." The lovers are transported back to the day that decided their fate, and they relive the moments that have left so indelible an impression on their souls.

Sir Edward places Zulma in his sister's arms and introduces her as his bride. General amazement. But James, Robert, and George can attest to the fact that this splendid girl saved their lives by her selfless devotion, and everyone congratulates the noble baronet on his choice.

Aditscha shall marry Tom, who in the eyes of the world will continue to be a mandarin. Sami does not dare show any opposition, but he can take some consolation in the fact that, together with several members of the Asiatic Division, he has been awarded the Grand Gold Medal of the Exhibition, and the ballet ends with a Great Exhibition Polka, which unites all nations and interests in peaceful joy.

* * *

THE WEDDING FESTIVAL IN HARDANGER
(Brudefaerden i Hardanger)

A Ballet in Two Acts
by
August Bournonville

Music by Holger Simon Paulli

Décor by Christian Ferdinand Christensen and Troels Lund

Costumes designed by Edvard Lehmann

First performed at the Royal Theatre, Copenhagen, March 4, 1853

Characters

ARNE, owner of the farmstead of "Vold" . . . . .Hr. Füssel, Sr.
GURI, his wife . . . . .Jfr. Larcher
RAGNHILD, their daughter . . . . .Jfr. Juliette Price
HALVOR } young farmers . . . . { Hr. Brodersen
OLA . . . . Hr. Gade
KIRSTI, a *saeter* maid . . . . .Jfr. P. Fredstrup

NIELS THE SEXTON .... Hr. Hoppensach
THE BRIDE from the farmstead of "Heja". .... Jfr. Amalie Price
THE BRIDEGROOM .... Hr. Hoppe
PARENTS OF THE BRIDE .... Hr. Nehm
Jfr. Andersen
PARENTS OF THE BRIDEGROOM .... Hr. Füssel, Jr.
Jfr. J. Fredstrup
NORWEGIAN PEASANT FOLK OF BOTH SEXES. FARMHANDS. CHILDREN.

Dances

Messieurs Stramboe, Lund, and Fredstrup; Miles, Rostock, S. Price, Borup, and Garlieb.

The scene is laid at the farmsteads of "Vold" and "Heja," as well as at Hardanger Fjord.

Foreword

Excited over everything beautiful and good I had seen and experienced in Norway, I felt compelled to express my impressions in my allotted sphere of poetry, which, in this instance, seemed to possess two essential advantages: (1) that of enabling me to treat a Norwegian theme *for the first time* and (2) that of being completely independent of linguistic differences.

While gratefully acknowledging how useful and instructive I have found Welhaven's and Østgaard's interesting national descriptions, I must also confess that, just as it was Marstrand's and Sonne's transparency for the Scandinavians' Christmas celebration that gave me my first idea for *Bellman*, so it was mainly Tidemand's superb genre pictures that furnished the material for the present ballet. It should therefore come as no surprise that this work has more of painting in it than of drama. May it, like its older brother, succeed in delighting the Danish public and at the same time show our hospitable neighbours that we continue to view their art, as well as their folkways, with love.

ACT I

SCENE ONE

A log room with beam ceiling at the farmstead of "Vold." Through the open door upstage a mountain landscape can be seen. To the right and left, doors leading to the other rooms in the house.

Guri is dozing at her spinning wheel. Her daughter, Ragnhild, is holding a book, a passage of which she has read, but her thoughts are elsewhere. Vibrating tones are heard; it is a harmonica. She recognizes the melody and perceives Halvor, who enters with noiseless tread. The lovers cautiously greet one another, for they must not awaken the mother. They have so much to say to each other but are at a loss for words, and the quivering but familiar sounds must express their feelings.

SCENE TWO

Arne comes from the woods, deep in intimate conversation with Ola. He bids him enter, but they are taken aback at the sight of the lovers. The father plants his axe so firmly in the door jamb that Guri is startled out of her sleep and the young couple springs apart. The parents express their anger at Halvor's forwardness, while Ola nonchalantly throws himself into a chair and lights his pipe. With tears and pleas, Ragnhild seeks to soften her father and mother. Halvor summons his courage and, as an honourable suitor, asks for the maiden's hand in marriage. Arne asks what he has to offer his daughter, and when he receives the reply "A strong pair of arms and a heart full of love and confidence," he scornfully shrugs his shoulders. The mother is already half inclined in favour of the fine lad, but Arne, who has other plans, pounds his fist on the table to signify that only a well-to-do man who can bring Ragnhild affluence and happiness shall have her as a wife. Moreover, here stands Ola, to whom she has already been promised.

The rich suitor thanks the father for entertaining such a good opinion of him, takes a drink which is offered him as a mark of welcome, and swaggers over to Halvor to show him his silver buttons and brooch, his pipe mountings, and his full wallet. With the mother's leave, he presents a magnificent prayer book as a betrothal gift to Ragnhild, who is sitting in a corner, brokenhearted and aggrieved.

Arne has shown Halvor the door, and when the poor lad bids him consider that he will have to answer to God and his conscience [for what he is doing], the old man loses his temper. But Ola violently pushes him aside and promises that he himself will settle the affair with Halvor. The latter, who will tolerate nothing from his brutal opponent, prepares to defend himself, and the womenfolk come between the antagonists just as the farmhands and maids come to announce that visitors have arrived.

SCENE THREE

It is the bridegroom from the farmstead of "Heja" and Niels the Sexton who have come to invite them to a wedding. The Sexton will do the talking, but he takes his time, has a drink, jokes with the girls, surveys the room with relish, and finally notices Ola and Halvor: they are chosen to be groomsmen and cannot refuse this honour. They are given staves as badges of honour, and Niels, assuming a pompous stance, now reads a formal invitation punctuated with strenuous gestures that cause beads of perspiration to stand out on his brow. They all promise to attend; the names are registered, they have another little drink, and the bridegroom offers his hand in thanks. He leaves, together with his spokesman and the groomsmen.

SCENE FOUR

The whole farm now becomes a beehive of activity. Presents or wedding gifts of provisions are taken from the *stabbur* [storehouse]. The old folks go inside to get ready, and the maids gather round Ragnhild to dress her for the celebration. But she does not share their delight, for she has received the silver-studded prayer book not from the man she loves but from Ola, whom she despises. The maids try to cheer her by telling her that perhaps she will meet Halvor at the wedding at "Heja" and be able to have a dance with him.

SCENE FIVE

Arne and Guri enter in their old-fashioned festal dress, and the mother is delighted to see Ragnhild so nicely turned out. But the young girl begs her parents to let her return the magnificent prayer book to Ola, since she cannot love him nor will she marry him. Her mother tries to mediate, but her father is unbending and, since he fears a meeting with Halvor, he decides that Ragnhild shall stay home from the feast. She puts her finery back in the coffer. The signal is given to depart. Arne goes on ahead while the mother puts the prayer book in her pocket, kisses her daughter good-bye, and follows the others. Silent and sorrowful, Ragnhild remains at home alone.

TRANSFORMATION

SCENE SIX

The mountainous region at Hardanger Fjord. On both sides, pine and birch woods. To the right, an old bell tower, and, behind it, a path leading up to the church, which cannot be seen. Some large stones are lying on the shore.

Peasants of various ages have flocked to this spot to view the wedding procession, which is expected to arrive here by water. They meet Kirsti, the young *saeter* girl, and greet her in friendly fashion. But she diffidently avoids them, and when the maids hand her a nosegay with which to greet the bridal party, she tears it to pieces, scatters the flowers at her feet, and indicates that thus have her youth and happiness been wasted. All regard her with sadness and sympathy.

Niels the Sexton has been busy calling people hither, rehearsing a choir of schoolchildren, and drilling the young people in how to welcome the bridal party.

SCENE SEVEN

Three decorated boats put in at the landing-place. Halvor arrives in the first boat with the musicians and shooters; the second one is filled with young peasants of both sexes; and the third bears the bridal couple and the old folk. They are greeted with jubilation. The musicians strike up a solemn march, and the Sexton joins in with the children. The bride, with a golden crown on her head, is congratulated by the women, while the men loyally shake the bridegroom's hand. Led by Halvor, the procession proceeds up the mountain slope to the church, while, as part of his duties, Ola takes care of the rowers and musicians and rather excessively refreshes himself.

SCENE EIGHT

Kirsti, who has watched the whole procession from a distance, fearfully draws near to speak with Ola. The latter is not happy to see her: it is immediately apparent that there was once a more tender relationship between them, but the faithless lover's embarrassment is expressed by scorn rather than regret, and when Halvor happens to enter just then, Ola even goes so far as to propose that he and Kirsti become a couple. Their indignation only increases his hilarity. He jumps into the boat, pulls out a jug of mead, pours some into a cup, and is about to drink to their health when the boat lurches and, in his half-drunken state, throws him off balance. He tumbles backward into the water. Kirsti and Halvor stand there, petrified with fright. But the brave lad quickly makes up his mind to take the boat and row out to help the unfortunate fellow. However, Ola cannot be seen on the surface, and Halvor must dive to the bottom to search for him. Kirsti hastens to the tower to ring the alarm bell.

SCENE NINE

Everyone comes running, dismayed at this unlucky omen on a wedding day. But Halvor has brought his rival up from the depths and, with the aid of some other young men, brings him ashore, half dead. Ola gradually regains consciousness. He stares about him in bewilderment, and his gaze comes to rest upon his saviour. Shamefaced and bowed down, he goes over to Halvor, shakes hands with him, gives Arne a pleading look, and indicates that Halvor is the proper son-in-law for him – the only man worthy of Ragnhild. Everyone presses the old man, who still raises objections. But at length he yields to something within him and opens his arms to the honest young man. Beside himself with delight, Halvor embraces the whole world, blesses his former rival, and, accompanied by the good wishes of all, hastens off to bring Ragnhild the happy news.

SCENE TEN

The wedding party prepares to set sail for home, but Ola remains behind. Guri gives him the betrothal gift that Ragnhild has rejected. He opens the prayer book, presses her hand, and wipes a tear from his eye.

The boats glide toward the fjord. On a stone near the church sits the deeply shaken and remorseful Ola. A consolatory spirit approaches him; it is his cast-off sweetheart. He sees her, takes her hand, offers her the prayer book, and all is well again.

ACT II

SCENE ONE

The log room with beam ceiling at the farmstead of "Vold."

Ragnhild, who has cried herself to sleep, is seated on a footstool with her head resting on the coffer. She starts up, awakened from a dream; she saw her beloved in danger, great misfortune seemed to threaten them both – but, thank Heaven, it was only a dream! Work will help to dispel these sad thoughts, and she takes out her sewing. It is a linen collar with scalloped edges which she had intended for Halvor, and she is embroidering his initials on it. Every once in a while, however, she becomes lost in gloomy reflections, for her love is opposed to her father's wishes.

She hears rapid footsteps. The sound draws nearer, and Halvor, out of breath, comes bursting through the door. He has run all the way to bring the glad tidings, but now that he is standing before Ragnhild, his strength deserts him and he sinks down on the stool, exhausted. The anxious maiden seeks to calm him and hands him a bowl of milk, which he drinks with his gaze immovably fixed upon her. At last he is able to tell her, with exclamations of joy, that their sorrow is ended and that her parents have consented to their union. Ragnhild can hardly believe it is possible, and the vehemence with which Halvor expresses himself makes her think that he plans to carry her off from her father's house by force. Halvor is offended by her suspicion. But even though she loves him more than anything in the world, Ragnhild will not disobey her father, and Arne has ordered her to remain at home.

SCENE TWO

Ola and his fiancée [Kirsti] appear just in time to corroborate Halvor's statements and explain everything. Delighted with her bold and faithful lover, Ragnhild gives him her hand and promises to go with him to the wedding, where her parents are. Kirsti helps her to don her festal dress, and amid dancing and merry jumps, the two happy couples hasten off to the celebration.

TRANSFORMATION

SCENE THREE

The parlor at the farmstead of "Heja," decorated as for a wedding.

The guests are seated at long, richly laid tables. The bride and groom, together with their parents, occupy the high seat. Toasts are delivered and drunk, and it is Niels the Sexton who, in high spirits, does the honours.

The meal is over, the fiddlers begin to play, and the floor is cleared for dancing.

First the bride and groom dance with each other, then the Sexton and the mother of the bride. The older men and women take part in the dance, and their serious steps alternate with the leaps of the young.

Three young fellows perform a comic scene which, under the name of "The Barber Dance," furnishes the opportunity for several characteristic episodes.

SCENE FOUR

The celebration is further enlivened by the arrival of Ola, Halvor, Kirsti, and Ragnhild. They are greeted with heartfelt joy, and Arne, whose stern expression has softened, embraces his children and gives them his blessing. Loyal handshakes welcome Ola and Kirsti, every trace of despondency has vanished, and cups are drained to friendship and love.

The most important moment of the celebration draws nigh. The golden crown is to be taken from the bride's head and she herself must designate the one who shall be the next to wear it. She chooses Ragnhild. She finds herself in the midst of the group of young girls, who, in airy dance, initiate the bride into the matrimonial state. While Ragnhild goes around the circle with the crown above her head, the married woman's hat is placed on the young wife, and at her husband's side she passes through the ranks of their friends, who, to the strains of a favourite melody, salute the couple and wish them happiness.

But in accordance with an old custom, the bridegroom must

undergo one more test before he may set his feet under his own table: he must seek out and capture his wife, who, with the help of all the guests, eludes him and hides. After several setbacks, he finally catches hold of her. With a mischievous expression, she presents him with the red "pixie hat," which is the hallmark of his new estate, and, following the advice of the other women, pulls it far down over his ears.

Now begins the *Halling,* wherein the young husband performs his daring kicks at the rafters with the bright hat on his head.

The hat is finally placed on a sword and the cleverest swain has to bring it down with his feet. They outdo one another in violent leaps, but it is Ola who wins the prize.

The guests applaud, and it is Halvor and Ragnhild who lead the *springdans.* Everyone, young and old alike, takes part in it. Joy has reached its height, and on jubilant groups the curtain falls.

* * *

A FOLK TALE
(Et Folkesagn)

A Ballet in Three Acts
by
August Bournonville

Music composed by Niels Gade and J. P. E. Hartmann

Decorations by Christian Ferdinand Christensen and Troels Lund

Costumes designed by Edvard Lehmann

Machinery arranged by Andreas Peter Weden

Performed for the first time on March 20, 1854

Characters

HILDA, a Mountain Lass . . . . .Jfr. Juliette Price
MURI, a Troll Woman . . . . .Mme. Møller
DIDERIK ⎫ her sons . . . . ⎧ Hr. Hoppensach
VIDERIK ⎭   ⎩ Hr. Stramboe

ELF MAIDENS. GNOMES. DWARVES AND TROLLS.

FRØKEN BIRTHE, heiress of "Højgaarden" . . . .Jfr. P. Fredstrup
JUNKER OVE, her cousin and fiancé . . . . .Hr. Funk
FRU KIRSTINE, their aunt . . . . .Jfr. Larcher, Sr.
HERR MOGENS . . . . .Hr. Gade

CATHRINE, the old housekeeper,
   former nurse .... Jfr. J. Fredstrup
MORTEN, the cook .... Hr. Füssel, Jr.
ELSE, a kitchen maid .... Mme. Stillmann
DORTHE, a lady's maid .... Jfr. Garlieb

LADIES AND GENTLEMEN. PEASANTS AND SERVANTS.

Solo Dance

Messieurs Hoppe, Lund, and Fredstrup; Mme. Kellermann; Mlles. Rostock, S. Price, Borup, and Bills.

The scene is laid in Jutland in the early sixteenth century.

ACT I

SCENE ONE

A piece of woodland at the foot of a hill covered with scrub.

The people of the manor are busy laying a table beneath an old oak tree. Hunting horns are heard nearby. It is the unpredictable Frøken Birthe, who has ordered the repast to be served at this spot. The old housekeeper is not at all pleased with this little whim of hers and recounts legends about gnomes and trolls; the girls are petrified, but the Frøken's arrival quickly gets them moving again. Their confusion and a number of mishaps bring out her shrewish nature, which is transformed into the most gracious amiability as the guests approach.

SCENE TWO

The party, consisting of the Frøken's aunt, the young Junker Ove, a number of ladies and gentlemen, and the stiff but chivalrous Herr Mogens, take their places at the richly laid table. Gamekeepers play spirited table music and peasants perform their rustic dances as entertainment for the distinguished guests.

The Frøken proposes several dances and games, in which she displays her bizarre humor. Herr Mogens seizes every opportunity to pay her compliments, in contrast to her cousin, who is cold and preoccupied. Birthe cannot hide her indignation at her fiancé's behaviour, and when darkness falls she gives Herr Mogens her arm and bids her guests accompany her to the manor house.

SCENE THREE

Despite Cathrine's warnings, the Junker stays behind in the forest and, brooding, sits down near the hill.

Subterranean music is heard, and the hill rises on four flaming pillars: gnomes are forging and dancing to the hammer strokes; in their midst sits the Troll Woman, and at her side stands a lovely maiden in dazzling raiment with a large golden cup in her hand. With gliding steps she approaches Junker Ove and gives him the brimming cup. He takes it with his gaze immovably fixed on the ethereal being, but pours its contents onto the ground, whereupon bluish flames spout from the grass. The Mountain Lass demands that he return the cup; she threatens and entices. But Ove is determined to keep it and there now ensues a struggle during which the Troll Woman finally loses patience and drags the maiden back inside, while giving a sign for the hill to close and calling forth the elf maidens from the depths of the swamp. In flowing garments, with rushes and water lilies in their unbound hair, they encircle Ove and sweep him along in their whirling dance. He tries to escape, but in vain. They entangle him in their veil of mist and, exhausted, he finally collapses at the foot of the hill, tightly clasping the cup.

ACT TWO

The Troll Woman's subterranean hall. Centre stage, a large hearth with forges on both sides.

SCENE ONE

Diderik and Viderik are each seated at a forge, fashioning jewelry for Hilda, who is spinning on her distaff. Muri is standing at the hearth, making pancakes. The brothers, who are both in love with the Mountain Lass, do not hide their jealousy but fly at each other at every turn; their mother has all she can do to restrain them. The most distinguished trolls of the surrounding countryside have been invited to a feast, and the most splendid household utensils shall be used. But Muri wonders about the golden cup which the Junker has kept as her eldest son, Diderik has been chosen to be Hilda's spouse, and Muri thinks it best that his proposal be made as soon as possible. Viderik becomes disconsolate and positively rebels. But old Muri picks up her big birch rod, grabs her vicious son by his frizzy hair, and drags him off to chastise him soundly.

SCENE TWO

Diderik's proposal, which essentially consists in bedecking his beloved with all the jewelry he and his brother have made for her, is not successful. Hilda gives him to understand that while she may be very fond of him, she will on no account have him for a husband. His transitions from flattery to indignation only serve to emphasize his ugliness. She dances rollickingly about him, and he runs off threateningly to complain to his mother.

SCENE THREE

Hilda gazes sympathetically after her rejected suitor but makes up her mind that she will never become his bride. On the other hand, she delights in thinking about the handsome Junker and longingly recalls their meeting near the hill. She feels weary and settles down to rest on the couch, where she soon falls asleep.

Out of the mist of dreams, a series of drifting pictures now unfolds to the soothing strains of a lullaby:

> A nurse sits rocking a tiny child. Next to her stands a table with a lamp and a golden cup. A group of angels, kneeling before the symbol of the cross, passes the cradle and the sleeping nurse.
>
> Small trolls arise from the floor, holding in their arms a babe, whom they kiss and caress. They cautiously approach the cradle and exchange the children. One of the pixies notices the golden cup, steals over to it, drains it, and puts it in his pocket. The trolls sink back into the earth with their changeling.

Hilda awakens. Everything has vanished. She strives in vain to recollect her dream. She remembers only one thing clearly, and, finding two sticks near the hearth, she fashions them into a Cross and kneels before it as did the angel in the cloud.

SCENE FOUR

Muri enters, is startled at the sight of Hilda's devotion, and intimidates her into throwing the sticks away. Diderik appears in his best clothes; Viderik, on the contrary, is red-eyed and plotting revenge.

The guests assemble for an imposing feast; the betrothed couple is presented and a toast is proposed in their honour.

Hilda must dance for the strangers, and Viderik is ordered to play his dulcimer. The trolls are delighted; the beer intoxicates them, and the party starts to get loud. But Hilda arranges to flee with Viderik when the troll dance is at its wildest.

They carry out their plan and disappear through the forge.

ACT THREE

The outskirts of a forest. To the left, a well with a picture of St. John. In the background, fields and meadows; farther off, the manor house, and, in the distance, the heath.

SCENE ONE

Harvesters are cutting and stacking grass in the field, while poor folk and invalids kneel at the well and enjoy its healing water. Hilda, in rustic dress, and Viderik, outfitted as a tinker, emerge from the thicket and behold this peaceful scene – with different feelings, however. The dwarf is amused at the old people's superstition, but Hilda, who remembers her dream and recognizes the Cross in the hands of the little St. John, chides her scoffing companion and is kind to the poor.

The harvesters, who have finished their work, settle down beneath the trees to partake of the luncheon Else brings them. They notice the strange girl and curiously gather round her but do not find her particularly fit for work. Viderik encourages them to dance and accompanies them on his dulcimer. Hilda takes part in their round dance, but displays such wondrous lightness that the peasants are astounded and simply forget to dance along.

SCENE TWO

With gracious condescension, Herr Mogens mingles with the merry groups and, as usual, becomes a victim of the girls' fooling. But their joy is silenced when Junker Ove approaches. His whole manner bears the stamp of quiet madness; everywhere he thinks he sees the elf maidens' dance and hears the hammer strokes of the dwarves. The peasants sympathetically move out of his way. Only Hilda remains and comes over to ask about the cup, which he is still holding in his hand. The Junker is startled at the sight of the young girl, but he is unable to recollect the memories her ethereal appearance evokes. Seized with an unconscious inspiration, Hilda fills the golden cup with the miraculous water of the well and brings it to Ove, who puts it to his lips as she kneels before the Cross the little St. John is holding in his arms. He is seized by a tremor; his eyes grow bright, his mind clears; he looks about him with joy and awareness and recognizes Hilda, whom he calls his Angel of Salvation. Viderik, who has followed their every move, indignantly comes between them, threatens the Junker, and tries to drag Hilda away with him. The lovers try in vain to placate him with entreaties and gifts. But when Hilda asks if he would prefer that she return to the gnomes and marry his brother, he shudders, and, rather than see this detested union take place, he gives the maiden to the jubilant Ove.

SCENE THREE

Herr Mogens – who has become suspicious of the tinker and the mysterious girl, and also does not like to see the demented Junker so close to Frøken Birthe's manorial seat – calls the peasants together in order to rid the countryside of these unwelcome guests. Ove tries to remonstrate with them, but now that he is once again of sound mind, they regard him as totally possessed. He becomes angry and tries to defend the girl but is overcome and led away with his hands bound. Light as a hind, Hilda eludes her pursuers, and by an ingenious trick Viderik upsets this entire army.

SCENE FOUR

Frøken Birthe's chamber in the manor house.

Dorthe, the lady's maid, is putting the Frøken's clothes in order and takes advantage of her absence to try them on. As she is standing in front of the mirror, the pantry maid enters with the Frøken's drink. She too wants to deck herself out; the other maids follow suit, and soon the whole wardrobe has been apportioned.

But their happiness is short-lived... A bell sounds... Birthe, in a dressing gown, enters and displays all her bad humor during her more than difficult toilette. A number of petty incidents send her into a rage. She strikes her servants, pushes old Cathrine away from her, and dismisses her aunt. The maids, who are now driven to extremes, rebel. The Frøken cries for help but is overcome by her vehemence and has a fit.

At this moment, Hilda comes flying into the room, carrying the golden cup in her hand. They all gaze at this strange girl in astonishment, but this place seems to remind her of her dream and the lovely cradle song. She sees the old nurse, slowly leads her over to the armchair, and places herself in her lap. The cup is recognized as the one that disappeared when the Frøken was but a babe. Fru Kirstine discovers a birthmark on Hilda's shoulder, and everyone joyfully acknowledges that she must be their true mistress. Birthe awakens from her swoon and again becomes enraged at the sight of the homage being paid to this strange girl. She orders them to chase Hilda away. But instead of obeying her, they turn on her and try to exorcise her, for she must be a troll. Birthe rings the bell and stamps her feet in vain; and since her anger is answered with nought but contempt and loathing, she tosses a cloak about her and, fuming with rage, rushes out into the forest to bring the farmhands back to the manor.

The aunt, the housekeeper, and all the maids surround Hilda with loving care and take her inside to dress her for the celebration.

SCENE FIVE

The wood near the well.

An old woman enters, pushing a wheelbarrow upon which a number of sticks and twigs are lying. She looks all around her and sounds a *lur* as a call to assemble. Diderik and all the dwarves crawl forth from the bushes. The woman casts off her hooded cloak. It is Muri, who informs the gnomes that now that their darling has returned to the Christian race they can no longer be happy here in Denmark. She hands out pilgrims' staves and bids them prepare for distant journeys. Diderik is disconsolate, and his mother must once again resort to her authority in order to allay his outburst of pain.

Noise is heard, and the gnomes sink back into the earth.

SCENE SIX

Herr Mogens, who has armed all the farmhands of the estate, divides them into various groups and sends them right and left to bring back the fugitives. Exhausted, he sits down beneath a large tree and ponders his love for the wealthy Frøken, whom he hopes to win by his personal merits. Viderik, who has gathered a handful of seed, comes slowly walking by. Mogens is not slow to call his people together. They come running from every side, but Viderik, who has climbed up into the tree, scatters the seed over them and at that very instant they stand as if turned to stone. The mischievous dwarf now takes out his dulcimer and amuses himself by watching his paralyzed opponents nodding and wagging their heads without being able to move their hands or feet.

Frøken Birthe comes rushing in to ask for help against her rebellious servants. But what can equal her surprise and indignation when, instead of defending her rights, Herr Mogens and the people he has armed look at her with pitiable expressions, nodding and wagging their heads. She discovers Viderik, who, with malicious delight, is observing the scene his wizardry has created. He freely and familiarly approaches Birthe, jovially claps her on the shoulder, and addresses her as "Sister," while shaking her hand and kissing her. She thrusts him away and tries to impress him with her dignity. But Viderik points out her frizzy hair and the other ways in which she resembles him, and her sudden outburst of ill temper, her clenched fists, and her stamping feet clearly confirm that *Birthe* is a *troll*.

The family ascends from the earth. The armed farmhands regain the use of their limbs, but use them only to save themselves by flight. Mogens is encircled by small trolls who dance about him and stick him in the ribs. Muri goes over to Birthe and opens her arms in a maternal embrace. Diderik and Viderik amiably greet their sister and ask her to accompany them on their journey. But Birthe would rather die than return to her race, and she cannot be coerced. Muri therefore wishes to see her provided for and turns to Herr Mogens, who she knows has proposed to her daughter. But things have changed: the manor no longer constitutes part of the dowry. However, Muri does not feel embarrassed.

She gives a signal, and the dwarves come in dragging coffers and sacks of money which they load onto the wheelbarrow and parade before the astonished suitor, who is soon convinced that this wealth is no delusion. Muri, her sons, and her entire household now sadly depart the country, while Mogens, who orders the dowry wheeled out in front of him, offers the Frøken his arm and takes the "troll for gold."

FINAL SCORE

Twilight spreads. Summer glows in all its radiance. The Midsummer procession draws near with its rustic splendor of banners, flower garlands, and sprays. The medieval Bacchus is seated on his cask, which is borne about in triumph. Jugglers and dancing gypsies accompany the people of the manor, and two waiters with wands and silver tankards head the procession.

Hilda, richly dressed and surrounded by distinguished kinsmen, enters and receives the homage of all. Ove chivalrously kneels before her. She once again presents him with the golden cup and and gives him her hand and her heart.

A seat of honour is erected for the young master and mistress.

Music sounds, dancing heightens the joy, and beneath the decorated Maypole, Midsummer is celebrated.

* * *

ABDALLAH

A Ballet in Three Acts by
August Bournonville

Music composed by Holger Simon Paulli

Scenery by Christian Ferdinand Christensen and Troels Lund

Costumes designed by Edv. Lehmann

Machinery arranged by Hr. Weden

Performed for the first time at the Royal Theatre on
March 28, 1855

Characters

ISMAEL, the Sheik, who first appears as
 a Stranger ....Hr. Füssel, Sr.

SELIME } his daughters .... { Jfr. Garlieb
GULNARE }   { Jfr. S. Price
FATIME, a townsman's widow .... Jfr. J. Fredstrup
IRMA, called "The Gazelle," her daughter .... Jfr. Juliette Price
ABDALLAH, a young shoemaker .... Hr. Hoppe
HASSAN, his comrade .... Hr. Hoppensach
PALMYRA, a Georgian slave girl .... Mme. Kellermann
AZELI, a serving maid .... Mme. Stillmann
OMAR, master of the seraglio .... Hr. Gade
CAPIDGI BACHI .... Hr. Füssel, Jr.
SADI, a little Negro slave .... Carl Price
SONS OF THE SHEIK, COURTIERS, JOURNEYMEN, COMMONERS, GUARDS, SLAVES AND SLAVE GIRLS.

Solo Dances

Messieurs Funck and Lund; Mlles. Fredstrup, Rostock, Bills, and Borup

The action takes place in Balsora, after the time of the Caliphs.

ACT I

An open square in one of the suburbs of Balsora. To the left, Abdallah's dwelling, with an awning over the door; to the right, Fatime's house, with a stone staircase. Upstage, a monumental well.

SCENE ONE

Groups of people are chattering and buying oranges at the well. Abdallah and Hassan are hard at work. The former is fashioning a pair of dainty lady's slippers, the latter a pair of enormous boots.

Abdallah is madly in love with little Irma, whose light dancing and vivacious eyes have earned her the name of "The Gazelle." Hassan is not in love and is trying to discover for whom his friend intends the richly embroidered shoes.

Two young maidens come to draw water from the well. They catch sight of Irma, who appears on the staircase at that very moment. They call her down in order to speak with her. Abdallah, who has carved some marks on an orange, tosses it into the basin of the fountain, thereby causing a quarrel among the girls. Hassan steps in to settle the dispute, and reads upon the face of this "apple of discord": "For the lightest foot." The maidens spurn this hackneyed compliment; but when they see the pretty slippers which are to be the prize for the competition, they are tempted to vie for it. The square is deserted. Thus they may safely proceed with this little jest, and there now unfolds a dance in which Irma (as Abdallah was hoping) walks off with the victory. The two vanquished maidens go away displeased, and Irma hurries in to her mother, delighted at her triumph.

SCENE TWO

A group of merry journeymen come to fetch their friends for an evening of fun. Abdallah declines, but, as usual, Hassan goes along for a drinking spree. The shoemakers perform a lighthearted dance, laugh at their infatuated comrade, and run off to the tavern.

SCENE THREE

Irma and Abdallah meet once again and confess their love for each other. Her mother enters and is surprised to see her daughter give the young man her hand. She hastens to throw a heavy veil over the maiden's head, but the opening made for the eyes is large enough for Abdallah to be able to read therein his future happiness. Fatime will have nothing at all to do with this proposal and resists the young couple's pleas with all her might.

SCENE FOUR

An alarming din comes closer and closer. A mob of people flock in; something new is going on: Sheik Ismael has been toppled from power and the Sultan has sent his Capidgi Bachi to fetch his head. A terrible punishment threatens anyone who does not surrender the fugitive, dead or alive. Everyone bows to the master's will and accompanies the guards, who hurry further on.

SCENE FIVE

The lovers and the mother remain behind, alarmed by this unfortunate warning. A Stranger approaches them and begs for refuge from his pursuers. The young people's hearts are moved, but Fatime sees only the misfortune that will befall them if they harbor a fugitive and, terror-stricken, turns him away. He raises his eyes to Heaven, wraps himself in his cloak, and resigns himself to the will of an inexorable fate. But Abdallah follows his heart, offers the Stranger a home in his humble dwelling, and swears to defend him with his life. Irma enthusiastically espouses her lover's generous purpose and, despite her mother's objections, leads the fugitive to his hiding place.

SCENE SIX

The mob of people returns. Hassan and his comrades are in the midst of the rabble. They have discovered that the Sheik is somewhere in the neighbourhood, and a house-to-house search is to be made. The leader comes to Abdallah's dwelling. But here the sounds of a zither and lively dance melodies can be heard. Capidgi Bachi stops at the door, and the people's anxiety dissolves into joy when they see "The Gazelle" jump out of the shoemaker's shop. She hovers playfully around the fierce Turk, who abandons his suspicions, strokes his beard, and, smiling, leaves with his executioners.

Abdallah's friends congratulate him on his pretty fiancée, and everyone goes home except Irma, who takes from her breast a little jewel which she hands her lover as a remembrance of this event and as a pledge of her eternal fidelity. Night falls. Irma and her mother say goodbye, and after his prayers and ablutions, Abdallah returns to his guest.

ACT II

The interior of Abdallah's dwelling. Doors on both sides; tools and simple furniture.

SCENE ONE

By the light of his lamp, Abdallah prepares a meal for his guest, who may now venture forth from his hiding place without fear. The Stranger climbs up from the cellar, pale and trembling with fever. Abdallah warms, refreshes, and nurses him, but refuses the gold which is offered him for his hospitality.

The Stranger, who intends to depart this very night, wishes, however, to leave behind a little token of appreciation for his kind host, and therefore asks him not to refuse a gift of lowly appearance – an old five-branched candlestick – but one which has the property of fulfilling a wish every time one of its candles is lighted. Only, one must guard against lighting all five of them, for then the magic will be gone and the good fortune lost. Abdallah is both astonished and distrustful. But the Stranger repeats his explanation several times and finally leaves, blessing the hospitable house and warning his young friend yet another time.

SCENE TWO

Abdallah is alone. Happy at the good deed he has done, he thinks of Irma, presses her gift to his lips, and almost forgets the one he has just received. To him the Stranger's suggestion appears so vague that he regards the whole thing as a clever joke. However, his lamp is nearly extinguished, and in order to replace it he lights the first candle.

SCENE THREE

A dazzling radiance fills the low room. There is noise outside, and black slaves enter to ask for Abdallah's commands. He tries to recover from his astonishment and asks that they bring him new clothes. The slaves hurry away and return immediately with complete dress for a distinguished gentleman: caftan, turban, shoulder scarf, pipe, and whip; nothing is forgotten. But the humble surroundings do not correspond to this magnificence. He therefore lights the second candle, and his hut is transformed into a sheik's palace, the couch into a divan; a richly laid table comes up from the floor, and the candlestick rises into the air on a bronze pillar. Noisy table music and numerous servants, with Omar at their head, surround the stupefied Abdallah; delicious dishes and choice fruits are set before him; only wine and women are lacking. He jests about this with Omar. But the black master of the seraglio recoils in horror: the Law forbids the use of strong drink, and he dare not open his master's harem. Abdallah, who now knows the way to the fulfillment of his wishes, lights the third candle.

SCENE FOUR

A curtain is drawn aside and one sees a dazzling hall where a host of women in splendid dress are reclining on Persian carpets in luxuriant groups. Enthroned in its midst sits Palmyra, who at the sight of Abdallah descends the broad staircase and dances toward him. She pours wine for him, strews his divan with flowers, and places garlands on his head while the other slave girls embrace him with caresses and intoxicate him with smoking incense. Completely enthralled, he follows Palmyra up into the enchanting hall, where refreshments are brought forth.

SCENE FIVE

The rumor of Abdallah's elevation has spread throughout Balsora. Hassan hastens to congratulate his comrade and share in his luxurious living. His boisterous gaiety ceases momentarily at the sight of all this magnificence. But he asks the slaves to inform their master that his good friend wishes to speak with him. The slaves laugh at Hassan and Omar threatens him with his stick. But he is not disconcerted. He trips the big Negro, and in all friendliness, steps over him in order to pour himself a glass of wine.

SCENE SIX

Upon hearing this noise, Abdallah comes rushing in and is unpleasantly surprised at encountering this self-invited guest. But his embarrassment becomes even greater when he sees Irma enter with her mother. He turns away and assumes such a haughty air that for a moment they doubt whether it is really he. However, on Hassan's repeated assurances he is recognized by Fatime, who, delighted with Abdallah's power and wealth, embraces him and leads her daughter over to him. But Irma, who is painfully aware of the change which has taken place in his disposition, asks him with loving anxiety if he has forgotten his little "Gazelle." Abdallah cannot resist her charm. He throws off his tiresome finery, rushes toward her, and shows her the keepsake she gave him. He has retained it even in the midst of all this splendor. Joy returns. Irma dances about and the three are happy once more.

SCENE SEVEN

Astonished, Palmyra and the slave girls appear and ask who this strange maiden can be. Irma greets them in a friendly manner and indicates by executing a few steps that she is the one who among all the maidens of Balsora has received the name of "The Gazelle." But she stops, unpleasantly affected at seeing the intimacy with which these beautiful women surround Abdallah. He, who is somewhat gauche himself, thinks he is doing everything right and showing Irma great honour by having costly clothes brought to her and giving her a place in his harem. But Irma rejects his offer with resentment, casts a sorrowful and reproachful glance at the bewildered man, and rushes off.

SCENE EIGHT

Abdallah stands there brokenhearted, but the mother will not let the matter rest. She showers her unfaithful son-in-law with threats and curses and seeks help from Hassan. He, however, has drunk so much that he has finally fallen asleep over his cup. Fatime rouses him in order to avenge her daughter's honour. Hassan pounds the table and tries to run to help, but his steps are faltering, his notions vague. He is not certain whether a compromise is to be reached or if the matter should come to blows; finally, Abdallah sees no other means of ridding himself of these tormenting spirits than to light the fourth candle. A crash is heard, and the unwelcome guests disappear through the floor.

SCENE NINE

Cups are filled and emptied again. Cymbals and drums sound, and, intoxicated, Abdallah whirls around in a bacchantic dance with Palmyra, who is still vainly questioning him about Irma's gift. Everyone kneels before him, and the stupefying incense robs him of the last vestige of reason. The slaves carry him on their shoulders in triumph, and in a frenzy of presumption he lights the fifth candle. Everything is transformed. The candlestick tumbles down and is extinguished in the fall. The slaves spring up with anger and scorn; the women flee; magnificence and joy, cushions and table, music and incense-all vanish before Abdallah's eyes, and a hail of blows is the sad ending to his lost splendor. He is lying once again in his poor room and sees the Stranger standing threateningly at the threshold.

ACT III

A large garden with a fountain and flower beds. The foreground forms a splendid veranda with entrances on both sides.

SCENE ONE

Selime and Gulnare, Sheik Ismael's daughters, are at home. Morning. Their father's fate fills them with anxiety, and it is in vain that their serving maid, Azeli, tries to cheer them while little Sadi brings them fruits and various birds. They leave in order to seek solitude.

SCENE TWO

The indifferent slaves, on the other hand, give themselves up to joking and playing games. Azeli dresses the Negro boy as a lady in order to deceive Omar, who is on the verge of becoming angry, when all of a sudden the sounds of martial music, which gradually draws closer, are heard. The master's return is announced, and Omar hastens to remove the women.

SCENE THREE

Dressed in magnificent armor, Ismael appears, surrounded by his eight sons, whose bravery has given him victory over his enemies. He resumes the seat of his power. His daughters throw themselves into their father's arms. The people flock to the palace and everyone gives thanks to Heaven. Ismael has brought with him a sister for his daughters. It is Irma, to whom (next to Abdallah's help) he owes his salvation. From now on she shall remain in his household and he will see to her future. "Forget your faithless lover," he tells her, "and choose a husband worthy of you from among my brave sons." The young warriors vie to please her, and the sisters try to guide her choice. But although she gratefully acknowledges all the kindness that is shown her, she confesses to the Sheik that she cannot drive the image of Abdallah from her heart. Ismael gestures to Omar, who hurries off, and to his daughters, who lead Irma away with them.

SCENE FOUR

A signal is now given for the games to begin, and, with javelins in their hands, the young chieftains perform a martial dance, which ends in reclining groups.

SCENE FIVE

Omar brings an announcement, and Ismael bids the assembly

withdraw. They bring in Abdallah and Hassan, blindfolded. When the blindfolds are removed for a moment, they rush into each other's arms, firmly convinced that death awaits both of them. Hassan tries to see whether it might be possible to escape, but the guard seizes him and he is dragged away, while Abdallah, who calmly resigns himself to his fate, is led around in circles to the same spot where they have, in the meantime, erected a throne upon which a veiled woman is sitting, surrounded by a numerous court.

Abdallah is waiting to hear his death sentence. Omar walks toward him with a deadly serious expression on his face, but breaks into a smile when he asks the young shoemaker to sew a pair of slippers for the princess. Abdallah can breathe once more, and with profound humility he approaches to take the measurement. But he knows this foot. It is impossible to mistake it, for there is only one such pair of feet in all Balsora. He recoils, trembling. He neither can nor will obey the given order. The Sheik gives a sign and they leave Abdallah alone with the veiled lady.

SCENE SIX

His suspicion now becomes certainty. It is Irma, who lets him know how deeply he has hurt her. Abdallah acknowledges his fault and wishes to escape from her sight forever. In bidding farewell, he wishes only to return to her the jewel she gave him in happier days. The sight of it arouses Irma's fondest memories and melts her heart. She forgives her contrite lover. Ismael is summoned to witness their recaptured happiness, and everyone gathers round to see and to congratulate the young couple.

SCENE SEVEN

Outfitted with ridiculous magnificence, Fatime comes to embrace her daughter, who has been elevated to such a high estate; but she is still firmly opposed to her union with Abdallah. She is interrupted by Hassan, who has once more eluded the guard and prostrates himself before the Sheik. But the latter also has a pleasure in store for Hassan: the entire court orders shoes from him, and he rushes off, delighted with his dignified new occupation. Fatime softens upon seeing Abdallah dressed in magnificent attire and received as the Sheik's foster son. With her consent, Ismael unites the young couple, and their wedding festivities shall be celebrated to the strains of the same music that was heard on that fateful night when "The Gazelle" saved the ruler by her dancing.

* * *

IN THE CARPATHIANS
(I Karpatherne)

A Ballet in Three Acts by
August Bournonville

Music composed by Holger Simon Paulli

Scenery by Christian Ferdinand Christensen

Machinery by Hr. Weden

Costumes designed by Edvard Lehmann

Performed for the first time at the Royal Theatre on
March 4, 1857

Characters

COUNT BATHYANI, a Hungarian magnate	Hr. Füssel, Sr.
JUNKER PAUL, his son	Hr. Brodersen
COUNTESS SOPHIE, his niece	Jfr. S. Price
GREGOR ⎫ peasants born on the	⎧ Hr. Scharff
LASLO ⎭ Count's estate	⎩ Hr. Stramboe
MATTHIAS, a tenant farmer	Hr. Füssel, Jr.
WILMA, his daughter	Jfr. Juliette Price
ANDREAS, the farm bailiff	Hr. Hoppensach
FARKAS, the Count's hussar	Hr. Gade
POLGAR, a gypsy chieftain	Hr. Funck
WANDA, his mother	Jfr. J. Fredstrup
ERZI, his wife	Jfr. P. Fredstrup
NORA, her sister	Hr. Ring

A PITMAN, MINERS, PEASANTS AND DOMESTICS.

Dream Pictures

The Action

ACT I: The gold mines in Schemnitz
ACT II: Gypsy life
ACT III: The wine harvest in Tokay

The Dances

ACT I

"The Dream"

Spirits of Luxury: Miles. Garlieb, Bills, Borup, Holm, Hammer, Eydrup, Nielsen, Juul, Olsen, Walbom, Thorberg, and Hansen

Spirits of Avarice: Miles. J. Fredstrup, Larcher, Wering, Eggersen, Andersen, and Larsen

Elf-maidens: Juliette Thorberg, Johanne Petersen, Alvide Møller, together with nine other children

Wilma: Jfr. Juliette Price; Laslo: Hr. Stramboe; Gregor: Hr. Scharff

ACT II

"The Prophecy"

Jfr. Petrine Fredstrup

Mme. Stillmann; Jfr. Bills; Jfr. Borup; Miles. Holm, Werning, Eggersen, Hammer, Juul, Larsen, Olsen, and Thorberg

"The Gypsy Polka"

Messieurs Funck, Stramboe, Fredstrup, Andersen; Mile. Fredstrup, Mme. Stillmann, Mile. Bills, Mile. Borup, together with the corps de ballet

ACT III

The Three Suitors: Messieurs Nehm, Sr., Busch, and Ring
The Three Mothers: Miles. J. Fredstrup, Larcher, and Andersen
CZARDAS: Hr. Brodersen and Jfr. Sophie Price; Hr. Scharff and Jfr. Juliette Price, together with the corps de ballet
SLOVANKA: Messieurs Funck, Gade, Stroboe, Fredstrup, and Andersen; Mmes. Fredstrup, Garlieb, Stillman, Bills, and Borup, together with the corps de ballet
CHANGING DANCE: Hr. Hoppe and Jfr. Juliette Price
FRISCHKA: All of the soloists and the corps de ballet

ACT I

The stage represents a pit in the mines at Schemnitz. Sloping ladders lead upward through the shaft, and a waterwheel serves to hoist up the baskets containing the ore. The cave is dimly lit by lamps.

SCENE ONE

Hammer strokes can be heard in the shaft to the left. Gregor comes out and informs the pitman that he is going to leave the mines in order to return to his home. The latter is reluctant to see him go but, when all persuasion proves fruitless, pays him the wages that are due him for his work.

SCENE TWO

The miners announce that everything is ready for the explosion. The sulphur thread is lighted, and a deafening roar is heard inside the mountain. The loosened block is drawn out of the shaft and is found to be rich in ore.

The pitman distributes money to the workers, and Laslo brings the meal, which is devoured amid merry conversation.

The mood is momentarily clouded by a subject which the pitman touches upon: he warns them against the temptations of gold. But down through the thousand-foot-high shaft come the strains of gypsy music from a rural fête. This awakens in the miners' breasts an inexpressible longing, and they receive permission to ascend to the surface, so long as one of them remains behind to look after the waterwheel. This lot falls to Gregor, who must resign himself to his fate and put off his journey until the following morning. Laslo, who wishes to go along with the others, is disappointed when the ladder is drawn up and the basket ascends before he can get ready. He is beside himself with vexation.

SCENE THREE

Gregor consoles his comrade, who must keep him company against his will. While Laslo examines the contents of the food basket, Gregor daydreams about the keepsakes his beloved girl has given him. He is delighted with the money he has earned, and with it – in accordance with native custom – he hopes to redeem his bride.

Above them the lively dance melodies resound, calling the two friends to their longed – for home. They wrap themselves in their cloaks, and each falls asleep on his stone bench.

SCENE FOUR

The mist of dreams hovers over the sleeping men, but the mountain is soon radiant with dazzling brightness. Everywhere, gold gushes forth and assumes the most varied forms. Young maidens with golden bows adorn themselves with pearls and flowers, drink from precious cups, and whirl about in voluptuous dances. A second band of female creatures, old, haggard, and with flowing hair, burst forth from the cave, scoop up gold from the ground, and cram it into sacks amid quarrels and struggling.

Laslo and Gregor appear in the midst of these groups and are attracted, in turn, by the forces of Luxury and Avarice.

A violent thunderclap frightens away all these fantastic characters. The back of the cave opens, and Gregor once again sees his home, while Laslo anxiously guards the moneybags he has captured from the old women.

Gregor sees his beloved: the graceful Wilma is standing on the bridge which leads from the vineyard to her father's farm. She tosses him a bouquet and rushes into his arms.

Laslo, who cannot bear to tear himself away from his riches but is unable to carry them alone, tries in vain to get the young couple to help him with his precious burden. He will even share it with them if only they will carry the sacks away from here. But they smile at him with pity and by their dancing and caresses indicate that gold means nothing to them: Love is everything. A new clap of thunder is heard; the heaps of gold vanish before Laslo's eyes, and three children dressed half as fairies and half as gypsies come skipping toward him, playing on flute and zither; they transform his despair into vivacity. It seems that he can play a number of instruments, and he forgets his vanished wealth by joining in the dance which is performed by Wilma, Gregor, and a host of child musicians.

The images are confused. The Spirits of Luxury separate Gregor from Wilma, who is surrounded by the old women with their moneybags. Bouquets fly between the lovers, who are drawn farther and farther away from each other. Laslo yearns once more for gold. Darkness falls again. The landscape disappears. Everything resumes its old form – the dream is over.

SCENE FIVE

Gregor and Laslo awaken and try in vain to remember what they have dreamt. High above the shaft the morning bell sounds; the miners return and express their sorrow upon learning of the friends' decision, for Laslo has decided to accompany his comrade. The pitman gives them his blessing. Everyone shakes hands with the men who are leaving, and they decorate the basket which is to carry them up to the surface. The wheel is set in motion, the basket ascends, farewells resound from above and below, and the men hurriedly set to work in order to banish their sad thoughts.

ACT II

A wild woodland area with mountains in the background.

SCENE ONE

A band of gypsies has camped at the side of a public highway. It is nearly dawn. The men are asleep under the open sky; the women, in tents. Polgar is awakened by his old mother, who reminds him of the day's business and orders the entire band to rise. Everyone gets up;

morning prayer is read and breakfast is prepared. They will break camp today, but first the common treasure must be buried in a safe place.

SCENE TWO

Gregor and Laslo, who are on their way home, happen to be passing by at this moment and are taken for spies. Their knapsacks are searched, and Gregor, who offers some resistance, is on the verge of being maltreated.

SCENE THREE

Erzi emerges from her tent and halts the confusion. She has immediately perceived their innocence, and commands that they be treated hospitably. She examines Gregor's hand and brow and assembles her girls in order to read his horoscope in a fantastic dance. She shows him the name of his beloved and prophesies good fortune for him.

SCENE FOUR

Gregor thanks the chieftain and his wife and is about to proceed with his journey. But they persuade him to tarry for a bit, while the men go hunting and the women pick berries in the forest. Laslo, who has taken great delight in Erzi's sister, the pretty little Nora, has no objection to staying here, though he is teased incessantly by boys and girls alike. They spread out on all sides, while Gregor tells Erzi, Wanda, and Nora his plans and what has befallen him.

SCENE FIVE

The sound of horses at full gallop draws nearer. Gregor looks across the highroad and hurries away. Polgar, Laslo, and the gypsies come running and, startled, look toward the public highway, where a travelling carriage is being dragged toward a precipice by a pair of runaway horses. The men rush to help, and Nora reports that the fearless Gregor threw himself on the horses' bridles and saved the travellers from death. He is carrying an unconscious woman, who is given over to the women's care, while the men crowd around an old gentleman who is still deathly pale and trembling. Both these people think they have fallen among robbers, but Polgar calms the strangers and Erzi kisses the hand of Count Bathyani as a sign that she and the whole band acclaim the magnate as their august protector.

Gregor is introduced as the courageous rescuer of the Count and his niece, and the Count assures him of his gratitude.

The gypsies are invited to glorify the celebration of the wine harvest on the Count's estate with their music and dancing.

They gladly accept the invitation and weave a sedan chair for the young Countess. The entire camp pulls up stakes and forms an escort around the Count, who is jubilantly accompanied to his castle with drums beating and banners flying.

Filled with hope and longing, Gregor and Laslo hasten onward to their home.

ACT III

The stage represents a vast mountain landscape. To the left, Matthias's tenant farm. In the background, vineyards and a bridge leading across a waterfall to the Count's castle. The atmosphere and lighting are those of a lovely autumn day.

SCENE ONE

Matthias is busy with the wine harvest. Andreas presents himself as a suitor for his daughter's hand. But Erzi and Nora tell Wilma that her true love will soon return. The ridiculous suitor becomes the object of the maidens' mischievousness and goes angrily away.

SCENE TWO

Accompanied by his servant – the merry hussar Farkas – Junker Paul is keeping company with the young girls; he is surprised by the arrival of his father and flees.

Count Bathyani brings with him his pretty niece, whom he has destined to be his daughter-in-law. Countess Sophie notices that her cousin is somewhat frivolous, and the Count himself is disheartened by this. Erzi has devised a means of capturing the inconstant fellow. The Count agrees to the plan, and Wilma and Nora lead the Countess into the courtyard of the tenant farm.

SCENE THREE

Erzi welcomes Gregor, who, with deep emotion, asks for his beloved and wishes to see her at once. But when at the same time the gypsies march past to the dream melody, Erzi makes him sit down at the table with his hands over his eyes, while she leads Wilma to the bridge and gives her a bouquet, which she tosses to Gregor.

A scene expressing the joys of recognition.

Gregor and Wilma show each other the keepsakes which they have faithfully retained. The money pouch she embroidered for him also appears. It is empty! But what is gold in the face of true love?

SCENE FOUR

Assailed by wealthy suitors, Matthias decides to give Wilma to the man who can offer the largest wedding gift. Gregor, who has concealed his wealth from his beloved, rejoices in the hope of being the victor.

SCENE FIVE

Countess Sophie, dressed in Wilma's village costume, is given her instructions by Erzi and Nora, and sent to the vineyard. Count Bathyani informs his son of the marriage plans he has in store for him, whereupon he goes off with Andreas and Matthias, who have come to ask him to honour the harvest festival with his presence. Farkas calls his young master's attention to a young maiden who is coming from the mountain with a basket of grapes on her head. Paul finds her attractive and is ever more captivated by her charms; but he is interrupted by Farkas, who announces a whole flock of mothers and daughters. As the Junker gazes after them, the pretty maiden slips away, and he hurries after her in order to seek her out.

SCENE SIX

Laslo, who has not failed to take advantage of the money he has acquired, is now considered a good match and is especially sought after by mothers with marriageable daughters. Farkas's gallantries are scornfully rejected, and every means is employed to focus Laslo's attention on this or that young maid who might be a fitting wife for him. The supposed "goldfish" puts on all sorts of airs, flatters and rejects, and from this arises a dancing scene in which Laslo finally has difficulty in making a choice. But Nora breaks off this jest and tells how he paid court to her. The mothers become angry, and Nora must defend the unfaithful swain.

SCENE SEVEN

The inhabitants of the neighbourhood crowd around in order to witness the competition of Wilma's suitors. Three well-to-do farmers present their bridal offerings in turn, and Matthias proudly nods as he directs meaningful glances at Andreas. Then Gregor appears and announces himself as the man who has captured the maiden's trust. General astonishment. Wilma clings to him, and both plead with her father; but the latter obstinately states that he will give his daughter only to a rich man. Full of confidence, Gregor now lays his entire little fortune on the table; but Andreas outbids him. Laslo, who has long wrestled with his natural tightfistedness, now makes a magnanimous gesture by helping his friend with all that he possesses… Andreas outbids them and triumphs! He shakes hands with Matthias and runs off to prepare everything for the exchange of vows. The crowd disperses, displeased.

Weeping, Wilma is led home by her father; and Gregor stands crushed, surrounded by a few of his friends.

SCENE EIGHT

Paul pursues the beautiful maiden who, moved by his pleas, accepts a ring and shakes hands with him as she enters the farmyard. Gregor, who, deceived by the costume, thinks he recognizes Wilma, angrily hurls himself at the Junker. People flock to the spot; Farkas and the servants overpower Gregor and lead him away. The Count appears and Wilma throws herself at his feet.

An explanation is demanded. Gregor is led forth; Bathyani recognizes him as the man who saved his life and promises him his protection. The ridiculous farm bailiff cannot become Wilma's husband; the Count himself will provide the trousseau. Every misunderstanding is cleared up when the young Countess, in a dress befitting her station as a lady, emerges from the farmyard and shows Paul the ring he gave her as the harvest maiden. He happily kneels at his bride's feet. The harvest festival seals the covenant of love. Everyone is happy.

The gypsy band strikes up and the ball is opened, by Junker Paul and his bride on one side and Gregor and Wilma on the other, with the Magyars' favourite dance, the Czardas.

A mixed quadrille of Hungarians and gypsies, headed by Polgar and Erzi, performs a lively Slovanka.

A large wreath of grapes is brought in and hoisted up beneath the leafy canopy. A young huntsman hands a thyrus to Wilma, with whom he performs a Changing Dance as a prelude to a festive finale.

The Count offers a cask of his finest wine, and with a pistol shot personally opens the source of the sparkling Tokay. Tankards are filled and jubilant cries of *"Elien"* (*Vivat*) are given for the Count and the bridal couples.

A merry Frischka ends the ballet.

* * *

THE FLOWER FESTIVAL IN GENZANO
(Blomsterfesteni Genzano)

A Ballet in One Act
by
August Bournonville

Music by Edvard Helsted and Holger Simon Paulli

Scenery by Christian Ferdinant Christensen and Troels Lund

Performed for the first time at the Royal Theatre on December 19, 1858

Characters

ROSA	Jfr. Juliette Price
PAOLO, her fiancé	Hr. Scharff
GELSOMINA	Mad. Kellermann
VIOLETTA	Jfr. P. Fredstrup
LILA } ....her friends	Jfr. Sophie Price
GIACINTA	Mad. Stillmann
FIORABELLA	Jfr. Garlieb
PATER FRANCESCO, a monk	Hr. Hoppensach
FELICE, a Corporal	Hr. Füssel, Sr.
GASPARO, a bandit	Hr. Gade
CHRISTOFFANO } .....his boon companions	Hr. Andersen
MATTEO	Hr. Stendrup
GIACCOMO } .... young peasants	Hr. Stramboe
PASQUALE	Hr. Fredstrup
MARIANNA, an old woman	Jfr. J. Fredstrup
BENVENUTTO, an innkeeper	Hr. Füssel, Jr.

PEASANTS, MONKS, CARABINIERI, VILLAGERS.

Dances

WALTZ: Mesdames J. Price, Kellermann, Fredstrup, Stillmann, S. Price, and Garlieb
BALLABILE: Messieurs Hoppe, Funck, Brodersen, Stramboe, and Fredstrup; Mesdames Stillmann, S. Price, and Garlieb
PAS DE DEUX: Jfr. Juliette Price and Hr. Scharff, together with the corps de ballet
FLOWER DANCE: Madame Kellermann, Jfr. Petrine Fredstrup; Messieurs Hoppe and Funck, together with the corps de ballet
SALTARELLO: Messieurs Hoppe, Funck, Brodersen, Stramboe, Fredstrup, and Andersen; Mesdames Kellermann, Fredstrup, Stillmann, S. Price, Garlieb, and Borup; Jfr. Juliette Price and Hr. Scharff, together with the corps de ballet.

The action, which is based in an actual occurrence, takes place at the beginning of this century.

SCENE ONE

The stage represents a wooded area near Arricia. To the left, Rosa's house, with a picture of the Madonna. In the background, a spring rising from a grotto, above which is the road leading to Genzano.

Young girls are binding wreaths for the festival. An old woman gathers arcs and garlands into a heap.

Gelsomina and Rosa bring baskets with bouquets, which they distribute to their friends.

Two little boys destined for the clerical estate enter embroiled in a violent quarrel. Their parents separate them and lead them away. The girls laugh and go on with their work amid playful joking and merry dancing.

SCENE TWO

Pater Francesco surprises the young folk as they are indulging in a diversion he has strictly forbidden, for to him, dancing is the Devil's invention. He reproaches the young girls for their frivolity. They beg his forgiveness and offer him refreshment; while he tastes the wine they continue to dance and hover round the good-natured Father with roguish glances that begin to remind him of the temptation of St. Anthony.

SCENE THREE

Paolo, the finest marksman in the entire district, enters with his rifle slung about his neck, and hastens to his fiancée, the lovely Rosa, in order to bring her the gold watch he has won as the prize for the best shot. His friends Giaccomo and Pasquale can attest to his victory, and only the women's fright keeps him from giving an impromptu demonstration of his skill.

Pater Francesco, who continually comes between the lovers, gives Rosa and Paolo to understand that this day should mainly be one of holy prayer and solemn procession, and orders them to appear at the Flower Festival in humble pilgrim dress. He gives them several more admonitions and exits with the young folk.

SCENE FOUR

The lovers soon forget the Father's prohibition. They cast off the bothersome cloaks and hats and rush into each other's arms. They express their mutual tenderness, and feelings of solemnity alternate with innocent jesting.

SCENE FIVE

A confused-looking man, showing every sign of terror and desperation, rushes toward Rosa and Paolo, who recoil in fear when they recognize the notorious bandit Gasparo. But the latter allays their fears, indicates that he is being hotly pursued, and that his life is at stake unless compassionate people will give him refuge. He is ready to drop from exhaustion. The lovers are moved by his plight and give him aid and refreshment. Gasparo thanks Paolo and fixes a burning glance on the young girl. They hear noises coming from every direction. There is no avenue of escape, but Rosa hides the fugitive under the mass of flower garlands which have been bound for the festival, and the lovers agree not to betray the unfortunate man.

SCENE SIX

The *carabinieri* come rushing forth from all sides, led by their corporal Felice, who zealously inquires after the man they are pursuing. However, neither Paolo nor his friends can give him any information. Pater Francesco learns that a reward of 500 *scudi* is being offered to anyone who turns in the bandit dead or alive.

Felice, who by the significant glances which pass between Paolo and Rosa has begun to suspect the young sharpshooter, tries to tempt him with the promised reward. His suspicions are strengthened by the indignation with which Paolo rejects his offer. The good young man will have to go with the *carabinieri* and remain under their surveillance until Gasparo has been caught. Everyone implores Felice, but he remains adamant. Paolo only has time enough to give his beloved a meaningful sign before he must follow the guards.

SCENE SEVEN

The rest of the people vie to comfort and console the griefstricken Rosa, and they crowd around Pater Francesco, who promises to use all his influence to secure Paolo's release. The young girls are about to remove their flowers from the pile when Rosa, remembering that Gasparo is hidden underneath them, violently prevents them from doing this. But she regains her composure, begs them to invoke the aid of the Madonna for her, and arranges to meet them here in a little while. They sadly exit; and Rosa, who wishes to do what her fiancé charged her to do, fearfully steals a glance at fhe bandit's hiding place and enters her house.

SCENE EIGHT

Pale and trembling, Gasparo rises from the heap of flowers and looks around him. He reflects on the danger from which he has recently escaped and admires the young couple's generosity. But Rosa's beauty has kindled a flame in his breast. He tries to combat his passion, but to no avail. Here the sacred law of gratitude and hospitality pleads its cause in vain. He sees himself as the serpent in the Paradise of Innocence – but everything must yield to his burning desire. He is still wavering when his cronies Christoffano and Matteo steal forth from the thicket in order to show him a means of escape. Gasparo reveals to them his plan to abduct Rosa. They promise to help him, and step aside when they hear her coming. Gasparo, pondering his evil designs, sits down at the stone table in a dark and pensive mood.

SCENE NINE

Rosa emerges from the house, tremblingly approaches Gasparo, and hands him a pilgrim's robe in which he will be able to seek safety and escape. She pities his misfortune, comforts and admonishes him, but darts back, appalled, when he pours out his guilty love for her. She tries to flee, but Gasparo stops her. His strong arms entwine her, and despite her cries of distress and desperate resistance, he drags her away with him toward a distant mountain cave.

Paolo rushes in to save his bride, but Christoffano and Matteo hold him back. A violent struggle ensues, and the courageous youth is about to succumb when Felice appears... the bandits flee... the order to fire is given but Paolo stops the *carabinieri* – he himself will risk the dangerous shot, and as Gasparo flees across the mountain path carrying Rosa in front of him as a shield, he is hit in the head by Paolo's bullet. The criminal lets go of his prey and falls to the ground mortally wounded.

SCENE TEN

The *carabinieri* set off in pursuit of the bandits and seize the dying Gasparo. Felice leads Rosa to her bridegroom, who, overcome with emotion, has fainted in the arms of his friends. The caresses of his beloved restore him to consciousness. She is saved! She is alive! His joy is boundless. Everyone surges forward to congratulate the young couple and to praise Paolo's bold deed, but he explains the whole thing as a miracle of the Holy Madonna, before whose picture they now thank Heaven.

The bandits, bound, are brought forth, Gasparo on a cart. The ladies draw back. Felice consigns the bandit to Pater Francesco's care and the mournful procession moves on.

Joy returns once more. The festival beckons. The young girls gather the rich store of flowers and everyone sets off for Genzano.

Rosa and Paolo hold each other tightly by the hand and follow the happy procession at a distance.

SCENE ELEVEN

The stage is transformed into the interior of an *osteria*. The innkeeper, Benvenutto, welcomes the guests who have come to refresh themselves before the procession. Felice displays the reward he has won for arresting the brigands and tells the story of the entire manhunt. But a solemn march is heard in the distance and everyone rushes out.

TRANSFORMATION

We see the main street in Genzano, magnificently decorated for the Flower Festival.

SCENE TWELVE

The procession to the church and a jubilant return. Happiness, gaiety, and dancing, which ends with:
A *Saltarello*.

* * *

THE MOUNTAIN HUT, OR TWENTY YEARS
(*Fjeldstuen eller Tyve Aar*)

A Romantic Ballet in Three Tableaux
by
August Bournonville

Music by August Vinding and Emil Hartmann

Performed for the first time at the Royal Theatre, May 13, 1859

Characters in the First Tableau

JON GRIMSTAD, a freeholder	Hr. Füssel, Jr.
SIGRID, his wife	Mme. Møller
THAIS, his elder son	Hr. Brodersen
SARA, his daughter-in-law	Jfr. Hammer
SVEND, his younger son	Hr. Gade
ELNA, a servant girl on the farm	Jfr. P. Fredstrup
CHRISTOFFER, a corporal	Hr. Füssel, Sr.
HENNING, a ship's mate	Hr. Fredstrup
GULDBRAND SKAFFER, a peasant	Mr. Hoppensach

PEASANTS OF BOTH SEXES.

The scene is laid in Norway toward the end of the last century.

Characters in the Second and Third Tableaux

SIGRID, an aged widow	Mme. Møller
THAIS JONSON, a freeholder	Hr. Borderson
SARA, his wife	Jfr. Hammer
THORKILD, their son	Hr. Scharff

THREE OF THORKILD'S YOUNGER SIBLINGS	Gold, Tardini, Bryde
GULDBRAND SKAFFER, a peasant	Hr. Hoppensach
KARIN, his wife	Jfr. J. Fredstrup
INGRID, their daughter	Jfr. S. Price
THE OLD MOUNTAINEER	Hr. Gade
ASTA, his daughter	Mme. Stillmann
ERIK, Thorkild's companion	Hr. Stramboe

PEASANTS OF BOTH SEXES.

The action takes place twenty years after that in the first tableau.

FIRST TABLEAU

The stage represents a farmstead. To the left, the main dwelling; to the right, the *stabbur*,* sheltered by pine and fir trees. The farmyard is enclosed by a fence made of diagonal boards, and from the gate the path slopes down to a valley which appears in the background, surrounded by high mountains. Deep in the valley can be seen scattered farms and the gables of a stave church.

SCENE ONE

It is Sunday morning. Sigrid summons the farm maids, sends them to the *stabbur*, and orders them to lay a table outside the house. She gently chides Elna, who stands lost in thought, but soon softens and, in honour of the impending celebration, gives a small silver brooch to Elna and some other finery to the rest of the maids.

SCENE TWO

Thais, in festive dress, enters and thanks his mother for all she has done. His child is to be christened today. Everyone is happy, but Sigrid perceives that her second son is missing. Those present shake their heads, but Elna tries to excuse his absence. At this very moment Svend appears at the fence. His pale face and disheveled clothing give evidence of his debauchery. Sigrid calls him over and in a slightly reproving tone asks him where he has been. Ashamed, Svend remains silent, but when his mother rails at him he takes a playing card out of his pocket, angrily tosses it on the table, and curses his bad luck.

Sigrid is distressed at this. Thais tries to reprimand him and reminds him of the solemnity of the occasion; Svend turns everything

---

* A storage building or crib, with its sills and floor raised above ground by means of pilings.

he says to scorn, takes a swig from his bottle, and bangs the table with his fist. When he hears the church bells ring he roars with laughter and is about to utter a blasphemy, but Elna stops him. Sigrid, who is amazed at the power this humble servant girl has over the lad's wild spirit, gives her an authoritative sign, which Elna respectfully obeys. Filled with milder feelings, Svend embraces his mother and, with his face averted, shakes hands with his brother.

SCENE THREE

Old Jon comes out and gives some orders to the farmhands. He affectionately greets his wife and elder son, but his countenance darkens when he lays eyes on Svend, who shamefacedly lifts his cap. The father cannot refrain from making some bitter remarks while on the other hand praising Thais's sobermindedness. Sigrid and the maids go into the house. With feigned cheerfulness, Svend replies that he has made up his mind to try his luck in the world. Jon regards him with a mixture of pity and indignation, and, laying his hand on the shoulder of his elder son, he gives him a paper turning the farm over to him. Svend can no longer contain his resentment. He accuses his father of partiality and hatred and goads him into a rage with his defiance.

SCENE FOUR

Sigrid quickly comes between them and holds Thais's little son, in his christening dress, before his grandfather's eyes. Jon's anger completely disappears. He embraces his elder son and daughter-in-law and gives the child his blessing. The bells call them to the church in the valley. The inhabitants of the farm set off, and Jon promises to follow them directly. But first he goes inside the house. Elna is standing alone, looking at Svend, who is seated at the table with his clenched fist beneath his chin. He sees her shake her finger at him and he stamps his foot on the floor in return. She is about to sadly go away when he calls her back and silently presses her hand.

Jon comes out of the house again. He gravely sends Elna away and coolly and calmly goes over to his son:

"We two cannot be reconciled... You want to make your way in the world... well then, take your inheritance and the Lord be with you." Svend is about to thank his father but the latter cuts him short, gives him a wallet filled with money, and goes off to the christening.

SCENE FIVE

Deeply moved and ashamed, Svend puts the wallet away and hides his face in his hands. Loud noise and merriment can be heard: it is the two tipplers, Christoffer the Corporal and Henning the Mate, who have invited themselves to the fete and greet their comrade with noise and laughter. They take no notice of his dejection, but quickly snatch a couple of bottles from the richly decked table.

Elna, who is going to the ceremony, tries to warn Svend against such company as this. The impudent guests take the liberty of flirting with her, but Svend pushes them aside and defends the girl.

The bells start to ring, and Elna tries to persuade Svend to go with her to the church. Christoffer and Henning burst out laughing and hint that the pretty lass has considerable power over their friend. Moved by false modesty, Svend angrily tells Elna to go her way. She obeys, but looks back at him with sadness several times.

SCENE SIX

Christoffer compliments Svend on his firm and determined character. Henning, who discovers the playing card Svend had carelessly tossed on the table, proposes a game. Christoffer accepts his invitation. Svend is seized with the desire to wager on Henning's game, but luck is against him.

A number of times, sounds of devotion can be heard from the church in the dale, but they are drowned out by stormy passions. Christoffer offers Svend his place against the unlucky Henning and stations himself behind his chair. Svend plays impetuously and loses everything. Furious, he throws his cards on the table and curses. Hymns are heard once more but are lost amid the clinking of glasses, the winners' cries of jubilation, and the loser's despair.

Christoffer, who has been waiting for this moment, displays a fistful of money, praises Svend's handsome physique, and promises him glory and advancement if he will become a soldier. Svend, whose state of excitement is further heightened by frequent trips to the bottle, accepts the King's shilling, signs the recruiting papers, and immediately sits down again at the table, where dice have now replaced the cards. Svend is lucky with the first throw and grows wild with delight, but the tables quickly turn and soon, out of money and suspecting that he has been taken, he picks a fight, grabs a bottle, and rushes at Henning, who defends himself with chairs. They hear the festive procession returning from the church. Svend must cover up what has happened here. He makes peace with his cronies and, at a loss as to what he should do, runs into the house. As the guests enter the farmyard he comes out onto the steps with a Hardanger fiddle and welcomes the procession with wild and violent music which expresses the storm that is raging within him. Christoffer and Henning retire to a remote corner, where they divide their winnings.

SCENE SEVEN

The young lads, with Guldbrand Skaffer (the liveliest dancer in the district) in the lead, immediately accede to Svend's request, perform breathtaking leaps, and fill the farmyard with resounding hurrahs. Mother Sigrid stops this merriment and, frowning with disapproval, takes the fiddle away from her delinquent son just as Jon Grimstad and the young parents arrive with little Thorkild. Elna reprimands him and persuades him to go inside and put on his Sunday clothes.

Jon thanks all who are present and invites them – Christoffer and Henning included – to the feast which is about to begin. The elders sit down at table while the young girls and children gather round the newly christened babe, who, rocked in his mother's arms, becomes the focal point of a dance in which he is fanned with nosegays and birch twigs.

Christoffer invites Sigrid to dance a minuet. She declines, but when Jon gives his consent, Thais and his wife also join in, and the guests form a circle around them and drink a toast to the family.

Henning and Guldbrand, each with two of the farm maids as partners, dance a reel.

SCENE EIGHT

Svend appears, neatly dressed and well behaved, he respectfully greets his parents and offers his congratulations by embracing his brother and sister-in-law. Elna nods her approval, and a wistful smile plays about his lips. But Sigrid, who is keeping a sharp eye on their familiarity, sends the maid over to pour a glass for the corporal and for the ship's mate, who feel obliged to address coarse jokes to Elna. Svend cannot stand this and starts to fight, but Christoffer stops him by reminding him of his military duty. Suspicious, Sigrid leads Elna over to the other side of the stage, and when she encounters her husband she whispers to him something at which he shakes his head in disapproval.

The fiddler strikes up a tune, and all the men choose their partners for the merry *Springdans*. Elna stands alone and deserted. Svend goes over to her and asks her to dance. His mother tries to prevent this and reminds him of Elna's humble rank, but Svend looks at her with amazement and defiance. Contrary to her prohibition, he dances with the maiden he loves best of all.

SCENE NINE

Evening falls. The long chain of dancers forms numerous curves and circles and disappears into the house.

Svend holds Elna back, and a brief conversation, in which the young couple confess their love for each other, ensues.

SCENE TEN

Christoffer and Henning enter from offstage, bringing with them Svend's equipment. He is to be off this very night. This news comes as a shock to Elna, who has not the faintest suspicion of his enlistment. The old folk must know nothing of it either, and Henning goes inside with Svend while he fetches his clothes and fiddle.

Alone with Elna, Christoffer tries to console her in his own way. He becomes obnoxious, and the girl resists him. Svend returns just as Christoffer is trying to force a kiss. In vain Henning tries to restrain the infuriated Svend; but he is hurled to the ground by a forceful blow from Svend's fist, and the corporal, who has visions of being treated in the same manner himself, draws his saber. Imploring, Elna throws herself between them, but Svend's saber flashes. He lunges at Christoffer. A brief clash of arms is heard... Pale and distraught, Svend rushes across the farmyard... he has his revenge!

SCENE ELEVEN

At Henning's cries of alarm, all the guests emerge from the house. From Elna's despair as well as the general horror, Jon, Thais, and Sigrid quickly realize everything that has happened. Svend is a murderer! He has fled, but all the hatred and condemnation fall on Elna, who was the unwitting cause of the bloody quarrel. Terrified, the guests depart, while the family stays behind to console the unhappy father.

Elna vainly begs for mercy. Everyone scorns her, and Jon Grimstad has just taken her by the hand in order to show her the gate when Svend jumps out of the bushes and defends the maid. Now Jon's anger knows no bounds. He vents his wrath on his son and his contempt on the young man's beloved. Svend is once more roused to defiance. Beside himself with rage, he pays no heed to entreaties or admonitions, and as the despairing family returns to the house, Svend and Elna are cursed by the old father.

Elna collapses at Svend's feet. He stands rooted to the spot, as if struck by lightning.

SCENE TWELVE

All is still in the light summer night. The church bell strikes twelve. Svend looks about him and ponders his fate. Elna opens her eyes but cannot really pull herself together.

Svend has slowly put his knapsack on his back and picked up his Hardanger fiddle. In doing so he involuntarily strikes several faint notes which are reminiscent of the hymns he heard that morning. Elna kneels and prays. She then rises, lays her hand on the shoulder of the unfortunate man, and promises to follow him, even to the ends of the earth. They wander off, and the curtain falls.

NOTE

In the interval between the first and second tableaux, twenty years have gone by. Jon Grimstad is dead and Svend, who has led a wandering life and dwelt in lonely places, has lost his wife, the faithful Elna.

SECOND TABLEAU

The stage represents a *saeter* [summer pasture] situated on high ground, with an extensive view. To the right, a hut.

SCENE ONE

The mountaineer, an elderly bearded man, is busy trimming a spruce tree he has felled. He pauses, wipes his brow, and surveys the glorious landscape which lies before him in the morning sunlight. Filled with sad memories, he stands lost in thought, leaning on his axe. A young girl (clad in a red skirt, with her hair braided across the top of her head) pops out of the hut, jumps up onto the log behind the graybeard, and leans over his shoulder. From their mutual greeting one can immediately perceive that they are father and daughter. She notices that he is dejected and uses all her childish caresses to comfort him. She will even help him with his woodchopping. He looks at her tenderly, kisses her brow, and turns away from her with a deep sigh. "Are you always thinking about my mother?" "Yes. Alas, I can never forget her!" "Did I ever see her?" "Yes, when you were very small." "Was she pretty? Do I look like her? Was she as fond of you as I am?" "She loved me until death. Now she sleeps in the cold ground!" "No, she lives in the radiance of Heaven!" The father gives his daughter a memento of her deceased mother. It is a little silver brooch, which she receives and admires with the utmost delight as she catches sight of her reflection in the rippling spring. But she suddenly remembers her household duties and blows on the *lur* to call home her cows, whose bells can be heard in the distance. She takes her milk pail and hurries off.

The old mountaineer gazes after her with sadness, for he must soon leave her and go off to earn something to keep both of them. He fetches an old fiddle, sits down on a tree stump, tunes the instrument, and plays a few melodies. His daughter returns, accompanying the sounds of the fiddle with some very singular steps. After they have enjoyed a humble meal, the father departs, leaving the little girl alone at the *saeter*.

SCENE TWO

Asta – for that is the young girl's name – waves until her father is out of sight and then tries to amuse herself in her solitude. She delights in gazing at her reflection and rejoices over the lovely brooch she has been given as a memento of her mother. She tosses stones at the birds flying past and blows on the *lur* so weirdly that it resounds in the distance. Noise is heard in the bushes; Asta is frightened but pleasantly surprised when she sees some children's heads come into view among the stones as they ascend the mountain.

She draws the children to her, gives them milk, plays her *lur* for them, and gets them to dance about her. But some older children soon appear and are horrified at the sight of the girl in the red skirt.

It can be none other than the *huldre* [the troll maiden]! Besides, this *saeter* is said to be bewitched. They anxiously gesture to the little ones and fearfully hasten away down the mountain. Asta tries in vain to get them to stay; they flee, and, weeping, she sits down on the log.

SCENE THREE

Two young lads, one of whom is armed for bear-hunting, enter from stage left. Erik, the hunter's companion, approaches with great trepidation and warns his comrade against proceeding any further in these ominous mountains. Thorkild laughs at him but is the first to perceive Asta, and he cannot hide a feeling of astonishment upon seeing the little girl standing alone on the spruce log with an axe on her shoulder. Erik, who is convinced beyond any shadow of a doubt that this is the *huldre* herself, threatens her with a stone, but she springs at him with her weapon raised, and he falls to the ground, terrified. Her hostile attitude does not frighten Thorkild. He waves to show her that he wishes to make peace and lays down his gun on the grass. Asta imitates him and places her axe in a tree. They curiously approach one another, and there now ensues a scene in which the idea of a supernatural being gradually takes possession of the young men's minds; it ends with Asta suddenly running away from them and locking herself inside the hut.

SCENE FOUR

Thorkild is really charmed by this curious revelation, but Erik soon gives him something else to think about by pointing off to the side of the stage from which they entered. The object of their search is quite close to them, and they must either strike or flee. Thorkild checks his flintlock, puts in new gunpowder, and crawls off to the left after his prey. Erik keeps an anxious eye on him. A shot is fired. Erik jumps for joy, but a moment later he is terrified, claps his hands, and saves himself by climbing a tree.

Thorkild comes rushing on in flight, pursued by an enormous, wounded bear. The bluff hunter is about to strike his pursuer with the butt of his gun, but the beast of prey overthrows him, lifts him between his front paws, and squeezes him so that he almost has the wind knocked out of him. But in that same moment, Asta has come out of the hut, seized her axe, and struck the bear such a deep blow in the back of its head that it is forced to let go of Thorkild and falls to the ground swimming in its blood. Thorkild is saved; Erik jumps down from the tree, the bear is slain, and Asta sounds a triumphant call on her *lur*.

SCENE FIVE

Thorkild thanks his saviour and, despite Erik's warnings, invites her to come to his parents' farmstead where she will be given a fine welcome. She is reluctant to do this and with a pensive look sits down on a stone in front of the doorpost of the hut. Erik implores his friend to be wary of this sorceress, but it suddenly dawns on Thorkild that there are ways of freeing her from the powers of darkness. In a friendly manner he approaches Asta and, addressing a few words to her, carves a cross in the doorpost and plants his knife firmly in the beam above her head. Asta rises, having decided to accompany them. She shows them a sledge to which they can lash the dead bear, tosses an animal skin over her head and shoulders, picks up the *lur*, and, as the young men triumphantly pull the sledge, she triumphantly takes her place atop the bear and goes off with them to Grimstad.

THIRD TABLEAU

The main dwelling room at the Grimstad farm. To the left, a large fireplace. Doors to the left and right, with the main entrance upstage. Furnishings and domestic utensils suggest affluence.

SCENE ONE

Old Mother Sigrid is spinning near the hearth, surrounded by three of her grandchildren. One of them holds a portrait which is crudely painted but bears such a striking resemblance to its subject that one immediately recognizes Father Jon. The old woman regards it with silent tears, while the children take turns kissing it, and the eldest of them hangs it on the upstage wall.

SCENE TWO

Some neighbours' children peek in the window and call to the three. Sigrid bids them enter, and they now tell how they were up on the mountain and met the *huldre*. One of the little girls even shows how the troll maiden danced, and Sigrid, with horror, warns them against such encounters.

SCENE THREE

Thais and his wife enter from opposite sides, greet their mother, and give the children permission to play outdoors.

Guldbrand Skaffer and his wife come in through the door with their daughter Ingrid. Thais greets them and sits down to have a serious talk with Guldbrand. The women keep Ingrid with them and treat her with a graciousness that evokes a rather awkward response from her.

SCENE FOUR

The children skip merrily in, followed by a whole crowd of neighbourhood swains, who welcome Thorkild and Erik back from the hunt and toss the fallen bear on the floor. Parents, brother, and sisters gather round Thorkild, who is unusually quiet compared with Erik, who is boasting and joking. Thais and Guldbrand take Thorkild by the hand and lead him over to Ingrid, who is standing between the two mothers. The parents have decided that they shall marry, and their betrothal will take place this very day.

Erik's gaiety suddenly vanishes and he plucks at Ingrid's skirt; but, out of shyness, she avoids him.

All are invited to celebrate the betrothal and the successful bear hunt. They hasten away to put on their best clothes and to fetch their neighbours.

SCENE FIVE

Thorkild tells what happened to him on the perilous hunt and introduces Asta as the girl who saved his life. All are taken aback at the sight of this strange girl, but they soon become more kindly disposed toward her and vie to thank and embrace her. But Asta does not respond to their kindness. She pushes them away and fearfully clings to Thorkild. Sara points out to her husband, "Thorkild's father." Asta is delighted and strokes his cheek. Sara then shows her Ingrid, "Thorkild's fiancée." This is not to her liking. She thrusts the betrothed couple apart and, dissatisfied, goes over and settles down by the fireplace. They coax her, but she lashes out at everyone except Thorkild. She calls him over to her and whispers something in his ear. She notices Ingrid's pretty clothes, rushes over to examine them more closely, and compares them with her own. Sara promises to give her similar apparel if she will come inside with her. Asta jumps for joy and runs off with the women. Thorkild wants to go with her but is held back by his mother, who tries to calm his troubled spirit, while Erik and Ingrid bemoan the fate that will part them forever.

SCENE SIX

Erik, who during the previous scene has been sitting despondently in a corner, stands up to speak to Thorkild. But the latter gives him a very confused answer, and when Ingrid returns, he takes flight.

Conversation between Erik and Ingrid; he utters charges and reproaches, which disconcert the poor girl.

Guldbrand and his wife enter and are greatly displeased with this intimate meeting. They reject all of Erik's ideas but are horrified when they learn that Thorkild has been led astray by another love. And who is she? A *huldre*! They will soon see for themselves.

They hear the stranger coming and hide in a corner.

SCENE SEVEN

Asta, in a pretty peasant costume and with a kerchief on her head, happily comes in with Sara, who hardly gets a chance to complete her toilet. She never tires of the handsome costume and is dying to show Thorkild how she looks. Sara holds a little looking glass up in front of her. Asta is startled when she sees her reflection, thinks the mirror is water, makes several naive experiments, and fearfully hands it back. She notices the portrait of the old man, finds that it resembles her father, and climbs up on a table to kiss it.

At this moment Mother Sigrid enters with the brooch, which Asta forgot when she was getting dressed. The old woman thinks she recognizes it and would like to question the stranger. But Asta jumps down from the table, grabs the piece of jewelry, and when both mothers try to find out where it came from, she bursts into tears and violently pushes them away. Together with Guldbrand, Karin, and Ingrid, Erik emerges from his hiding place. "Beware, it is a *huldre*!" The women are terrified, and the mothers make exorcistic signs at the supposed enchantress. But Thais and Thorkild hasten to pacify them and defend the girl.

SCENE EIGHT

The sounds of drum and fiddle can be heard outside. The guests march in in festive procession and are welcomed with shining silver tankards of the finest ale the farm has to offer.

The walls are decked with garlands and green sprigs, and the dancing is opened by Guldbrand Skaffer, who kicks the rafters in the *Halling* as briskly as he did twenty years before.

The young girls dance Ingrid out of maidenhood, and the married women whirl her into wedded life. Thorkild must go through the same thing with the young lads and the men, all this in the midst of a polska,* during which Asta has sat quietly near old Sigrid with her

---
* A popular Swedish dance of Polish origin.

head in her lap. But when the betrothed couple come together to dance, she suddenly starts up, throws herself between them, and asks to dance with Thorkild herself. General amazement! A mysterious whisper runs through the whole assembly. Thais and Sara shield their son, who is deathly pale and trembling. Ingrid takes refuge with her parents, and Erik hides behind her.

Asta looks around her in astonishment. "Is there no one who will dance with me?" Everyone recoils. "Well, then, I will dance alone"... But the fiddlers, hesitate to play. Then the old mountaineer enters and takes her in his arms. "If no one will dance with you, my daughter, and no one play for you, your old father will come to your aid. Take off this kerchief, let your beautiful locks flow freely, and show these people dancing such as they have never seen." He now takes up his Hardanger fiddle, encourages his daughter, and strikes up a fantastic dance to the sounds of which Asta moves with such wildness that a shudder runs through all assembled. They flee through every exit. Erik drags Thorkild away, and as the dance ends, Asta falls unconscious at the feet of the old mountaineer.

SCENE NINE

Thais and Sara have stayed behind with Sigrid, who has been following everything that has happened from her place by the fireplace. They have recognized those wild tones! The old woman goes over and takes the fiddle out of the musician's hand, while Thais takes the portrait down from the wall and holds it before his brother's eyes.

Svend falls to his knees, brokenhearted. Sigrid holds Asta tightly in her arms. Thais informs his brother than their father's dying words were ones of forgiveness and benediction. The curse is lifted, and the prodigal son has returned to his mother's heart.

SCENE TEN

The glad tidings are joyously proclaimed. Happiness reigns supreme in the mountain hut. Thorkild and Asta shall be wed. Guldbrand units Erik and Ingrid.

All must make merry, and a splendidly laid table is carried in. The joyful company drinks to their future happiness, while old Jon Grimstad's portrait smiles down on them from amid a garland of fresh flowers.

The curtain falls.

*   *   *

FAR FROM DENMARK, OR A COSTUME BALL ON BOARD
(Fjernt fra Danmark eller Et Costumbal ombord)

Vaudeville-Ballet in Two Acts
by
August Bournonville

Music, in part, by Joséph Glaeser, Jr.

Scenery by Troels Lund and Christian Ferdinand Christensen

Costumes designed by Hr. Edvard Lehmann

First performed at the Royal Theatre, April 20, 1860

Characters

FERNANDEZ, the Consul	Hr. Füssel, Sr.
ROSITA, his daughter	Jfr. Juliette Price
ALVAR, her suitor	Hr. Funck
CAPTAIN OF THE DANISH FRIGATE	Hr. Holst
WILHELM, a lieutenant in the Danish Navy	Hr. Scharff
POUL } EDWARD } Danish naval cadets	Jfr. Petrine Fredstrup / Mme. Stillmann
THE FIRST LIEUTENANT	Hr. Ring
NAVAL LIEUTENANTS	Messieurs Paetz, Eckardt, C. Price, and Gerlach
THE CHIEF BOATSWAIN	Hr. Füssel, Jr.
THE STEWARD	Hr. Hoppensach
OLE THE BARGEMAN	Hr. Gade
JASON } MEDEA } Negro servants	Hr. Fredstrup / Jfr. Borup

LADIES AND GENTLEMEN OF SPANISH ORIGIN. SAILORS FROM THE WARSHIP, NAVIGATING APPRENTICES, AND SHIP'S BOYS. NEGROES.

The action takes place on the coast of Spanish South America. In the first act, the scene is laid in the home of Fernandez; in the second, on board the Danish frigate.

Character Dances and Disguises

ACT I

Negro Dance: Hr. Fredstrup, Jfr. Borup. Messieurs V. Price, Stendrup, and four children

ACT II

Eskimo Dance:	Gold, Jeanette Tardini
Chinamen's Dance:	Messieurs Hoppe, Stramboe, Fredstrup. Mile. P. Fredstrup. Mme. Stillmann
Dance of the Bayadères:	Miles. S. Price, Garlieb, Petersen, Thorberg, Walbom, Hammer
Fandango:	Jfr. Juliette Price. Messieurs Funck, Hoppe, Stramboe. Miles. S. Price, Garlieb, Petersen
Indian War Dance:	Hr. Gade, Messieurs Busch, V. Price, Stendrup. Mme. Møller. Jfr. Juul
A Balladmonger:	Hr. Hoppensach
Neptune:	Hr. Füssel, Jr.

Interpolated Musical Numbers

"Negro Dance," after Gottschalk
"Indian War Dance," composed by Lumbye
Act Two "Finale," composed by Lincke

ACT I

The stage represents the veranda of a splendid villa commanding a view of the roadstead, where a Danish frigate is lying at anchor.

SCENE ONE

As the curtain rises, Rosita is seen resting in a hammock, surrounded by Negroes. A young lady is seated at the piano, to the sounds of which two other young women, friends of Rosita, dance, while alternately running from Rosita to a naval officer who is sketching the aforementioned group.

Wilhelm, the Danish naval lieutenant, has finished the sketch and shows it to Rosita, who gives her approval and expresses a desire to own it. But Wilhelm, who wishes to retain it for himself, offers her two other works as compensation, namely, a picture of his native Copenhagen and one of the world-famous Øresund, with Kronborg Castle in the background. Enraptured, the young ladies look at these sketches, and Rosita, who is aware of the power she already exercises over the infatuated seaman, deliberately expresses an indescribable longing to see that far-off land.

SCENE TWO

Fernandez brings in Don Alvar, who hands Rosita a bouquet, which she graciously accepts. Fernandez introduces Wilhelm and Alvar to one another, and each views the other as a rival. Rosita is aware of this feeling, which amuses her and affords her the opportunity for new coquetry.

SCENE THREE

The Negro Jason announces two young naval cadets. Poul and Edward enter, give dignified salutes, and deliver an invitation to a ball to be held on board the Danish man-of-war. Great delight among the women. Influenced by Don Alvar, Fernandez expresses some misgivings, but Rosita has soon managed to overcome them. She takes Wilhelm by the arm, the [other] ladies take hold of the two cadets, and they all hasten away to prepare for the festival.

SCENE FOUR

Alvar tells his prospective father-in-law how dangerous the presence of the Danish naval lieutenant might be for their future plans. But Fernandez tries to calm him by interpreting the whole thing as childish fantasies on Rosita's part. "Besides, surely Wilhelm will soon be travelling home again. Right now let us think of nothing but the coming pleasure trip." He exits.

SCENE FIVE

Jason and Medea are very busy. Still preoccupied with his jealousy, Alvar tries to question them, but one after the other they look at him, show their white teeth, shake their heads, and slip away. Alvar is beside himself with rage and contemplates revenge on his rival.

Medea soon returns and, with a mysterious look, delivers a little box from her mistress: it contains a pair of castanets. Overjoyed, Alvar presses them to his lips, promises to use them in the lovely lady's service, and begins to dance.

The two cadets, who enter just at this moment, cannot resist making fun of the infatuated bolero dancer, but Alvar gives them a look of cold *grandeza* and rushes off.

SCENE SIX

Poul and Edward confide to each other the intoxicating impressions they have received from bewitching Spanish eyes. "But as for Lieutenant Wilhelm, he is really in a bad way."

Ole the Bargeman brings the mailbag, which is inspected with excitement. There is a letter for Poul, one for the Lieutenant and one for himself, several for his comrades, but none for Edward.

The latter sadly sits down at the piano and involuntarily plays the melody of the familiar song:

> Across the wide ocean whose mirror so blue
> Gives back every beauty, reflected,
> I am drawn by my longings to my mother dear;
> In her I can see not a flaw.
> Her glance makes me fearless and brave,
> At the sound of her name my heart thrills with pride.
> Everywhere – in my soul, in my thoughts,
> I see her dear features before me.

With joy and emotion, Poul reads a letter from his beloved mother. Edward buries his face in his hands. Then guns boom in the distance – it is the frigate saluting. The Danish flag waves festively in the breeze. The young friends, feeling that their common "mother" is near, enthusiastically throw themselves into each other's arms.

SCENE SEVEN

Wilhelm enters, in despair over Rosita's caprices, and does not notice the cadets, who approach with military salutes. With an air of importance, Poul hands him a letter – from home! – from *her*! Wilhelm starts and turns pale. The ring he wears on his finger reminds him of the one he had forgotten in the throes of passion. Edward, who repeats the last stanza of the song, adds to his confusion and feeling of shame, and he asks Poul to keep the letter for him until a more tranquil moment. He himself takes the ring from his finger and, when he hears someone coming, puts it in his breast pocket. He starts to leave, but an irresistible sorcery holds him back.

SCENE EIGHT

Jason and Medea bring in several trunks. Rosita, in ball dress, enters on her father's arm. Alvar appears in native Spanish costume, Fernandez in his Consul's uniform. The party gathers for its departure. Wilhelm takes out his handkerchief in order to signal the bargemen. But in doing so, the ring falls out of his pocket and rolls onto the floor. Jason picks it up and gives it to Rosita, who tries in vain to find out who owns it. Wilhelm does not have the courage to claim it, and, accepting it as a gallant gesture, she ties the ring to her fan and takes Wilhelm's arm.

The bargemen fetch the trunks and parcels, and the party leaves, Wilhelm happy, Alvar fuming with rage and jealousy.

SCENE NINE

Poul and Edward express their disapproval of the Lieutenant's behaviour. Jason and Medea, who have noticed that Edward can play the piano, decide to take advantage of their master's absence in order to take a little whirl, and they persuade the naval cadet to play for them a dance, which they perform with immense delight. The children enter with their drums; two other Negroes join them, and the gaiety mounts until Ole interrupts the dancing to summon the laggards to the beach in the greatest haste. Poul and Edward run off with Ole, followed by the vociferous thanks of the Negro family.

ACT II

The stage represents the quarter-deck of a frigate. To right and left, gun ports, shrouds, and hammock netting. At centre stage, the descent to the gun deck. Further back, the mizzenmast, the steering wheel, and the roundhouse. In the foreground, a gaily decorated awning.

SCENE ONE

It is quiet on deck. Ole stands leaning on a gun, reading a letter, while other sailors are writing or sitting around in contemplative attitudes. Sentries are posted at both accommodation ladders, and the boatswain is on the lookout.

The quartermaster's whistle blows, and the men come crowding around from all quarters. A festival is announced. There is to be dancing and mummery, and distinguished guests have been invited aboard. The Captain, who is inspecting the arrangements, expresses his hope that all the men will do honour to their flag by their order and good discipline.

The officers assign the roles and decide that the younger men are to dress up as ladies. A chest with embroidered costumes is carried out, and Ole distributes the costumes, which are tried on with much laughter and provide the opportunity for hilarious jokes.

SCENE TWO

They hear the splash of oars from the barge which is bringing the guests. Someone whistles for the gangplank, which is set in place with due ceremony. The officers, in dress uniform, help the ladies and gentlemen aboard, and the Captain bids them welcome. Rosita and Wilhelm are the last to come aboard, and everyone crowds around the beautiful Argentine maid. Wilhelm is pale and distracted, and his comrades notice how his gaze wanders from Rosita to her hated suitor. Refreshments are offered, and the ladies take their seats beneath the awning.

SCENE THREE

Trumpets announce the opening of the festival. The ship's band heads a procession of seamen, in whose midst Neptune and the Four Winds appear in grotesque form. During a merry reel, two young candidates are brought in for a navigation examination but receive very low marks. Neptune respectfully approaches the Captain and asks him to set the course. The Captain goes along with the joke and indicates on the map: Buenos Aires! At that very moment the Argentine colours are run up and the band plays the national anthem. This compliment is enthusiastically accepted by the guests, who reply by giving a cheer for his Majesty the King of Denmark.

SCENE FOUR

After a quadrille danced by the naval officers together with the visiting gentlemen and their ladies, there follows a series of character dances in the following guises:

1. *an Eskimo Bride and Bridegroom*, portrayed by two ship's boys
2. a *pas de cinq* in Chinese style, by three Spanish gentlemen, with Poul and Edward as the ladies
3. a *bayadère dance*, by Rosita's friends.

This last dance furnishes the opportunity for a toast to the ladies, proposed by the Captain.

SCENE FIVE

The clacking of castanets is heard, and Rosita, in Andalusian costume, comes out of the cabin, thanks the Captain on behalf of her countrywomen, and begins to dance

4. a *Fandango*, in which Don Alvar, the ladies, and their cavaliers take part.

Rosita, who captivates everyone with her grace and lightness, takes a rose from her hair and designates it as the prize for the best dancer. The gentlemen are vying for it when Lieutenant Wilhelm, in Spanish dress, suddenly appears in the ranks of the competitors. The dancing now takes on an ever more dramatic character. None of the rivals will give in, and Rosita always knows how to spur them on with new hope. In her hilarity, she promises to give the prize to the one who can retrieve her fan, and with an easy swing she tosses it overboard.

Everyone is startled, but Wilhelm, who recalls that a precious token is attached to this fan, does not stop to think, and, despite his comrades' protests, dives in after it. General commotion, anxiety, and dejection.

SCENE SIX

Although both the men and the officers think Wilhelm bereft of his senses, they rejoice at seeing him come up with the fan, which he has resued from the waves. He tosses a cloak about him, chivalrously walks over to the proud beauty, and, with a meaningful look, detaches the ring from the ribbon, places it on his finger, and hands her the fan. Rosita looks at the hotly contested rose with embarrassment, but Wilhelm designates Alvar as the winner of the dancing prize, gives a dignified salute, and retires, conscious of having overcome his dangerous infatuation.

SCENE SEVEN

Wild, shrill music is heard, and a new procession appears. It is Ole and five of his comrades. They perform

5. an *Indian War Dance*.

Their menacing, passionate gestures work on Rosita's already overwrought feelings, and she suggests to her father that it is time for them to go. With mutual courtesy, guests and hosts take leave of one another. The Captain places the barge at his guests' disposal, and they leave the frigate at eventide as coloured lanterns are hung about the gaily decorated ship.

SCENE EIGHT

The Captain and his officers seat themselves atop the roundhouse, where they form a jolly group. The men have received permission to make merry on deck. The chief boatswain, still dressed as Neptune, serves punch. Toasts are drunk to the loved ones back home. At the same moment, a familiar melody is heard from down on the gun deck, and a Copenhagen ballad monger (the steward in disguise) pops up and is led forth in triumph among his old friends, has some punch, and distributes ballads. The singing is accompanied by dancing and coquetry. The gaiety mounts, and the popular Muse is soon assailed with importunate homage. Neptune seizes his trident and commands silence. A host of grotesque mermaids ascend from both gangways and form a circle about the mast. They beckon to the good seamen and lure them thither, but the men steadfastly resist them. At a given signal, the fantastic costumes fall away and Danish peasant girls from Sjaelland applaud the astonished sailors. (This scene has as its musical motif the ballad:

> Even though, proud ocean,
> Thou art many a seaman's grave,
> He loves thee.
> But if his native soil he sees,
> Then wide his arms he opens,
> And cries aloud his sweetheart's name –
> In short, is happy.)

An impetuous *longenglesk* replaces the serious song, and the merry couples dance about in whirling circles. The dancing is interrupted by sounds from the coast – it is the guests, who have reached shore and pay their respects to the Danes by having a bugler blow:

> Wave proud on Codan's swells
> O blood-red Dannebrog.

Everyone listens devoutly, and at this moment Wilhelm, in uniform, steps into the foreground. Moved, he stands and looks at the ring he had come so close to losing. A little Amager lass goes over to him and hands him a letter. It is Poul, who has seized the right moment; for while the patriotic song echoes in the distance, Wilhelm reads and kisses the lines, which restore peace and happiness to his soul.

NINTH AND LAST SCENE

At the Captain's orders, bonfires are lighted, the music strikes up a tempestuous gallopade, and the dancing continues with gladness and jubilation on the deck of the frigate – far from Denmark.

The curtain falls.

* * *

THE VALKYRIE
(Valkyrien)

A Ballet in Four Acts
by
August Bournonville

Music by J. P. E. Hartmann

Scenery by Christian Ferdinand Christensen

Costumes by Edvard Lehmann

Performed for the first time at the Royal Theatre,
September 13, 1861

Characters

SVAVA	Jfr. Juliette Price
BRUNE	Herr V. Price
HEIMDAL	Herr A. Fredstrup

HARALD HILDETAND	Hr. Füssel, Sr.
HELGE, his grandson	Herr Scharff
BJØRN, Helge's friend	Herr Gade
NICETAS, a Greek chieftain	Herr Funck

IVAR		Herr Füssel, Jr.
GUTTORM	Vikings	Herr Hoppensach
EIGIL		Herr Andersen

DANISH WARRIORS AND HOUSECARLS. GREEK CHIEFTAINS AND FIGHTERS. BRETON AND GREEK WOMEN. VALKYRIES. GODDESSES. MERMAIDS AND DWARFS.

In Act I the action takes place in Sjaelland; in Act II, on the coast of Brittany; in Act III, in Sicily; and in Act IV, at Braavalla Heath.

The time is the early eighth century.

Dances

ACT I

Valkyries: Miles. Garlieb, Petersen, Thorberg and nine Ballet Dancers
Dwarfs and Mermaids

Act II

Greek Chieftains: Messieurs Hoppe, Brodersen and Stramboe
Greek Danseuses: Jfr. Fredstrup, Mme. Stillman, Miles. S. Price, Rostock and eight Ballet Dancers

ACT IV

Finale of twenty-four *einherjar* and twenty-four Valkyries
The entire corps de ballet

PREFACE

Nowhere in our legendary history does heroic life appear with greater force or with a closer connection to Norse mythology than in the Staerkodder ballad dealing with the battle of Braavalla Heath. Odin himself is said to have provoked the struggle, which was fought to win immortality for Harald Hildetand.* He won this immortality over all the

---

* The Staerkodder ballad deals with the death of Harald Hildetand. Staerkodder is a legendary hero of enormous size and bravery much praised in heroic songs known as the Staerkodder ballads.

kings of pagan times, and if we consider the honour shown his body, and the radiance which the victor's son, Regnar Lodbrog, shed upon the name of Denmark, we care little whether this gigantic mythical combat was a victory or a defeat.

These reflections might seem superfluous were it not that the present mimed work met with the objection that it centres around an event which might prove hurtful to Danish national feeling since it is a well-known fact that the battle of Braavalla was won by the Swede-king, Sigurd Ring!

I confess that it had no more occurred to me to view the matter in this light than it had to consider Rolf Krake, or the unknown chieftains who rest in our burial mounds, as vanquished or conquered. From the time I was a child, the impression I have received from Oehlenschläger's heroic poem about Hildetand who, fighting, goes to Valhalla, has been one of greatness and triumph. Thus I could do nought but regard the memories of Norse antiquity as a common treasure and a bond of kinship between the nations.

The central idea of the ballet *The Valkyrie* is that of depicting in a series of scenic pictures the Viking and his *fylgia* [guardian spirit]. And since these two lovers could not be united save in Valhalla, the great battle – which calls the sons of the North to follow their heroic king and ride with him, as *einherjar* [Odin's companions], to Odin – had to be my best means of solving the problem successfully.

Although this fantasy picture does not claim to possess any real historical value, I have nonetheless striven to reproduce, as far as circumstances would allow, the impressions that accounts of the customs and beliefs of the old Northmen have imprinted on my soul and which I have carefully and lovingly grouped around that brilliant nucleus.

I pictured the hero of my ballet as Harald's grandson; for since among all the warriors named in the Staerkodder ballad there is no mention of any son of Harald Hildetand, while other legends speak of Thrond and Rerek, who probably died before their father (he lived to an unbelievably ripe old age), it would seem quite natural that it is Rerek's son, Helge, who rushes home from his Viking expedition to fight and die at his grandfather's side. In various guises Svava follows him, watches over his destiny and, through the fight for king and country, leads him to the bliss of Valhalla.

As grandiose as this subject may seem to the reader, it is still my hope that the benevolent and approving spectator will quickly discover that the composition does not make greater demands, either upon the mimic art or the Theatre's talents, than those which, given a certain amount of industry and skill, can and ought to be satisfied on the Danish stage. On the other hand, should it turn out that I have exceeded my own capabilities and failed to bring the production to the heights to which I aspired, then must the honourable public's imagination and love of our native land – but, above all, its kind indulgence – compensate for the shortcomings of the work.

[**Translator's note:** One of the hallmarks of Bournonville's genius as a writer of ballets was the way in which he was able to penetrate to the heart of a topic, extract its meaning (preferably allegorical), and then weave it together with story elements of other fables or myths until, under his hand, the total ballet became a perfect vehicle for ideas he wished to express. Bournonville, as his memoirs reveal, was thoroughly conversant with popular histories by Danish scholars of the Romantic school and had a particular fondness for the colourful intricacies of Norse mythology.

In *The Valkyrie*, as in *The Childhood of Erik Menved*, Bournonville exercised to the full his artistic privilege of *licentia poetica*, interweaving episodes from the twelfth-century historian Saxo Grammaticus' account of the death of Harald Hildetand in the battle of Braavalla Heath and Oehlenschläger's heroic poem on the same theme with episodes from the saga *Helgakvitha Hjorvarthssonar* (*The Lay of Helgi the Son of Hjorvarth*). From this *Lay*, which forms part of the Icelandic literary classic, *The Poetic Edda*, the choreographer derived the names of his hero, Helge, and the Valkyrie Svava. For a fine, detailed account of the creation of *The Valkyrie*, see Sidsel Jacobsen, "Bournonville's Ballet *Valkyrien*," in *Theatre Research Studies* II, Copenhagen, 1972.

The actual existence of Harald Hildetand is uncertain. In *The Story of Denmark*, historian Stewart Oakley says, "Though all such legends must, of course, be treated by the modem historian with great caution, some of the characters mentioned in them, like Harald Hildetand ('Wartooth'), who is said to have united the country and to have been killed fighting the Swedes at Bravellir, may have actually lived in the late sixth or early seventh century."]

ACT I

SCENE ONE

Hemidal sounds his Gjallor-Horn.*

Valkyries perform martial dances. The clouds part, and one beholds Odin at Hlidskjálf.† Goddesses bring him his food, but he will

---

* The "shrieking horn" with which Odin's son Heimdal, god of light and sentinel of the gods, called them to their final struggle against the giants.

† "Gate shelf," Odin's watch tower in heaven. From here he could survey the nine worlds.

take nought save wine from the golden horn handed him by Svava. Other Valkyries feed his wolves.*

From distant lands Valhalla's bellicose maids bring tidings of battles and heroic deeds. Svava alone stands pensive and crestfallen. Odin has perceived this. He hands his spear† to Heimdal, removes his sky-blue cloak and entrusts his golden ring to the goddesses. At his command the Gjallor-Horn is sounded once more, and the Valkyries hasten away. Only Svava is detailed, and when the clouds part, she and Odin are standing in a forest on the coast of Sjaelland.

SCENE TWO

Odin orders Svava to hide the golden drinking horn beneath a bush near an upright menhir. Dwarfs array him in mortal garb, with arms and ornaments, and mermaids bring him a golden harp [*Straengeleg*].‡ They dance around their august guest and, at a sign from him, disappear.

SCENE THREE

Svava has carved a rune on a beech tree. Odin (who will henceforth walk among mortals under the name of Brune) has seen through her and condemns the weakness which holds her in thrall. She throws herself at her master's feet and names the young hero to whose destiny her heart has become attached.

> *Brune.*   Thou canst never be his.
> *Svava.*   Let me follow him, watch over his life.
> *Brune.*   Thou shall bring him to me.

Svava trembles at the thought of the horrors of death, but asks whether, in the next world, she will be united to the one she loves.

> *Brune.* That is in the hands of the Norns.

A sound is heard. It is Helge and his friend Bjørn who are approaching. Brune and Svava hide in the woods.

---

* Odin himself drank only wine, while his pet wolves ate his food. They were called *Freki*, "The Greedy," and *Geri*, "The Ravenous."

† Odin's spear was called *Gungnir*; it was forged by dwarfs and nothing could deflect it from its mark.

‡ Odin was not only the Lord of Battle, he was also the God of Poetry, pawning one of his eyes, so the sagas say, to learn the nine sacred songs.

SCENE FOUR

The young warriors enter, fully equipped for the impending Viking expedition, and rejoice at the splendid long ship that is to carry them to distant shores. Helge pauses upon seeing the rune freshly graven in the tree bark and is seized by a hitherto unknown emotion. Bjørn laughs at him and ridicules the written characters, the meaning of which he does not understand. He goes to gather his boon companions while Helge lingers at the menhir which covers the ashes of his father, Rerek. He kneels and begs the gods for victory and good fortune. Unseen by him, Brune and Svava come forth and extend their hands above Helge's head; but when he rises he sees the airy being fly away among the bushes. He is about to rush after her, but the approach of the King is announced and Helge halts.

SCENE FIVE

Deeply bowed with the weight of years and sorrow over his son Rerek's death, Harald Hildetand comes to have runes carved on the menhir of the fallen warrior.

Helge steps forward and delivers his farewell. Harald seeks to detain his grandson, sadly pointing to the grave which houses the dust of him who fell victim to the bloody fray.

> *Helge.* It is precisely to avenge my father and to emulate him that I go forth into the world, and I would rather lose my life on the field of battle than die of old age and decrepitude.

The brave young man, however, quickly realizes that he has spoken rashly and, kneeling, he asks his royal grandfather's forgiveness.

SCENE SIX

Bjørn enters with Helge's men. They salute him respectfully, point toward the beach and strike their shields.

Brune steps forward and offers his services to the departing men. Bjørn and his Vikings smile scornfully at the stranger and his harp, but Brune plants a spear in an old oak tree and challenges the valiant men to test their might by pulling it out. Bjørn reserves the first attempt for himself, but all his efforts fail to dislodge the spear. He regards the stranger with astonishment and cools his ire.

The old King makes Brune one of his housecarls and bestows upon him a precious ring. He now turns his attention to Helge's expedition and, while outfitting him with Rerek's sword and shield, he is troubled by the ignominious thought of dying in his bed. "We shall never meet again! Nor shall we meet in Valhalla, for I shall belong to the Kingdom of the Shades."

Brune beckons the warriors, who noisily set off. But Helge returns once more to receive the old King's blessing.

The ship weighs anchor. A stiff breeze carries it away from land. But Svava, her arms laden with flowers, stands on the shore, sending the Vikings a last greeting from home.

SCENE SEVEN

Harald sinks into a profound melancholy. His housecarls withdraw, and Brune, who remains alone with the grieving King, strikes some chords on his harp. But nothing can lighten the King's dark mood. Svava places a spray of flowers in his lap and tries to put a garland on his head. But Harald scatters the blossoms on the ground and indicates that for him they have lost their beauty and their fragrance.

Now Brune vigorously sweeps the strings of his harp. It sounds like another *Bjarkamál*.* Harald rises and listens to Svava, who bids him gather hope in his breast and strength in his arm. "Tell me, fair maid, who art thou?" he asks. But Brune orders her to bring forth the golden horn and present it to Harald, who accepts it with trembling hand and raises it to his lips. Scarcely has he tasted the invigorating drink than a thrill of divine enthusiasm surges through him. The harp is still, but the air is vibrant with powerful tones... The broken old man feels the strength of youth and involuntarily reaches for his sword. Alas, it is gone. Once again he is on the verge of dejection, when Brune points to the spear which is planted fast in the old oak. Harald pauses in mistrust... There is a thunderclap... Heimdal sounds his Gjallor-Horn. With heavy tread, Harald goes over to the tree and, with the arm of a warrior, jars it loose so that the tree trunk splinters. Brune enfolds him in his embrace, and in the twinkling of an eye they are surrounded by a host of jibilant Valkyries, who once again initiate their favourite into Hildur's [another name for the Valkyrie Brynhild] fierce game.

Harald follows them to battle and glorious deeds. Helge's *fylgja*, transformed into a swan,† soars away over the sea.

ACT II

A rock cave on the coast of Brittany. In the background, the sea.

---

* A poem attributed to Bjarki, the warrior-skald of Rolf Krake, a legendary Danish king.

† According to the *Larousse Encyclopedia of Mythology*, "Valkyries were sometimes depicted as maidens in swan's plumage who could fly through the air. Every swan-maiden was not necessarily a Valkyrie; but a Valkyrie always had the power to turn herself into a swan-maiden."

SCENE ONE

Followed by Bjørn and a band of Vikings, Helge enters with wild exultation. They have triumphed and are bringing their booty ashore to divide it and to refresh themselves after battle. Helge has been wounded in the arm. Bjørn perceives this and wishes to dress the wound. But as their eyes meet they are both struck with the same idea: they will become blood-brothers. The warriors form a circle about them and, with the solemnity which attends this ancient custom, Helge and Bjørn vow to live and die as loyal friends. A Viking brings news that there is new booty to be won.

Bjørn gathers his men. Helge wishes to lead them, but his friend, who realizes that he is in need of rest and care, persuades him to stay behind in the cave.

SCENE TWO

Helge feels tired and drowsy and lies down on a slab of rock, where he soon falls asleep.

The strains of a harp resound, little mermaids come into view. Svava flies over the sea, dives down and rises from the waves in another guise. Mermaids gather round her while she tenderly beholds the wounded Helge, pours balsam on his arm and heals it. Helge awakens – the mermaids flee – but Svava remains standing at the entrance to the cave. Helge thinks he is still dreaming when he sees the airy being who appeared to him at his father's grave. He is amazed to find his arm perfectly sound and hardly dares give himself up to reality when Svava stretches forth her hands to him. He beckons her; she draws near but flees once more. He threatens and cajoles, becomes gentle and angry by turns, but feels subject to the power of love. "Be mine!" he exclaims. "Come with me to the land of my ancestors."

Svava indicates that he must first win a hero's name. "Wilt thy love then be my reward?" Svava points toward the heavens. Helge ponders the meaning of this sign, but a hollow noise is coming closer.

SCENE THREE

Helge and Svava hasten to the exit of the cave and are met by the glow of red flames. They hear the clash of arms and piteous cries, and Svava recoils, trembling. Helge crows with delight, but when his eyes meet Svava's reproachful look his ferocity ceases.

Women and children burst into the cave, seeking refuge from the fury of their enemies. They are terrified at the sight of Helge, and flee to Svava who has seized Helge's sword and now stands as a bulwark against the advancing Vikings.

The crude assailants stop dead in their tracks, astounded at the sight of the brave woman who dares to defy them. They recoil when she scornfully hurls the sword at their feet and tells them how ignoble it is to attack the weak and defenseless. They all stand as if under the influence of some higher power... then Bjørn rushes forward, pale, his eyes staring and his hair standing on end.

In his *berserker* frenzy he cannot tell friend from foe, and when Helge, with a commanding air, places himself next to Svava and the women, he goes for his blood-brother with sword and axe. But the latter disarms him and Bjørn's boon companions jump in to wedge the madman between their shields.

Svava has disappeared; the women kneel before their magnanimous liberator. They may now go in peace, and the trembling group slowly returns to the burning town. Bjørn, who has come to his senses, sinks down, filled with remorse. But Helge raises him up and presses him to his breast.

ACT III

A magnificent garden at Catania, on Sicily. In the background, can be seen the bay, and, to the right, a kiosk in the form of a temple.

SCENE ONE

Helge has been given a friendly reception by the Byzantine Viceregent, Nicetas, who has arranged a feast in his honour.

At a splendid table the Nordic sea-king is served. The Greek chieftains vie to pay him the most flattering homage. Slaves bring forth costly dishes, wine is poured in abundance from golden pitchers, and loud music intoxicates the overwhelmed senses.

Nicetas gives a signal, the table is taken away, the slaves and honour guard withdraw. The temple opens and out steps a chorus of graceful maidens, who shall heighten the festivity by their dancing.

The music sounds, and the dances alternate with hilarious jesting, during which the maidens hide Helge's weapons in the kiosk and adorn him with flowers.

SCENE TWO

An unknown young woman brings a basket of fruit, which she distributes among those who curiously gather round her. Only an apple does she keep, and lifts it just as she pauses in front of Helge.

So intoxicated with pleasure is he, that he has failed to notice her presence. Thus his surprise is all the greater when he recognizes the gentle features which, at home and on the coast of Brittany, made such a deep impression on his heart! The men are captivated by her dancing, even though it is quite different from that of the Greek women. The latter express their jealousy over the applause accorded the foreign maid.

Helge, troubled by the burning glances of the Greeks, tears himself loose and goes over to Svava, who refuses to give him the apple he desires. He hotly pursues her but is hindered and whirled about by the dancing girls. However, they cannot hold him back, and when Svava flees he rushes after her.

SCENE THREE

Nicetas now reveals his malicious plot and, together with his friends, decides on the downfall of his brethren-in-arms. He gives his orders, and all promise to aid him. They see a foreigner approaching, and the conspirators scatter in every direction.

SCENE FOUR

In vain has Bjørn scoured the woods along the coast, searching for his blood-brother. Tired and irritated, he calls to right and left, but only Echo answers. He suspects foul play, but consoles himself with the thought that if any harm has befallen Helge, he will surely be avenged.

He decides to wait and sits down on a bench near the steps of the temple.

Greek women steal up behind Bjørn and poke fun at the boorish Norseman. They soon go further and offer him wine. Bjørn thanks them and inquires after Helge, but they answer evasively and continue to fill his cup while dancing about him. His countenance gradually softens. He drinks one glass after another, allows himself to be disarmed and entwined with garlands and dances off with the maidens in a bacchantic chain that winds its way through the sinuous garden paths.

SCENE FIVE

Helge continues to pursue the fleeing Svava who, lightly leaping, eludes him and aggravates his impatience. But as he kneels and begs her to halt, her manner suddenly changes. She sadly goes over to him and bids him eat of the coveted apple. Helge tastes the refreshing juice and, as if by a stroke of magic, his wild intoxication disappears and profound shame enters in its stead.

At this moment Bjørn returns. Slightly befuddled and blowing kisses to the merry maids, he whirls around several times and comes face to face with Helge.

Svava walks upstage and looks out over the sea. Bjørn and Helge can hardly look each other in the eye. All at once their hands come into contact with the garlands, which they toss far away from them. Helge hands the apple to his friend, and when Bjørn eats of it he hears the strains of a harp. In the bewitching Sicilian heavens there now appears a singular mirage depicting the Danish coast with its beech wood, while high upon a barrow covered with runic stones can be seen a blazing beacon.

SCENE SIX

Helge's men come rushing to point to the wondrous sign on the horizon, but it is already fading in the air.

The clash of arms can be heard. The Vikings perceive that they are surrounded by a menacing horde and that it is Nicetas who has instigated this treachery. Only now do Bjørn and Helge remember that their weapons are hidden in the kiosk. They hasten thither with their men and prepare to offer strong resistance.

SCENE SEVEN

Nicetas, who thought he could take the unarmed Norsemen by surprise, flies into a rage when he learns that they have ensconced themselves in the temple. His warriors wish to storm it, but he knows a surer way of coercing the foreigners: their place of refuge is surrounded with bundles of brushwood, trees and other combustible materials which are lighted by the women who, with their torches, dance about the mounting flames. But suddenly the temple doors fly open and the Norse warriors toss their shields over the fire, leap through the crackling flames and, with heavy blows, cut into the terrified Greeks. Helge and his Vikings reach the shoreline. Nicetas gathers his men in order to pursue them when, like a gust of wind, a host of shield-maidens darts forward against the traitors, causing them to flee in every direction. Svava stands triumphant among the proud Valkyries. Yet again the distant coast appears behind the reddening evening clouds and Helge's ship heads home to the great battle of the North.

ACT IV

Braavall Heath at dawn. To the right, King Harald's tent; to the left, a rampart with the King's standard and some military engines. The extensive backdrop shows distant, wood-covered hills.

SCENE ONE

The army stands ready for battle. Harald's chariot is encircled by a numerous bodyguard. Brune is seated on a stone, playing his harp for the skalds who surround him. Svava, armed as a shield-maiden, stands at his side.

Harald Hildetand, in full battle dress, emerges from his tent. Small boys carry his helmet and shield. He is greeted by the clanging of arms and responds with dignity to the army's jubilant acclamation.

He turns to Brune and expresses how deeply he feels the absence of his valiant grandson in this hour.

Svava announces that from every side warriors are flocking to the army to take part in the great battle. They wish to be reviewed.

Harald mounts his chariot. Led by their chiefs, the countless phalanxes march past him, brandishing their swords and striking their shields.

Brune calls and a host of shield-maidens appears before the King. They vehemently demand to fight against the enemy, and Svava promises that none of them shall fail in the hour of peril.

SCENE TWO

From his high-seat, Harald calls upon the gods for assistance, and the enthusiastic army promises to follow him to victory or to death.

The sacrifice is over. The altar is removed, and Harald is descending to gird himself for battle when a new host of troops is announced. It is Helge, Bjørn and their bold Vikings. Odin has heard Harald's prayer! Beside himself with joy, the old man embraces his grandson, and Brune orders that the charge be sounded.

Harald sends Bjørn to the left wing; Brune, Svava and the shield-maidens shall fight on the right; and Helge shall remain with the King to bear his standard at the centre of the army.

Helge vacillates for a moment when Svava on the one side and Bjørn on the other ask him to remain with them. But to him, honour is the most precious thing of all. He heeds its call and obeys the command of his grandfather and king.

War trumpets sound in the distance. Harald's *krummhorn* players loudly answer. Helge waves the Dane-king's standard; spears and arrows fly through the air, and with a terrible din the combatants come together.

TRANSFORMATION

A spruce forest. (The tumult of battle is expressed by the music throughout the ensuing action.)

SCENE THREE

With wild delight, the Valkyries dash through the forest. They meet, brandish their spears and point toward the heath, where death is raging. They hasten away in jubilant dance.

Dwarfs enter, laden with helmets, byrnies, arrows and swords, but mainly with golden ornaments they have gathered on the battlefield. They are now returning them to the bosom of the earth, to hiding places thousands of years old.

SCENE FOUR

Brune enters, well satisfied with the day's work. He gives his earthly weapons and ornaments back to the dwarfs and orders them to take refuge in their caves. They sink into the ground. Violently agitated, Svava comes from the scene of battle. All is lost and in vain she begs the Lord of Battle to come to the aid of her beloved.

SCENE FIVE

Bjørn, with tattered coat of mail, stumbles in and stands astonished at seeing Brune unarmed and tranquil amid the horrors of battle. He calls him a coward and traitor and is about to run him through with his sword. But a look from Odin renders him powerless. The din of battle grows faint, but the air is filled with the victors' loud cries of jubilation. Bjørn now remembers his blood-brother's oath, rises with strength and rushes off to fulfill his promise.

Brune seizes the despairing Svava's hand and leads her away with him to the opposite side.

TRANSFORMATION

SCENE SIX

Darkness has settled over the heath, and the roar of the storm has replaced the dying din of battle. Ravens wheel above the corpse-strewn battlefield.

Bearing a torch, Bjørn enters to search for Helge among the fallen. He finds him with the standard in his arms, lifts him up, places a fraternal kiss on his brow and falls on his sword.

THE FINAL SCENE

Heimdal's Gjallar-Horn sounds. The mist of night vanishes and the fallen heroes cast off their bloody garb.

Radiance surrounds them, and they stand in Valhalla as *einherjar*, clad in light, glittering armor with winged helmets.

Valfather [Odin: Father of the Slain] has called his chosen ones to him. He welcomes Harald Hildetand and shows him the ring that the skald Brune received from his royal friend. He takes Harald with him to his High-Seat and gives him a place at his side.

Svava hands Helge the cup of immortality. Now she shall belong forever to the hero whose *fylgja* she was.

The Valkyries step forth and pour Heidrun's* mead for the warriors. The *einherjar* perform warlike games and acclaim Heerfather [Odin: Father of the Host] with a shield dance, which shall daily be renewed and lead them, through Ragnarok [the Fall of the Gods] to the eternal bliss of Gimle.†

*   *   *

PONTEMOLLE
(An Artists' Party in Rome)
(Pontemolle-Et Kunstnergilde i Rom)

A Vaudeville-Ballet in Two Tableaux
by
August Bournonville

Music for Act I composed and arranged by Wilhelm Holm; for Act II partly by A. F. Lincke

Scenery painted by Christian Ferdinand Christensen

Costumes arranged by Edvard Lehmann

Performed for the first time at the Royal Theatre, Copenhagen,

April 11, 1866

Characters

ALFRED	⎫	Hr. Brodersen
CESAR	⎬ .... painters	Hr. V. Price
HYPPOLITE		Hr. Stramboe
EDOUARD	⎭	Hr. C. Price
FULVIA, their landlady	....	Frk. J. Fredstrupt
CAMILLA	⎫ .... her daughters	Frk. Petersen
ANNINA	⎭	Fru Stillman
FABRICCIO, Camilla's sweetheart	....	Hr. Scharff
CHAUVIN, regimental drummer, fencing and dancing master as well as model	....	Hr. Gade
PAOLUCCIO, *scrivano*	....	Hr. Hoppensach

---

*   The she-goat who daily furnishes mead for Odin's *einherjar*.

†   The Paradise of the pagans.

A FOREIGN GENTLEMAN ....Hr. Ring
A FOREIGN LADY ....Fu Gade
PIETRO, innkeeper ....Hr. Füssel

ARTISTS. COUNTRY FOLK. FRENCH OBOISTS.
CHARACTER FIGURES

The scene is laid in Rome in modern times.

FIRST TABLEAU

An artists' atelier in Rome. The locale was once a splendid hall opening onto a perron and garden. In the background can be seen a portion of the city. Doors to right and left. The light, which comes from above, is filtered through a sunshade. Picturesque disarray. Sketches, busts, weapons, old furniture, and ethnographic objects.

SCENE ONE

Alfred is seated at his easel, in the process of completing a genre picture. He is painting draperies from a female lay figure [a painter's dummy].

Hyppolite is comfortably stretched out on a couch, smoking his pipe.

Cesar is standing on a stepladder and drawing with charcoal on a large cartoon which is to represent Achilles dragging the body of Hector behind his chariot.

Chauvin, in the underclothing of a military uniform but with antique breastplate, helmet, and spear, is standing on a table as a model.

Enthusiastic over his work, Cesar tries in vain to evoke a sympathetic response from Hyppolite, who is far more interested in Alfred's painting. However, it is not so easy to cheer the latter, who is in the throes of homesickness.

Chauvin, who has received permission to rest, jumps down from the table and accepts a cigar from Hyppolite, to whom he gives a little fencing lesson in return. With an air of a connoisseur, he gives his approval to Cesar's historical picture, drains a glass of wine, and resumes his academic pose.

To dispel Alfred's melancholy, Hyppolite fetches his guitar and strums a few chords – an echo of his distant homeland. Alfred goes out onto the perron in order to hide his emotion.

SCENE TWO

Camilla and Annina come dancing in, lured hither by the merry waltz, and Chauvin, who has hastily thrown a jacket over his torso, performs an Allemande with the young girls. Though at first irritated at this disruption, Cesar himself now gets the urge to dance. He takes Annina as his partner and Hyppolite selects Camilla, while Chauvin seeks his consolation in a pearly Orvieto.

SCENE THREE

Fulvia comes on an important errand, which she forgets the moment she catches sight of her daughters dancing away. She is about to scold them, but Chauvin puts his arm about her waist, Hyppolite plays a prelude on his guitar, and Fulvia's anger is allayed. The waltz continues with the three couples.

All of a sudden Fulvia stops. She remembers the real reason she has come here and summons Alfred in order to give him two letters. He opens them with a trembling hand. The first contains a bill of exchange, which he gives to Hyppolite; the second, on the other hand, is from his beloved, with her portrait and a message calling him home to marry her. Jubilation and congratulations. Hyppolite reminds him to cash his bill of exchange, and, arm in arm, they hasten outdoors.

Chauvin follows the ladies inside through the door to the left.

SCENE FOUR

Paoluccio brings in a foreign lady and gentlemen who have come to see the atelier. Cesar receives them with particular affability and shows them a number of his works, which they view with indifferent expressions, while Paoluccio momentarily mistakes the seated lay figure for a live model and approches it, bowing deeply. The foreigners are about to leave when the lady notices Alfred's genre picture and leads her husband over to it. He is delighted with it and immediately wants to purchase it, but Paoluccio calls his attention to the fact that the painter is not there. The gentleman takes out his note case, writes a word or two, tears out the note, and asks the *scrivano* to announce him as the purchaser. The foreigners politely nod to Cesar and depart. Outraged at this presumed failure to appreciate his talent, the latter appeals to Paoluccio, who, however, does not display any enthusiasm for his works. Cesar flies into a rage, stamps his feet, and rushes out. Paoluccio gives vent to his delight.

SCENE FIVE

Camilla beckons to the old *scrivano* and dictates a letter to him. Fabriccio slips in from the perron and hides behind Cesar's cartoon in order to spy on them. Paoluccio receives his fee, bows, and departs.

SCENE SIX

A scene of amazement, frolicking, jealousy, and reconciliation between Fabriccio and Camilla. They hear someone approaching and hide behind the large cartoon.

SCENE SEVEN

Annina enters, pursued by Chauvin, who is assuring her of his sincere love. At first she will hear none of it, but when he praises the life of a soldier and promises her a future as a vivandière with the Cross of the Legion d'Honneur on her breast, she is won over to his marriage plan, takes his arm, and marches about with him. But Camilla and Fabriccio halt them with bitter reproaches. However, the one pair of lovers will not allow themselves to be lectured by the other and there arises a lively quarrel which is interrupted only by the entrance of Fulvia and Paoluccio.

SCENE EIGHT

The mother's amazement and anger. The lovers' futile pleas, and Paoluccio's unsuccessful mediation.

SCENE NINE

Alfred returns, accompanied by Hyppolite, Edouard, and a host of artists who, while congratulating him, lament his hasty departure. He soon becomes aware of the sad and serious faces, and discovers the sorrow that lies so heavy on the young hearts. From every side they try in vain to move the mother to forgiveness, but every attempt is countered by the practical objection that "the lovers have nothing to marry on."

At this very moment the foreign gentleman and his wife, who have made an offer for Alfred's painting, enter. The latter politely returns their greeting, but has not the faintest idea what they want from him. Only now does Paoluccio remember the bank note on which the gentleman had written. He hands it to Alfred, who, seized with a happy inspiration, goes over and fetches the picture and presents it to the young ladies. With delight and gratitude, they both accept the proffered prize and obtain their mother's consent.

Everyone admires Alfred's magnanimity, but he lives solely for the thought of his beloved native land, where the supreme happiness awaits him, and it would grieve him deeply to leave behind distress, in this hospitable house where he mastered his art. They agree to celebrate his farewell party with a splendid *Pontemolle*.

Chauvin is appointed *maître de plaisir*, and all those present are invited.

SCENE TEN

Cesar enters and offers his congratulations, but his grand work is the main thing on his mind and he is anxious to know his colleagues' opinion of this composition. They all move downstage to view it more closely, and the frame is moved out into the centre of the floor. A pregnant silence ensues. One person looks inquisitively at another. Finally, with a nimble leap, Edouard jumps through the cartoon, and, imitating his example, the whole laughing crowd follows him out through the open door.

Crushed, Cesar drops into a chair. Paoluccio, with glass in hand, mischievously peeps out of the torn masterpiece. Cesar gathers all his strength of mind, drains the full glass, and with a proud "All right!" he follows Paoluccio.

SECOND TABLEAU

A landscape outside Rome (in the vicinity of the old Pons Milvius, well known from the defeat of the Emperor Maxentius, and later christened Ponte Molle). To the left, the inn called La Storta, where artists' parties of welcome and farewell are customarily held. To the right, in the foreground, the ruins of an ancient temple.

SCENE ONE

A crowd of curious country folk, who are gathered outside the inn, from which comes the sound of music accompanied by the clinking of glasses.

Pietro, who is extremely busy, comes out and looks to see if everything is in order for this outdoor fête.

Paoluccio, slightly intoxicated and wearing a napkin around his neck, rushes after the offended Cesar, who is threatening to leave the party. He vainly tries to reason with him as much as circumstances will permit, but when a couple of boys enter with a chest of costumes, he lays hold of a sword and helmet, which he presents to the overwrought artist; the latter is soon carried away once more by his heroic illusions and enthusiastically accompanies Paoluccio back to the feast. Fanfares sound, and the country folk take their places as spectators on stones and benches.

SCENE TWO

A grand procession headed by Chauvin, in dress uniform, and the French military band. Several character figures form a jubilant group around Pietro, who is borne in triumph as Silenus, foster father of the god of wine.

Fabriccio and Camilla, in festive dress, accompanied by a host of lads and lasses, bring up the rear of the procession. A signal is given for the dancing to begin, and in the following order are performed:

> *A Pas de Deux* and *Saltarello* – Music composed by W. Holm
> *Ancient Rome* – Gladiators and Flower Maidens
> *The Age of Art* (from the sixteenth century) – *Roccocco Quadrille*,

music arranged by Carlsen
Pulcinello – an indispensable grotesque figure
Old Age and Folly (mimetic waltz) – music composed by F. Neruda

SCENE THREE

The hour for departure is drawing nigh, and Alfred's travelling bags have already been taken away. He bids a heartfelt good-bye to his dear friends, to beautiful Italy, and to Rome – the Eternal City!

Toasts are drunk to a happy homecoming, and from Camilla and Annina Alfred accepts small gifts which shall adorn his bride –the Northern woman. From the temple ruins emerge three little girls dressed as genii representing: AMORE! GLORIA! PATRIA!

They encircle Alfred, and while Love hands him a beautiful rose, Glory presents him with a wreath of fresh laurels. But his native land beckons him with its waving flag. The men bare their heads and the women kneel in prayer. Deeply moved by this unexpected and solemn moment, Alfred hangs the wreath on the sacred symbol of his native land, presses the sweet genii to his breast, once again throws himself into the arms of his friends, and hastens off – to the North! to the North!

SCENE FOUR

Joy appears to have been struck dumb by Alfred's departure.

All stand downcast and dejected, but Chauvin orders the drum to be beaten, and the French military band strikes up a thunderous galopade. Life springs anew into the numerous crowd, and dancing helps to dispel the heavy clouds of sadness. But there is yet another pause!

It is the train signal, and in the distance the express train can be seen puffing out of the station. Every hat is in motion, every kerchief aflutter. No one can see the departing passenger, but out of the window of one of the coaches, *the Danish* flag is waving!

* * *

THE LAY OF THRYM
(Thrymsqviden)

A Ballet in Four Acts with a Final Tableau by
August Bournonville

Music by Johan Peter Emilius Hartmann

Scenery by Christian Ferdinand Christensen and Fritz Ahlgrensson

Costumes by Edvard Lehmann

Machinery by Andreas Peter Weden and Lindstrom

Performed for the first time at the Royal Theatre, Copenhagen
on February 21, 1868
With a Prologue

THE NORNS
by
Hans Peter Holst

[**Translators' note**: As we know from his writings, Bournonville was quite well versed in Danish literature and history and from the time he was a child devoured the poetical and dramatic works of Adam Oehlenschläger. In later years, whenever circumstances permitted, he tried to bring this rich legacy to life on the stage. The *Lay of Thrym* was one of Bournonville's most ambitious ballet projects. In composing the work, he wove together various myths from various sources. Among these sources were Oehlenschläger's Eddaic cycle, referred to below, Petersen's Norse mythology, and the historical writings of Finn Magnussen and N. F. S. Grundtvig. The choreographer's own account of the ballet's production may be found in his autobiography, *My Theatre Life* (Wesleyan University Press: Middletown, Conn., 1979), on pages 349–353.

There are several fine translations of the original Icelandic sagas from which the above-mentioned histories were drawn. Two particularly readable ones are *The Norse Myths, Introduced and Retold by Kevin Crossley-Holland* (Pantheon Books: New York, 1980) and the more scholarly version, *The Poetic Edda*, translated by Henry Adams Bellows (New York: American Scandinavian Association, 1957). They also contain glossaries which are most helpful in finding one's way through the bewildering array of Aesir (gods) and Vanir (giants) who people *The Lay of Thrym*.]

PREFACE

The rich allegories and moral undertones of Old Norse mythology fall mainly within the sphere of thought and study. But, for Art, its vivid pictures still provide a vast and relatively uncultivated field [for inspiration].

The first thought which strikes even the most ardent supporters of the scenic art is: How dare the poet venture onto such slippery ice as the *Edda*: Can its grandiose figures ever be compressed into a frame as narrow as that of a ballet?

To this I reply: When an artist is obsessed by a subject day and night, that subject usually ends up assuming a form peculiar to the artist; thus we have Oehlenschläger's great epic, *Gods of the North* and, following that, Freund's frieze, *The End of the Gods*.* Between the creation of the poem and the bas-relief, the proportions [of the epic figures] were modified to the degree that the element of grotesqueness, which is so disturbing to contemplate, almost entirely disappeared. It is harder for the human mind than for the eye to comprehend the enormous dimensions in which the giants, and often the gods themselves, are manifested. And it staggers the boldest imagination to entertain the possibility of a union between the Wane Freir and the giant-maid Gerda, or Thrym's proposal of marriage to the lovely Freia! But, if we view the struggle of the Ases against the giants and sorcerers *historically* (cultivated folk against rude barbarians) or *mythologically* (the power of the spirit against *the forces of Nature*), there emerge proportions which are consonant with our own concepts of beauty and greatness, and the picture takes shape of its own accord.

It is one thing, however, to reflect poetic images with chisel or brush; it is quite another to make them come alive on stage, and many are bound to consider it presumptuous of *the Ballet* to think it has the ability and power to succeed where lyric and dramatic means have proven inadequate. But, next to the invaluable support the mime and character dancing derive from the instrumental music which puts us into the mood more readily than either song or recitation – it should be noted that the Gods of the North and their gigantic opponents, as they have come down to us in the *Edda*, are *creatures of action* not much given to declamation and whose primitive tongue, when they sometimes speak among themselves, is quite unlike the language with which we strive to make ourselves understood on the stage.

The main problem in this daring, though not hazardous, undertaking is, consequently, not only to make the story clear and intelligible but

---

* Adam Oehlenschläger's Eddaic cycle, *Gods of the North*, was written in 1818. Hermann Ernst Freund's frieze, "The End of the Gods," was begun in 1825, and completed after the sculptor's death (1840) by H. W. Bissen. The frieze was destroyed when Christiansborg Palace, in Copenhagen, burned in 1884. Today, parts of it may be seen in casts preserved in the Copenhagen Glyptotek. A fragment also appears as an illustration on page 281 of the *Larousse Encyclopedia of Mythology* (Prometheus Press: New York, 1959).

to give some sort of dramatic coherence to these fragments of a magnificent *epic* poem.

With respect to the first point, I have, like the pantomimes of old, sought the aid of the spoken word and, to this end, persuaded my highly esteemed friend, the poet H. P. Holst, to serve as *Prologus* to my ballet through the medium of an orientational curtain-raiser. As for the second, no less important, requirement: I spent a long time mulling over various titles to describe the action and nature of the story. *Aegir's Banquet, Thor's Hammer*, and *Loke and Sigyn* occurred to me in turn. But when I finally realized that the most important plot complications arose from the giant Thrym's proposal which, owing to Loke's outrageous trick, leads to Vola's predictions of the fall of the gods and their glorification in a new and better world, I decided upon the name which had already been sactioned in Iceland's ancient literature, namely,

Thrymsqviden [The Lay of the Giant Thrym].

I hope that the honourable public will find that the seriousness of the subject has not prevented me from using all the scenic effects our Theatre has at its command. To what extent strict antiquaries will see their expectations disappointed or exceeded, I dare not say. They will in any case be able to note that, to Art and the imagination, the *Edda* is not a dead treasure. And should there happen to be some deeper meaning or other in the series of pictures I have sought to present, I leave it to the perspicacity of my esteemed and benevolent audience to discover it.

AUGUST BOURNONVILLE

*   *   *

THE NORNS

Prologue to August Bournonville's Ballet

The Lay of Thrym
by
Hans Peter Holst

Characters

```
EIGIL, a young sea-king  . . . . . . . . . . . . . . Hr. W. Wiehe
AUSA, his wife  . . . . . . . . . . . . . . . . . . . . . Frk. Lange
URDA      ⎫   . . . . . . . . . . . . . . . . . . . . . . Frk. C. Bournonville*
VARANDA   ⎬ Norns  . . . . . . . . . . . . . . . . . Frk. Nielsen
SKULD     ⎭   . . . . . . . . . . . . . . . . . . . . . . Fru Jacobson
```

---

*   Charlotte Bournonville, the choreographer's daughter and an opera singer at the Royal Theatre in Copenhagen for many years, created the role of Urda.

A mountainous region near Silavaag. Sunset

EIGIL (*entering with Ausa*) Wherefore art thou silent? Thou art as somber and still as if some great stone lay heavy on thy breast.
AUSA. And so it does.
EIGIL (*smiling*) And can I not help to lift it from thee?
AUSA. Thou canst not or *wilt* not.
EIGIL. In riddles speakest thou, like Gestur Blinde.*
AUSA. But riddles, so thou sayest, thou canst fathom. Gudrun of Halogaland, thy mother, was a seeress, both well and widely known. From her didst thou learn minstrelsy and magic spells to cast.
EIGIL. What my mother taught me, I remember not.
AUSA (*bitterly*) Far more than that, I fear, thou hast forgot.
EIGIL. Say not so. Thou makest me sore distressed. Behold, mine Ausa, behind yon lofty cliff my long ship rideth gently on the waves, while evening's sun doth shimmer on the shields along its sides. It waits for me. Wherefore, wilt thou, wife of mine, make doubly hard this parting? When last I did a viking go, to this very spot thou camest. Cheerful and glad wert thou back then, but my courage now thou sappest.
AUSA. How wrong thou art, o husband mine. A *different* Eigil 't was I followed then.
EIGIL. A different Eigil?
AUSA. Aye. The youth who knelt beside me in the temple, to light the torch before fair Freia's image, was not a morbid, melancholy dreamer.
EIGIL. How hardly dost thou judge.
AUSA. But, surely, not too hard. It is not I who slays thy courage now. Nay, dead it was e'er ever thou returned. I know not if it be the Southland – its beauty, air and tones, its violet hills – which hath thee rendered spiritless and soft. Or, if it be
EIGIL. Come, say it!
AUSA. Or, if it be a woman who hath charmed thee, and caused thee to forget thy sacred vows. But goddess Lofn† unto thee hath harkened, and breaking of an oath she'll surely punish.
EIGIL. Thou know'st not what it is thou sayest.
AUSA. This I know for certain: thou art false, and traitorous art thou, such as few men are. Whose picture holds thy gaze when none can see it? To whom, perjurer, are sent thy sighs and musings?

---

* Gestur Blinde: one of Odin's disguises.
† Lofn: a Scandinavian love-goddess whose special province was smoothing over the difficulties of love.

Who is that youthful mother with her child? Give it me. I'll crush it in the dust, along with every though I've wasted on thee!

EIGIL. O, trespass not!

AUSA. Against whom? 'Gainst her who hath stolen thy love through arts infernal?

EIGIL. She taught me what it really means to love.

AUSA. Hold thy tongue, o shameless man! Thou heapest sin on sin! *She* taught you? She? Tremble before Freia! For thy faithlessness she shall punish thee, and I (*hiding her face*) why, I shall grieve to death!

EIGIL. (*taking her hands in his*) Thou shalt not, if thou wilt only hear what did befall me on my latest expedition, and what, through my compassion, I have tried to hide from thee. My ship had landed in distant Sicily, at the foot of the giant mountain, which, like a silver shield, reflects the sun's rays from its snowy peaks. While my ship lay waiting for a fair wind to blow, up the mountain, alone, I did wander – to a marvelous spot where a temple so white glistened high on the side of the hill. I strolled among myrtles, while around me I saw golden fruits that we don't even know here. Turning round, I beheld the cornflower blue sea, and to home and to thee my thoughts travelled.

AUSA. To *her*, meanest thou.

EIGIL. To thee, Ausa mine. A fresh chestnut tree promised me shadow; but 'neath it I'd hardly set foot when villainous robbers – full twenty or more – shrieking wildly descended upon me. Lightarmed with a dagger and also an axe, I was caught with my back to a tree, but made up my mind they should not take my life, save with utmost difficulty. I struck with my dagger, I lunged with my axe, mowing down whatever came near me. It lasted a while, 'twas a merry game, yet I saw it could only end poorly; for blood streamed from my wounds and I quickly began to feel my strong resources desert me. Then seized I my broadaxe with both of my hands and broke into the fine "Ballad of Bjarki,"* in order to die with a song on my lips, as is truly befitting a hero. I struck once again and, just as I did, to my wondrous surprise – help was there!

AUSA. *She* saved thee!

EIGIL. Thou art wrong. Nay, a prince of the Roman Church it was, with snowy hair and beard of white, who, followed by his retinue, through the woodland came ariding. With angry mien he confronted me, and with menace stretched forth the golden cross, round his neck, to the impudent fellows: "Ye murdering cowards! Bend ye the knee to the

---

* A poem attributed to Bjarki, the warrior-skald of Rolf Krake, a legendary king of Denmark. Some of the names that occur in "The Lay of Thrym" have already been identified in notes to Bournonville's libretto of "The Valkyr," in *Dance Chronicle*, Vol. 4, No. 4.

cross that I hold up before ye! On thy knees, to be saved! On thy knees, to appeal for mercy, before clemency's door close upon ye." And, lo and behold! they heeded him; in the dust they were humbled before him. What next befell I cannot say, for a cloud then descended upon me. And when I awoke, my wounds had been dressed; by my bed sat the priest gazing at me. But this time his look was quite gentle and mild, and sweet, pious words flowed from his lips. He spoke to me then of the miracle which had recently happened to me, and prayed God – his God for another which greater, far greater, would be. Then, filled with both terror and loathing, I anxiously turned me away. But he stayed there – just for me to hear him – and soon –

AUSA. I tremble. Soon? Go on, go on.

EIGIL. Like the bee who sucks nectar out of a plant, I drank into my ears all the sweetness that lay in his words. And when I arose from my sickbed, I was sound both in body and soul. The gentle teaching had melted my heart. My faith, it found roots – my soul, wings. When, reborn, eventually I sailed away, he tearfully kissed me goodbye and gave me this picture of which thou didst speak, God's mother's image, which calls to my mind that in faith alone is life and salvation.

AUSA. (*horrified*) O, godless man, dost thou not fear that the air thou breathest shall sicken; that Thor from the heavens shall send thee his bolt; the earth open and Nastrond* swallow he who scorns the gods of his fathers?

EIGIL. I do not fear, for my fate I have placed in the hand of a far greater power.

AUSA. Thou blasphemer, hast thou forgot that this very spot is holy, that this grove is sacred to angry Norns? Within this mountain – as a child thou knew it – spin they their web from life's morning until its evening; that great web which conceals all our destinies. Stand in dread of their doom, o thou, who wast fearful of nought!

EIGIL. It cannot fell me. (*Harkening*) Ha! What's that?

AN UNSEEN CHORUS

Alas! We must fall –
Valhalla, the shining
Delight of the gods,
Into ruins shall crumble!

AUSA. (*who has listened with horror*) O, dreadful news! Whence comest those tones which the death do portend of Valhalla? It shall fall into ruins and, then, like a star, it shall be extinguished forever! Oh, no, the whole thing's an invention! (*turning toward the mountain in desperation*)

---

* Nastrond: the shore of corpses in the underworld.

Ye powers who dwell in this place, who canst fathom dark runes of the future, if ye can hear me, O make me reply: Shall Loke then triumph? Can Thor never more defend Gudheim with heavy hammer? And, last, is All-father's sovereignty done?

THE UNSEEN CHORUS

Done! Done!

AUSA. O, hateful refrain of my own gnawing fear, I cannot believe what thou sayest; for if thou spake true, my life – it would be nought but torment from this moment on!

EIGIL. Nay, then wouldst thou start to live. But hush! Be still!

During these last lines darkness has fallen. One hears some chords, which increase in intensity. The mountain opens, and in a rock hall one sees the Norns at their web, in a magical illumination.

URDA.
    Ases and Giants
    Struggle for power,
    The last battle it is
    That I sing of here.
    Deep in the ocean
    Hath Thor lost his hammer,
    And now feel the Ases
    That danger is near.
    Skirnir the nimble
    To fetch it is sent,
    And with haste doth deliver
    The will of the gods.
    Thrym doth defy them,
    Doth promise the hammer,
    If only they'll give him
    Fair Freia to wed.

THE UNSEEN CHORUS
    Thrym doth defy them,
    Doth promise the hammer
    If only they'll give him
    Fair Freia to wed.

VARANDA.
    Loke to falsehood
    The Ases doth lure.
    Wickedness triumphs,
    Respectfulness dies.
    Clad as fair Freia

> To Thrymheim* doth go
> Thor, in the fluttering
> Veil of the bride.
> The giant, enamored,
> His sweetheart now greets.
> While the hammer he gives
> Back quite happily.
> Thor hastens to seize it.
> The giants do quake;
> And, mortally wounded,
> They give up the fight!

THE UNSEEN CHORUS

> Thor hastens to seize it,
> The giants do quake;
> And, mortally wounded,
> They give up the fight!

SKULD.
> Heimdal his trumpet
> Now desperately sounds.
> The Ases come flocking
> All round to the fray.
> The first to fall's Odin,
> And, next, Aukathor;
> Geirsodden now wheteth
> The edge of the swords.
> Then comes a stillness,
> And Yggdrasil† burns.
> The stars are extinguished,
> The goddesses die.
> Soon, though, a loving
> And fatherly eye‡
> Once more shines upon
> Plain and sea.

THE INVISIBLE CHORUS

> Soon, though, a loving
> And fatherly eye
> Once more shines upon
> Plain and sea.

---

* Thrymheim: home of the giant Thiase.

† Yggdrasil: the world tree.

‡ Fatherly eye: The eye of Odin, a possible reference to the sun. Odin was supposed to have exchanged one of his eyes for wisdom.

> Music. The mountain closes. The moon comes out.

AUSA. O, how appalling! No dream is it, then! I behold them, the terrible three. And the sound of their voices turns my blood into ice. Nay, nay, there's no hope of salvation!

EIGIL. There is, there is, my Ausa. At the feet of Him who taught us God is love, and love the only thing we really need. Look, the ship is beckoning, out there upon the water, and now the wind doth flutter so lightly through thy hair! Come, O come, along with me to that far off land, where the Saviour lived and taught and suffered! There shall thy soul now sick and weak, be bathed in the balm of his teachings. And then thy eyes shall clearly see what now lies hid in dark and gloom!

AUSA. I follow thee, my husband! Lead on, I follow!

THE LAY OF THRYM

Characters

ACT I: THRYM'S PROPOSAL

THRYM, King of the Giants	Hr. Gade
ASA-LOKE	Hr. Scharff
VOLA, a prophetess	Frk. P. Fredstrup
SIGYN	Frk. Schnell
and Her Five Sisters — Vola's foster's daughters	Fru Stillman, Frk. S. Price, Frk. Cetti, Frk. Jansen, Frk. Poulsen
THOR	Hr. Price
VIDAR	Hr. Emanuel Hansen
FREIA	Fru Eckardt
FREIR	Hr. Krum
SKIRNER	Hr. Fredstrup
GERDA, Freir's bride	Frk. Petersen
THIASE	Hr. Stramboe
FTIHNFNINN fire spirits	Hr. Hoppensach
TWO GIANTS	Messieurs Füssel and Busch

FIRE SPIRITS. GIANTS. DISIR. ELVES.

ACT II: AEGIR'S BANQUET

THOR, VIDAR, LOKE, FREIR, SKIRNER, FREIA, GERDA, SIGYN AND HER FIVE SISTERS. ELVES AND DISIR.

ODIN	Hr. Hoist
TYR	HR. Brodersen
BRAGE	Hr. Ring
HEIMDAL	Hr. Emil Hansen
AEGIR	Hr. Döcker
FRIGGA	Frk. Eydrup
IDUN	Fru Mentzell
AEGIR'S DAUGHTER	Fru Gade

AEGIR'S SERVANTS AND MERMEN

ACT III: LOKE'S CUNNING

THOR, LOKE, FREIR, SKIRNER, HEIMDAL, FREIA, GERDA,

SIGYN, ELVES AND DISIR

ROTA, a Valkyrie .... Frk. Juul
FREIA'S PRIESTESS .... Frk. J. Fredstrup
FREIA'S HANDMAIDS { Frk. M. Price
Frk. Scholl
Frk. Dehn

EINHERJAR AND VALKYRIES.

ACT IV: SLAUGHTER OF THE GIANTS AND THE END OF THE GODS

THRYM, VOLA, THOR, LOKE, SIGYN, ODIN, VIDAR, TYR, FREIR, SKIRNER, HEIMDAL.

EINHERJAR AND VALKYRIES. GIANTS AND FIRE SPIRITS.

FINAL TABLEAU: GIMLE

ALL AESIR AND ASYNJR

BALDUR .... Hr. Dorph-Petersen
NANNA .... Frk. Bryde

*   *   *

BLISSFUL SPIRITS

ACT I

A cave inside a mountain. The prevailing half-lights broken by swirls of flame rising from the ground.

SCENE ONE

Fire spirits dance around the wise-woman Vola. They receive her commands, light a fire and help her prepare a magic potion.

SCENE TWO

Asa-Loke appears. All bow to his power and, at a sign from him, Vola is forced to summon her five young foster daughters.

To the first, Loke hands *a mirror*;
To the second, *an arrow*;

To the third, *a brimming cup*;
To the fourth, *fragrant flowers*;
And, finally, to the fifth, *a glockenspiel*.
(This test of the senses provides the opportunity for a dance in which Loke takes part while Vola and the fire spirits serve as a mimic frame for it.)

Flowers are tossed into Vola's magical cauldron and, at Loke's behest, the sisters set off for the feast of the Aesir, where he intends to bring them before Odin and Freia.

SCENE THREE

Vola has a *sixth* foster daughter, the gladsome Sigyn, whom she has endeavored to keep from Loke's notice. But he demands to see her and, when Vola anxiously and suspiciously points to the drink which has already been poured into golden cups, he assures her that Sigyn shall be sacred to him, for he has chosen her to be his wife. Vola hesitates to fulfill his wish, but with a single sign the Lord of Fire conjures up an extraordinary brightness which fills the vaults of the cave with the dazzling light of day.

SCENE FOUR

Sigyn comes dancing in and asks her mother what has caused this radiance. Vola tries in vain to caution her and to check her gaiety. But Loke steps forth, reassures the astonished maiden and, with a pious look and expressions of tenderness, tries to win her heart. Sigyn is easily deceived by the cunning god's entreaties and declarations. He binds her to him with a golden chain and, paying no heed to Vola's forebodings, she confidently places her hand in Loke's.

SCENE FIVE

A tremendous thunderclap is heard. It grows dark; the background of the cave opens and one sees the foaming sea illuminated by close flashes of lightning: Sigyn seeks refuge in her mother's arms while Loke hides himself.

A boat is tossing on the rough waves. Vidar is at the helm; Thor stands tall in the stern and, with all his might, pulls the Midgard Serpent* up from the deep. The monster's head has already risen above the surface of the water. But Loke who, unperceived, has slipped away to the seashore, releases an arrow from his bow, severing the rope in Thor's hands. The Serpent sinks back into the abyss and Thor, beside himself with wrath, hurls his hammer, Mjollnir, after his escaped quarry. The

---

* Midgard Serpent: Jormungand, the serpent, was an offspring of Loke and the giantess Angrboda. He encircles Midgard, the World of Men, and bites his own tail.

storm increases, and the cave closes amid heavier peals of thunder.

The fire spirits rise with Thor's hammer, Mjollnir, lying on a stone in their midst. Loke shares their wild and radiant delight. A reddish glow lights up the cave, and Sigyn turns to her bridegroom who, mild and amiable once more, comforts and caresses her.

SCENE SIX

Heavy footsteps herald the approach of the Thursar.* They enter, led by their king, the rich and mighty Thrym. Finn and Thiase show him their important catch. Delighted at having Mjollnir in his power, he immediately tries to seize it, but is repeatedly repulsed by electric shocks. Outraged by this disappointment, he mistreats his thralls and pushes away any of them who tries to pacify him. Loke introduces his young bride. Thrym regards her with haughty indifference and orders his entourage to leave him alone with Loke.

SCENE SEVEN

Thrym expresses his dejection at finding himself alone. Without a wife! Without love! Loke promises to show him the ideal woman and, touching the giant's eyelid, he puts him into a deep trance.

In his mind's eye a magnificent sight unfolds: Freia's hall, where the goddess, surrounded by the Disir† and light elves, receives her brother who brings a bride from the realm of the giants to the home of the Vanir. The lovely Gerda kneels before Freia who raises her up into her embrace and bestows her blessing upon her and upon Freir. The Disir remove Gerda's subterranean headdress and adorn her with the bridal wreath.

Skirner announces the arrival of Thor. The mighty As is sorely distressed by the loss of his mighty hammer; not even Freia's gracious smile can console him and he rejects any replacement. Gerda finds a way! Relying upon her kinship with the giants, she bids Skirner take her golden head-ring as security on his mission to Jotunheim‡ and, in her name, demand the return of Mjollnir. This proposal wins unanimous approval. Skirner hastens away on winged Sleipnir,§ and the elves' dancing restores joy and hope to lovely Folkvang.'¶

---

* Thursar: a name for the Giants.
† Disir: fate-goddesses, supposed to control an individual's talents and defects; it also means any Scandinavian goddess.
‡ Jotunheim: the realm of the Giants.
§ Sleipnir: Odin's eight-legged steed.
¶ Folkvang: the hall of Freia in a portion of Asgard, realm of the gods.

SCENE EIGHT

Excited over what he has seen, dreamt or experienced, Thrym awakens from his hypnotic sleep! Freia's divine beauty has aroused in him the most violent passion. She must be his, and, calling his warriors to arms, he prepares to carry her off by force. Vola tries in vain to prevent him from this rash undertaking, but Loke points out to him that Thor's hammer is a valuable pawn which can be redeemed in return for Freia's hand. Thrym readily accepts this idea. He makes up his mind to propose to the goddess, takes off his great arm-ring, and looks around for a suitable messenger.

SCENE NINE

Hoofbeats are heard outside, and the fire spirits proclaim Skirner's arrival. Thrym orders a high-seat erected; behind it Loke conceals himself in order to surreptitiously give counsel to the King of the Giants.

Skirner enters, presents Gerda's ornament and demands the return of the hammer. Thrym, who has received the emissary of the Aesir with haughty self-importance, states his terms and gives him his arm-ring as a betrothment gift for Freia. Shocked at this proposal, Skirner threatens him with the vengeance of the gods and tries to seize the hammer with his own hands. But at a sign from Thrym it sinks into the bowels of the earth and a loud roar of laughter causes the walls of the cave to shake.

In the meantime, Loke has summoned Sigyn and given her a golden pitcher containing the drink which shall cause Freia to become favourably inclined toward her boorish suitor, and, as Vola prevents the angry Skirner from leaving the cave, Sigyn steps forth and offers to accompany him to the feast of the Aesir. Skirner eventually allows himself to be persuaded to deliver the detested message and hastens away, followed by Sigyn.

Thrym is already savouring his triumph. Sleipnir's hoofbeats are heard once more, then fade in the distance. The proposal will soon be made, and at a merry drinking bout, the Thursar celebrate their monarch's anticipated betrothal to the fair-haired Freia.

ACT II

Aegir's palace on Hiesey.* To the left, a colonnade with an awning. In the background, the open sea bounded by an embankment adorned with coral and marine flora. Broad daylight.

---

* Hlesey: an island near which the gods Aegir and Ran lived in a hall beneath the sea.

SCENE ONE

Aegir's daughter calls the servants together and announces the impending celebration. There is a flurry of preparations for the reception of the exalted guests.

The five giant-sisters turn up for the wedding of Freir and Gerda, and Loke himself intends to appear at the banquet.

SCENE TWO

Skirner and his young companion dart across the upper portion of the stage on the lightning-fast steed and dismount at the palace. Sigyn rushes over to Loke, who is greeted rather coolly by Skirner but remains undeterred. In fact, he does quite the opposite; he advises the envoy of the gods and Thrym to put off his unpleasant errand until a more opportune moment in order not to disrupt the festal joy.

SCENE THREE

Aegir comes forth from his hall to welcom Odin and his kin, who draw near the strand in a splendid ship and are hailed by the servants and sons of the sea. Out climb Heimdal and Tyr, Freia and the bridal couple with a retinue of Disir – into whose midst Sigyn is admitted as a servant – Brage and Idun, Odin and Frigga, and, lastly, Thor and Vidar. Aegir bids them welcome, and golden horns are passed around. But the mood is darkened when Loke boldly jumps out and is about to seize the horn of welcome. Bitter memories of his guile are called to mind, and wherever he turns he encounters wrathful and contemptuous looks. But he reminds Odin of the blood brotherhood they swore to each other in earlier days, and though it goes against the grain to do so, Heerfather grudgingly gives him his hand and bids him drink. All the guests go up to the palace and take seats in its colonnade while Loke, fuming with revenge, empties the contents of the golden horn onto the sand.

SCENE FOUR

Freia, Brage and Idun bring Freir and Gerda to the bridal dance in which Sigyn and Aegir's servants also take part. After having introduced Sigyn into the circle of the Aesir, Loke calls forth the five sisters, invites them to dance and pours each of them a cup of the drink Sigyn has brought with her from Vola's cave. Aegir's servants are lured into their midst, taste the drink and share their mounting intoxication, which is manifested in violent actions and movements; this attracts everyone's attention and shocks Freia, who orders the dancing stopped and reproaches Loke for his shameless jest. He, however, remains unperturbed, calls for the frolic to continue and bids the goddess herself taste of the magic brew. She hurls the cup at his feet and hides her face, but the impudent rascal steals over to her and snips off a long lock of her blonde hair. General exclamation of indignation and disgust. Odin expels Loke from the company of the gods, but is met by nothing more than his scornful smile. Even Thor cannot escape his biting insults; anger mounts to rage, and Loke is about to fall victim to righteous vengeance when, resorting to sorcery, he transforms himself into a snake and throws himself into the sea.

Group registering dismay and wrath. Sigyn and her five sisters kneel before the indignant Freia. Aegir reprovingly threatens his daughters, and the exalted guests promise to obtain satisfaction for the insults which disrupted his joyous feast.

ACT III

Freia's sacred grove. To the left, her altar; to the right, flowering shrubs and flower-beds. In the background rises a wooded hill.

SCENE ONE

Sigyn, in the service of the goddess, waters her flowers and sadly dwells on the one she cannot tear out of her heart in spite of all his faults. Loke, who has witnessed her lamentation, suddenly appears and responds with feigned tenderness and repentance to the reproaches she levels at him for all the offence he has caused. He soon succeeds in mollifying her, and she promises to obtain for him the infuriated Freia's forgiveness.

Gentle, undulating tones can be heard close at hand, and Sigyn seeks a hiding place for her husband.

SCENE TWO

Elves bring the newly-wedded couple to Freia's grove.

Priestesses receive the offering Freir and Gerda place at the goddess's altar, and Freia herself comes to accept their homage. Sigyn takes advantage of this moment to throw herself at her mistress's feet and is just about to stammer out her plea when Skirner appears, somber and serious.

SCENE THREE

Everyone wants to know the outcome of his mission. After some hesitation, he delivers Thrym's proposal and presents Freia with the golden arm-ring-the betrothment gift from her suitor! Surprise and indignation! Freia's ire knows no bounds. She vehemently berates Skirner, who has dared to bring her such an offer. She tears asunder her starry veil, hurls her precious collar (the marvelous Necklace of the Brisings)* at his feet, and, in despair, swoons on the steps of the altar.

SCENE FOUR

Thor has seized Loke and brings him to the goddess's altar to have him expiate his guilt. Sigyn throws herself between them, and Freir shows him his poor sister, while Skirner informs him of Thrym's harsh terms for returning Thor's hammer.

With Sigyn's help, however, Loke has implored Freia's forgiveness. He wipes away his crocodile tears and, to show his gratitide, comes up with a strategem which shall benefit Thor and Freia – indeed, all of Asgard. Gathering together Freia's jewels, her veil and Thrym's broad arm – ring, he proposes that Thor, clad in the goddess's raiment, journey to Jotumheim and redeem the precious pawn himself. Thor scorns his proposal, but Loke will not give up his scheme and, laughingly beholding the prevailing dejection, he drags Sigyn away with him into the beech grove, with an air of mystery.

Martial tones draw near with mounting intensity. It is Heimdal, sounding Gjallar Horn, and the Valkyrie Rota, calling Valhalla's warriors to fight against Surt's† might.

Gerda painfully takes leave of her beloved Freir, who commits her to his sister's care. But Thor, deprived of his Mjollnir, feels weak and defenseless. The warrior-maids surround him; the clanging of shields deafens him; he is bewildered; tears gush from the strong man's eyes! Then, two feminine beings glide into the midst of the battle-eager host. Sigyn is immediately recognizable, but who can that taller, sturdier creature be? It is Loke, disguised as a maidservant.

For a moment, the profoundly serious mood is overcome by his dancing and roguish gestures. Thor himself bursts into divine laughter and is finally persuaded to follow Loke's clever advice. Gerda and Sigyn hasten away with them to complete their disguises.

SCENE SIX

Surrounded by her priestesses, Freia ascends the altar and calls down success upon Heerfather's sacred host. Freir, Skirner and Heimdal, together with Valkyries and *einherjar*, perform a weapon dance in honour of the goddess. It is soon announced that the transformation is complete, and, hailed by the striking of shields and the flashing of swords, Thor and Loke, in Freia's chariot, hasten off to Jotunheim.

---

* Necklace of the Brisings: a beautiful necklace which Freia managed to obtain from four dwarves.

† Surt: guardian of Muspell, the realm of fire.

ACT IV

Thrym's subterranean royal hall, whose ceiling is supported by pillars of strangely carved rock. In the background, a wide, arched door with a grille through which can be seen a deep ravine with a waterfall.

SCENE ONE

Finn and Thiase are arranging a feast, and the fire spirits are busy laying the table. The former comment on their lord's ridiculous marriage proposal.

Thrym enters, mooning over the lock of hair Loke has sent him as a pledge of the goddess's consent. He is pleased with the preparations for his bride's reception but impatient with Vola's continual warnings. In her mind she sees that Thrym's passion will lead to great misfortune, but the King of the Thursars turns a deaf ear to all her notions and finally sends the wise-woman away. She exits, furious and threatening.

SCENE TWO

Lurs sound, and the coming of the bride is announced. Thrym goes to greet his fair guest. The lofty bride, accompanied by her handmaid, majestically steps forth (only her eyes are unveiled). She is greeted with shrill jubilation, and Thrym is delighted to see his betrothal ring on her arm. He kisses her hand but is amazed at its size and the muscular strength of her arm! The eager maidservant praises the goddess's lovely countenance and, burning with curiosity, Thrym tries to lift the starry veil, but a daggerish look scares him out of doing so! Piqued, he turns once again to the servant, who reminds him of the cup of welcome, which he must taste before presenting it. Thrym has a great mead-horn brought in, puts it to his lips, then offers it to the bride. But what can equal his surprise when it is returned to him with every drop drained! He now leads his proud guest to the place of honour and seeks to console himself through his ravenous appetite. But why isn't the bride eating? Her handmaid replies that she is waiting for her betrothment gift. Thrym hastens to atone for his act of negligence by proffering a nosegay of the most precious stones. But this gift is contemptuously refused, and Thrym is about to lose his patience when the maid reminds him of the pawn which is to be redeemed with Freia's own hand.

After some hesitation, Thrym gives the order for *the fetching of the hammer* and presently the fire spirits bring it forth from the bowels of the earth. The handmaid cautiously lifts it and places it in the bride's lap... Mjollnir has scarcely been gripped by the hand which is accustomed to wielding it when the mountain gorges are rocked by peals of thunder.

The bride's raiment vanishes, and mighty Asa-Thor leaps up onto the table, defiant and challenging. Astonishment and alarm! The fire spirits take cover in their secure hiding places, while Loke himself finds shelter beneath the thunder god's feet. Fright, however, soon gives place to the rage of revenge, and while the Thursars brandish their clubs against Thor, Loke is dragged forth to pay for his guile. But Thrym is the first to fall beneath the hammer's blows; they fall crushingly in every direction. The grille is forced open and Thor leads Loke out into the open.

The pillars of the hall give way and, in falling, the vault buries the whole host of Thursar, while on the far side of the smouldering pile of rubble, in the moonlight, Thor and Loke can be seen on the bridge across the foaming waterfall.

The foreground is covered by dense clouds. A musical interlude fills the time it takes for the fog to disperse, and we find ourselves in Vola's cave.

SCENE THREE

The seeress is seated on the stone bench with the rune stick in her hand; the golden cup with the magic potion is standing at her feet. She gazes into the distance, and before her eyes appears the Plain of Ida, where Odin is assembling his warriors and shield maidens, who enthusiastically hasten to the decisive battle. Thor is the last to arrive but hopes to be first in the fray. He brings Loke with him, but the latter fails in the hour of peril, and Thor desists. The cavern closes.

SCENE FOUR

Alarmed about the outcome of the battle and her husband's fate, Sigyn has recourse to her foster mother in the rock cave. Vola beholds her with deep compassion and, tearing off her golden chain and casting it far away, she bids her forget her shameless spouse. Pale and dispirited, Loke bursts in, seeking protection from the powers of darkness. But these no longer obey him: he has betrayed both them and the Aesir, and now the hour of punishment and reckoning has come! In vain, Sigyn begs them for mercy. They bind him with the very chain with which Loke captivated her. She clings to him tightly while the angry spirits drag him away. But Vola tears her from his embrace and the unhappy wife swoons in her foster mother's arms.

SCENE FIVE

What the Norns have preordained is now fulfilled. To the eye of the seer the last battle is revealed through red swirls of flame and murky clouds of smoke. Surt's might triumphs: Odin is torn asunder by the wolf Fenrir* while Thor is overcome by the Midgard Serpent. Odin is, to be sure, avenged by the striking Vidar. But the snake's venom and the all-consuming force of the fire have completed the downfall of the gods: Everything is lost in Ragnarok!†

From the midst of this chaotic destruction rises a dead tree, from whose branches a poisonous snake hangs down over Loke, who is bound to the rock by fire spirits. Lightning flashes. The earth trembles, and Sigyn, awakening from her stupor, beholds her husband condemned to everlasting torment! The faithful wife will share his suffering! She seizes the golden bowl, climbs the steep rock and, supporting Loke's head, she holds the bowl beneath the serpent's jaws in order to catch the dripping venom. Vola sinks into the depths of the earth.

FINAL TABLEAU

The tempestuous storm dissolves into celestial harmonies. The dark clouds part, and through the breaking dawn appears a lovely landscape, resplendent in the fresh glory of Spring.

SCENE ONE

At a flower-decked altar stand Baldur and Nanna. Elves and blissful spirits dance about them to the gentle strains of harps and flutes.

Day dawns, and from both sides emerge Aesir and Asynjr, *einherjar* and Valkyries.

SCENE TWO

Odin and Frigga embrace their beloved son, whom they have sorely missed. The gentle Baldur bids them all lay down their arms before the Altar of Peace. Thor offers his hammer; helmets and shields are decked with flowers and green palms while elves adorn the brows of the blessed with wreaths of stars.

Nanna assigns Freia the supreme place in the kingdom of Love. Hope and joy pervade every heart, and the happy elect adoringly kneel before the eye of All-father which, sparkling brightly, rises above the eternal home of the good and the beautiful in

GIMLE.‡
* * *

---

* The Wolf Fenrir: another of Loke's offspring who, in the words of Kevin Crossley-Holland, "is bound by the gods and will remain so until Ragnarok, the end of the world." (*The Norse Myths*, Pantheon Books: New York, 1980).

† See previous note.

‡ Gimle: the Paradise of the pagans.

CORT ADELER IN VENICE
(Cort Adeler i Venedig)

A Ballet in Three Acts and a Final Tableau
by
August Bournonville

Music by Peter Arnold Heise

Scenery by Fritz Ahlgrensson

Performed for the first time at the Royal Theatre, Copenhagen, January 1870

Characters

CORT SIVERTSEN ADELER, Norweigian sailor, *Capitano*, later Admiral, in the service of Venice	Hr. V. Price
JOHANNES, his brother	Hr. Scharff
IBRAHIM PASCHA	Hr. Gade
FRANCESCO MOLINO, the Doge	Hr. Hoist
DOLFINO, *proveditore*	Hr. Brodersen
ISEPPA, his daughter	Frk. Schnell
LELIA, her friend	Frk. Petersen
VALERIO, nobleman	Hr. Fredstrup
BENEDETTO, prelate	Hr. Emanuel Hansen
GUIDO, attendant at the Doges' Palace	Hr. Hoppensach
CONCETTA, his wife	Fru Stillmann
A PIRATE CHIEF	Hr. C. Price
THE MASTER OF THE HAREM	Hr. Iversen
MESSENGER OF THE STATE INQUISITION	Hr. Ring
A TURKISH BOATSWAIN	Hr. Carpentier

VENETIAN NOBLES. HALBERDIERS. SBIRRI. MONKS. NUNS. GONDOLIERS AND COMMONERS. SEAMEN OF SEVERAL NATIONS. NAVAL OFFICERS. TURKISH OFFICERS AND SAILORS. VISIONS FROM CORT'S BIRTHPLACE.

Solo Dances

Dances in Act I

La Gondoliera: Mmes. Fredstrup, Stillmann, Larsen, and Hansen; Messieurs E. Hansen, Krum, Stramboe, and Kliiver, together with the corps de ballet.

Dances in Act II

A Sorcerer:	Hr. Busch
Scarramuccia:	Hr. Stramboe
La Schiavona:	Messieurs Hansen, Klüver, Iversen, Lense, and Smith; Mmes. Hansen, Viberg, Jeppesen, Jansen, and Madsen
La Capitana (Barcarole):	Mlles. Schnell, Petersen, and Larsen
La Sorpresa	Hr. Krum and Frk. Scholl

Dances in Act III

Dance of the Odalisques: Mmes. M. Price and Gade, together with the corps de ballet

In Act I, the scene is laid in Venice; in Act II, at Dolfino's villa; and in Act III, first on the island of Rhodes, then in the dungeons of the Doges' Palace.

The final tableau takes place in the waters off Tenedos. The time is the summer of 1654.

[**Translator's note**: August Bournonville had long been fascinated with the life and exploits of Kurt (or Cort) Sivertsen, whose Norwegian surname of honour-Adeler-means "eagle." Among the manuscripts of Bournonville's choreographic works is a draft of a ballet entitled Cort Adeler, dating from July 1832; this early "ballet poem" bears a dedication to the sculptor Bertel Thorvaldsen, that other Nordic hero whose fame and fortune were made in Italy.

By way of a postscript to Bournonville's biographical note on Cort Adeler, given below: Following his years of service in Venice and the Netherlands, Adeler returned to Denmark and, in 1662, accepted command of the Danish fleet from King Frederik III. During the reign of Frederik's successor, Christian V, he was to have led the fleet against Sweden but died suddenly in 1675, before the expedition got under way.]

Foreword

The portion of the life of the renowned naval hero Cort Sivertsen Adeler that has furnished the material for the present series of mimed pictures is described by the contemporary author Mylius and offers the following historical features:

His father, Sivert Jensen, was overseer of the Royal Salt Works at Brevig in southern Norway. Cort (born 1622) went to sea in his fifteenth year and travelled to Holland, where he was enrolled as a Cadet (in Dutch, Adelhorst, from which his later name appears to have been derived).

There he served under the great Admiral Tromp, and when peace was concluded he went into merchant shipping with Captain Reiersen. On a voyage to Italy he came to Venice, where he took service with the fleet of the Republic, advancing from grade to grade so rapidly that by 1645, at the age of twenty-four, he was appointed *chef de vaisseau* (*Capitano*).

In this capacity he took part, under Admirals Morosini and Molino, in all the naval battles fought against the Turks in the bloody war for Candia, and won undying glory at Tenedos (July 6, 1645), where with his flagship, the *San Giorgio Grande*, he victoriously contended against superior forces and with his own hand felled the Turkish admiral, Ibrahim Pascha.

In this famous battle, where a host of Christian slaves were freed, Cort had the sorrow of seeing his younger brother fall. What the latter was called, the biographer fails to say. Furthermore, history tells nothing of how matters stood for Cort Sivertsen during his stay in Venice, nor of how he was thought to be Flemish (*fiamengo*) and went by the name of Don Curtio Suffrido. It is therefore quite within the realm of dramatic probability that his younger brother might have been spurred on to heroic deeds by a violent passion and that Cort's appointment as admiral and a Knight of Saint Mark, as well as his Protestant faith, had come to be viewed with an evil eye.

The friendship that bound him to the ship's chandler, Iseppo Dolfino, under whose special guidance he won his greatest laurels, is sufficient motivation for the situations which mold the various scenes of the ballet into a dramatic plot.

ACT I

The Captain's cabin on board the *Giorgio Grande*. To the right, the after gallery, with windows; to the left, the entrance from the deck. In front, a cabin with curtains. The walls are hung with weapons and nautical instruments. Mid stage, a table with naval maps, writing implements, and documents.

SCENE ONE

Cort gives orders to officers and messengers; foreign seamen apply to serve under his command and are given the king's shilling.

One of them, who modestly holds back, refuses to accept the piasters handed him and will not obey the officer who sternly orders him to leave. The young man boldly steps before the captain. The latter recognizes his brother Johannes and joyously opens his arms to him. At a polite sign from Cort, the officers retire.

SCENE TWO

Left alone, the two brothers rejoice in their reunion. Cort asks for news of Norway, for the sounds of home are ever in his thoughts. Johannes brings him a letter from his aged parents. He reads it privately, while the new arrival admiringly observes the magnificence that surrounds his distinguished brother.

He, too, hungers for fame, now more than ever. Cort perceives the youth's sudden melancholy and seeks to learn its cause.

Johannes now tells him how, immediately upon arriving in Venice, he saw a lovely maiden who made a deep impression upon him. From the balcony on which she was standing she tossed a nosegay, which he picked up and hid in his breast as a memento of this celestial vision! Cort points out to him how dangerous such infatuations can be and bids him banish these romatic notions, which do not accord with the vigorous life of a sailor.

SCENE THREE

A salute of guns announces the arrival of distinguished guests, and Cort leaves to bid them welcome, first ordering that his brother be given clothing consistent with his rank. Attendants busy themselves, partly with bringing refreshments, partly with outfitting Johannes in his new garb, and he soon appears, dressed as an officer, with plumed hat and sword.

SCENE FOUR

The *proveditore* Dolfino and his party, among whom are his daughter Iseppa and her intended bridegroom, Don Valerio, are led in by Cort and respectfully saluted by the officers. Johannes is thunderstruck at the sight of Iseppa. " 'Tis she! My ideal, my tutelar goddess!" Cort introduces him to Dolfino, who, on Cort's recommendation, issues a diploma for the young officer and bids his daughter deck Johannes' sword with the colours of the Republic. Valerio views this situation with a jealous eye and observes with great anxiety the feelings that Johannes does not bother to hide.

With special significance, Dolfino invites Cort and his officers to the Doge's festival. All accompany him except Johannes, who stays behind, dreaming of love and glory, until his brother, half in anger and half in jest, comes and leads him away.

TRANSFORMATION

The Piazza San Marco, with a prospect of the Grand Canal. To the right, a throne has been erected; to the left, a marble staircase leads up to the Doges' Palace.

Accompanied by work people, the attendant Guido arranges everything around the throne. Curious gondoliers and commoners flock to the spot. Concetta, the attendant's young wife, mingles with the throng, to the great indignation of her petulant and jealous husband, who soon becomes the object of teasing on the part of the crowd. He tries in vain to drag her away from the young folks' dancing and merriment and goes threateningly away, while *La Gondoliera* drives the rest of the people mad with delight.

SCENE SIX

The sbirri come to clear the square, and the people recoil in fright.

The prelate Benedetto approaches, reading his breviary. He meets Valerio, who kisses his hand and receives his blessing. He gives Guido the key to the Lion's Mouth, near the palace steps. But today the container is empty. "Denunciations are few at present, and the prisons stand empty!" Guido bemoans this fact. Benedetto consoles him, while Concetta curiously harkens to their conversation.

The proveditore and his party come from the canal. Benedetto goes to meet them, and Dolfino presents Iseppa to him as the intended bride of Valerio. She receives his congratulations with noticeable coolness and disdain. General cries of jubilation greet Don Curtio (the name the Italians have given the Norwegian naval hero). Concetta is one of the most enthusiastic, and garlands and bouquets are handed him from all sides.

SCENE SEVEN

Gun salutes and fanfares announce the Doge's arrival. Pages and halberdiers station themselves near the throne, and the Council of Ten takes its place.

The aged Francesco Molino walks out onto the steps of the palace and is greeted with profound respect. Dolfino leads him to the throne, and with banners flying, a numerous procession marches past the leader of the Republic, who receives the oath of allegiance of all classes. Among the several corporations appears that of the Dominican Order, whose banner bears the motto: "Damnation to heretics!" Everyone kneels at the sight of this emblem; only Cort remains standing, a smile on his lips and his hat on his head. Benedetto and Valerio have noticed this, and the latter is not slow to seize a welcome opportunity to harm the hated foreigner.

The festivity continues; rewards are distributed to the valiant officers of the latest naval campaign, and Cort receives the accolade from the hand of the Doge himself. This is the day of the annual ceremony in which the chosen Prince of Venice weds the Republic to the Adriatic! Molino produces the ring with which he intends to perform the ceremony and invites Cort as well as the august nobility to accompany him aboard the flag-decked galley. The procession starts off. People throng to the quays; and, while amid cries of jubilation, salutes, and shrill music, the gilded Bucentaur glides past the Grand Canal and out into the lagoon, Valerio tosses a mysterious slip of paper into the Lion's Mouth.

The curtain falls.

ACT II

Dolfino's villa (on the mainland by the Adriatic Sea). Groups of trees and shrubbery, statues, and flower beds. To the right, the ascent to the main edifice; to the left, in the background, an avenue through which one glimpses the sea.

SCENE ONE

A fête champêtre has been arranged in honour of the newly created Admiral and Knight of Saint Mark. Iseppa and her friends are preparing several surprises for the honoured guest, and Valerio is arranging the whole thing with a zeal and pomposity that mask his perfidious designs.

SCENE TWO

Dolfino announces that the guests are approaching. Iseppa and Lelia hastily slip behind the curtain that has been hung between the trees to form an open-air theatre.

Cort and his brother, together with a select circle of noblemen and officers, are presented to the ladies. Refreshments are carried round, and the company are invited to take their seats.

The strains of an unseen orchestra are heard. The curtain is drawn aside, and the pantomime begins in the usual way, with a sorcerer who draws a magic circle about him and conjures up Scarramuccia, to whom he entrusts the distribution of the programme.

The dances succeed one another in the following order: first, *La Schiavona*, performed by five couples; next appear two young seamen carrying a model of Cort's flagship, the *San Giorgio Grande*; Iseppa and two of her friends, dressed as sea nymphs, adorn the vessel with garlands and perform a barcarole, which in honour of the exalted guest is called *La Capitana*. Scarramuccia announces two amorous maskers, and they spin out a little intrigue which ends with *La Sorpresa;* that is to say, the foreigners are greatly surprised to see the masked figures transformed into a Norwegian couple who perform a lively *Springdans* to melodies of their homeland. The brothers are both moved and happy at this lovely mark of attention, and Johannes can hardly suppress his desire to dance.

Iseppa, who has changed her clothes in the meantime, invites him to dance a sarabande, in which Cort and Dolfino, as well as the whole company, take part.

SCENE THREE

The festivities are interrupted by the arrival of three sinister masked figures, who are immediately recognized as messengers of the State Inquisition. All are filled with misgivings. Only Valerio maliciously smiles when the chief of the sbirri touches Cort with his baton and asks him to hand over his sword. Dolfino demands an explanation, and the masked figure hands him a written order, to which the *proveditore* must yield. Appalled by such injustice, Johannes wishes to offer resistance, but Cort tells him to keep his head, embraces him, shakes hands with his friends, and goes off with the messengers as a prisoner.

Visibly disheartened, the company follow Dolfino up into the palace, while Johannes sinks down onto a bench in despair. Suddenly. he hears the splash of oars, as from an approaching vessel. There may be a possibility of his brother's release! He rushes off in the hope of saving him.

SCENE FOUR

It grows dark. The vessel noticed by Johannes is manned by Levantine pirates. The latter now steal forth and express their intention of plundering Dolfino's villa at nightfall, felling anyone who dares to block their path. The leader gives his orders, and his men fan out in several directions.

SCENE FIVE

Servants bearing torches escort the departing guests. But Iseppa asks her father's permission to tarry in the garden with Lelia for a moment. She is sincerely distressed at what has just happened and is thinking of the brave young officer who has lost his sole support, his brother.

Johannes returns without having accomplished his mission. Cort was taken away in such inexplicable haste, and he himself is now left alone in the midst of foreigners! Iseppa consolingly approaches him and promises not only to pray Heaven for Cort's salvation but also to ask her father to petition the Doge for his release. Johannes sees her as a guardian angel and takes leave of her with thanks and benedictions.

SCENE SIX

Lelia warns her friend about the feelings she is unable to hide. Iseppa admits that she is in love with the stalwart young seaman and that she abhors Valerio. Lelia trembles at the thought of the impending dangers and Dolfino's wrath.

A dull noise is heard in the direction of the palace. A red glare is spreading this way; frightened, Iseppa and Lelia are about to hasten thither, but see the pirates coming from the villa laden with booty. Dolfino, who tries to stop the vandals with weapon in hand, receives a stunning blow. He falls unconscious on the staircase, and the young women are carried off as priceless captives!

Johannes, who is not yet far from the villa, rushes to help. But he is overpowered and thrown to the ground, and is about to receive the fatal thrust when the leader orders his men to bind him and to bring him along as a slave. They hurry off to the beach.

The curtain falls.

ACT III

Part I

A landing place on the island of Rhodes. The foreground is formed of a large tent, through the open sides of which one sees the ocean and the Turkish fleet lying at anchor.

SCENE ONE

A boat, rowed by chained slaves, is moored, and the boatswain orders carpets and cushions to be brought to the tent. Pascha Ibrahim intends to rest here, surrounded by his harem.

The leader of the pirates, who is anticipating an advantageous sale of the captured beauties, deferentially approaches the master of the harem. But at the same moment he notices Johannes, who, chained to another galley slave, is listening to his proposal with uneasy looks and strained attention. The unwelcome listener is chased away, and some gold pieces settle the business between the parties concerned.

SCENE TWO

Ibrahim and his headman come ashore. The Pascha proudly surveys his fine fleet and dismisses his retinue. At a signal from the master of the harem, the Pascha's women emerge from the adjacent tent, humbly bow before their master, and try to brighten his dark mood by their dancing.

SCENE THREE

The slave dealer is announced and brings with him two veiled maidens: Iseppa and Lelia. Ibrahim orders them to raise their veils, is immediately struck by Iseppa's beauty, and tosses a purseful of gold to the seller. Lelia, the dealer may keep. But, bathed in tears, the two friends beg the Pascha not to separate them. He agrees to buy Lelia too. The slave dealer is dismissed. Ibrahim desires his chosen one to be adorned with jewels, and the women gather round her in friendly fashion. But she repels their consolation and caresses.

SCENE FOUR

Ibrahim tries to win the affection of his new maiden with chivalrous tributes, but she responds to his amorous outbursts with fear and loathing and asks only to be returned to her father. A rich ransom will be paid for her and Lelia. The latter implores him not to abuse his power but to give Iseppa back to the one she loves! Ibrahim loses patience, angrily sends Lelia away, and invokes his right as Iseppa's lord and master. The desperate girls tightly cling to each other and implore the aid of the Madonna. At this moment Johannes appears at the entrance to the tent. He has broken his chains and rushes to the aid of his beloved. Ibrahim seizes his dagger and tries to hurl the daredevil to the ground. But the powerful youth wrests the steel from his grasp. Raging, the Pascha calls to his slaves, who come rushing forth, overpower Johannes, and prepare to carry out their master's death sentence. Iseppa throws herself at Ibrahim's feet and pleads for mercy, until he finally relents and orders the foolhardy slave taken back to the chains of the galleys. Johannes gives the disconsolate Iseppa a look filled with pain and despair, and is carried off by his executioners, while in his gondola the Pascha takes Iseppa and Lelia onto the flagship with him.

Part II

The prison vault beneath the Doges' Palace in Venice. To the right, a curtained niche, a wooden table, and a chair; to the left, cells with iron-bound doors. Upstage, a wide iron gate leading out to the little canal near the Bridge of Sighs. The exit door is to the right; beneath the ceiling burns a dim lamp.

SCENE ONE

Keys jangle. Guido enters with bread and a jug of water for the prisoner in cell Number 1. He is in the process of reflecting upon the vicissitudes of fortune when Concetta steals in and pesters him to find out who this important state prisoner is. After long and futile resistance, he is finally forced to reveal this, and his wife, prompted by dismay and the liveliest sympathy, demands that a decent meal be brought in place of the prison fare. Guido starts to object, but Concetta's authoritativeness overrides him.

She takes advantage of her husband's absence to inform the prisoner of her presence, and when Guido returns with the collation, the cell door is opened and Cort emerges. Concetta bursts into tears upon seeing the admired hero in this state. She reverently kisses his hand and bids him accept the proofs of devotion they can offer him without violating their strict duty.

Guido thinks he hears a noise outside and hurries off to see what it is. Meanwhile, Concetta hands Cort a piece of paper and a pencil. She bids him write his wishes and asks if he desires to see a spiritual adviser, as there is surely no hope that he will ever see daylight again. Deeply moved, Cort thanks her and writes a couple of words, which she conceals in her bodice; but, pointing to his evangelical psalter, he signifies to her that in this he finds his strength and consolation. Guido enters and anxiously summons his wife. She pours another glass of wine for the admiral, then follows her husband, who carefully locks the exit door.

SCENE TWO

Cort finishes his meal and stands up, contemplating his situation with mixed emotions. He searches for a psalm that can prepare him for his final journey. Its sacred tones hover before him, and his mind finds the needed peace. Little by little, the sounds die away. Overcome by sleep, he dozes off on the folding bed in the recess of the wall.

He dreams that the large iron gate is thrown open, and a Norwegian landscape appears in glorious sunlight. His old parents are sitting at their family prayers, thinking of their son. A rustic celebration is at hand, and a young bridal couple comes to receive the old people's congratulations. A boat pulls up to the shore; a tall man in noble dress, with the chain of an order of knighthood about his neck, steps out and is recognized by Sivert Jensen: it is his eldest son, Cort, who, after an absence of many years, is returning home covered with glory! Enraptured, his parents embrace him, and he is given a jubilant welcome by friends and relatives.

All of a sudden the sky grows dark, a thunderstorm breaks, and a burning city is seen in the distance! It is Copenhagen, which, hard-pressed by the enemy, calls upon her sons for heroic defense! Nothing can hold Cort back. He says good-bye to his parents, embraces them, and hastens away. But suddenly the horizon clears, and in a cloud there descends a crowned woman, leaning upon the Danish coat-of-arms with one hand and holding the sacred Dannebrog in the other. She signals Cort, and, handing him the flag, which he enfolds in his embrace, she crowns him with the laurels of glory. Darkness enshrouds the kneeling group. The vision fades, and the iron gate once more becomes the boundary of the prison.

SCENE THREE

The keys jangle anew: Guido and Concetta enter in the utmost haste to remove the table and put Cort back in his cell. They are terrified at not finding him, but finally discover him asleep in the niche. He is awakened to receive Benedetto, who, accompanied by four masked men, has come to pronounce the death sentence. But there is still a way to obtain mercy: he can abjure his Protestant falacies and bend his knee before the banner he scorned with his defiance. With dignity, Cort rejects this offer and points to the psalter, which contains the faith in which he will live and die. Benedetto flies into the most violent rate. With fanatical zeal he tears the clasped book from Cort's hands, treads it underfoot, and showers his anathema on the head of the sinful man. Cort has now sealed his own doom. The indignant prelate leaves the prison with his somber retinue. Only one of them stays behind to savour the pleasure of revenge. As he lifts the hood from his face, we recognize Valerio.

SCENE FOUR

Cort is now perfectly calm. He thanks Guido and Concetta for their kind sympathy and sends yet another thought to his far-off native land.

The iron gate opens with a thud. A gondola glides forth by torchlight, and one expects that the executioners have come to fetch their victim. On the contrary, it is Dolfino, who, accompanied by noblemen and pages, has come to bring tidings of freedom and honour! He opens his arms to the astonished Cort, tells him of the misfortune that has befallen his house, speaks of the captivity of his daughter and Johannes, and announces that, placed in peril, the Republic has given Cort supreme command of the fleet which is to be sent against the Turk.

The prison resounds with cries of jubilation from Cort's officers and men, who crowd in to hail and congratulate their valiant admiral, and, promising to follow him to victory or death, they happily rush off to the impending battle.

The curtain falls.

FINAL TABLEAU

The foreground is occupied by the quarter-deck and by part of the deck of the Turkish flag ship, with the starboard guns facing upstage, where the Turkish and Venetian fleets a redrawn up in line of battle; the *Giorgio Grande* is closest to the left.

The prelude already expresses the violence of the battle, and when the curtain rises everything is in full swing. Ibrahim and his headman encourage their people, and the fire from both sides steadily increases, accompanied by all the episodes that are part and parcel of a heated conflict. In the midst of the tumult, Iseppa finds the opportunity to release Johannes, who lies bound in the battery down below. They signal the Venetians by waving their scarves, and the *San Giorgio* ceases fire in order to send out its boats. Ibrahim, who perceives that something is amiss, is astonished to see Iseppa on deck. He orders her to take cover on the poop deck and suspects some treachery when she refuses. At this instant, the first grappling irons are dug into the ship, and with Cort in the lead, the Venetian sailors soon swarm over the bulwark. Only a few shots fall, but fierce hand-to-hand combat with sidearms ensues. Ibrahim, who sees that his defeat is imminent, wishes to punish the infidel woman who spurned his love and betrayed him to the enemy. When she tears herself loose from him, he fires his pistol at her but hits Johannes, who has thrown himself between Ibrahim and Iseppa.

Meanwhile, the attacking Venetians have forced the Turks to retreat in the direction of the ship's stern and up toward the stairway of the quarter-deck. At mid-deck a life-and-death struggle takes place between Cort and Ibrahim, while Dolfino hastens to his daughter, who is holding the mortally wounded Johannes in her arms.

Cort has felled the Pascha, who is weltering in his blood. Those Turks who have not been killed fall at the victor's feet and are given quarter. The crescent flag is lowered, and the Lion of Saint Mark flies from the captured ships.

The victor's joy is dampened by the inevitable death of his gallant young brother. But Johannes still has life and enthusiasm enough to congratulate Cort on his heroic deed. He himself has only one remaining wish: to receive in his last moments his brother's and Dolfino's blessing with Iseppa's hand in his. This sorrowful ceremony is performed while everyone thanks the Lord for the victory they have won. Smiling, Johannes gives up his spirit, and Cort, sober and griefstricken, stands surrounded by the radiance of his glory.

To the booming of victory guns, the blaring of trumpets, and the beating of drums, the Venetian Admiral's flag is presented to the famous naval hero, and sorrow must give place to the warrior's duties.

Jubilation resounds from deck and masts, marking the victory of Tenedos, which upheld the ancient renown of Venice and crowned the name of Cort Adeler with unfading glory.

* * *

THE KING'S VOLUNTEERS ON AMAGER
(Livjaegerne paa Amager)

An Episode from 1808
A Vaudeville-Ballet in One Act by
August Bournonville

Music composed and arranged by Wilhelm Holm

Scenery by Valdemar Güllich

Costumes designed by Edvard Lehmann

First performed at the Royal Theatre, Copenhagen,
February 19, 1871

Characters

EDOUARD, musician and Lieutenant		Hr. V. Price
STEFFEN, *Overjaeger*		Hr. Gade
OTTO		Hr. Scharff
EMIL	*Jaegere*	Hr. Krum
CARL		Hr. E. Hansen
LOUISE, Edouard's wife		Fru Stillmann
SOPHIE	fiancées of Otto and Emil	Frk. Petersen
ANDREA		Frk. Scholl
TØNNES		Hr. Ring
THAYS	farmers	Hr. Carpentier
CORNELIS		Hr. Busch
BODIL		Frk. Juul
SIDSE	their respective wives	Frk. Bydrup
ANE		Fru Thygesen
ELSE	servant girls	Fru. Hansen
TRINE		Frk. Jansen
JAN	bachelors	Hr. Stramboe
DIRK		Hr. Fredstrup

VOLUNTEERS. PEOPLE OF AMAGER. GUESTS FROM COPENHAGEN. CARNIVAL MASKERS.

The scene is laid in Kastrup at Shrovetide.

Dances and Pageantry

Polonaise and Hoop Dance: Corps de ballet and twelve couples belonging to the cast

Polka Militaire: Mmes. Stillmann, Gade, Price, and Larsen (masked);

Messieurs V. Price, Gade, Scharff, and E. Hansen

Pas De Trois: Hr. Krum (Prince Carnival), Frk. Petersen, and Frk. Scholl (Goddesses of Folly)

Reel and Molinaski: Messieurs Stramboe, Fredstrup, and Kluver; Mmes. Hansen, Jansen, Viberg, and Madsen, together with the corps de ballet

Holberg Quadrille (masked):

JEPPE	Hr. O. Poulsen
THE BAILIFF	Hr. Carl Price
JEAN DE FRANCE	Hr. Brodersen
DIDERIK MENSCHENSCHRECK	Hr. Gade
NILLE	Hr. Hoppensach
THE BAILIFF'S WIFE	Hr. Scharff
MADAME LAFLECHE	Frk. Bryde
THE OFFICER'S WIFE	Hr. Eckardt
THE WEATHERCOCK	Fru Stillmann

Finale

Carousel Galop: The entire corps de ballet

The stage represents the parlor of a prosperous farmhouse (in which a Lieutenant and an *Overjaeger* of the King's Corps of Volunteers are billeted). To the right a stove fed from another room [*billaeggerovn*], a piano, and a bed in an alcove. To the left, an oak table and cupboard. Doors on both sides; the right-hand one leads outdoors, while that to the left gives access to the other rooms. The background is formed by a garden door and two windows, through which can be seen a flat winter landscape and, in the distance, the seashore. Along the walls, old-fashioned furniture and benches which can be used for sleeping[*slagbaenke*].

SCENE ONE

Tønnes, owner of the farm, is seated at the large table, playing cards with his neighbours Thays and Comelis. Else and Trine are decorating a ridiculously outfitted doll. Bodil comes in with punch for the men. Jan and Drik, who are looking forward to the merry Shrovetide celebration, pay their respects to the master and mistress of the house, and, giving the girls their hats to decorate, they ask permission to celebrate the occasion with dancing and beating the barrel.

At first Tønnes is unwilling to give his consent, but when he sees the funny doll the girls have made, he bursts out laughing and gives in.

In the meantime, the farmhands have had their hats decked out with multicoloured ribbons and now play up to the girls, whom they have an eye for. But their advances are coolly received, and they cannot refrain from making some insinuating remarks about the good-looking Lieutenant who charms the girls with his amorous melodies.

SCENE TWO

Sidse and Ane enter with the children, who are clad in their Sunday best. The men joyfully greet them. Bodil, who has her whole apron filled with buns, distributes them to the youngsters and proposes a game which consists in striking an earthenware pot while blindfolded. The crock with all the buns tips over, and the merry horde pounces upon them in a disordered crowd.

SCENE THREE

The Volunteers are heard returning after having made their rounds of the coast. They halt outside the farmhouse. Everyone rushes to the windows, and the garden door is opened for Lieutenant Edouard, who, after turning over his command, enters, accompanied by his *Overjaeger*, the jolly Steffen, whose haversack always contains a bit of candy or some sweets for the children and whose merry jesting is always welcomed by the Amager lasses.

Edouard, who is billeted in Tønnes' house, is cordially welcomed by the host and his guests; but since Bodil is sure the Lieutenant must be in need of rest after the strenuous march, she asks the company to join her in another room. Steffen leads the way, and with the doll and the punch bowl, they march off in triumph.

SCENE FOUR

Edouard sits down in an armchair and reads himself to sleep, but is soon disturbed by a melody that continues to haunt him. He tries in vain to find some peace, but it is no use; he must get up and confine his fantasies to the piano.

Else steals into the room, lured by the strains of the melody. She beckons Trine, and they both harken to the tender harmonies which each girl believes to be a sign of the Lieutenant's infatuation for her. They start to slip away, when they are noticed; but Edouard detains Else, tells her how pretty she is, and, as usual, assures her of his ardent love. Trine returns, stands there astounded, and begs pardon for having interrupted their conversation. Edouard tries to pacify her, but she reproaches him for his unfaithfulness, since he has also played up to her a good deal. (This evolves into a dancing trio, wherein Edouard tries to convince each girl in turn that she is the one he prefers.)

SCENE FIVE

Outside, a snowball fight arises between the Volunteers and the Amager lads, and, amid laughter and din, a host of young people bursts into the room. Steffen enters and lectures them about how unfitting it is to burst into the Lieutenant's quarters in such a way. But Edouard finds the whole thing amusing, and, since the Volunteers are off-duty for the moment, he invites them to dance with the girls while he plays a waltz for them on the piano.

SCENE SIX

Gunshots in the distance announce that something important must be happening. The assembly is sounded, and Edouard orders the Volunteers to arm. They rush out to don their gear. Fright among the peasant folk. Edouard reassures them but cannot hide his delight at the thought that there might be action. The Volunteers enthusiastically gather around their lieutenant, who encourages them to uphold the reputation of the Corps, then hurries them off at a run.

SCENE SEVEN

The Shrovetide banquet seems to have gone to pieces. Troubled, the older people retire; Else and Trine sit down in a corner to weep while the lads anxiously pace the floor. They give vent to their dejection by reproaching the girls for their coquetry. Else accuses Trine, and vice versa. The lads become abusive and box one another on the ears. The dispute threatens to become really serious, when the women enter and make peace. But the young folk withdraw their allegiance from one another and take turns throwing their presents at each other's feet.

SCENE EIGHT

The jingling of bells announces the approach of a sleighing party, and four sleighs bearing guests from Copenhagen soon pull up in the farmyard. The hospitable Amager folk amicably greet them, and a party of four gentlemen and seven ladies enters – all of them in furs and some of them quite frozen. They have come to celebrate Shrovetide out here on Amager and have brought with them costumes for a carnival. The Lieutenant's wife, Louise, together with Sophie and her friend Andrea – both of whom are engaged to members of the Corps – form the core of the merry circle and anticipate great enjoyment from this festival. "But what of the war and the enemy?" ask the anxious inhabitants. The Copenhageners have heard nothing of this – it is probably a false alarm! Fear gives place to brighter prospects, and the steaming coffee pot summons the guests to the parlor.

SCENE NINE

Louise stays behind and approaches the piano, on whose music rest she discovers the score of Edouard's latest composition. She pages through it and finds her favourite romance. She summons her young friends and shows them the piece of music, convinced that Edouard thinks only of her and is dying to see her. Sophie and Andrea perceive Else and Trine, and sympathetically ask them the cause of their distress. The girls are reluctant to answer, but Jan and Dirk step forward to give an explanation, from the confused details of which it appears that the Amager lasses are given no peace by the Volunteers, all of whom are outrageous philanderers. Then it must be true of Otto and Emil! The two young ladies are indignant at such behaviour. They decide to break off with their fiancés. They are going to return to the capital immediately and ask Louise to give their rings back to their unfaithful lovers. The good-natured Louise tries to cool their anger and, advising them to put up with the men's folly, she smilingly states that "they are all the same!"

SCENE TEN

Steffen peeps in the window. The girls open the door for him, and he is just about to begin his roguery when he discovers Fru Louise, who asks for her husband and is delighted to learn that he is expected to return soon. Else and Trine wish to learn something about the expedition. "Not the slightest trace of the enemy!" Otto and Emil, impatient to see their fiancées, come running but are astonished at their cool reception. They try in vain to explore the reason for this change of heart; but when the young ladies haughtily put Else and Trine before them, they comprehend the droll misunderstanding and can hardly keep from laughing. The girls now explain that it is not these two gentlemen who are responsible for the farmhands' jealousy but, rather, the Lieutenant who was always talking and singing of love! It is now Louise's turn to become angry and distressed; but her tenderness and good humor overcome her legitimate grounds for complaint. "But, the false [lover] shan't get away with it!" He has no idea she is here, so, swearing the others to secrecy, she resolves to play a practical joke which shall serve to punish and, if possible, reform him. She now makes peace between the young couples, and they go off with her to carry out the plans for the proposed masquerade.

SCENE ELEVEN

Led by their band, the Volunteers return, followed by a host of children and young people. The neighbours arrive for the banquet, and Tönnes invites the Volunteers to take part. Edouard, who is not really pleased at the peaceful outcome of this *promenade militaire*, thanks his host for his politeness and orders the band to enhance the festivities with its music. Everyone wishes everyone else a "Happy Shrovetide!" Glasses of punch are passed around, a wreath of spruce and artificial flowers is hoisted up to the ceiling, and the signal is given for the commencement of the dances, which are performed in the following order:

POLONAISE AND HOOP DANCE

performed in turn by the older people, the young folk, and the children.

POLKA MILITAIRE

(Four masked hussar *vinandières* ask the same number of Volunteers to dance – namely, Steffen, Otto, Carl, and Edouard.

The last is artfully deceived by Louise, to whom he is attracted without knowing her identity. She vanishes, and after trying in vain to find her amid the throng of merrymakers, he leaves the celebration.)

PAS DE TROIS

performed by Emil, Else, Trine, and a whole corps de ballet made up of natives of Amager and Volunteers. After this comes

A QUADRILLE BY CHARACTERS FROM HOLBERG

called forth by Prince Carnival, while the goddesses of Folly hover round. The Weathercock is represented by Louise, who once again attracts Edouard's attention and captivates him to the degree that he implores her to give him her heart. She hands him the butterfly which adorns her belt and gives in to his plea that she unmask... to his shame he recognizes his own wife! A gently reproving glance meets his eye. The waltz whirls about them; through the music of the dance can be heard the strains of that favourite romance as Edouard, unnoticed, obtains forgiveness and promises to mend his ways in the future.

SCENE TWELVE
(FINALE)

Joy mounts with every moment and is expressed in a thunderous Carousel Galop in which everyone takes part; and while the dance moves from room to room, outside the barrel is beaten... the grotesque doll finally falls out through the bottom and is brought inside by the winner to form the pinnacle of the final tableau.

The curtain falls amid rejoicing and the clinking of glasses.

*   *   *

IN MEMORY OF WEYSE*
(Weyses Minde)

An Epilogue with Tableaux
by
August Bournonville

Music arranged by Voldemar Holm, after compositions by Weyse

Performed for the first time at the Royal Theatre in honour of the hundredth anniversary of Weyse's birth, March 5, 1874

Characters

Scene One

WINTHER	Hr. Hoppensach
MADAME SOMMER	Fru Thygesen
PETER	Hr. Klüver
CHRISTINE	Frk. Egense
LITTLE GIRLS	Mesdames Hansen, Møller, Viberg
SOLDIERS	Messieurs Iversen, Valbom, L. Hansen

CHILDREN OF BOTH SEXES.

Scenes Two and Three

PHANTASUS	Hr. Krum
EUTHERPE	Frk. Petersen
POLYHYMNIA	Frk. Poulsen
MELPOMENE	Fru Mentzell
THALIA	Fru Stillmann
TERPSICHORE	Frk. Westberg

Scene Five

First Tableau

LEICESTER	Hr. V. Price
EMMY ROBSART	Frk. G. Petersen
GYPSY DANCE	Hr. E. Hansen and Frk. Scholl
THE ELF KING	Hr. Gold

---

* **Translator's note:** The setting for this tribute to the popular Danish composer Christoph Ernst Friedrich Weyse (1774–1842) is the gardens of Rosenborg Castle, which was then on the outskirts of Copenhagen and a popular resort. The gardens provided the setting for one of his six operas and operettas – his librettists included Oehlenschläger, Hans Christian Andersen, and Heiberg. The music for this tribute draws on five operas and his incidental music for *Macbeth*.

THE ELF QUEEN	Fru Gade
DANCE BY TWO ELVES	Miles. Flammé and Mibach

ELVES AND GNOMES

Third Tableau

ROBIN	Hr. Ring
GEORGE	Hr. Carpentier
SCOTTISH REEL	Ida Bertelsen and Virginie Monti

Fourth Tableau

MACBETH	Hr. Gade
BANQUO	Hr. C. Price
THE WITCHES	Mesdames Frederiksen, Eydrup, and Jensen
ELVES' DANCE	Mesdames Schousgaard, Madsen, Viberg, Jeppesen, Flammé, Mibach, Nielsen, Kempf, and Vick

Fifth Tableau

FARUK	Hr. Lauenberg
THE FLOWER MAIDEN	Frk. Larsen
KURUM	Hr. Lense

Final Tableau

SAINT CECILIA	Frk. O. Petesen

ALL THE FOREGOING FIGURES.

SCENE ONE

The stage represents a portion of the Rosenborg Gardens, with the castle in the background. It is toward evening.

Children are playing while their nursemaids chat with some young soldiers.

Meeting of old Winther and Madame Sommer, and of Peter and Christine.

The bugle sounds roll call, and a bell signals closing time.

The various groups depart. It grows dark, and the Gardens stand empty.

(Music: Overture to *An Adventure in Rosenborg Gardens*.)

SCENE TWO

The night mist hides the castle from view (Romance: "The sun goes down, etc."). When day breaks once more, we are transported to the Temple of Hercules, and Phantasus consecrates the spot as the assembly hall of Memories.

(Allegretto from the above-mentioned operetta.)

SCENE THREE

The strains of a harp and an invisible chorus can be heard coming from the temple. Euterpe and Polyhymnia emerge from the woods, Thalia and Melpomene from the flower garden. Phantasus bids them welcome, hands them garlands, and calls upon them to praise in unison the composer's memory.

(Elves' Chorus from *Floribella*.)

At a signal from Phantasus the statue of Hercules is replaced by a bust of Weyse, and the Muses enthusiastically hasten to the temple to adorn the statue of their favourite with flowers.

(Patriotic song: "There is a land, etc.")

SCENE FOUR

Terpsichore comes dancing in, waving her tambourine. She too wishes to pay the celebrated artist the homage of remembrance.

But her more earnest sisters seem to want to prevent her from taking part in this honour. However, she will not be deterred, and as Phantasus enters with a basketful of flowers, she says in a jocular vein: "Just go into the temple, august Muses; I shall stay out here and strew blossoms about the bust of the glorious composer." The four fair goddesses enter the temple and, together with the bewinged Phantasus, Terpsichore performs her task.

(Allegro: Ballet music from *The Festival at Kenilworth*.)

SCENE FIVE

From the temple come the sounds of delicious harmonies.

The curtain is drawn aside, and, as in a tableau vivant, there is depicted a scene from

THE FESTIVAL AT KENILWORT
(Leicester and Emmy [sic] Robsart)
Melody from the same opera

The curtain is drawn once more, and a gypsy dance from the same opera fills the interval between this and the ensuing tableau,

FLORIBELLA

At their master's command, elves forge a helmet and sword for

Fernando.
(Elves' Chorus.)
The tableau vanishes, and Terpsichore joins in the dance of the elves.
A new picture appears, representing a merry drinking scene from

LUDLAM'S CAVE

(Ballad: "If thou wilt be strong and free, etc.")
The gaiety must now give way to a more somber mood, and the next tableau depicts a scene from Shakespeare's

MACBETH

The three Witches prophesy the fates of Macbeth and Banquo.
(The Witches' Sabbat from the tragedy.)
But the merry elves soon perceive the disquieting impression this last scene has made, and by their dancing they conjure up a picture from

FARUK

The Maiden of the Well hands Prince Faruk the enchanted rose.
(Elves' Chorus and dance from this opera.)

SCENE SIX

Solemn tones are heard. The Muses form a group around Weyse's bust. All the figures who have been seen in the tableaux now come to the fore, while deep within the cloud-enshrouded recesses of the temple sits enthroned

SAINT CECILIA AT HER ORGAN

surrounded by cherubs singing and playing stringed instruments. Weyse's genius reaches its height in his

"Hymn of Thanksgiving."

The curtain falls.

*   *   *

THE MANDARIN'S DAUGHTERS
(Mandarinen Døtre)

A Ballet Divertissement by
August Bournonville

Music arranged and composed by Wilhelm Holm

Scenery by Valdemar Gillich

Performed for the first time at the Royal Theatre on
April 23, 1873

Characters

YANG-TCHOONG, Imperial Prince	Hr. V. Price
KAO-LI, Mandarin	Hr. Gade
WENKJUN, his consort	Fru Stillmann
PING-SIN, her daughter	Frk. Westberg
THE MANDARIN'S THREE OTHER WIVES	Fru Gade / Fru Hansen / Frk. Møller
THEIR RESPECTIVE DAUGHTERS	Frk. Petersen / Frk. Scholl / Frk. Price
AN IMPERIAL MESSENGER	Hr. Ring

In addition, dances are performed by Messieurs Krum, Hansen, Stramboe, and Kliiver; Mesdames Larsen, Skousgaard, Madsen, and Wiberg.

THE PRINCE'S RETINUE. LIVING CHESSMEN. BRIDESMAIDS. DOMESTICS AND SLAVES.

The scene is laid in the province of Chung-King. The time is the middle of the sixteenth century.

MOTIF

In addition to his consort, the Mandarin has three other wives who live in mutual discord, and when any of them has a marriageable daughter, there are endless quarrels as to which of these young girls ought to be given precedence if a distinguished suitor should present himself. Old Kao-Li has all he can do to keep peace.

An imperial messenger announces that Prince Yang-Tchoong will visit the Mandarin's home and choose a wife from among his daughters. Everyone is in a state of anxious expectation. Only Ping-Sin, Wenkjun's daughter, does not seem to receive this news with joy.

The sound of shrill instruments proclaims the Prince's approach in grand procession. Kao-Li hastens to receive him, and the women disappear. Refreshments are served, but the Prince, anxious to see the pretty daughters, declines, and Kao-Li summons his family while the Prince bids his retinue retire.

The mothers bring their veiled daughters before the Prince. The veils are lifted, and the Prince is dazzled by the beauty that meets his eye. But shy Ping-Sin has captured his heart at first sight. He gives his necklace, his medallion, and his beaver skin to the three sisters, but to her he offers only a simple golden ring. Trembling, she hesitates to accept it, and both the Prince and her parents are greatly astonished at her behaviour. "It must be she or no one!" exclaims Yang-Tchoong, and he begs the family to withdraw for a bit so that he may obtain her consent without the influence of others. He succeeds in convincing her of his true love. Kneeling, he hands her the golden betrothal ring and she places it on her finger. Enraptured he calls hither her family and his retinue in order to show them his chosen bride, who now receives the acclaim of all with becoming modesty.

The bridesmaids appear with fans and flowers, and Wenkjun adorns her daughter with the meaningful emblems of the fan, the wreath, and the lotus blossom. After the Bridal Dance ends, Wenkjun bids Kao-Li and the Prince seal the marriage contract with a cup of wine and a game of chess. The cups are drained with the heartiest congratulations, but, smiling, the Prince shakes his head at the sight of the little chessboard. He knows of a completely different set of chessmen, and, at a signal from him, pawns, bishops, knights, kings, and queens come dancing forth. A carpet of chess squares is placed on the floor, and the living chessmen assume their proper places.

The match begins between the Prince on the one side and the Mandarin on the other. The latter is mated after several moves, and delight is expressed at the Prince's victory. Two of the sisters are united with the gentlemen who have played the kings in the game.

The third daughter declines the knight's proposal and will remain with her father, who, while the young folk were dancing, was enjoying the wine and losing a little of the dignified bearing of a mandarin.

The dancing continues until darkness falls, and ends with the Festival of Lanterns, beneath which Yang-Tchoong leads the charming Ping-Sin home as his bride.

*   *   *

A FAIRY TALE IN PICTURES
(Et Eventyr i Billeder)

Ballet in Three Acts
by
August Bournonville

(Motif from Hans Christian Andersen's "The Steadfast Tin Soldier")

Music composed and arranged by Wilhelm Holm

Scenery by Valdemar Güllich

First performed at the Royal Theatre on December 26, 1871

Characters

RICHARD	J. Bertelsen
JENNY	J. Petersen
THE FATHER	Hr. Ring
THE MOTHER	Fru Gade
THE GRANDMOTHER	Fru Stillmann
THE MAID	Fru Hansen

PARTY OF CHILDREN AND ADULTS.

The scene is laid in England, at Christmas time.

In the Realm of Fantasy

A FAIRY	Fru Stillmann
OSCAR, soldier in a Highland regiment	Hr. V. Price
ROSALIE, ballerina	Frk. Scholl
MONTPLAISIR, solo dancer	Hr. Krum
SULIVAN, régisseur	Hr. Gade
BELTON, capitalist	Hr. Gundersen
HAWKINS, writer	Hr. C. Price
A STAGE HAIRDRESSER	Hr. Hoppensach
A DRESSER	Fru Thygesen

SOLDIERS. CANTINIÈRES, SYLPHIDES.

SOLO DANCES

Messieurs Hansen, Stramboe, Fredstrup; Mesdames Petersen, Price, Larsen, Hansen, and Jeppesen.

FOREWORD

The title of this ballet is apt to modify considerably the demands an audience usually makes with respect to "dramatic action." The motif, which is taken from one of our famous countryman's most naive fairy tales for children, merely contains the seed from which a larger plant has sprung in the fertile soil of the imagination. Indeed, the series of pictures conjured up by the love of "the steadfast tin soldier" for "the little ballerina" gains scenic importance only through the trials and tribulations both these lovers must endure before they may be united.

A little romance such as this is most at home in the fairyland of dreams, which is, in fact, the most convenient framework for a ballet. Here it is set in motion by two small children, a brother and sister, before whose childlike imaginations Andersen's fairy tales and stories vividly appear.

One may perhaps object that the dramatic coherence necessary in even the lightest genre of scenic production is not to be found in a dream, where images generally drift by in hazy confusion. Yet to this one may reply that could we but retain and record all that hovers before the ever-wakeful soul during our hours of repose, many a man would rise from his bed a poet, a painter, or a novelist.

By now my fantasies have once and for all assumed the form of ballets. May this unpretentious work – like the ingenious fairy tales that have inspired me – find a receptive audience; and, even though it may not be fully understood by children, I hope that it may entertain and amuse them as well as adults.

August Bournonville

ACT I

The stage represents a nursery. To the left, a door; to the right, a window. In the background, two settees in curtained alcoves; an old-fashioned clock on a commode, above which hangs a magnificent picture. On both sides, tables with playthings. Midstage, a large armchair.

SCENE ONE

Richard is playing with his tin soldiers; Jenny is busy with her dolls. *He* beats a drum and drills his troops while *she* dresses a little ballerina and teaches her to perform graceful steps. Richard laughs at his sister's fantasies, which gives rise to mutual banter. He makes fun of her doll, while she scoffs at his warriors. Richard seizes his gun and tries to shoot the innocent ballerina. Jenny flees with her protégé and, in passing, wreaks havoc among the tin soldiers. Richard becomes angry and is about to avenge the fall of his gallant men when Grandmother intervenes.

SCENE TWO

She makes peace between the children and tells them that "if they promise to be good," she will show them pictures. They jump for joy and nestle close to Grandmother, who takes her place in the armchair and opens a book with illustrations of the Danish writer's fairy tales, which have so often filled their childlike imaginations.

They see "The Mysterious Stork," "Thumbelina on the Water Lily," "The Chinese Nightingale," "The Little Mermaid," "The Ugly Duckling Transformed into a Swan," "The Swineherd," "Ole Shuteye," and finally, "The Angel"!

By the time they come to "Ole Shuteye" ["The Sandman"], the children have grown sleepy, and the angel hovers above their heads while Grandmother carries them over to the settees and offers a prayer for these dear little ones. She herself sits down to rest in the armchair, the picture book in her hand.

SCENE THREE

The room is shrouded in darkness. A melody that sounds like a lullaby fills the room, and its strains lead the sleeping children into the Realm of Dreams. The room is transformed in to a Hesperidian garden, and the old Grandmother into a beautiful Fairy who, with a signal, summons from the doll table a graceful little ballerina and from Richard's fallen army a lifelike soldier dressed in the Highlanders' picturesque uniform.

SCENE FOUR

At her mistress's command, the ballerina (who bears the doll's name of Rosalie) climbs down from her lofty perch and assumes some pretty poses, which are intended to capture the soldier's attention. But Oscar remains unmoved and executes his maneuvers with dignity and precision. The Fairy's magic wand brings the table down to ground level, and he is soon forced to yield to the power that hovers round him. His eyes follow Rosalie's movements. He is captivated by her grace, kneels before the benevolent Fairy, and, piece by piece, allows himself to be disarmed.

The Fairy beckons to a small winged elf (in whom we immediately recognize Jenny) and departs in order to allow the young couple to find an explanation, with the help of the mischievous genius. In a scene wherein dancing alternates with expressive mime, they confess their love for each other and are about to swear eternal fidelity when the Fairy interrupts them and gravely signifies that only after they have withstood hard trials and tribulations can they hope for a happy union. The lovers promise to be true, and sadly part. The Fairy leads Rosalie away, while Cupid jocosely warns against the dangers that threaten our young soldier.

SCENE FIVE

Oscar remains alone and presses to his lips the ribbon Rosalie has given him. He suddenly hears the beat of drums, and a little drummer boy comes toward him, salutes, and announces the arrival of a troop of his comrades, who wish to rest at this spot. Oscar bids them welcome but refuses to take part in their game of dice. The game soon degenerates into a brawl, and sabers are drawn in order to settle a quarrel between two of the players. Oscar tries in vain to pacify them, but only succeeds in increasing their indignation. Swords have already been crossed when the little drummer boy (Richard himself) rushes in, followed by a troop of young *cantinieres* who by their dancing and coquetry soothe the ruffled tempers and pour schnapps from their kegs as a token of reconciliation.

They also try to tempt Oscar, but he steadfastly resists them. And yet, for a moment he is almost caught up in the whirl of the dance; but the drum quickly restores him to his senses. A new detachment of Highlanders, with their colours in the lead, comes marching in.

They all hasten to get under arms and, amid a lively *Stormgalop*, they depart, to go where duty calls.

ACT II

The ballet *foyer* in the Drury Lane Theatre. To the right, the stairway leading to the stage; to the left, the general exit. In the background, a broad balcony window with large mirrors on either side.

SCENE ONE

The danseuses are finishing their toilette and are getting ready to appear as sylphides. The hairdresser and the dresser are busy trying to satisfy all their demands. Rosalie, who is recognized and acclaimed as the prima ballerina, is the object of her sister artistes' envy, while mischievous little Cupid buzzes about among the various groups.

SCENE TWO

Dressed in a grotesque shepherd's costume, M. Montplaisir, the leading male soloist, enters, jumping and doing pirouettes. He brings Rosalie a bouquet and proposes that they rehearse the dances to be performed this evening. All the ladies take part, and, together with her cavalier, Rosalie displays all her graceful talent. The rehearsal is barely over when the régisseur's bell summons the sylphides for the performance. They put the finishing touches on their toilette and scurry on stage.

SCENE THREE

Montplaisir has been unable to resist his partner's charm, and, finding himself alone with her, seizes this opportunity to declare his tender feelings and offer her his hand. Rosalie dismisses the whole thing as a joke and assures him that she can never be his. He becomes passionate, suspects that she loves another, and threatens to kill both himself and his rival.

The bell in the foyer rings violently, and Sulivan, the régisseur, comes rushing in to summon the desperate *danseur* for the next scene. Montplaisir finally regains his composure, glares at Rosalie, collects his strength, and hurries off.

SCENE FOUR

The astonished régisseur asks Rosalie the reason for this emotional behaviour and learns that Montplaisir has made her an offer of marriage, which she is unable to accept. Sulivan thinks he has now found an opportunity to present *himself* as a suitor. However, he meets not only with the firmest of refusals but with an ironic smile that almost makes him burst with spite. Rosalie skips off to perform her role on stage.

SCENE FIVE

Angry and disappointed, Sulivan paces up and down the foyer. Two *amateurs*, Mr. Belton, a capitalist, and Mr. Hawkins, a writer, come storming in through the exit door and try to force their way up onto the stage in order to pay their homage to the celebrated prima ballerina with bouquets and wreaths. Sulivan informs them that outsiders cannot be granted admittance. They try in vain to overcome his opposition, both by force and by cunning. But when he calls for help they are forced to leave, consoling themselves with the thought that from the auditorium they can toss both their flowers and their laurels to the ballerina. Sulivan and the hairdresser scamper up into the wings.

SCENE SIX

Hidden behind a curtain, Cupid has witnessed this last scene. He now emerges, laughing and dancing, and gloats over the unsuccessful suitors and admirers. He notices a veiled woman stealing into the foyer and asks what errand brings her her. But what can equal his delight when he recognizes the Good Fairy! He throws himself into her arms and answers her questions about Rosalie by pointing toward the stage, where they can hear the music for her solo, which is rewarded with rounds of thunderous applause. These sounds have also been heard outside and have lured hither the little drummer boy, who has clambered up onto the balcony window. The Fairy opens it for him and wishes to know what has become of Oscar. Richard indicates that the faithful lover is standing guard at the entrance to the theatre and that his thoughts are constantly fixed on his little ballerina.

Rosalie has finished her *pas* and returns. The Fairy exits left, taking Cupid with her. Richard hastens off in the direction whence he came.

SCENE SEVEN

Tired and out of breath, Rosalie returns from the stage rejoicing over the triumph she has celebrated. The dresser brings with her all the bouquets and wreaths, which she has gathered in her apron, and casts them once again at the ballerina's feet. Rosalie modestly accepts them, but confesses that her heart is more attached to her first love than to the acclaim that has now been showered upon her talent. She thanks the dresser, dismisses her, and pensively sits down in an armchair.

SCENE EIGHT

The two *amateurs* enthusiastically return and assail Rosalie with panegyrics and declarations of love. Hawkins introduces himself as an author whose articles shall sound her praises, and now hands her the very laurel he tossed onto the stage. Belton, on the other hand, has a bridal basket brought in, filled with genuine shawls, laces, and jewels, which he lays at the feet of the one he adores. Rosalie, who is impervious to splendor and false renown alike but loyal to the oath she has sworn her valiant soldier, contemptuously dismisses the pressing suitors and their gifts. The rivals fly into a rage and blame one another for their lack of success. They challenge each other to a duel with pistols, but turn back once more and, kneeling, try to soften the heart of the relentless beauty.

SCENE NINE

The performance is over. The sylphides, Sulivan, Montplaisir, the hairdresser, and the dresser come down into the foyer and are outraged at the scandal, of which (in their opinion) Rosalie has been the cause. The uninvited guests are scornfully ushered out and, the exit door is locked behind them. The régisseur, who takes the key, now pours forth a torrent of reproaches against the misunderstood woman. All join in his castigating remarks. Rosalie tries in vain to justify her behaviour, but she is repulsed by everyone. As they leave the foyer, Sulivan, in his wrath, pounds on the locked door.

SCENE TEN

Left alone, Rosalie sadly reflects on her plight, bemoaning the lack of understanding she must endure and lamenting the perishability of the garlands she has won with her ephemeral art. She begs Heaven for strength to bear this opposition, thinks of her beloved friend, and feels encouraged by this deep inner knowledge. All of a sudden she is filled with longing, and bursts into tears.

A commotion can be heard somewhere close at hand. It increases with dreadful force. She can hear bells clanging, drums beating, and horns blaring! Rosalie is frightened and runs to the exit. The door is locked; nor will the stage door yield to her efforts. She rushes over to the balcony window, pulls the curtain aside, and sees smoke and flames leaping from the floor below. Terrified, she recoils and calls for help from every side. The flames are already beginning to come through the floor, and she is on the verge of swooning when, at the same moment, a ladder is placed against the balcony and Oscar comes into view on the balustrade.

He seeks and discovers his beloved, who joyously clings to him in the hope of salvation. He shatters the door with his axe, but everywhere the fire rages toward them. There is but a single means of escape: the ladder outside the balcony window! Rosalie shudders at the thought of this daring act, but Oscar lifts her in his powerful arms and carries her over the balustrade. Thick clouds of smoke enshroud the stage!

ACT III

The setting from Act One.

SCENE ONE

The lullaby is heard once more, and we find ourselves in the familiar nursery, where everything stands as it did when Grandmother carried the sleeping Jenny and Richard over to the settees. The room is still quite dark, but within the large picture frame there now appears a radiant image showing Oscar and Rosalie united and blessed by the Good Fairy. Little by little, this picture also fades. The enchanting melodies die away, and the maid, with a candle in her hand, comes in to waken the children.

Richard and Jenny get up, but for a little while they are still under the influence of their dreams. They try to remember what they have learned of the fate of the tin soldier and the doll, but can relate only a few scattered details, which seem to amuse the astonished maid. Finally their beloved Grandmother comes. They have so much to tell her, but time is precious. A large company has gathered, and the children are to take part in a merry Christmas party. They are led out by the maid, and Grandmother rejoices at the surprise that is in store for the little ones. She follows after them.

SCENE TWO

TRANSFORMATION

A splendid *salon*. The servants are busy arranging chairs and settees and decorating a magnificent Christmas tree.

The Master and Mistress (Richard's and Jenny's parents) enter. They give orders and express their satisfaction with the arrangements. Grandmother announces that the flock of children is assembled in the room to the right. A numerous company of guests now enters from the left. They bring friendly Christmas greetings and are full of respectful attention to their host's venerable mother. The children of most of these families are in the adjoining room. They are awaiting the moment for the festivities to begin. The signal is given, the doors fly open, and in swarm the jubilant children. led by Richard and Jenny.

This reality surpasses the most beautiful dream, aye, even the most enchanting fairy tale! Music is heard, the spirit of childhood animates young and old alike, and all join in the grand Round Dance which ends with a group expressing *Christmas joy*.

The curtain falls.

*   *   *

ARCONA

A Ballet in Four Acts
by
August Bournonville

Music by Johan Peter Emilius Hartmann

Scenery by Valdemar Güllich

Performed for the first time at the Royal Theatre, Copenhagen,
on May 7, 1875

Characters

LADY INGE OF FJENNISLØV .... Fru Nyrop
ABSALON   ⎫
ESBERN SNARE ⎭ .... her sons .... ⎰ Hr. Gade
                                             ⎱ Hr. Valdemar Price
HULDFRIED, Esbern's bride .... Frk. Schnell

SAXE LANGE, a clerk of Sorø . . . . Hr. Ferslew
WETTEMANN, a sea rover . . . . Hr. Ring
KNUD, a young merchant . . . . Hr. Carl Price
RASMUS, an innkeeper . . . . Hr. Hoppensach
JØRGEN, a young peasant . . . . Hr. Krum
ELSE, his fiancée . . . . Frk. Scholl
RADBODE, a Wendish princess . . . . Fru Stillmann
HELLA, her foster daughter . . . . Frk. Westberg
ULF, a leader of the Wends . . . . Hr. Fredstrup
WENDISH VIKINGS . . . . Messieurs Stramboe and Emil Hansen
AGDA } . . . . Wendish girls . . . . { Frk. Petersen
YRSA }   { Frk. Schousgaard
THE SACRIFICIAL PRIEST OF
SVANTEVIT . . . . Hr. Carpentier

SUPPORTING ROLES AND DANCES

ACT I

THE INNKEEPER'S HOUSEKEEPER . . . . Fru Thygesen

    PROPOSAL DANCE: Hr. Krum, Frk. Scholl, together with the corps de ballet

    WEAVERS DANCE AND FINALE: corps de ballet

ACT II

MAITRE DES PLAISIRS . . . . Hr. Eckhardt
COOK . . . . Hr. Døcker
JESTERS . . . . Messieurs Klüver, Lense, and Lauenberg
DWARF . . . . Christian Christensen

    FLOWER DANCE: Miles Flammé and Mibach

    BRIDAL DANCE OF KNIGHTS, LADIES, AND MAIDENS: corps de ballet

    JESTER DANCE: Messieurs Klüver, Lense, Lauenberg, and Christian Christensen

ACT III

    SACRIFICIAL DANCE: Miles Westberg, Petersen, and Schousgaard

    FINALE: Messieurs E. Hansen and Stramboe; Miles Petersen and Schousgaard

DANISH KNIGHTS AND LADIES. WARRIORS AND PEASANTS. WENDISH VIKINGS, SACRIFICIAL PRIESTS. COURT AND COMMONERS.

The scene, in Acts One and Two, is laid in Sjaelland; in Acts Three and Four, in the Temple of Svantevit, at Arcona, on the island of Rugen.

The year is 1168.

[**Translator's note**: In 1874, the old Danish Royal Theatre, for which most of Bournonville's ballets had been created, was replaced by a larger, more modern house. To introduce the company to this broader, deeper stage, the ballet master devised *Arcona*, a spectacular patriotic work based on a dramatic episode from the golden age of the Valdemars.

For years, the Baltic coast was harried by Wendish pirates; finally, Valdemar the Great (reigned 1157–82), after having consolidated the Danish kingdom and put an end to decades of civil war, turned his attention to ridding his territory of this threat.

Many campaigns, bearing the papal sanction of Crusades, were launched against the Wends; the most important, however, was that of 1168–69, which is depicted in *Arcona*. This raid, like many others, was led by the King and Absalon (the warrior-bishop whose equestrian statue today dominates the Copenhagen waterfront) and aimed at nothing less than the Christianization of the Slavs of Riigen and the destruction of Arcona, their chief fortress and the principal temple of the four-headed god, Svantevit, or Svantovit.

In *Arcona*, Bournonville remained fairly true to his historical sources. The temple is said to have contained a colossal figure of the deity of war and plenty, and each year the statue's golden horn was examined to see if the year would be fruitful. The saddle, bridle, and white steed also played a part in the cult. The people were told by their priests that every night Svantevit rode out to persecute Wendish foes, and every morning they were shown the sweating white horse to confirm their belief. Radigast and the Black God, Czernebog, or Cherebog, mentioned in the story, were likewise part of the Slavonic pantheon.]

ACT I

A cell in the monastery of Sorø. To the right, in front of an arched window, a large table holding folios, parchment scrolls, writing implements, and an hourglass. On the walls, old pictures, arms, and antiquities. To the left, exits.

SCENE ONE

Saxe Lange sits writing. He ponders, rises pensively, paces the floor, then seizes his lute in the hope that the strains of a heroic ballad will carry him back to the time of the sagas.

His mind conjures up pictures from the pagan past, and, playing and writing by turns, he chronicles historical memories of *Thyra Dannebod and Gorm the Old, the saintly Rimbert* ransoming Christian captives, and *the women of Denmark* offering their jewels to free Svend Forkbeard.

SCENE TWO

Absalon, in clerical garb, enters and surprises the industrious historian, who deferentially shows him his works. The Bishop admires and approves his accounts, and cannot refrain from fixing his attention on the various objects that fill the confined space. Saxe shows him a number of curious items, but when he seizes an old battle axe, his passionate yearning for deeds of arms is aroused, and he brandishes it with relish. The ringing of bells, however, sounds the call to Mass, and service at the altar bids the prelate cool his ardor. He sets off for the abbey church, accompanied by the learned scribe.

TRANSFORMATION

A village square near the shore. To the right, an inn; to the left, a churchyard wall, shaded by willow trees and hawthorn. Centre stage, a large linden tree. The whole is situated on a hill, at the foot of which can be seen houses of a fishing settlement and the open sea.

SCENE THREE

It is the festival of Midsummer. The innkeeper is expecting guests, and his housekeeper is busy making arrangements. Peasants and fishermen with their wives, children and sweethearts arrive for the joyous rendezvous; neighbourhood musicians are fetched, and "there is merry dancing in the grove."

SCENE FOUR

Knud, whose mother has recently died, comes to place a wreath on her grave. He cannot share the delights of the festival, but displays to the sympathetic group *the golden cross*, which has become his most prized inheritance. With a melancholy salute, he goes up to the churchyard; the innkeeper enlivens his guests, and the dancing continues, with several interruptions, until darkness falls.

The final performance before the move to the present Royal Theatre, June 1, 1974 was *A Folk Tale* and an epilogue called "Farewell to the Old Theatre," which ended with this scene, showing the transfer of the theatre's artists, led by the Muses, to the New House.

SCENE FIVE

A distant tumult is heard. On the horizon can be seen columns of smoke rising from burning villages. The Wends have landed and are harrying the coast! Universal terror and fright. Knud, however, halts the fugitives and encourages them to resist. Arms are procured; old men, women, and children are made secure, and their defenders place themselves under Knud's leadership.

SCENE SIX

The Wends rush in but, to their amazement, are repulsed by the unexpected opposition. They send a hail of arrows from hidden ambushes; the Danes are overcome, and Knud and several of the most stalwart fellows are pinned between shields, taken prisoner, and dragged away. Ulf gives orders to set the inn on fire; first, however, it is plundered, and by torchlight the Wends hold a celebration.

ACT II

Fru Inge's manor, with a staircase and landing leading up to the main edifice on the left. Through the broad castle gate can be seen the village of Fjennisløville, with the twin church towers.

SCENE ONE

Everything is ready for a celebration. The cook gives his orders, a platform is erected for the musicians, and servants hang flower garlands to right and left. Fru Inge enters the courtyard and fully approves the arrangements. She also wishes the poor to share in the delights of this festival and commands that they be fed in Abildgaarden. The cook has covered tables brought out, and all bless the noble lady.

SCENE TWO

Absalon and Esbern come out onto the landing and are greeted with jubilation. Affectionate and respectful, they meet their mother, who reminds them of their childhood and alludes to the birth of the twin brothers by pointing out the towers of the village church.

Huldfried is led forth by Fru Inge. This very day she shall be wed to Esbern; before the altar of the Lord, Absalon shall bless their union, and he now goes to array himself in his pontificals. His mother goes with him.

SCENE THREE

Tender conversation between Esbern and his bride. He points out to her the manor and all the manorial rights she shall soon enjoy. But she asks only his faithful heart and Heaven's aid.

A maidservant announces some little girls who wish to bring the bride a floral tribute. They are greeted kindly and perform a little dance in honour of the bridal couple.

Esbern gives further orders and goes up into the castle with Huldfried, while the house jester offers his homage and plays tricks on the cook and the domestic servants.

SCENE FOUR

Hoofbeats and wagon wheels are heard outside, and the *Maître des plaisirs*, followed by the servants, hastens out to greet the guests.

Fru Inge and Esbern come out onto the landing to salute the distinguished wedding guests who arrive with large retinues of esquires, men, jesters, and a dwarf. These latter remain down in the courtyard, where they are welcomed and entertained by the house jester, who arouses their mirth.

SCENE FIVE

Music sounds from the bandstand; the background is filled with commoners, and two by two the wedding procession winds its way down the castle stairs and around the decorated courtyard, which resounds with jubilation and shrill fanfares. The *maître des plaisirs* bids the company take their places while a bridal dance is performed by noblewomen and maidens. A merry interlude is presented by the jesters and the dwarf, who with their droll capers arouse the laughter of the assembly, especially the common folk.

SCENE SIX

The ringing of bells and the strains of the organ sound from the church, whose reverend servants, together with Saxe Lange, come from upstage to lead the bridal procession. Absalon descends into their midst. He is in full pontificals, with his crosier in his hand. The *maître des plaisirs* marshals the procession, which sets off through the closed ranks of the devout.

SCENE SEVEN

The sound of an approaching troop of cavalry. Everyone halts and listens. Ridder Wettemann and his men, accompanied by fleeing peasants, report that the Wends have landed. Esbern Snare is urgently requested to meet the enemy with all the forces he can hastily muster. There is a moment of hesitation; some people feel that the wedding should not be interrupted. But Absalon, who has immediately divested himself of his miter and handed his crosier to the priests, indicates that the defense of the fatherland supersedes all else. The wedding should be put off until happier times. He encourages his brother and the other noblemen to take part in the holy fight and goes off to don his own armor.

SCENE EIGHT

The men rush off; the women encircle the grieving bride, and while Fru Inge, overcoming her dejection, has refreshments brought to Wettemann and his people, Huldfreid makes a swift decision, which she secretly confides to Saxe, who promises his assistance.

SCENE NINE

Drums and trumpets mingle with the clangor of the alarum bell. Knights and their men enter in full armor. Absalon steps into their midst with the banner of the Cross, and Esbern swears to lead them to victory over the fierce heathens. Hail and farewell! Accompanied by prayers and blessings, the warlike host marches off with drums beating and banners flying.

ACT III

The great Temple of Svantevit, at Arcona, on the island of Rugen. At centre stage, the colossal statue of the idol, with a bow in its left hand and a golden drinking horn in its right. Above the doors to right and left, images of the Black God (Czernebog) and the goddess Radegaste. Through the pillars of the temple (when the curtain is drawn aside) the ocean can be seen in the background.

SCENE ONE

Dawn. Sacrificial priests have spent the night in prayer around the statue of Svantevit. At the first rays of sunlight they rise from their kneeling position, sound trumpets, and draw aside the curtain. People pour into the temple and adoringly throw themselves down before the idol.

The priests lead forth the white steed and point to the saddle and bridle to indicate that this very night Svantevit has ridden out to wage war on the enemies of the Wends.

SCENE TWO

The Wendish princess, Radbode, followed by a troop of young girls adorned with flowers – her foster daughter, the fair Hella, among them – brings offerings of gold pieces, which the sacrificial priest accepts. To the sound of trumpets, harps, and cymbals, *a sacred dance* is performed during which the idol's empty golden horn is exchanged for a new one, brimming with wine.

The priests withdraw for a time while, at Radbode's request, the girls continue the dance.

SCENE THREE

It is Radbode's intention to initiate Hella into the service of the temple – that is, of Radegaste. The priests return, bringing with them the head-ring, belt, and veil for the initiation of the young priestess. But the area resounds with tumultuous jubilation. It is the victorious Vikings returning home, laden with the spoils of war. Their chieftain, Ulf, leads them before Radbode's throne, and, with the clashing of arms, they give thanks to the mighty lord of battle the all-triumphant Svantevit.

The booty is divided and the priests receive their share. The Danish prisoners, including the brave Knud, are brought forward, scorned and plundered. Ulf seizes Knud's golden cross, which catches Hella's eye and is presented to her by Ulf. In vain Knud begs to have it returned. He is led away along with the other prisoners. No sooner has Hella hung the cross around her neck and fixed it on her breast than her whole being is suffused with a religious feeling hitherto unknown to her. It is as if her eyes have been opened to a totally new existence! Everyone beholds her in amazement, and when she is once again asked to dance, she swoons in Radbode's arm.

SCENE FOUR

Hella regains consciousness and Radbode, who has dismissed her retinue, reminds her of the calling into which she is to be initiated and warns her against falling away from the gods of her fathers.

Hella, alone, gives vent to her loathing of the menacing idols, and, regarding the mysterious ornament, she involuntarily falls to her knees and presses it to her lips.

SCENE FIVE

Ulf, who has noticed how warmly she regards his gift, thinks this a favourable moment to declare the passion he feels for her. But she contemptuously spurns him and flees.

SCENE SIX

The indignant chieftain conceals his wrath and encourages the crowd to celebrate the victory with drinking and dancing.

The curtain falls amid the wildest exclamations of delight.

ACT IV

The dungeon beneath the Temple of Svantevit. In the background, to right and left, steps leading up to the temple. In the left foreground, an iron-plated door.

SCENE ONE

The dejected Danish prisoners are seated on stone benches and at tables upon which dull lamps are burning. Knud tries to console his comrades-in-misfortune, who, in bitter sorrow, are thinking about the beloved native land they shall never see again! With a piece of charcoal he draws *a cross* on the prison wall and leads his friends toward this holy symbol of hope and salvation.

SCENE TWO

Radbode, accompanied by armed men, enters from the background and threatens the prisoners with the fate that is in store for them. But there is still a way out, if they will worship the Wendish gods. The sacrificial priest brings forth Svantevit's golden horn and bids them kneel before this symbol. Knud contemptuously spurns the princess's offer and points to the cross: the Danes' consolation in life and death! At a sign from the outraged woman, the armed men throw themselves upon the defiant Christians. But the sacrificial priest restrains them, indicating that they shall pay for this insult before Svantevit's altar! He drags Radbode away with him, and, threatening the prisoners, the armed men follow him.

SCENE THREE

Knud and his friends prepare to die; they kneel down to pray and bid farewell to one another with the fraternal kiss. An inspiring hymn expresses the solemn mood, and Heaven seems to open to them its embrace.

SCENE FOUR

Ulf and his people enter from the side door to conduct the condemned prisoners to the sacrificial stone. They are ready to follow him and stride rapidly toward the exit. But Knud is held back; he is to be kept for a more painful punishment, since it was he who urged his countrymen to resist. The latter are halted yet again with the offer of life and freedom if they will serve in the Wendish army. They are tempted and vacillate for a moment, but a sign from Knud reminds them of the vow they have made, and their reply is a unanimous "Never!" They are taken away.

SCENE FIVE

Knud is left alone in total darkness. He ponders his fate and seems to steel himself against the horrors that are to come. But his strength deserts him. He gropes his way over to a stone block and falls into a trancelike sleep. In a dream, he sees the cross on the wall glowing with dazzling radiance.

SCENE SIX

Hella, accompanied by Agda, her playmate, enters from the stairway on the left and approaches Knud, who awakens and stares at her in amazement. She places her finger on her lips as a sign that he is to be quiet, sets down the burning lamp, humbly begs his forgiveness, and returns the golden cross that was stolen from him. But there is not a moment to lose! There is a way out, and he must follow her! Agda shall help them; but when they are halfway up the stairs, they hear the hymn that the Christian prisoners are singing at the place of sacrifice, and Knud turns back to share his brethren's lot. Hella tries in vain to pull him away with her, but the solemn song holds them fast to the spot. They harken to its dying tones. At last it ceases altogether... It is over!

Knud lapses into profound sorrow, and Hella kneels by his side.

SCENE SEVEN

Ulf enters and can hardly believe his eyes when he finds Hella with the prisoner. Radbode and her women come rushing in, but start back, astonished, at the sight. Hella begs Ulf to have mercy on the unfortunate man and beseeches her foster mother, who indignantly thrusts her away. With proud firmness, Hella rises, takes Knud's hand, and declares that she will go with him to death.

Radbode tears her away from him and turns her over to her women, while Ulf orders the condemned prisoner to be taken to the sacrificial stone. Hella breaks loose, frees Knud from the hands of his executioners, and, pointing to the cross Knud extends toward Heaven, she professes that to this sacred sign alone will she bend her knee! Thrilled, Knud raises her up, and their hearts are united in this last solemn moment.

The onlookers, who have stood as if turned to stone by this scene, now fly into a wild fury. Knud is led away, and the women seize Hella.

A muddled commotion is heard outside, and presently the news arrives that a Danish fleet is approaching the island and threatens the fortress of Arcona. Ulf and the other chieftains rush off to summon people to defend the fortress and the temple. Radbode calls upon the gods and utters imprecations against the hereditary Danish foe.

TRANSFORMATION TO THE TEMPLE OF SVANTEVIT
(Storm, thunder and lightning.)

SCENE EIGHT

Universal confusion. The fleeing commoners surround the pedestal of the statue, and the sacrificial priests call down vengeance upon the advancing enemy. Bands of armed men hasten to battle, and, in a flurry of activity, Radbode gives orders and receives news from her chieftains.

Knud is led forward and is designated as a propitiatory offering to allay the wrath of the gods. The sacrificial knife is already directed at his breast when Hella darts forward and stays the fatal steel. At this very moment, Ulf and his men enter and demand that the temple be cleared, since the fighting will probably be fiercest at this very spot. Terrified, the sacrificial priests flee, together with the crowd. Radbode, beside herself, seizes the lost knife and will complete the sacrifice with her own hand. But her women hold her back and force her up toward the throne, which is surrounded and defended by the most valiant Wends.

SCENE NINE

The Danes surge forward with irresistible might. Esbern and Wettemann are at their head, and all opposition is crushed. Hella has freed Knud's bound hands, and he grabs a sword in order to take part in the fray. He confronts Ulf and deals him a death blow. The fighting is hottest around the throne, where Radbode, with sacrificial knife uplifted, promises her defenders that the gods will aid them. Terror spreads among them when they see the gigantic idol fall to the ground in pieces, shattered by Absalon's war club. They fly from the temple, pursued by the victors, and in a rage of desperation, Radbode kills herself on the ruins of the fallen deity!

SCENE TEN

Hella throws herself on her fallen foster mother's body, but Knud pulls her away from this sorry object, which is removed by the women. Absalon, who has climbed down from the lofty pedestal of the statue, orders his men to carry away the fallen and see to the wounded. Knud and Hella approach him; they state that they are Christians, and Absalon enfolds them in his embrace.

Drums and trumpets proclaim the victory. Esbern Snare and Wettemann lead the jubilant troops before Absalon, who praises their bravery and promises them honour and rewards from King Valdemar.

At this moment the sun breaks forth and illumines the banner of the Cross, which is planted on the base of the statue by a shield-maiden –"accompanied by a clerk." It is Huldfried and Saxo [sic], who, unbeknown to Esbern, have followed the fleet on the Wendish campaign. They are greeted enthusiastically. The astonished bridegroom embraces his lovely bride. Absalon blesses their union, and festive rejoicing proclaims the triumph of Faith and Denmark's Honour.

* * *

FROM THE LAST CENTURY
(Fra det Forrige Aarhundrede)

A Ballet Divertissement by
August Bournonville

Music arranged by Wilhelm Holm

Performed for the first time at the Royal Theatre, Copenhagen, on the occasion of the unveiling of Holberg's statue,
October 31, 1875

Characters

THE KING	Fru Nyrop
THE QUEEN	Fru Poulsen
THE HOFMARSKAL	Hr. Gade
THE COMEDY WRITER	Hr. Meyer
M. DESLARCHES, the Court Dancing Master	Hr. V. Price
STOLLE, the German Solo Dancer	Hr. E. Hansen
HIERONIMI } .. Italian dancers	{ Hr. Krum
MME HIERONIMI }	{ Frk. Westberg

COURTIERS. CORPS DE BALLET. MUSICIANS. SERVANTS.

Ballet Characters

PRINCE PARIS, as a shepherd	Hr. Krum
MERCURY	Hr. E. Hansen
VENUS	Frk. Westberg
JUNO	Frk. Petersen
MINERVA	Fru Mentzell
CLIO	Frk. Madsen
FAMA	Frk. Schousgaard
HELEN	Frk. Scholl
HARLEQUIN	Hr. Lauenberg

CLOG DANCE

Hr. Stramboe, Fru Stillmann, and the corps de ballet.

HOLBERGIANA

HERMANN v. BREMEN	Hr. Busch
JACOB v. THYBO	Hr. C. Price
JERONIMUS	Hr. Ring
LEANDER	Hr. Gold
HENRIK	Hr. Fredstrup
ARV	Hr. Poulsen
OLDFUX	Hr. Hoppensach
CHRISTOFF	Hr. Walbom
PEER DEGN	Hr. L. Hansen
THE DOCTOR	Hr. Jensen
GEDSKE	Frk. Eydrup
THE FRU	Frk. Sørensen
MAGDELONE	Fru Gade
LEONORE	Frk. Egense
PER NILLE	Frk. Flammé
ANNEKE	Frk. Golodnoff
A GIRL	Frk. Petersen
A GIRL	Frk. Oppenhagen
ANE THE TINKER'S WIFE	Frk. Frederiksen
INGEBORG THE PLUMBER'S WIFE	Frk. Stendrup

The scene is laid in the gardens of Fredensborg Castle in May 1747.

[**Translator's note:** The ballet is set at Fredensborg Castle, the summer retreat of the Danish Royal family near Hillerød. It was built in the early eighteenth century at about the time that the great Norwegian-born playwright Ludvig Holberg (1684–1754) was writing the thirty-two comedies that have remained classics of the Danish stage. In the 1850s Bournonville established his home at Fredensborg, where he died and is buried. The occasion for this divertissement was the dedication of Theobald Stein's statue of Holberg, which still stands before the Royal Theatre as companion to the statue of Bournonville's revered Oehlenschläger.]

SCENE ONE

The stage represents a *rond-point* in the Castle Park at Fredensborg, with the castle in the background. The open space, which is surrounded by shrubbery and flowers, appears to be arranged for a fête *en plein air*. To the left, a dais for the spectators of the forthcoming spectacle.

The Court Dancing Master, M. Deslarches, to whom the entire arrangement has been entrusted, enters, followed by his *répétiteur*, and mentally runs through the most important features of his ballet scenario.

The Hofmarskal gives his orders to the servants and approves Deslarches' plans and arrangement. A lackey announces the Comedy Writer, who has been summoned to Court. He brings with him a deluxe edition of his comedies, which he intends to present to Her Majesty the Queen. The Hofmarskal welcomes him most graciously and introduces M. Deslarches as the man who will illustrate the writer's masterworks with his corps de ballet. With ironic modesty, the Comedy Writer thanks him for this honour and follows the Hofmarskal up to the castle.

SCENE TWO

Deslarches calls his corps de ballet together and shows each person the role and the character he or she is to perform. A little rehearsal is held, but it is almost disrupted because of the obvious superiority he accords Mme Hieronimi. It not only arouses her husband's jealousy, but that of her female rivals as well. However, this is not the time for bickering. The Court is approaching, and at the signal from their master, the *danseurs* and *danseuses* take their places.

SCENE THREE

Distinguished ladies and gentlemen gather for the court reception and are received by the Hofmarskal, who observes the proper ceremonial. The King and Queen draw near and graciously acknowledge the most humble greeting. The Comedy Writer walks at their side. In most gracious fashion, the Queen thanks him for the gift he has brought her, and in the presence of all, the King promises him his patronage. The Hofmarskal bids the royal visitors take their seats on the dais, and, presenting Their Majesties with the festival programme, he signals the musicians.

SCENE FOUR

A Ballet in Rococo Style

Prince Paris, in the guise of an Arcadian shepherd, dances into the circle, plants his staff – which is adorned with ribbons and flowers – in the ground, and, amid entrechats and pirouettes, variously expresses his deep longing for a loving heart to which he may be amorously united. He hears noise and hides on one side of the stage. It is the goddesses Juno, Minerva, and Venus quarreling over the apple that was tossed into the midst of the guests at Thetis' wedding with the inscription: "To the fairest of the fair." Each of the three goddesses thinks she has the right to possess the apple, but Mercury, who has followed after them, snatches the apple of discord away from them and designates Paris as the one who shall be the arbiter in this conflict. The goddesses and Paris are astounded for a moment, but Juno is the first to try to influence the young judge by offering him *wealth* and *power*. Minerva summons Fama and Clio, with offers of glory and renown. Venus, surrounded by cupids and flower maidens, promises him the pleasures of love. Paris is drawn to Minerva, then to Juno; they are both lovely, but in the end, Venus emerges triumphant. To her he presents the golden apple, while her rivals depart, fuming with ire and revenge.

Venus calms the trembling Paris, and, sending the little genii of love away, she repeats her promise and smilingly bids him farewell.

SCENE FIVE

The cupids being Helen forward, entwine her with garlands, blow kisses to her, and vanish. Enraptured and inflamed by the most passionate love, Paris tries to overcome the fair lady's chaste resistance in an expressive pas de deux and finishes by abducting her.

SCENE SIX

Harlequin, who is attracted by the abducted woman's cries for help, reflects for a moment and comes to the conclusion that it is best to let the mythological characters fend for themselves. He takes out his violin, and, asking permission to call forth the lusty peasant dances that have lain so long in hibernation, he beckons to a troop of Sjaelland lads and lasses who, in their clogs, perform a merry Polish dance.

SCENE SEVEN

The climax of the festival is near, and shrill fanfares announce a series of stock characters from the plays of Holberg. Advancing in pas de menuet, they salute respectfully and form all sorts of figures, each in keeping with the physiognomy of his or her particular character. Lines and semicircles are formed, and as the King leads the Poet down among these creations of his genius, the entire corps de ballet comes forward to crown him with garlands.

Pages bring forth on velvet cushions the diploma and sword which raise the poet and man-of-letters to the nobility. Everyone hastens to congratulate the newly created baron, and the Queen asks if she may take his arm for the walk back to the castle.

The King expresses his royal satisfaction with the delightful festival. He orders the Hofmarskal to present M. Deslarches with a purse of gold and departs, followed by cries of jubilation.

SCENE EIGHT

The Hofmarskal gives orders to the servants that refreshments are to be served, and as a toast is drunk to the royal couple, the day's solemnities end with dancing and hilarious gaiety.

* * *

FROM SIBERIA TO MOSCOW
(Fra Siberien til Moskau)

A Ballet in Two Acts
by
August Bournonville

Music by Carl Christian Møller

Scenery by Valdemar Gillich and Fritz Ahlgrensson

Performed for the first time at the Royal Theatre, Copenhagen, on November 29, 1876

Characters

TSAR PAUL PETROVITCH	Hr. C. Price
THE TSARINA	Fru Mentzell
SMIRNOV, an exiled nobleman and writer	Hr. V. Price
NATHALIA, his daughter	Frk. Westberg
IVANOV, a young officer in exile	Hr. Krum
PETROV, a Cossak leader	Hr. Gade
THE HOFMARSKAL	Hr. Carpentier

COURIERS. OFFICERS. GUARDS. SERVANTS AND PAGES. COSSACKS. TARTAR VILLAGERS. CORPS DE BALLET.

In Act One, the scene is laid in Siberia in 1798. Act Two takes place in the Imperial Palace in Moscow in 1799.

DANCES AND PAGEANTRY

ACT ONE

MAZURKA: Frk. Westberg and Hr. Krum
COSSACK DANCE: Messieurs Klüver, Walbom, Iversen, and Lense; Mmes Flammé, Madsen, Hansen, and Güllich, together with the corps de ballet

ACT TWO

POLONAISE

The Imperial Couple and the entire court.

DIVERTISSEMENT REPRESENTING THE RIVERS

THE RIVER DEITY: Hr. Ring

UNDINES: Frk. Milbach, Frk. Egense, and six pupils

THE RHONE (Provengal fisherfolk): Hr. Iversen, Frk. Petersen, and corps de ballet

THE THAMES (English jockeys): Messieurs E. Hansen and Klüver

THE GUADALQUIVIR (Andalusian *danseuses*): Mmes Tychsen, Schousgaard, and Flammé

THE RHINE (vineyard folk): Fru Stillman, Hr. Walbom, and corps de ballet

THE NEVA (Russian character dance): Frk. Westberg

ACT ONE

The stage represents a room in a log hut in one of the milder places of exile in Siberia. To the right, a large stone oven with a crackling fire; to the left, the entrance to the other rooms. Upstage, a wide door and windows through which a frozen lake and distant mountains can be seen.

Simple furnishings and a table with writing implements and papers.

SCENE ONE

Smirnov returns from the hunt with his quota of sable and fox skins. His mind is weighed down by his cruel fate, but his countenance softens at the sight of his daughter, who, together with young Ivanov, is skating boldly over the frozen lake. He hangs his gun on a peg and sets the skins aside, for the writing table lures him to his favourite occupation.

Meanwhile, Nathalia has taken leave of her friend, who unfastens her skates and promises to return soon. She lovingly approaches her father, who is writing, but to her sorrow discovers that his thoughts are once again filled with the ideas of the French Revolution – the old infatuation that was the very cause of their misfortune and exile. Smirnov enthusiastically jumps up and vows never to betray the sacred cause of Freedom, but soon falls victim to his former despondency upon considering his present desperate plight.

Nathalia seeks to console and calm him. With a pleading look, she brings him his harp. Its tones have a soothing effect, while the chords and melodies are soon transformed into a merry dance which, by his daughter's graceful rendition, carries his thoughts back to happier days.

SCENE TWO

Ivanov enters. He respectfully greets Smirnov and brings him books, which the latter gratefully accepts. The young couple's fondness for one another has not gone unnoticed by the father; but the prospect is dark and hopeless. Ivanov himself, who had the misfortune of killing his opponent in a duel, cannot expect any advancement, and Smirnov's literary activity has incurred the lasting disfavour of the Autocrat.

SCENE THREE

Accompanied by some of his Cossacks, Petrov enters with a brutality that bears witness to his half-drunken state, and, measuring Smirnov from head to foot with a distrustful look, demands that he give him the required bag of furs. He takes it and carelessly tosses it to his men.

Ivanov and Nathalia, who stepped aside when the Cossacks entered, now return and keep an eye on every movement made by Smirnov, who can hardly control his indignation. Meanwhile, Petrov has made his tour of inspection and discovered the books and papers on the writing table. He beckons to the Cossacks, laughingly shows then this unintelligible rubbish, and tosses everything into the blazing oven. Beside himself, Smirnov has picked up his gun but is restrained by the young couple.

Petrov, who only now becomes aware of Nathalia and Ivanov, bows to the young lady in courtly fashion, at the same time remembering that he has important business with the officer. Assuming an air of solemnity, he presents Ivanov with an imperial rescript repealing his exile and summoning him back to the army. Delighted, the brave young warrior receives his weapon and his orders, according to which he is to join Suvarov's army without delay. He embraces Petrov, waves his cap in a salute to the Tsar, and, tossing his purseful of gold to the Cossacks, bids them prepare a celebration and summon the entire neighbourhood to the farewell feast.

SCENE FOUR

Caught up in his overwhelming happiness, Ivanov has momentarily forgotten his friends and fellow unfortunates, who are now sitting dejectedly in the farthest corner of the room! He rushes over to them, and they congratulate him with highly different feelings. To be separated from the one he has sworn to love eternally is a thought that rends his heart and wounds his sense of honour. But Nathalia does not hesitate for a moment as to whether to follow her beloved or to share distress and need with her father: she unties a holy medal from her throat, gives it to Ivanov as a keepsake (perhaps as a protective talisman), and extends her hand in a gesture of farewell. But their fate is not to be settled in this way. A bold idea begins to dawn in the young man's mind, and with a combination of courage and ingenuity it can be carried out! He overcomes all their objections and urges father and daughter to make ready to flee at the same time as his departure.

SCENE FIVE

Violently shaken by conflicting emotions, Ivanov now realizes the full significance of the responsibility he is taking upon himself. He is overwhelmed by an involuntary apprehension. But in pressing his hand to his pounding heart, he encounters Nathalia's gift and kneels down to pray for strength and success in his bold undertaking.

Nathalia approaches and stands before him like a good angel. She tries to dissuade him from the proposed venture, but his decision has been made and, imploring Heaven for protection, they part, soon to meet again.

SCENE SIX

The invited guests-Tartars and their women as well as Cossacks and their sweethearts-gather in a most festive mood. Tables laden with food and drink are carried in, and a separate table for the leader is placed downstage right. All this takes place amid music, dancing, and merriment. Ivanov does the honours with exquisite politeness and welcomes Petrov in the most gallant manner. There are numberless bottles of wine on the leader's table, while kvas and vodka are served as refreshment for the simple folk. Toasts are proposed with cries of jubilation and hurrahs.

As an invitation to dance, a pleasant surprise is announced, and, together with Ivanov, Nathalia – who is enthusiastically greeted by the whole assembly – performs the very popular mazurka.

Petrov, who has frequently been dipping into the bottle, rises with difficulty to compliment the graceful young dancing couple and, staggering, cracks his whip and orders his Cossacks to perform their national dance. They joyfully obey, and, alternating between bouts of drinking and the ladies, they stomp and swing themselves about to the familiar melodies.

For a little while Nathalia and Ivanov continue to take part in the festivities, but finally manage to slip away, unnoticed by the noisy band.

Enraptured by the dancing, Petrov feels tempted to join in, is swung about by the mischievous girls, falls into his armchair, stupefied, and tries to gather new strength from the brimming glasses.

The Cossacks continue to drink, clink, and clout one another-all in good fun. Finally, they are about to call for three cheers for their leader but discover that Petrov has had to give in and has fallen into a deep sleep. The women now think it best to leave the feast and induce their menfolk to stumblingly accompany them—however, not before the tables have been duly plundered. They all depart, and one can hear their music growing ever more faint and distant.

SCENE SEVEN

The moon breaks forth and sheds its beams upon the vast winter landscape. Disguised as a coachman Ivanov steals into the room, regards the sleeping Petrov, and, convinced that they will not be discovered, signals to Smirnov and Nathalia, who, wrapped in furs, follow him to the readied sleigh, which, at tearing speed, carries all three of them to freedom!

ACT TWO

The stage represents the magnificent Great Hall of the Imperial Palace in Moscow. A gold-studded curtain separates the hall from its background, where a staircase leads up to the remaining apartments. To the right, a large writing table and gilt armchair.

SCENE ONE

Surrounded by her ladies in waiting, the Tsarina is engaged in discussing with the Hofmarskal the details of a party with which she intends to surprise her consort. The Hofmarskal presents his programme and summons the corps de ballet, who, in the guise of river deities and undines, are to perform the divertissement whose character dances should denote the rivers of Europe. The Tsarina approves his plan, graciously salutes him, and leaves with her retinue.

SCENE TWO

Everything is now a flurry of activity. The servants are sent hither and yon to light candelabra and to fetch vases of flowers. Drum rolls outside announce the return of the Tsar from parade. The guard enters at arms, and all station themselves at a respectful distance.

Followed by his staff, Paul Petrovitch enters through the door to the left. He returns the salute given and sits down at the writing table, where the Hofmarskal places before him a number of papers requiring his signature. The Tsar is astonished at the sight of these festive preparations, but smilingly shrugs his shoulders on persuing the Tsarina's programme. He invites his adjutants to the party. They bow and are just about to leave when a servant announces an imperial courier. The latter hands his dispatch pouch to the Hofmarskal, who opens it and delivers the report to the impatient Tsar. It contains news of a great battle,* but the victory is still undecided! The officers leave, and, left alone with the Hofmarskal, the Tsar sits somberly and pensively staring at the fateful report.

SCENE THREE

A clamour outside announces the arrival of a new dispatch from the army. It is Ivanov, who brings news of a glorious victory and lays the captured banners and standards at the feet of the Tsar. Paul's joy is indescribable, and since the report also contains praise of the bravery Ivanov has manifested, he enthusiastically embraces the young officer and bestows upon him a ring, signifying that whatever favour he desires shall be granted him by virtue of the same. The party shall now be held in honour of the victory. The Tsar hastens away to inform his Consort of the happy event.

SCENE FOUR

Congratulations flow in to Ivanov, and when the banners are brought in to the Tsar's apartments, the Hofmarskal asks the favoured officer what gift he intends to ask for. However, he recoils in dread when he learns the object for which Ivanov intends to beg the Tsar. Ivanov imparts his plan and asks if he may have the party programme in order to add an interesting number to the national dances already designated. The Hofmarskal reluctantly accedes to his wishes, but promises to lend his assistance. Ivanov hastens away, filled with the highest hopes.

SCENE FIVE

Festive music announces the approach of the royal guests. The curtain is drawn aside, and from the flower-decked staircase the Court, led by the imperial couple, advances in a polonaise, at the conclusion of which Their Majesties take their places on their thrones, and the members of the Court seat themselves on their appointed tabourets.

A signal for the commencement of the scenic and allegorical episodes included in the party programme, which the Hofmarskal now hands to the Tsarina.

The divertissement opens with River Deities and Undines, who in a Wave Dance call forth:

---

* The battle of Novi, in Northern Italy, in which the French were defeated by the combined Russian-Austrian forces under Suvarov and Melas.

THE RHONE
characterized in a Farandole by Provençal fisherfolk

THE GUADALQUIVIR
in a Jaleo by three Andalusian danseuses

THE THAMES
in the Horse Race and Reel by two jockeys

THE RHINE
in the procession and dancing of merry vineyard folk.

Under the impression that this last dance marks the end of the divertissement, the Tsarina expresses her satisfaction and thanks the Hofmarskal for the lovely arrangement. But he indicates that yet another surprise is in store, and the Tsarina returns to her seat. The Hofmarskal signals and two musicians enter, dressed in Russian peasant garb. The older of the two is a harp player, while the younger one plays the stringed instrument known as the balalaika. He himself leads before the throne a young Russian girl in white native costume. It is Nathalia, who timidly kneels before Their Majesties, who wave to her their encouragement.

The musicians strike up melodies that, like her dancing, are alternately sad or gay. Encouraged by the approbation of the imperial couple, her courage and strength begin to mount, and when, swinging her sky-blue scarf, she finishes her dance surrounded by a group of river dieties and undines, everyone enthusiastically recognizes

THE RIVER NEVA!

Thundrous applause rewards this illustration of Russian nationality. The Tsar, and the entire Court along with him, admire the idea as well as its execution, and the Tsarina bestows upon the undine of the Neva a precious jewel. Nathalia falls to her knees before the Tsarina and implores her to obtain mercy for her father!

(The old harp player is none other than Smirnov.) Her plea is granted, but when the Autocrat recognizes the man he has banished, his irreconcilable anger is aroused, and, despite everyone's intercession and the daughter's despair, he orders his guards to seize him.

At this moment, Ivanov (the younger musician) steps forth and hands the ring to the Tsar. The latter is startled but asks in a milder voice: "What do you ask of me?" "Mercy for Smirnov!" "What!" "I have my Emperor's sacred word!" "Well then, so be it!"

Exclamations of joy and gratitude. The orchestra strikes up the national anthem, and, accompaied by a benediction of all, the imperial couple leaves the room, where the celebration continues while the happy union of Ivanov and Nathalia Smirnova is sealed.

The curtain falls.

APPENDIX

The ballets in the appendix, with the exception of the recently recovered scenario for Soldier and Peasant, are Bournonville's adaptations of works by other choreographers that he had seen in Paris. In *My Theatre Life* he wrote of these works:

> In order to mount an unfamiliar work, such as The Sleepwalker, The Pages, Paul and Virginia, Romeo, or Nina, I first had to acquire the original music, then learn the details of the ballet, and finally adapt everything to suit our theatre's facilities. However, with La Sylphide it was quite a different matter. I saw the Parisian Sylphide but a single time and came away filled with nought but admiration for Mlle. Taglioni's extraordinary bravura and amazement at the splendid machinery. Both these things were equally unobtainable at our theatre and, even though I found the main idea of the ballet most appealing, I felt that I would benefit most by drawing from my own fund of inspiration. Besides, the score was entirely too expensive, and those who could have taught me the roles (for they had to be taught) did not seem disposed to do so just then. (p. 78)

The first two restagings were ballets by Jean Aumer, *La Somnambule* (1827, to music arranged by Hérold) and *Les Pages du Duc de Vendôme* (1820, to music by Gyrowetz). *Paul and Virginia* was based on Pierre Gardel's *Paul et Virginie* (1806); Bernardin de Saint-Pierre's enormously popular 1786 novel was first adapted to the stage as an opera with music by Rodolphe Kreutzer, who later also composed the score for the ballet. Bournonville's *Nina* was adapted from Louis-Jacques Milon's *Nina, ou La Folle par amour* (1813), with a score by Louis de Persuis derived from Nicolas Dalayrac's 1786 opera. In 1802 Galeotti had also created a ballet on this popular subject – a story in F. T. M. de Baculard d'Arnaud's *Delassements de l'homme sensible* – while Paisiello's 1789 Italian opera version was also widely played and is still revived occasionally. The scenario for *Romeo and Juliet* has not been included here, since Bournonville's 1833 restaging of Galeotti's great success of 1811 was actually more of a revival of the work than an adaptation of a ballet not originally intended for the Copenhagen company and theatre.

THE SLEEPWALKER
(Sqvngaengersken)

A Ballet in Three Acts by
Jean Aumer

Adapted for the Danish Stage by
August Bournonville

Music arranged by Ferdinand Hérold

Performed for the first time at the Royal Theatre, Copenhagen, on
September 21, 1829*

Characters

EDMOND, a rich tenant farmer ....Hr. Bournonville
THÉRÈSE, his fiancée, a young orphan
        girl raised by Madame Michaud ....Mad. Kraetzmer
MADAME MICHAUD, a miller's wife,
        Thérèse's foster mother ....Unknown
GERTRUDE LEBON, a young widow,
        proprietress of an inn ....Jfr. Werning
DE SAINT-RAMBERT, a colonel of the
        cavalry, lord of the manor ....Hr. W. E. Funck
OLIVIER, a trumpeter, his servant ....Hr. Stamboe
THE LOCAL MAGISTRATE ....Hr. Fredstrup
MARCELINE, serving maid at the inn ....Unknown
HUSSARS, PEASANTS, PEASANT GIRLS.

The scene is laid in Provence, on the island of La Camargue, opposite Arles.

ACT I

A village crossroads. To the right is the entrance to the farm; to the left, an inn with a signboard bearing the legend: "Garlands of Roses, The Widow Lebrun." Upstage is a portion of a house, which forms an angle with the inn; above the door it says: "The Widow of Miller Michaud." A ladder leads up to the trap door of the loft, wherein one can see a grain sack that has not yet been taken in. To the right stands a signpost with two arms; on one it says: "The Road to Aries"; on the other, "The Road to Tarascon." To the left, another signpost, with the inscription: "The Road to the Castle."

---

* Original Production: *La Somnambule, ou la Arrivée d'un nouveau seigneur*, ch. Jean Aumer, mus Ferdinand Hérold, sc Pierre Ciceri, cos Hippolyte Lecompte, 19 Sept. 1827. Vincenzo Bellini's opera *La Sonnambula* (Milan, 1831), with a libretto by Felice Romaani, closely follows the ballet's action.

When the curtain rises, we see a group of villagers taking their midday rest one day during haymaking. Some are sitting on the ground, eating or relaxing. The young men and maids dance. Edmond gives his people orders, indicating to them the hay that is to be brought in. From time to time he goes over to Thérèse and her foster mother, who are also present. He gazes at one woman with love, at the other with gratitude. Thérèse takes part in the young girls' dancing, but her eyes continually rest on Edmond, and it is always to him that she turns during the dance. In their blameless merriment, they express their love and happiness.

Gertrude, who emerges from her house at this moment, cannot hide her vexation when she beholds them. She calls Madame Michaud's attention to them, but the latter replies that the marriage contract will soon be signed and they are to be wed on the morrow. There is no harm in it, is there? Meanwhile, Thérèse and Edmond frequently and impatiently look toward the road leading up to the castle, as if they were expecting someone.

At last the Magistrate arrives. They hasten to greet him, and the dancing ceases. Edmond and Thérèse reproach him for not having come sooner. He excuses himself by saying that he was detained at the castle, where they are awaiting a new lord, a handsome young man and a fine soldier; but it appears that he will not arrive today. When he sees Gertrude, he compliments her on her appearance and charm. She, knowing that the Magistrate is in love with her, returns all his compliments with affection. Edmond, who is eager to sign the marriage contract, sets a little table in place while Thérèse roguishly takes the Magistrate by the hand, draws him over to the chair, and forces him to be seated. Offended by this, Gertrude tries to leave, but Edmond holds her back so that she can witness the contract.

They sit down, Edmond on one side, Madame Michaud and Thérèse on the other. Everyone forms a group around them. The Magistrate asks Edmond what he has as a dowry; to this he answers that he shall bestow upon Thérèse his dairy, his land – all that he possesses! When Thérèse is asked the same thing, she replies that she has nought to give as a dowry save her heart; for a long time now that has belonged to Edmond and her good mother, who raised her and to whom she owes everything. Edmond and Thérèse sign joyfully. The pen is handed to Madame Michaud, who does not know how to write and merely traces a cross instead of her name. "Never mind; it will do!" says the Magistrate. Edmond gives Gertrude the pen; she takes it with annoyance. "Ungrateful man! In spite of the love I felt for you, I shall sign my name to your alliance with another." She would like to toss away the pen, but when she sees that everyone, particularly the Magistrate, is looking at her, she signs and gives Thérèse many protestations of friendship. "My friends," says Edmond, "let us all go to our work. But this evening we shall gather here once more, and tomorrow comes the great day – tomorrow the wedding shall take place. The whole village is invited."

Everyone leaves. Edmond and Thérèse also start off, but slowly, and when they find themselves alone, they animatedly rush back to the foreground and display to each other their joy and delight. "Now thou art mine, nothing can part us!" In a pas de deux, during which the action progresses, Edmond places his betrothal ring on Thérèse's finger and then gives her a rose. He begs her for a kiss, which she denies him, saying, "Tomorrow!" When Edmond takes offence at this, Thérèse presses to her lips the rose he has just given her, and hides it in her bosom. Edmond is about to rush over to her when she tells him he should return to his work. Edmond obeys and goes toward the ladder, which he intends to mount. Thérèse is afraid he will hurt himself. Edmond climbs down, removes the ladder, and sets it up against one of the windows of the inn. Before leaving Thérèse, he again asks her for a kiss. She finally grants him one.

Madame Gertrude enters and displays her jealousy and animosity. "What kind of maiden are you! You behave like that with a man who is still only your fiancé?" The two women quarrel. Edmond tries to bring about a reconciliation. "Why are you angry at us?" he asks Gertrude. "Must you be our enemy because I will not become your husband? Let the three of us live in friendship and harmony. Come, come, dear children! Join hands!" In a dance, Edmond seeks to reconcile them, but soon one escapes, then the other. At length, Thérèse gives in and holds out her hand to her rival, who promises herself to get revenge at the first opportunity. Edmond ends their quarrel by making them embrace one another, whereupon he embraces each one in turn.

At this moment, Saint-Rambert enters, followed by Olivier. "Well done, comrade!" says Saint-Rambert to Edmond. "Don't let me interrupt you. You're a lucky fellow!" Edmond is surprised at the stranger's straightforwardness and asks what he wants. "To know the way to the castle." Edmond points out to him the road to the left. "That is it." "Is it far?" "Two miles." "I shall never make it. I am too exhausted." "Sir!" says Edmond, "it would give me great pleasure if you would be content to stay with me, even though my house is quite full; for I am to be wed on the morrow." "What! Might that be your wife?" "Aye, sir!" "And that is–?" asks the Colonel, pointing to Gertrude, who displays her annoyance as he continues: "I don't want to disturb you. Here is an inn. I shall stay there." "You do me great honour," Gertrude drily replies.

The Colonel now orders Olivier to proceed to the castle in order to tell them he will not arrive. But the latter, who has noticed the pretty serving maid and would rather stay, says that he injured his knee when the carriage in which they were riding overturned, whereupon he is allowed to remain. Overjoyed, he decides to pay court to the fair Marceline, who has taken his roguish looks and compliments in good part. Saint-Rambert commands Olivier to keep silent and not disclose their identities. Olivier salutes his colonel, as if to say, "I shall obey."

Madame Michaud, the Magistrate, and all the villagers enter. Evening has come, and everyone gathers. Madame Michaud and the old women form a circle to the left, and spin; on the right side, the old men sit at a table, gaming and drinking. The young lads and lasses, as well as Edmond and Thérèse and Gertrude, dance and play blindman's buff at centre stage.

After Olivier has tired of the dance, in which he has been an avid participant, he joins the men for a drink. With delight, Saint-Rambert beholds the young girls' dancing and groupings. Edmond follows him with his eyes, and every time the Colonel draws near Thérèse, he is at her side to thwart his designs.

After the joyful throng has danced for a time, Madame Michaud rises and announces that it is time to go home. Gertrude, who is fearful of catching cold, has Marceline fetch a red shawl, which she puts around her. After having said good-night to everyone, Saint-Rambert goes into the inn. Olivier, who has continued to drink toasts and flirt with the serving maid, has forgotten his military bearing, has gotten a bit drunk, and staggers into the farmyard, thinking he is following his colonel. Edmond escorts Thérèse and Madame Michaud, who enter the mill, and bids them good-night, expressing his delight at tomorrow's festival.

Everyone is gone, save Gertrude and the Magistrate, who have stayed behind and pay one another many compliments. Edmond, who has gone into the farmyard, now comes back and secretively informs them that he has important news. "Who is the stranger who has lodged with you and whom you have given such a poor reception? Do you know?" he asks Gertrude. "No." "The new lord of the manor, who is expected here." "Who told you that?" "His servant the trumpeter, in his intoxication, has just told me everything." Gertrude is frightened and declares that she will rectify her error by paying him twice as much attention. "And this very night I shall give him a surprise," says the Magistrate. Edmond says good-night and, sighing, gazes at Thérèse's windows. Gertrude goes inside, and the Magistrate, who is totally preoccupied with his plan, exits upstage.

ACT II

A room in the inn, with two side doors and a window in the background. In the right foreground stand a couch and an armchair. To the left, a table.

Smiling, Saint-Rambert regards the room and its furnishings.

He sits down in the armchair. Shortly afterward, he rises, filled with the memory of the young girls' charms – of the naive Thérèse and the snappish, captious Gertrude.

Marceline enters with a light, which she sets on the table. Behind her comes the proprietress of the inn, bearing two handsome silver candlesticks and scolding Marceline because she has given the lord of the manor so little attention. She orders her to leave and to take her light with her. Marceline goes over to Saint-Rambert to ask if there is anything he wishes. But Gertrude, taking her by the arm, informs her that she has decided to wait on the lord herself. Marceline curtseys and exits, after having said good-night to the Colonel.

The latter, surprised at this change in Gertrude's behaviour, takes advantage of it to make her a declaration of love. Gertrude listens with downcast eyes and pretends she wants to leave. Saint-Rambert detains her. She puts up such a gallant defense that he finally releases her, whereupon she walks to the door, but so slowly that he again runs after her and importunes her even more fiercely than before. He throws himself on his knees before her, and she becomes uneasy when a soft noise is heard just outside the window. Frightened, she flees into the small room to the right, thereby losing her shawl, which the Colonel tosses onto the armchair.

Annoyed at the noise that has interrupted him, Saint-Rambert hurries over to the window, which opens at the same time. We see Thérèse, clad in simple white garb, her arms and feet bare. Outside the window can be seen the end of the ladder Edmond placed there in Act I; it is by this that Thérèse has climbed up. She is walking in her sleep and slowly wanders down to centre stage.

The astonished Saint-Rambert can hardly believe his eyes. Thérèse thinks she is playing blindman's buff. She is afraid of being caught. She eludes her pursuer and presses close against Saint-Rambert, whom, in her dream, she takes to be Edmond; she gives him her hand to kiss. The ecstatic, bewitched Saint-Rambert is no longer master of himself; he runs over to the window and closes it.

At this very moment, Gertrude opens the door of the closet. Her eyes fall on Saint-Rambert's movement, and even more: she beholds a white-clad woman, though she cannot yet tell who it is. She makes a movement revealing her displeasure at this, and quickly returns to the closet.

Saint-Rambert approaches Thérèse. At this moment she thinks it is the following day, that she is in church with the wedding taking place. She imagines the priest is asking her if she loves Edmond. She points to her ring, places her hand on her breast and vows before Heaven that she will love her husband forever and always be faithful to him. "Heavens!"

cries Saint-Rambert, "What am I doing? What a crime I am thinking of committing! Such purity – such innocence, demands respect! I, who have been so well received by these good people; I, their lord – is this the way I should celebrate my arrival? Nay, here the only voice I shall heed is that of honour. Thus, the wisest thing for me to do is to leave." He goes over and opens the window. The moonlight is lovely. "I can travel to the castle on foot, briskly and merrily. We travel quickly when not weighed down by conscience."

Meanwhile, Thérèse has risen from the armchair and draws near the bed. She sits down on it, lays her head in her hand, and rests. Saint-Rambert, who is leaving, is involuntarily drawn back, halts, and gazes at her one more time. Then he exits through the window and vanishes.

Just then, the door to the right quietly opens. The Magistrate, Edmond, and a number of villagers, together with Madame Michaud, come tiptoeing in with bouquets. They approach the couch. General amazement. Abhorrence. Edmond's anger. Thérèse is awakened by this noise. Her dismay and astonishment at such an awakening. She does not know where she is or what has been going on. Madame Michaud is horrified, grabs the shawl from the armchair, and throws it around Thérèse.

In the meantime, Gertrude has quietly emerged from the little room. She mingles with the villagers and expresses even greater contempt for Thérèse than the others do. Overwhelmed by her taunts and Madame Michaud's reproaches, Thérèse looks at Edmond and rushes over to him to implore his aid. He thrusts her away, will not listen to anything she says, tears up the contract and tells her that their wedding is canceled, that he no longer loves but loathes and abandons her. They all run out in disorder, and Madame Michaud drags the all-but-lifeless Thérèse away with her.

ACT III

A lovely rural area of Provence. Upstage can be seen the mill with a tiled roof; a brook, which drives the mill wheel, runs between the mill house and a crumbling wall, which are joined together by a beam. To the left is an orchestra, and round about hang flower garlands and entwined monograms. All is ready for the wedding of Edmond and Thérèse.

Young lads and lasses adorned with ribbons and flowers cross the stage to fetch other wedding guests. The young girls point up to Madame Michaud's windows as if to say: "Thérèse is certainly lucky!" They view with delight the orchestra and the preparations for the festival. Lads and lasses bedeck the door of the house with flower garlands. They finally depart, and even in the distance can be heard the sound of tambourines and shepherd's pipes.

Madame Michaud comes out of the mill with Thérèse, who is completely bewildered and can hardly hold herself up. She looks around at the preparations for the festival, and this only adds to her pain. She weeps, loses heart, and assures her foster mother that she is innocent, that she has done nothing for which to reproach herself. "It is hard to believe, but when you tell me that, my child, I am convinced of it." "What! You forgive me! I have regained your esteem! O, now I am only half as unfortunate as I was." She sinks into the arms of the old woman, who sheds tears. "Dear child! It is not I you need to convince but" – pointing to Edmond, who enters – "him who comes; and that you can hardly do."

Wretched and dreamy, Edmond enters. He sees neither Thérèse nor her foster mother. He sighs and buries his face in his handkerchief. "O," says Thérèse to the old woman, "you see how unhappy he is. He weeps, he loves me still." She hurries toward him in order to explain. Edmond raises his eyes and gives her such a terrible look that she is immobilized with fright. "You dare to show yourself before me – you!" "Why this dreadful look? What have I done?" "You dare to ask me that?" He takes her violently by the hand and pulls her aside. "Behold these preparations for the festival that was to make us happy. I loved, I adored you – everything I had was yours – and you deceived me! The love that was my joy, my bliss, is today my misfortune and dishonour! I curse it – and you along with it!" Overwhelmed with torment, he sinks down on a bench and gives himself up to despair.

Merry music announces the arrival of Saint-Rambert, in uniform, with ladies and gentlemen from the castle, and, surrounded by villagers and musicians, Olivier at the head of the whole crowd. Some chambermaids carry a basket of wedding gifts. All congratulate Saint-Rambert, who gives orders to Olivier and makes a sign to the girls that they should carry the basket, intended for Thérèse, into Madame Michaud's. Saint-Rambert's gaze falls on Thérèse. He approaches her. He is highly astonished to find her in tears and Edmond in the utmost misery. He bids the bystanders leave him alone with the bridal couple.

At the sight of Saint-Rambert, Edmond can hardly refrain from venting his wrath and jealousy. He tries to leave, but the Colonel holds him back. "What is the matter with you? This is a strange way for a bridegroom to look. Are domestic troubles beginning even before the wedding?" "O, my lord," says Thérèse, "you know if I am guilty. Protect me, defend me against this raging, jealous man. He did find me in your room. It is true, I was there. But tell me how I got there, for that I do not know." Saint-Rambert bursts out laughing and tells Edmond that in her sleep, Thérèse wandered through the window into his room. "You can tell that to someone else," says Edmond, "for you won't get me to believe it. I will never believe that people can walk while still asleep. She went there, but wide awake." Saint-Rambert assures him that what he told him is true. "Your reassurances do not help," replies Edmond, "and if you were not our lord, I should know how to avenge myself. But since I now know only one revenge that is permitted me, I shall use it: I shall wed another this very day. It is all settled with the woman I prefer to Thérèse!"

Thérèse trembles with dread. "Aye, I have made haste to fall in love with her; I do love her and she will be faithful. It is to her I have given hand and heart!" At the same moment, he grabs Thérèse's hand and removes his betrothal ring. Thérèse is horrified, looks at the hand from which he has taken the ring, and sinks unconscious into the arms of her foster mother, who takes her into the mill. Saint-Rambert, who feels the most intense pain, blames himself for their misfortune. He ponders a way to convince Edmond. "Will you not believe a soldier's word of honour?" he says to Edmond, placing his hand on his medal as if swearing upon it. "Leave me alone," replies Edmond. "Just postpone this new wedding – don't be in such a hurry. The truth will come to light." "Nay, I long to avenge myself by marrying another." "And who is she?" "The most sensible, the most virtuous woman in the entire village. Here she comes."

At this very moment, Gertrude enters, dressed as a bride and accompanied by Marceline, who is also decked out. Saint-Rambert can hardly refrain from laughing at this new choice. With downcast eyes, Gertrude quite bashfully bows to Saint-Rambert, who is about to tell Edmond how she behaved toward him, when, unseen by the latter, she animatedly puts her finger to her lips to hush him, and Saint-Rambert remains silent. "It is not I who should betray her," he seems to say to himself; and looking at Edmond, he goes on: "Married men are strange! Why should a man who would not allow himself to be persuaded of Thérèse's innocence permit himself to be convinced of this woman's coquetry?"

Olivier enters at the head of the whole bridal party. On his trumpet, he accompanies the musicians, who walk behind him. Edmond has the flower garlands torn off the door of the mill and orders that the monograms made of entwined flowers be taken apart and replaced by the letters G. E. General amazement. Gertrude's delight. Edmond presents her to everyone as his new bride. The Magistrate, whose hopes are dashed by this, stands brokenhearted. Edmond takes Gertrude's hand and starts off for the church. Olivier is asked to lead the musicians, but he gives a flat refusal since it is no longer pretty little Thérèse who is to be wed. Gertrude remarks that they can certainly do without him and go to the church quite nicely with no trumpeter. They are about to depart when Madame Michaud comes from the mill, saying, "Poor child! She is sleeping. And, indeed, she needed to sleep." She runs into Edmond and Gertrude, who are about to leave. "Where are you going?" "To the church," he replies. "With whom?" "With Gertrude." "With Edmond!" "What! It is for her you have abandoned Thérèse?" "And doesn't he have reason to?" asks Gertrude. "A girl who behaves like that!" "You accuse her – you accuse my child? Well then, Madame, I shall follow your example." She pulls out Gertrude's shawl and goes on: "Who owns this shawl that I found tonight in an armchair in the Colonel's room? Thérèse? No? It belongs to a far more virtuous woman, and that is you."

Edmond, who has been holding Gertrude by the hand, drops it and stands crushed. She is disconcerted. Saint-Rambert turns around to keep from laughing. "What!" exclaims Edmond angrily, "not merely one! The lord of the manor has come here to rob us of all of them." "Nay," says Saint-Rambert, taking his hand, "for I assure you once again that Thérèse is innocent." "And what shall convince me of this?" "Your own eyes," replies the Colonel, looking toward the mill.

Everyone turns and beholds Thérèse, who emerges from a dormer window of the mill. She walks in her sleep along the edge of the roof. The mill wheel is turning swiftly and threatens to crush her should she make a false step. Terrified, Edmond is about to run toward her. Saint-Rambert puts his hand over Edmond's mouth to muffle his cry of alarm. He tells him that if they wake her she will inevitably be lost; they cannot give her any help but must allow her to do what she will.

Everyone is petrified with horror and follows her every move with dismay. She slowly continues her course and steps out onto the beam. At this awful moment, Saint-Rambert and all the villagers fall to their knees and offer up their prayers. Moved and affected, Gertrude, too, follows their example. She goes down on her knees and prays for her rival.

The uneven stones of the crumbling wall almost form a staircase; in this way, Thérèse makes her descent. She stands at centre stage. She listens and thinks she hears bells ringing for Edmond's wedding. She kneels and prays for him: "May he be happy! And I? O, for me there is no longer any happiness, and even though I am innocent – " She gazes at her hand. "My ring? It isn't there any more. He has taken it from me to give to another. But what he can never rob me of is the memory of him, the image of him that is imprinted on my heart; and so" – she looks to every side – "no one will see me." From her bosom she takes the flower Edmond gave her; it is dry, withered. She waters it with her tears and covers it with kisses.

Gertrude, touched by such love, feels all hatred vanish from her breast. She yields to compassion and magnanimity. She hands Saint-Rambert the promise of marriage that Edmond had given her and asks him to unite the two lovers. Edmond throws himself at Thérèse's feet and puts back on her finger the ring he took from her. In the meantime, Saint-Rambert makes a sign; they open the basket intended for the bride and take out a white veil and bridal wreath, with which Gertrude adorns her during her prolonged somnambulism. Saint-Rambert presents her with a bouquet.

The musicians are in the orchestra. 'The dancers have arranged themselves in rows. Edmond takes Thérèse's hand. Saint-Rambert gives the signal and the music begins. At this sudden noise, Thérèse wakens, petrified, dazzled by everything around her. The splendor, her lover on his knees, her friends gathered about her, the noise of the instruments, the cries of joy – all this makes her believe this is a new dream. She holds one hand in front of her eyes, and the other seems to say: "Don't awaken me!" But this happiness is no dream; it is real. Groups of joyful, sympathetic friends surround her. Saint-Rambert unites her to Edmond and presents them with a deed of gift. The Colonel, who knows the Magistrate's feelings for Gertrude, sets his mind at ease with regard to the shawl, and the good-natured jurist holds out his hand to the pretty widow, who takes it in obedience to her lord.

All now express lively joy, and Olivier no longer refuses to play for the wedding, but, together with four of his comrades, steps forward to open the festivities with a merry dance, after which he is rewarded with Marceline's hand. The happy hour has come, and, led by her bridegroom, Thérèse hastens to the altar accompanied by jubilation and congratulations from all.

*   *   *

THE PAGES OF THE DUKE DE VENDOME
(Hertugen af Vendômes Pager)

A Pantomimic Ballet in Two Acts
by Jean Aumer

Produced for the Danish Stage, with newly composed dances
by August Bournonville

Music by Adalbert Gyrowetz

Performed for the first time at the Royal Theatre, Copenhagen, on
September 4, 1830*

Characters

THE DUKE DE VENDOME	Hr. Fredstrup
MADAME DE ST. ANGE, his sister	Mme. Schouw
ELISE, her daughter	Mme. Bauer
THE COUNT DE MURET	Hr. Hammer
COLONEL MARIMON	Hr. Villeneuve
VICTOR, his son	Hr. Bournonville
EUGENE	Hr. Bentzen
AUGUSTE ... Pages	Mme. Haack
PHILIPPE	Jfr. Larcher
SIX OTHER PAGES	
PEDRILLO, a miller	Hr. Stramboe
MOTHER PEDRILLO	Jfr. Brunn
ROSINE, their daughter	Jfr. Werning
AN OFFICER	Hr. Weile

Solo Dances

Hr. Larcher, Mme. Kraetzmer, Hr. Funck, Jfr. Møller.

The action takes place in a small town in northern Spain.

Some public newspapers have announced that this ballet was *composed* by me; others, as necessary justification, have termed it *arranged* by me. If the first designation suggests the original idea and the second the arbitrary treatment of that idea, then neither of them is applicable to this ballet or to *La Somnambule*, both of which are by M. Aumer (a splendid artist and my especial patron). The most faithful rendering of plot and situation is the product of six years' choreographic studies, which can be made only by means of observation and retentiveness. The dances in

---

* Original Production: *Les Pages du duc de Vendôme*, ch. Jean Aumer, mus. Adalbert Gyrowetz, des Auguste Garneray, 18 Oct. 1820.

these ballets, on the other hand, are entirely of my own composing and are, to some extent, more in agreement with the situation and with many local circumstances.

Should these works, then, be favourably received, the only thing I shall venture to take credit for is that I have understood my author and, aided solely by my imagination, have (for the most part) trained performers to fit his roles instead of tailoring the roles for consummate artists. I have also made the dancing interesting in places where, even in Paris, it interrupted or delayed the action.

In conclusion, I hope that these patrons who believe me capable of treating a subject will not object to the fact that I, being inexperienced, unselfishly offer the Theatre a repertoire of the finest French ballets until such time as my own products shall have attained the requisite maturity and are worthy to be performed.

A. BOURNONVILLE

The stage represents a landscape with mountainous background. To the left, Madam de St. Ange's dwelling, whose walls are adorned with an espalier which, to the right of the house, forms a bower. In the right foreground, a mossy bank; farther off, on a vine-clad hill, Pedrillo's mill.

ACT I

The page Eugene presents Madame de St. Ange with a letter containing the glad tidings that her brother, the Duke de Vendôme, who has victoriously entered Spain, will this very day pay her a visit with his staff. While she is relating this news to those standing around, the cunning page has slipped a letter to Elise and also casts amorous eyes at the little miller's daughter, who, as it happens, is strictly watched over by her parents. Madame de St. Ange arranges for the hero's festive reception; Elise distributes flowers to the young girls; martial music is heard, and young and old flock to greet the Duke.

French troops march past upstage. Vendôme enters and rushes into his sister's arms. She and Elise sympathetically ask how he is and present him with laurels, which he modestly shares with his brethren-in-arms. He introduces the Count de Muret and the intrepid old Marimon to the ladies.

The latter's son, Victor, who wishes to acquit himself with credit in front of his beloved, has captured an enemy standard during a skirmish, and he lays the banner at the feet of the Duke. The Duke praises and rewards his courageous act and shares the pleasure of Marimon, who proudly and delightedly embraces his son. With heartfelt satisfaction, Elise beholds her honoured sweetheart who, repressing the expression of his feelings, respectfully bows before her.

The Count de Muret has been promoted, and he receives his diploma from the Duke, who also presents him as a suitable match for his niece. Madame de St. Ange is in complete agreement with her brother, and both hope to surmount the obstacles they expect to encounter as a result of Elise's bashfulness.

Refreshments and a little rustic festival are offered to the exalted guest. Toasts are drunk to new triumphs, and merry dancing by pages and villagers enlivens the scene. Victor is burning with the desire to dance with Elise, but is prudent enough to ask one of her playfellows to join them. All three now take turns dancing together, although Victor cannot help but accord Elise a noticeable advantage.

The dancing is interrupted by the announcement that the enemy has attacked the outposts. Fright spreads among the women and villagers. Vendôme calms them and orders Marimon and a detachment of troops to repulse the enemy. Victor asks to accompany them. Elise trembles for his life but is soothed when she hears his father firmly deny his request.

Marimon rushes off to battle. The Duke, after having escorted the ladies [off], gives his pages six hours' rest and leisure. "But don't create a disturbance!" The Count accompanies him on his rounds.

The Duke is hardly out of sight when the pages start to pursue the young girls. Eugene has an eye for Rosine, and her parents have their hands full trying to watch her. He tries to follow them into the mill, but they slam the door in his face.

The young gentlemen have not had any supper. This is taken care of, but Victor is unusually quiet. His gaze is fixed on the balcony. The pages quickly guess his secret and force him to own up. A toast to his darling is proposed and drunk amid cheers.

In the meantime, the miller's daughter has stolen out to hunt for the little page. Frightened when he locks her parents in, Rosine rushes into the midst of the other pages; they are delighted to see her and each tries to steal a kiss. Eugene demands that his fugitive be handed over, and Victor returns her.

But the miller Pedrillo, who has managed to escape through the cellar window, flies into the most violent rage when he catches sight of his daughter among these madcaps. He rushes down to them, but is surrounded, pinched, forced to sit down at table; and when he finally breaks loose and runs home, he finds Eugene embracing Mother Pedrillo without so much as a by your leave or with your leave. Furious, he rushes at the bold fellow. But Eugene eludes him and, almost dying with laughter, returns to his comrades.

Night falls. They are about to set off for camp, but Victor has contrived to have a tent fetched and erected near Madame de St. Ange's dwelling. The pages intimate that they have guessed why. Well, everyone will try to make himself a comfortable bed. Victor rests on his captured standard. They bid one another good-night and go to sleep. Victor alone is wakeful. He must speak with Elise, no matter what the cost. He steals out of the tent. Harp strains tell him that Elise is still up. He risks clapping his hands. The harp sounds once more, and Victor is on the balcony. He taps softly on the jalousie. The blind opens, along with the balcony door, and Elise cautiously steps out. Victor trembles at his own daring, but his love must be his excuse. However, they have hardly exchanged a few words before they hear the [Duke returning from his] rounds and notice the sentry challenging him. Elise hastily closes the balcony door while Victor hides in a corner of the balcony.

Astonished to find the pages' tent, the Duke is about to enter the house when Victor jumps down from the balcony and steals over to his bench. The surprised Vendôme quickly pulls himself together and figures out what has been going on. "But who is the culprit? He must be pretty excited. The pounding of his heart will betray him." He softly approaches the sleeping pages and soon finds a heart beating violently. "This is he! But no thoughtless outburst which might compromise Elise." He removes Victor's aiguillette and promises to clear up the whole matter in the morning. When he finds the door locked, he returns to camp.

Victor is in the most dreadful trouble; Elise has seen everything and trembles for herself and for him. But he thinks of a way to deceive the Duke. He hastily snatches the aiguillettes of all his comrades and shows them to Elise in order to comfort her. He sends her many a kiss and a thousand assurances of eternal love. They hear someone coming. Victor hurries back to his place, and Elise closes her window.

Madame de St. Ange, who has heard noise outside her house, comes out to see what is going on and is quite astonished when she beholds the pages' tent. She has all kinds of misgivings and hurries away. When August, who has been awakened by Victor's bumping into him in the dark, notices her, he takes her for a young girl and hastens to stop her. She tries to flee, but he holds her back, giving her no time for explanation but importuning her with declarations of love. Victor realizes and laughs at August's mistake, encounters Elise, who would follow her mother, and in the bower renews his vows of faithfulness and love.

August has recognized Madame de St. Ange and flees in confusion and embarrassment. Two other pages have also glimpsed a female figure; they both move toward her at the same time, one on either side. The old woman is utterly astounded at this increase in admirers and does not know whether to be amused or angry because of it. On bended knee they swear undying love, but when they become bold enough to try to steal a kiss, her anger is aroused and with two deft cuffs on the ear she reveals herself. The pages fly to the tent, and Elise follows her mother into the house.

ACT II

Day is dawning. Vendôme enters, accompanied by the Count de Muret. He is showered with complaints, first from Pedrillo, then from Madame de St. Ange. The Duke informs them that he has come to punish the offender. He orders his pages to come forward but is startled to hear that three of them have harassed his respectable sister. However, he shall begin by learning the identity of his own nocturnal wanderer and orders de Muret to seize whichever page is missing his aiguillette. The Count makes a move to obey but discovers that all the aiguillettes are missing and, with the utmost seriousness, calls the Duke's attention to this fact. The latter can hardly refrain from laughing at this cunning trick. Nevertheless, he retains a stem expression and states how amazed he is that his pages would dare to appear before him without their honourable badges of rank. All the pages feel their shoulders and are astonished not to find the cord there; they search the tent, but in vain. The Duke, who has by now told his sister of his nocturnal adventure, informs the pages that in one hour's time they must appear with their aiguillettes or expect to be dismissed. He goes inside with Madame de St. Ange.

Partly through persuasion and partly through random conjecture, the Count de Muret seeks to elicit a confession. But all too quickly he realizes that the pages are making a fool of him. He is very displeased, threatens to report their scandalous behaviour, and departs, pursued by the pages' roguery. The pages' predicament is not at all a pleasant one, and Victor does not hesitate to tell the whole story and to return each of their badges. But his own is missing, and where is it to be found? His comrades promise to aid him and help to find a trick. But it is a difficult thing to do. No matter! Victor borrows a cord with which he alone will go before the Duke! Cupid must do the rest. They hear the Duke. All the pages flee except Victor, who is immediately noticed and called forth. He approaches with feigned shyness, but suddenly loses his composure when he comes face to face with Elise, who is led forth by her mother.

The Duke is sure he has found his man and is about to force a confession when Victor, to justify himself, pulls out an aiguillette; this once again confounds the Duke's suppositions. Elise's courage revives, and Madame de St. Ange assures her brother that he must be mistaken. Vendôme tries to get Victor to denounce the culprit; but Victor has his reasons for keeping silent and asks for the cord in order to free his comrade of suspicion. The Duke refuses and puts the aiguillette in his pocket. But here chance comes to Victor's aid: the cord has slipped out of the side of the Duke's pocket and onto the ground, unnoticed. Victor seizes a favourable moment to snatch up the cord and rushes off in triumph.

While the Duke and his sister rack their brains trying to figure out whether or not Victor is the culprit, Muret receives a definite refusal from Elise, who everywhere evades him. The Count is terribly disheartened just as Vendôme bids him call the pages together.

They enter and line up before the Duke, who is startled to see them all wearing aiguillettes – and his pocket is empty! "Ah! This time it can't be anyone but Victor! Step forth, page!" Victor obeys. But when the Duke questions him in greater detail, all the pages declare themselves to be equally guilty.

This pleases Vendôme, who will now spring the last mine. He declares that he had intended to give Elise's hand to the one who was bold enough to climb up to her window. The pages, who obey only the call of their hearts, wish Victor well, and the latter throws himself at his master's feet. Elise kneels, too; but the Duke has put on his serious face again, and Victor is handed over to two grenadiers.

Martial music and victory fanfares now proclaim that Marimon has driven back the enemy. He himself has trophies brought before the Duke and receives his commander's expressions of gratitude. But when the Duke points out to him Victor, who has so grossly offended him by compromising Elise's reputation,

Marimon becomes indignant, and, although the Duke himself proposes that he pardon his son, he disowns Victor and gives himself up to his grief. But when Muret voluntarily renounces his claim to Elise's hand, and Vendôme, with his sister's consent, unites the young lovers, the father's face brightens. He forgives and general rejoicing spreads among all the bystanders. Amid dancing and martial exercises, the curtain falls.

* * *

PAUL AND VIRGINIA
(Paul og Virginie)

Pantomimic Ballet in Three Acts
by Pierre Gardel

Produced for the Danish Stage, with newly composed dances,
by August Bournonville

Music by Rodolphe Kreutzer

Performed for the first time at the Royal Theatre on the occasion of the august birthday of Her Majesty the Queen, October 29, 1830*

Characters

M. DE LA BOURDONNAYE, Governor
   of Isle de France ....Hr. Hammer
MME. DE LA TOUR, widow of a French officer .....Mme. Schouw
VIRGINIA, her daughter ....Mme. Kraetzmer
MARGUERITE, her friend ....Jfr. Bruun
PAUL, Marguerite's son ....Hr. Bournonville
DOMINGO, a Negro in Marguerite's service ....Hr. Larcher
MARIE, his wife ....Mme. Haack
CANDOR, a priest ....Hr. Villeneuve
DORVAL, a planter ....Hr. Fredstrup
ZABI, his Negro slave ....Hr. Stramboe
ZABI'S TWINS .... {Rinda / Augusta

Solo Dances

Hr. Funck. Jfr. Møller (Negroes)
Mme. Bauer. Jfr. Weming (Creoles)

Ensemble Dance Numbers

Bamboula: Hr. Füssel, Hr. Hoppe
Stick Dance: Messieurs Funck, Friis, Bentzen, Weile, Holm, Jacobsen, Füssel, Stramboe, Nehm, Borch, Pio, Lund
Creoles: Mesdames Bentzen, Larcher, Weiner, Bechman, Johnson
Negresses: Mesdames Worre, Fredstrup, Rasmussen, Wolstrupt, Skaarp, Møller, Freyman
Sailors: Messieurs Lundgreen, Holm, Füssel, Lund

* Original Production: *Paul et Virginie,* ch Pierre Gardel, mus Rodolphe Kreutzer, 24 June, 1806.

ACT I

A landscape on the coast of Isle de France. To right and left, the dwellings of Mme. de la Tour and Marguerite. In the remote background, a section of Port-Louis.

It is morning. The weather is fine, but from time to time distant thunder betokens the fact that this tropical clime is visited by frequent storms. Paul and Virginia are already busy in the garden. They show their solicitude for the twin palm trees that were planted in their childhood, and in whose shadow they have been raised like brother and sister. In the attentiveness with which Paul anticipates each of Virginia's wishes and the satisfaction he feels when she is near, the eye can detect an emotion stronger than fraternal love. How fervently he kisses her hand! And how annoyed he becomes when she roguishly denies him this pleasure! Virginia delights in teasing him a bit. She evades him, makes him angry then amiable again, and finally gives him her hand, which he ardently presses to his lips.

Domingo, who, unnoticed by the young couple, has witnessed their innocent banter, heartily hugs himself over it. He fetches his little Marie to tell her what he has seen and repeats the childish scene with the most ridiculous gestures. Paul and Virginia break off their conversation and reproach them for eavesdropping. But the good blacks promise to perform their favourite dance, the lively bamboula, they are forgiven and delight their young masters with their singular movements. Paul and Virginia attempt to imitate this dance. Domingo fetches his drum, Marie her triangle. The noisy instruments heighten the merriment, and everyone expresses the liveliest joy. Paul and Virginia interrupt their dance to rush into their mothers' arms. Kindness and gratitude are expressed in a sincere "good morning," and tranquil delight animates the little group.

While the children and blacks prepare breakfast, Mme. de la Tour has, with more gravity than usual, called Marguerite's attention to the heights the twin palm trees have reached. Paul is seventeen years old, Virginia fifteen. They should no longer be considered children; furthermore, to leave them to their own devices might prove dangerous to their peace of mind unless a sacred pact were to unite them quite soon and thus secure their young hearts against the storms of passion. Marguerite's objections are soon overcome, and the tender mothers embrace each other with the most joyous hope.

Candor, a priest in the colony and the family's friend and counselor, approaches, followed by a band of Creoles and Negroes. The children happily run to meet him. He greets everyone in an amicable fashion and bids Mme. de la Tour accept some fruits from his hermitage. He accepts her invitation to the humble meal, and when the Negroes ask permission to entertain the good whites with dancing and merriment, he himself encourages them and gazes with delight at their distinctive dances, which are so different from those performed by Paul, Virginia, and the young Creole girls.

The dancing ceases and everyone departs, except Candor, with whom the mothers have something of importance to discuss. But since it concerns their children, and the latter are not to know anything about it just yet, they bid the priest accompany them to Mme. de la Tour's dwelling. When Paul and Virginia, curious, intrude, they are told to wait until they are summoned. The young couple give each other a searching look. They are both astonished and sad that people seem to be keeping secrets from them, and they are despondently setting off for the beach when, all of a sudden, wailing is heard and an old Negro, with his two children, breathlessly throws himself at their feet and begs them to hide and save them. Paul and Virginia sympathetically ask him to explain, and Zabi, as the old man is called, trembling, tells them in broken phrases that his master wants to sell him, take him across the sea, and tear him away from his beloved little ones. Driven to despair by the planter's maltreatment, he has taken flight. They are after him and, weakened by hunger and fatigue, he will soon fall prey to his cruel pursuers. Paul's heart is touched by this account. He will hasten to the planter, speak with him himself. But Virginia's first thought is to make sure the poor souls are safe. With a caress, she draws her friend back; in an out-of-the-way place they can find a safe haven for Zabi and his children.

Virginia takes one child on her arm; Paul takes the other. They allow the father to lean on their shoulders, while, deeply moved, he thanks Heaven for the angels it has sent to save him.

Mme. de la Tour and Marguerite emerge with the priest. They repeat what has already been decided concerning the wedding of their children. Candor promises to make arrangements so that the ceremony can take place the following morning. He accepts a present of flowers with which to adorn the Madonna's altar, bids them farewell, and departs.

Military music is heard, and Domingo announces that the governor is approaching with a detachment of grenadiers. Mme. de la Tour is most surprised at this visit and tries in vain to fathom the reason for it. The troops approach. M. de la Bourdonnaye very respectfully presents himself to Mme. de la Tour. He opens a dispatch case containing a letter for her – a letter from France! A letter from her aristocratic sister-in-law! What can it say?

The opening lines seem to please her greatly. But her countenance soon darkens, and she trembles spasmodically; she can hardly believe what she is reading. All too soon does she ascertain its dreadful meaning, and she swoons in Marguerite's arms. People encircle her with the liveliest sympathy and, after some difficulty, restore her to consciousness. The first thing to meet her eye is the detested letter. She tells the bystanders that they want to take Virginia to France and tear her away from her mother. She bursts into a flood of tears but rallies enough to rise and steel herself for the separation from her child. The governor shows her the presents he has brought and tells her how happy Virginia will be in dazzling Paris. He tries his best to console the despondent Mother and delays as long as possible delivering the firm orders he has received regarding Virginia's voyage. Tomorrow morning he will come to fetch her. He would be sincerely distressed to encounter opposition. He bows and takes his leave.

Mme. de la Tour abandons herself to her grief. Marguerite and the loyal Negroes share her anguish and are already bemoaning the loss of their beloved Virginia. The tender Mother cannot accustom herself to the idea of being parted from her child. Marguerite tells her how impossible it would be to defy authority. But what will become of poor Paul? Only now do they notice that their children are missing; no one knows where they have gone. A storm is brewing and the mothers tremble for them. But Domingo consoles them as best he can, and, assuring them that he will bring Paul and Virginia back without delay, he succeeds in getting them to take shelter.

Domingo actually does not know in which direction to look. He runs now to the right, now to the left, displaying the utmost uncertainty. Then he hears his dog. Things will be all right!! "With the help of Paul's jacket, Fidele will quickly pick up his young master's scent." Delighted with this aid, Domingo hastens to make use of it.

ACT II

Wild woodland.

Some Negroes are roaming through the brushwood. They are hunting for Zabi and shudder at the thought of the suspicion and punishment that await them should they fail to find him. Their rude, unfeeling master, Dorval, suddenly enters their midst and learns with mounting indignation that their search has been fruitless. Incensed, he brandishes his cane above their heads, sends them off again on the trail of the runaway slave, and continues his own hunt amid horrible threats!

Paul, Virginia, and the fugitive blacks come into view on the face of a cliff. But the group has changed. Virginia and Zabi are so exhausted from the long walk that they cannot go any farther. Paul is supporting them with his mighty arm while both children are seated on his shoulders. In vain, he encourages them to exert themselves. Virginia shows him her injured foot, and Zabi falls to the ground, unconscious. The children lament over the lifeless body. Paul and Virginia are horrified to learn that the old man has fainted from hunger and thirst. They hasten to his rescue. Some distance away, Paul discovers a fruit tree; he quickly returns with refreshment for the poor Negro. But Virginia has forestalled him; from a nearby spring she has fetched water, and Zabi has drunk new vitality from the palm of her hand. Paul is enchanted by this sight. In his delight, he drops the fruit, and tears of joy glisten in his eyes. The blacks devour the fruit and make ready to follow the kind whites.

All of a sudden, Zabi starts, points to the right, and, together with his children, falls prostrate. Dorval has found him and leaps out with his slaves. Paul snatches a branch, intending to defend singlehandedly those he has promised to protect. Dorval scoffs at his daring, orders him disarmed, and, with upraised cane, rushes at the trembling Zabi. But, like a protecting angel, Virginia stands before the unfortunate man! Quaking, with folded hands, she adjures Dorval to be kind and, for heaven's sake, not to do the poor souls any harm. She believes that she can lend strength to her entreaties by telling him who she and Paul are. But it is all in vain! The hardhearted planter laughs at her tears. His sole desire is to vent his wrath on Zabi. But Virginia does not lose heart. She seizes a child with each hand, and, with imploring sadness, as if to say "What is their offence?," she forces Dorval slowly to back down. He is startled by unfamiliar feelings of compassion that are suddenly awakened in his soul. He threatens no more; he even allows the children to embrace his knees, and averts his face in embarrassment while Virginia gently slips the cane out of his hand. Zabi cowers at his feet; Paul and Virginia, imploring, hang upon his neck. Moved, he can no longer hold back his tears, and, for the first time in his life, he forgives. Zabi shall not be sent away, shall not be punished, shall not be parted from his little ones. General rejoicing and benedictions in gratitude to the whites. Dorval has experienced the pleasure of a good deed; it will certainly not be his last, but he shall never forget Paul and Virginia. He and the blacks exit happily.

Never have Paul and Virginia felt a livelier joy than at this moment. Touched, they give thanks to heaven; they go back over what has happened; Virginia praises Paul's courage; he lauds her gentleness. They are both beside themselves with delight. Enraptured, they embrace one another, and, in an outburst of heartfelt tenderness, he imprints a kiss on her brow. Trembling, Virginia blushes and places a hand on her beating heart. She becomes aware of the fact that she is alone with Paul and anxiously appears to be looking for her mother. Never before was Paul like this; never before has she found him so handsome. But she timorously evades him, turns away from him, and weeps. Paul fears for his Virginia, but she regains her composure and points out to him that they are a long way from home; evening is drawing nigh; they do not know their way;

and the woods are full of wild beasts. Paul searches and calls out in vain; nevertheless, he comforts Virginia and still hopes to find the way home. Virginia's feet will no longer carry her, and he himself is too exhausted to lift her onto his shoulders. Virginia bursts into tears; from Providence alone can they expect their salvation, when all of a sudden the barking of a dog catches their attention. They hearken; the sound draws closer. It is Fidele, who has tracked them down, and now everything will be all right. Joy gives them new strength. They run off in the direction from which the noise is coming and meet faithful Domingo, who throws himself into their arms, speechless from fatigue and happiness. However, he soon feels strengthened and bids the young couple hasten home, telling them, in the same breath, about the officers, the presents, and the money; about the letter he says nothing. They set off, but bad weather has caused the nearby brook to swell, and the detour is long and hard. Distress and dejection. They hear resounding instruments. The report of Paul's and Virginia's noble deed has spread throughout the plantation; young and old rush out to behold the dear white children and to shower them with caresses and benedictions. Domingo is touched to learn of Zabi's deliverance. The Negroes learn that Paul and Virginia are worried about the journey home and delightedly seize this opportunity to display their devotion. They quickly weave a sedan chair; Virginia takes her place in it, along with Zabi's children. Paul walks at her side, and to the accompaniment of torchlight and the sound of drums, the troop of Negroes, happy to bear their precious burden, marches in triumph through the forest.

ACT III

Home.

Day is dawning and still the children have not returned. Marie expresses her alarm. She has searched in vain in every direction but can bring the distressed mothers no consolation! Her sharp ears, however, have detected a distant sound, and she hastens to find the Negroes, who emerge from the forest singing and dancing. Her cries of joy bring out the mothers; their minds are relieved; their children fly to them with a thousand demonstrations of filial tenderness. They would be scolded for their absence were everything not drowned out by the noisy narratives of the Negroes. The reunion is spoiled, however, by a presentiment of what is going to take place in a few moments. This very morning, Virginia is to depart. Mme. de la Tour tries to make this news less dreadful for her daughter by displaying the gifts that have arrived. Virginia, having no idea that a separation is imminent, takes childish delight in all this finery and, with her mother's permission, shares some of it with the bystanders.

Paul is not forgotten: to him she gives a fine watch. The Negroes, too, must have their curiosities, and while the mothers take Paul and Virginia aside to prepare them for what is to come, the blacks cavort endlessly in front of a mirror and delightedly skip off with it.

Paul comes rushing out of the house like a madman. He pays no heed to his mother's pleas nor to the Negroes who tearfully implore him to get control of himself. He fetches Mme. de la Tour and her daughter in order to shower them with reproaches; but his agitation renders him speechless, and he stands before them as if turned to stone while they, trembling, wait for him to give vent to his grief. A flood of tears loosens his tongue; he points to the wild ocean that will soon swallow the thing he holds dearest on earth. He begs Virginia, for heaven's sake, not to abandon him, for it would kill him to lose her. Everyone weeps bitterly, but Paul is cheered by an idea: Yes! He will do it! He shall accompany Virginia, stay with her, save her from distress at sea, or die with her!! But he has a mother, a beloved mother. Who shall console her when he, too, is gone? Paul is crushed with despair.

Seamen come to fetch Virginia. The wind is fair, they are waiting only for her before weighing anchor. The governor approaches; Paul entreats him to let Virginia stay, or at least to allow him to go with her. But a cold and definite refusal chills his blood. A gunshot announces that the ship is about to leave. The family prepares for Virginia's departure, but Paul embraces the governor's knees; only when he remains adamant and the guns have fired for the fourth and final time does Paul rise in desperation and throw himself into Virginia's arms. Both declare that they will never be parted. The governor calls in the guard. Paul fights like a tiger, swings Virginia onto his shoulders, and tries to flee. But they are seized and forcefully torn apart, and during this last effort to cling to one another, they lose consciousness. The swooning Virginia is carried off to the ship; her mother is overwhelmed with grief, and Marguerite throws herself on her unconscious son.

The priest comes as he had promised, bringing with him a band of Creole and Negro men and women, festively adorned with flowers and fluttering ribbons. Two banners bearing inscriptions in honour of Paul and Virginia and lively dances express the joy that animates the entire troop. Candor is the first to discover Paul lying lifeless in his mother's arms. Everyone is dismayed to learn the cause. With the utmost effort, they succeed in bringing the unconscious youth back to his senses. He opens his eyes and seems to have forgotten what has taken place. He starts at finding himself surrounded by people; astonished, he reads the inscription on the banners and wrings from Candor an explanation. Heavens! it was his wedding, and the ship bearing Virginia is far, far away. Paul falls into the most profound sadness, and all the consolation that religion, his mother, and his friends can afford him is of no avail.

The thick clouds that have formed, unnoticed, gradually come together, spreading an awful darkness. A flash of lightning followed by a dreadful clap of thunder rouses the group from its mournful stupor. The storm breaks and the hurricane churns the foaming sea. Everyone seeks shelter save Marguerite and Candor; they remain with poor Paul, whose only thought is of Virginia! His fear is not unfounded. Flashes of lightning reveal the ship, which is the sport of the waves and cannot stay afloat or return to harbor. It is being violently driven toward the rocks. The distress shots are answered from the coast. The drum is beaten, the alarm bell sounds, and the shoreline teems with rescuers. Paul anticipates that the ship will sink; he slips away from his mother, rushes toward the ocean, and dives in to save Virginia. The ship founders and is crushed. Zabi enters just as M. de la Bourdonnaye offers his purse to anyone who saves the shipwrecked. But the Negro proudly rejects his offer, grabs a rope, and swims out with it to the wrecked ship. Domingo follows him into the waves.

After several moments of silent expectation, the rope has been made fast. Everyone sets to work hauling it in. Clinging tightly to a yard are Zabi and Domingo, and in their arms lie Paul and Virginia. People crowd around them; they are given every possible attention but show no sign of life, and the mothers wail over their chidren's bodies.

The storm is over, yet everyone is still standing silent and grief-stricken near the lifeless couple, when, all of a sudden, Zabi and Domingo spring up and cry, "Console yourselves! Paul and Virginia are not dead! They breathe! They live!" Rejoicing, and the wildest delight seizes everyone when they behold the lovers embrace their mothers, recognize one another, and fall into each other's arms. The governor gives his word never to part them. Candor blesses their union, and Dorval bestows upon the Negro Zabi that noble Danish gift – Freedom.

*   *   *

NINA, OR THE GIRL DRIVEN MAD BY LOVE
(Nina eller Den Vanvittige of Kaerlighed)

A Pantomimic Ballet in Two Acts
by Louis Milon

Adapted for the Danish Stage
by August Bournonville

Music arranged by Louis de Persuis, after Nicolas Dalayrac

Performed for the first time at the Royal Theatre on September 30, 1834*

Characters

THE COUNT	Hr. Fredstrup
NINA, his daughter	Fru Heiberg
GERMEUIL, his kinsman, an officer	Hr. Bournonville
THE GOVERNOR OF THE PROVINCE	Hr. Hammer
BLINVAL, his son, an officer	Hr. Fülssel
GEORGE, the Count's steward	Hr. Stramboe
GEORGETTE, his daughter	Mme. Kraetzmer
VICTOR, the gardener	Hr. Larcher
ELISE, Nina's nurse	Mme. Schou[w]
THE BAILIFF	Hr. Nehm

LADIES AND GENTLEMEN. FISHERMEN AND PEASANTS.
ORDERLIES AND SERVANTS.

Solo Dances

Hr. Hoppe, Mme. Bauer, Jfr. Weming, Jfr. Grahn

The scene is laid in the neighbourhood of Marseilles, on the count's estate.

ACT I

The stage represents the garden of the château of the count's manor. In the background, a terrace, at the foot of which can be seen the sea.

Peasant folk are bustling around. They are making ready for a feast that the Count will give in honour of the Governor's anticipated visit to the château. That is to say, this man, the supreme military authority of the province, has had his name sent in to his old friend, the Count.

* Original Production: *Nina, ou la folle par amour*, ch. Louis Milon, mus Louis-Luc Loiseu de Persuis, after Nicolas-Marie Dalayrac, des Pierre Ciceri and Louis Daguerre.

Germeuil, the Bailiff, and George arrange everything, and the latter is doubly busy since he must also keep a sharp eye on his daughter, Georgette, who lends a willing ear to Victor, the young gardener. After the farmhands have taken up their posts, the girls stay behind to await Nina.

Nina enters, followed by Elise. Germeuil offers her his hand and shows her the preparations for the feast. He then leads her into the bower where they have often sat in intimate conversation. At this spot they pledge to be eternally faithful to one another. Nina receives a ring and a kiss, which she declares to be a sacred pledge of this.

In the meantime, the Count has entered and drawn near the bower, where he surprises his daughter and Germeuil. He himself appears to be no less amazed; for even though he has long suspected the young people's love and is far from disapproving of it, he still wishes to gloat for a moment over their embarrassment.

They now confess that they love one another, and ask him to consent to their union. Touched by their mutual tenderness, the father promises to consider the matter, just as they hear the drum announcing the Governor's arrival and the start of the festivities. The Count hastens to greet the newcomers, and Germeuil and Nina joyfully follow him.

The Governor and his son, Blinval, enter, accompanied by the Count, Nina, Germeuil, and all the people of the manor. The Governor surprises the Count by handing him, in the King's name, a diploma that invests him with a new dignity. All express delight at this unexpected Royal favour that has befallen the Count. The celebration begins. After the dancing, the whole procession moves off for refreshments, but the Governor remains behind with his son and tells the Count that he would like to have a word with him. He then, on his son's behalf, asks for Nina's hand in marriage. The Count did not expect this offer. He does, indeed, remember the promise he half made to Germeuil; but the prospect of this brilliant match, and the friendship for the Governor he has cherished since he was a youth, determine his answer: he gives his consent. However, since he believes he should be the one to prepare Nina for this change in her destiny, he asks the Governor to keep the agreement secret for the time being.

But Blinval has not heard this condition and rushes to greet Nina, who comes with Elise to ask him and his father not to keep them waiting any longer at the feast; he cannot refrain from informing the beloved object of the Count's consent to their union. The Count is greatly embarrassed by this, but once the secret is revealed, he begs Nina to consider how much he owes the Governor and what great honour the Governor has done him. He brings Blinval over to his daughter and presents him as her bridegroom. Nina stands as if struck by a bolt of lightning; she can hardly believe that she is wide awake. She fixes her gaze on the Count and falls to her knees before him. He raises her up and orders Elise to take her to her room. He then asks the Governor and his son not to attach too much importance to the girl's strange behaviour. He repeats his promise and requests them to honour the feast with their presence.

After having been left alone, he enters a pavilion of the château to write a letter to Germeuil, in which he informs him of his altered decision and asks him to leave the castle, for it is no longer fitting that he remain. George is commissioned to deliver this missive to Germeuil and to add that the Count does not wish to speak with him before his departure. The Count exits; George stays behind, highly astonished at the errand that has been imposed on him.

Meanwhile, Germeuil, delighted with his joyous expectations, enters, and George hands him the letter. He opens it with misgivings, but after having read it, he can hardly believe his own eyes. He reads it again; he looks at the address to convince himself that it is really he the Count is dismissing. He wants to see him; he wants to speak with him; but George holds him back, telling him that the Count does not wish to take leave of him. His despair is augmented by this scornful treatment. And when Elise arrives and beholds his condition, she is moved and cannot deny him the fulfillment of his wish: to have a secret meeting with Nina in order to bid her a last good-bye. But this arrangement is no secret to Blinval, who, after having long since suspected that Germeuil was his rival, has now received positive assurance of the fact; for he has heard the entire conversation with Elise while standing hidden behind the trees.

After Germeuil, Elise, and Blinval have gone, the people of the manor return amid merry dancing. George bids them cease their merriment and tells them what has happened. Next come Victor and Georgette, no less jolly, and performing just as gay a dance, which no less outrages George, who takes the opportunity to forbid Victor to go near Georgette. The Bailiff approves this prohibition and presents himself as a man worthy of the young girl. George is of the same opinion, but Georgette will not hear of it and steals away. Her father threatens her and follows her in order to scold her. Everyone disperses.

In the meantime, darkness has fallen. Blinval and Germeuil enter, each from a different side: the latter for a rendezvous with Nina, the former to surprise and humiliate his rival. They run into each other, draw their swords, and are fencing just as Nina arrives, and by her cry draws the Count and the Governor to the spot. The Count angrily reproaches Germeuil and threatens to hand him over to the law if he does not immediately quit the château and promise never to show himself to him or Nina. In the utmost despair, Germeuil runs onto the terrace upstage and hurls himself into the water. Nina faints. Blinval and several fishermen rush out to come to his aid.

The Count hastens to Nina. She awakens from her swoon but can no longer remember what has happened. She does not recognize her father, but is afraid of him. She becomes calmer when she does not see him. Presently, she even seems gay; she begins to dance, thinking she is dancing with Germeuil. But when she does not see him, she again becomes distressed. The father, who cannot endure his daughter's fear of him, once again approaches to see if she recognizes him. But she again withdraws from him, regarding him with timorous glances. She then places Elise and, after her, all the peasant girls between her father and herself; and, after having hidden behind the last of the maids, she suddenly takes flight.

ACT II

The stage represents a rural area. On one side, in the foreground, is a grass seat beneath some trees.

Nina is slumbering on the grass seat. Elise keeps vigil by her side. The Count, accompanied by George, comes to gaze at his daughter as she sleeps. But as soon as she gives a sign that she is about to awaken, the unhappy father must remove himself from her sight. Yet he can hardly bring himself to do it; George and Elise must almost drag him away by force.

Nina awakens. She peers around uneasily. But when her eyes fall on the bouquet she has recently made to present to her beloved when he returns, she is reassured, and her anxious watching turns into tranquil reverie. She takes the bouquet, looks at it, and expresses the contents of the romance "Quand le Bien-aime Reviendra,"* which the orchestra plays in the meantime. When the romance has ended, she gazes around again to see if her lover has come. She listens for his footsteps and shushes the birds in the trees. But when he does not arrive, she falls back into her melancholy.

Elise has young peasant girls come to keep Nina company and to distract her. The mad girl asks them all if they have seen her lover; but when each of them answers nay, she bids them join their prayers to hers that Heaven will soon permit her to see him again. She then thanks the young girls for their sympathy and distributes money among them; but when she comes to Georgette and discovers that her purse is already empty, she offers her a precious ring as compensation. However, Georgette, who finds this gift too fine, tells her that she would be content with the simple ring Nina is wearing on her second finger. But the mad girl has not forgotten that it is Germeuil who gave her this pledge of his

---

* From [Nicolas-Marie] Dalayrac's opera *Nina* – A. B.

fidelity; therefore she can never part with it.

Victor enters and starts to walk across the upper portion of the stage. When he sees Georgette he halts, yet dares not approach her. Nina calls him to her and promises to plead the two lovers' case with George. Delighted at this, they now take part in a dance with which Nina intends to welcome her beloved when one day he returns. She, however, becomes despondent and weary of the dance, and loses herself in her old reveries.

George, who has in the meantime entered with the Bailiff, becomes very angry when he sees Victor in Georgette's company. He separates them and breaks off the dancing. But Nina intercedes for the lovers. She tells George how hard it is to be parted from the person one holds dear – a grief that no one knows better than she herself. All are moved by this, especially the Count, who, hidden in the background, has witnessed the entire scene. He now softly emerges, orders the Bailiff to leave, and gives George a sign, after which the latter, in obedience to his master's will, gives Victor and Georgette his consent. Both of the young people are beside themselves with delight and gratitude.

Meanwhile, Nina's gaze has fallen on the Count. She asks Elise: "Who is that man?" The Count can no longer refrain from rushing to greet her with open arms, saying: "I am your father!" But she evades him and will not recognize him as her father. Then, pointing to George, who at the same moment presses Victor and Georgette to his breast, she declares: "If I had a father like that, I would not be so unhappy as I am." At length she makes a sign to Elise to accompany her and slowly walks away, looking fearfully and anxiously behind her. Everyone follows her, except the Count and George.

The Governor approaches. The Count, who, when he found himself alone with George, allowed his tears to flow freely, feels troubled by the presence of his old friend. But the latter hopes that everything will still be all right; for he has brought with him Germeuil, accompanied by Blinval, who has saved his rival from the waves. The Count, who at first can hardly believe his eyes, runs to greet Germeuil, embraces him, and calls him son. Germeuil can scarcely believe his good fortune but is soon wrenched from his happy dream when he realizes that Nina has gone mad. In his despair, he showers the Count with reproaches and blames him for everything, without thinking that if this should be the case, the unfortunate man has sufficiently expiated his guilt. At this very moment George announces that Nina is returning, and they all hasten away.

Nina enters once again, peering anxiously around her, once again grieved when she does not find what she is seeking. Elise tries to distract her and consoles her with her favourite thought: that her beloved will return. In this hope, Nina watches for him and sees Germeuil standing before her. She is astounded; she trembles; she flees to Elise. She then gazes at the spot a second time and for the second time beholds her beloved. She cannot believe her own senses. Elise reassures her that it really is Germeuil. Little by little, she approaches; she looks at him closely; her fear vanishes; he presses her hand, and she notices with amazement that his handshake is just like Germeuil's. He leads her over to the grass seat and picks up the bouquet that is lying there. She is surprised that he dares to take it, for she made it for her beloved. But when he tries to give it back to her, she bids him keep it.

He now sits down beside her, and the entire scene between the lovers that took place in the bower (at the beginning of Act I) is repeated: the declaration of love, the vow of fidelity, and, finally, the ring, which Germeuil merely goes through the motions of presenting to her, since she is already wearing it on her finger. All this gradually reawakens her consciousness; but it is the kiss, in particular, that heals her completely. Now she remembers everything; now she recognizes her beloved.

The Count, the Governor, Blinval, George, Victor and Georgette, and all the villagers have, in the meantime, been slowly and cautiously drawing near. Nina sees her father, recognizes him, and throws herself at his feet. With indescribable delight, her father raises her up and, amid general rejoicing, unites her with Germeuil.

* * *

LA SYLPHIDE
(Sylfiden)

A Romantic Ballet in Two Acts
Composed by August Bournonville

Music by Herman Severin Løvenskjold

Performed for the first time at the Royal Theatre on November 28, 1836*

Characters

THE SYLPHIDE	Lucile Grahn
ANNA, a tenant farmer's widow	[Unknown]
JAMES, her son	August Bournonville
EFFY, her niece, James's bride	Jfr. R. Lund
GURN, a peasant lad	Hr. Stramboe
MADGE, a fortuneteller	Carl Fredstrup

SCOTTISH PEASANT FOLK. SYLPHS. WITCHES.

The scene is laid in Scotland.

Preface

The subject, taken from a Scottish ballad, was first treated as a ballet by Taglioni, to music by Schneitzhoeffer. The lack of materials needed in order to mount a production of the Parisian *Sylphide* on the Danish stage, together with the experience that a smaller theatre often possesses talents that, if carefully used, will make up for the shortcomings of its facilities, have led me to treat this theme in a completely *original* manner so as to give my work that freshness which a copy can never obtain.

Just as in any art a problem may be solved in various ways, so I have composed this ballet after a foreign idea, to entirely new music by a Danish artist; the dance, mime, groupings, and a number of changes in the plan are of my own invention. Therefore, admitting that this younger *Sylphide* owes its existence to an older one, I commend this light product to the kindness and indulgence that have up to now constituted my happiness and reward.

Copenhagen, November 1, 1836.

Most gratefully,

AUGUST BOURNONVILLE

* Original Production: *La Sylphide*, ch Filippo Taglioni, mus Jean Schneitzhoeffer, sc Pierre Ciceri, cos Eugène Lami, March 12, 1832.

ACT I

A spacious room in a farmhouse. In the background, a door and a staircase leading to the sleeping chamber. To the right, a window. To the left, a high fireplace. Dawn.

James is asleep in a large armchair. A feminine being in airy raiment and with transparent wings is kneeling at his feet. Her arm is resting on the seat of the chair. With her hand beneath her chin, she fixes her loving gaze on the sleeping youth. She expresses the joy she feels in being near the one she loves. She hovers round him and flutters her wings in order to cool the air he breathes.

James slumbers restlessly. In his dreams he follows every one of the air creature's movements, and when, carried away with tenderness, she approaches him and lightly kisses his brow, he suddenly wakens, reaches out to grasp the lovely image, and pursues it about the room as far as the fireplace, into which the Sylphide vanishes.

Beside himself at the sight of this vision, which has already enchanted him several times in dreams but now stood alive before his eyes, James awakens and questions the farmhands, who are sleeping in the same room. Confused and sleepy, they do not know what he is saying and do not understand his questions. He rushes out the door to see whether the Sylphide might still be outside; but he fails to notice that in his haste he has run into Gurn, who has already been out hunting. Gurn and the farmhands regard one another with astonishment, but when James immediately returns to overwhelm them with questions about the airy figure who knelt by his couch, kissed his brow, fluttered about the room, and flew up the chimney, their wonder dissolves into laughter and they strive to convince James that the whole thing has been a dream.

James comes to himself again and remembers that this very day he is to be betrothed to his cousin, the amiable Effy. Vexed, Gurn leaves him, bemoaning the injustice he must suffer because of the superiority Effy accords this daydreamer.

James sends the farmhands away to make everything ready for the celebration and quickly finishes dressing in order to please his lovely bride. But as he draws closer to the hearth, he falls ever deeper in thought. Effy is brought in by her aunt. Her first glance is directed at James, who takes no notice of her. Gurn, on the other hand, is immediately at her service. He begs her not to reject the spoils of the hunt and gives her a bouquet of fresh wildflowers. Effy rather absent-mindedly accepts his compliment and goes over to the pensive James to ask him what he is brooding about, whether he is distressed, and why. He begs her to forgive him for being so distracted and assures her that he is really very happy, especially today, when he shall be united to the one he loves and whose he shall be for eternity. Tender and happy, Effy gives him her hand to kiss. Gurn also tries to take one of her hands, but she quickly withdraws it. James threateningly steps between her and Gurn, who, ashamed and distraught, goes away in order to hide the tears he can no longer hold back. His sorrow is further augmented by seeing Anna unite the young couple, who, kneeling, receive her blessing.

Some young girls, friends of Effy, come to congratulate the loving couple. They bring presents for the bride: a plaid, a scarf, a wreath, a veil, a bouquet – in short, everything that can delight her. Gurn begs them to put in a good word for him, but they make fun of him and offer him their love amid laughter and teasing. Weeping, he tears himself loose and goes over to sit down in a corner.

Effy thanks and embraces her childhood playmates while James once more becomes lost in thought. He approaches the fireplace – but what does he see! A loathsome figure! Old Madge, the fortuneteller, who has stolen in among the young girls. "What are you doing here?" "I am warming myself by the fire!" "Get away from here, witch! Your presence is an evil omen." James is about to drive her away, but the girls plead for her. Gurn bids her to be seated and offers her a glass of spirits, which she greedily swallows.

Madge knows hidden things, and the girls cannot resist their desire to know what lies in store for them. They surround the witch and hold out their hands to have her predict their fortunes. To one she promises happiness in marriage, while she tells the other she will never be wed. This one is but a child and gets no prediction at all, but another has her fate whispered in her ear, and walks away blushing. Finally, Effy asks if she will be happy in marriage. "Yes!" is the answer. "Does my bridegroom love me sincerely?" "No!" James begs her not to believe this hateful old woman. Gurn also gets the desire to question Madge. "Ah!" she says, "this man loves you with his heart, and you will soon come to regret the fact that you have spurned his love." James now becomes furious, seizes the fortuneteller, and hurls her to the door. Gurn quotes her utterance and makes yet another effort to hinder the wedding he detests so much, but everyone laughs him to scorn and calms James by reassuring him that they do not believe at all in the prophecy.

Anna and the young girls follow Effy to her room to array her in festive dress. Gurn goes sadly away, looking back at Effy all the while. James wishes to accompany his beloved, but the girls hold him back and Effy blows him a parting kiss. James is delighted with this amiable bride, but the memory of the Sylphide soon returns to his mind. He cannot account for the nature of this being. Perhaps she is his good angel, a powerful fairy who watches over his destiny! With this, as if by a gust of wind, the casement opens. The Sylphide is in the corner, melancholy and hiding her face in her hands.

James bids her approach, and she glides down from the wall. He asks the cause of her grief, but she refuses to answer. When he continues to demand her confidence, she finally confesses that his union with Effy constitutes her misfortune; from the first moment she saw him her fate was joined to his, and this hearth is her favourite refuge. She hovers above him, visibly and invisibly, night and day; follows him on the hunt among the wild mountains; watches over his sleep; wards off evil spirits from his bed; and sends him pleasant dreams. James has listened to her with mounting agitation. He is touched by the Sylphide's love, but does not dare to return it. Effy has received his vow: his heart belongs to her alone. The Sylphide rushes desperately away. She has nothing to hope for, only death to desire. James calls her back. He cannot hide his confusion; he does not understand what sorcery is controlling him; but despite his love for Effy, he is enraptured by the Sylphide.

She expresses the liveliest joy, regains her airy lilt, and hovers about the youth, fluttering her transparent wings. She tries to use his agitated state of mind to lure him away with her, but he shudders at the thought of deserting Effy, tears himself loose from the Sylphide, and spurns her. But the Sylphide has wrapped herself in Effy's plaid, and when he turns around he finds her at his feet, reminding him of his beloved. James is intoxicated at this sight. He raises the Sylphide, presses her to his heart, and enthusiastically kisses her.

Gurn, who has witnessed part of the foregoing scene, hastens to acquaint Effy with everything that has happened, but when James hears a noise he hides the Sylphide in the armchair and covers her with the plaid. Gurn has summoned Effy and her friends in order to take the unfaithful bridegroom by surprise. At first, they see nothing at all. However, suspicion soon falls on the covered armchair. James is bewildered; Effy turns pale with jealousy and, together with Gurn, lifts the plaid aside. The Sylphide has vanished. The girls laugh. Effy becomes angry at Gurn, who is ashamed and startled.

All the villagers arrive to celebrate the betrothal of James and Effy. The old folk sit down at table, while the young ones enjoy merry dancing. James is so distracted that he forgets to ask his bride to dance. It is she who invites him. But in the midst of the dance, he perceives the Sylphide, who shows herself to him alone, then disappears once more. He forgets everything in an effort to seize her, but she always eludes him, and the guests think it is high time James was married, since he stands in danger of losing his reason from sheer affectionate longing.

The dancing ceases and the bride is adorned for the ceremony. Anna gives her the ring that she shall exchange for that of her bridegroom, and everyone surrounds her with congratulations and expressions of sympathy. James alone is melancholy. He stands apart from the others with the betrothal ring in his hand. The Sylphide emerges from the fireplace, snatches the ring from him, and indicates with an expression of utter despair that she must die if he marries Effy.

The bride is ready. She has given her girlhood friends a parting embrace. They summon the bridegroom, but he is nowhere to be found. General astonishment. Gurn has seen him flee to the hills with a woman. Effy is plunged in grief. Anna expresses indignation; everyone, anger and disapproval.

Gurn triumphantly mentions what Madge had predicted for him. He still talks of love and now finds support among the young girls. Effy is overwhelmed with grief and despair. She is indifferent to all consolation and leans helplessly on Anna's breast. Gurn kneels at her feet, and all express the liveliest sympathy.

ACT II

The forest at night. A dense fog permits only a glimpse of the foremost trees and cliffs. To the left, the entrance to a cave.

Madge makes ready for a meeting with other witches. They come from all quarters, each with lamp and broomstick, each with her familiar spirit. They dance about the fire in a circle, hail Madge, and by way of welcome empty a cup of the glowing brew she has prepared for them. Madge calls them to work. Some spin, wind, and weave a rose-coloured drapery, while others dance and fence with the broomsticks. The spell is complete. They drink a farewell, and the flock of witches disappear into the cave.

The fog disperses. Dawn gives way to sunrise, and the landscape presents a charming blend of woods and mountains. The Sylphide leads James down from a steep mountain path, which he fearfully treads while she scarcely seems to touch the cliff with her foot. This is her domain. Here she will live for the one she loves, hide him from the eyes of the world, and allow him to share the joys she prizes most highly. James is enraptured with delight and admiration. The Sylphide seems to fathom his every desire, brings him the loveliest flowers, and refreshes him with fruits and spring water. James regards her with rapture. He forgets everything for the one he loves, and lives and breathes only to possess her. But she is more retiring than usual. She will not sit with him, easily disengages herself from his arms, and eludes him every time he ardently tries to embrace her. James is on the verge of becoming annoyed, but then she hovers about him in the most delightful attitudes. James's movements unwittingly acquire a more airy lilt. He follows the Sylphide in her easy flight, and their dancing blends together in harmony.

Despite his love for the Sylphide and the magical power that irresistibly sweeps him away with her, the memory of Effy still returns, impressing upon him the injustice he has done her. He grows melancholy once more and feels as drained as if he had been intoxicated.

The Sylphide perceives his state of mind and seeks to dispel his dark thoughts with her innocent merriment. She knows a way: her sisters shall help her to cheer her beloved. At a signal they all come into view through bushes, on boughs, and over the cliffs. Young sylphides with wings of blue and rose soon chase away the youth's distress. Some of them swing on airy draperies that they hang between the trees, while others stand on the tip of a bough and bend it to the ground with their weight, to have it raised into the air again by a puff of wind. Their dancing and delightful groupings arouse James's enthusiasm. He is more than ever taken with the Sylphide, but she eludes his embraces and, after having disappointed him several times, disappears at the very moment he thought to grasp her. In vain he questions the remaining sylphides. They do not answer him but fly away one after another. Anxious and grief-stricken, James cannot remain alone but rushes after the enchanting creature.

James's friends come into view on the hill. Gurn is with them. They seek and question one another about the runaway, but until now their search has been fruitless. They spread out, and Gurn discovers a hat. It belongs to James. He is about to call the others, but Madge steps out of the cave, seizes the hat, and flings it away. Gurn is frightened by the witch's sudden appearance, but she calms him and orders him to be silent and clever, pointing to the hill whence Effy is coming with some of her friends. Nobody has found James, and Madge now tells them of his unfaithfulness. He is lost to Effy, but her prophecy will be fulfilled; for Gurn, that fine, goodhearted young fellow, is destined by fate to be Effy's husband. All the others, outraged at James's behaviour, support Gurn's pleas. Effy, although deeply distressed, is nevertheless moved by the slighted Gurn's affection and allows him to escort her home. Madge remains alone. James returns without having overtaken the Sylphide. His heart is a prey to regret and despair. He feels how deeply he has violated his responsibilities toward his bride, but he does not have the strength to tear himself loose from this being who, like a dream image, charms and confuses his senses and captures his thoughts. Old Madge has been watching him secretly and approaches with feigned compassion. He readily tells her everything and says that he would gladly give his life to capture the celestial maiden if only for a single moment. "But the one you love is a sylphide! Naught save a talisman can bind her to you." "Give it me! In return I will bestow upon you all that I possess." "But this morning you mocked me, cast me away!" Kneeling, James begs her to forgive him for his hardness and to give him life through the possession of the Sylphide. Madge suffers herself to be moved and meaningfully hands him the rose-coloured scarf: "Believe in its power and you shall succeed! Entwine her with this gauze. Then her wings will drop and she is yours forever." Beside himself with joy and gratitude, James kisses the scarf and follows the witch to her cave with a thousand expressions of thanks.

He spies the Sylphide on a bough with a bird's nest in her hand. He waves the scarf; she climbs down and offers him her catch, but James reproaches her for being harsh toward innocent creatures. Deeply moved, she regrets what she has done and hastens to replace the nest. She now pleads for the pretty scarf, which he purposely refuses her. She begs him for it and promises never more to flee from him. Greedily, she reaches for the scarf, but at the same instant he twists it about her so tightly that she cannot move her arms. The Sylphide is captured and, kneeling, asks for mercy; but James does not release the scarf until her wings have fallen off. The Sylphide puts her hand to her heart as if she felt mortally wounded. James presses her to him but she pushes him away from her. He throws himself at her feet... the pallor of death covers the Sylphide's brow. James, who had thought to possess her forever and in his outburst of joy gives her a thousand caresses, suddenly stops: what has he done! The unhappy creature! By taking away her freedom he has robbed her of life? "Do not weep! You, whom I have so dearly loved! I was blessed by your tenderness, but I could not belong to you, could not give you the happiness you longed for. I must die! Take your wedding ring. Make haste, return it. You can still marry her whom you loved before me... Farewell! I die with the hope of your future happiness..."

At this moment the fortuneteller enters to rejoice at James's despair and counters his reproaches with the icy laughter of revenge. She points to the background, where Gurn is leading Effy to the altar. The Sylphide's strength is decreasing little by little. James is at her feet. Her sisters surround her, and in their arms she breathes forth her spirit. Sylphs and sylphides veil the beloved body and carry it away through the air. Overcome with grief, the unfortunate James casts yet another look at his airy mistress and falls to the ground in a swoon.

INDEX

Abdallah 8, 169-176
Acclaim to the Graces 1, 12, 13
Aladdin 4
Arcona 10, 278-287

Bellman, or The Polska at Gronalund 5, 98, 99, 156
Bewitched, The 10
Blossom of Happiness, The 5
Bouquet Royal 9

Caprichio, El 8
Castle of Montenero, The 7
Cheval de Bronze, Le 10
Childhood of Erik Menved, The 5, 88-97, 211
Children's Party, A 5
Conservatoire, The 7
Conservatoriet 131-135
Corsican, The 10
Cort Adeler in Venice 9, 247-257
Cracovienne 4
Czaar und Zimmermann 6

Dame Blanche, La 11
Danes in China 11
Diamantkreuz, Das 6
Diamants de la Couronne, Les 5
Dieu et la Bayadère, Le 4
Divertissement in honour of Wilhelm of Hesse's Golden Anniversary 9
Domino Noir, Le 4
Don Giovanni 6
Don Quixote at Camacho's Wedding 3, 48-55
Dragons de Villars, Les 10

Earnest Maiden, The 8
Echo of Sunday, An 6
Elf Maiden, The 9
Entführung aus dem Serail, Die 11

Fairy Tale in Pictures, A 10, 271-277
Farewell to the Old Theatre 10, 282
Far from Denmark, or a Costume Ball on Board 9, 201-207
Fatherland's Muses, The 4, 69-73
Faust 2, 19-27
Federigo 6
Festival in Albano, The 4, 64-69
Fiancée, La 2
Fidelio 1
Fiorella 3
Fisher Girls, The 8
Flower Festival at Genzano, The 8, 184-187
Flower Maids of Florence, The 11
Folk Tale, A 8, 162-167, 282
From Siberia to Moscow 10, 293-299
From the Last Century 10, 289-291

Galop militaire 8
Gioacchino 5, 19, 33, 48
Guerrilla Band, The 2
Gustav III 7

Hamburger Dans 5
Hans Heiling 3
Healing Spring, The 9
Hermanas de Sevilla, Las 11
Hertha's Offering 3, 57
Holmen's Old Guard 7
Huguenots, Les 5
Hussar Dance 7

In Memory of Schall 3
In Memory of Weyse 10, 265-267
In the Carpathians 8, 177, 179, 181, 183
Iphigenia in Aulis 9
Iphigenia in Tauris 10
Irresistibles, The 7, 137-138
Isle of Fantasy, The 4, 58-63

Jean de Paris 11
Joseph et Ses Frères 11

Kermesse in Bruges, The, or *The Three Gifts* 7, 144-147
King's Volunteers on Amager, The 10, 259-263
Kirsten Piil 6, 109-113

Lay of Thrym, The 9, 227-231, 236-245
Little Kirsten 8
Lohengrin 10
Lucia di Lammermoor 8
Lucky Wheel, The 6
Lucrezia Borgia 8

Maçon, Le 11
Mandarin's Daughters, The 10, 269
Maritana 6
Marsk Stig 7
Masquerade 7
Matrimonio Segreto, Il 8
Meistersinger, Die 10
Memorial Wreath to Denmark's Great Poet, A 11
Merry Wives of Windsor, The 9
Moise 5
Mountain Hut, The, or *Twenty Years* 8, 189-199
Mousquetaires de la Reine, Les 6

Napoli 4, 81, 83, 85, 87
New Penelope, The 6, 122-123
Nina, or *The Girl driven mad by Love* 3, 301, 326-331
Nix, The 7
Norns, The 227-235
Nozze di Figaro, Le 5

Old Memories, or *a Magic Lantern* 6, 126-131
Oresteia, The 5, 100-109
Orpheus 6, 143

Pages of The Duke de Vendome, The 2, 301, 312-317

Parisian Polka 5
Pas de cinq from *The Raven* 2
Pas de cinq from *The Youth of Henry V* 2
Pas de Deux 'a la Taglioni 4
Pas de Deux de Retour 4
Pas de deux for Grahn's debut 3
Pas de deux from *La Muette de Portici* 2
Pas de deux from *Robert le Diable* 4
Pas de deux from *Zampa* 2
Pas de deux in *Herman von Unna* 3
Pas de deux in *The Carnival* 2
Pas de Deux Oriental 1
Pas de Deux, *retour de Fjeldsted* 5
Pas des Trois Cousines 7
Pas de trois from *Le Postillon de Lonjumeau* 3
Pas de trois, Johansson 3
Pascha's Daughter, The 9
Paul and Virginia 2, 301, 318, 319, 321, 323, 325
Petit Chaperon Rouge, Le 11
Polacca Guerriera 6
Polka Militaire 5, 259
Polketta 8
Polonaise, La 8
Ponte Molle 9, 221-225
Pre-aux-Clercs, Le 3
Preciosa 7
Princess Isabella 2
Prophecy of Love, The 11
Psyche 7, 68, 139-144

Raphael 6, 115-21
Robert le Diable 4, 10
Romeo and Giulietta 2

Sailor's Return, The 11
Sally from Classens Have, The 10
Scandinavian Quadrille 10
Sleepwalker, The 302-311
Soldier and Peasant 2, 12, 13
Somnambule, La 1, 301, 302, 312
Soprano, The 4
St. Olaf 3
Sylphide La 3, 332-337

Tannhiuser 10
Tarantella Napolitana 8
Templer und die Jüdin, Der 3
Toreador, The 4, 74-79
Trovatore, Il 9
Tyroleans, The 3, 33-37

Undine 5
Uthal 6

Valdemar 3, 37-47, 70
Valkyr, The 9, 231
Valkyrie, The 208-219
Ventana, La 8
Veteran, The, or The Hospitable House 2, 27-33
Victor's Wedding, or The Ancestral Home 2, 15-17

Wedding at Lake Como, The 7
Wedding Festival in Hardanger, The 8, 155-161
White Rose, or Summer in Brittany, The 6, 124-125
William Tell 5

Yelva 3

Zauberflöte, Die 9
Zulma, or The Crystal Palace 7, 149-153

www.ingramcontent.com/pod-product-compliance
Lightning Source LLC
Chambersburg PA
CBHW041307240426
43661CB00037B/1463/J